MW00508958

Born into a working-class family in 1949 in Basel, Switzerland – by the time that Bryce completed elementary schooling, his father, a self-made man left his wife for another woman. In the early seventies Bryce, after he completed his formation as a pilot left Switzerland, cruising down to Cape Town, where he was confronted with apartheid, before heading across to Australia where he worked as an airline pilot, at the same time living in the Victorian goldfields. He returns to Switzerland after the tragic event of 911, wanting to spend time with his aging father, accompanying him on his last journey.

Had you not been there that particular Sunday Moring – the 20 July 2014 – when my heart decided to have a cardiac infraction; had you not saved my life that day, I would not have been able to realised that I was still traumatised by the mental torture that Aunt Lulus behaviour has inflicted on us; had you not responded in the manner that you did that morning, this book would not have come into being, and I would not have had the opportunity to begin the process of mental healing. For this reason, in recognition and internal gratefulness, I have dedicated this book to you – my dear wife, Athina.

Bryce Cortney

# AUNT LULU: BOOK ONE

AUSTIN MACAULEY PUBLISHERS™

LONDON * CAMBRIDGE * NEW YORK * SHARJAH

**Ordering Information**
Quantity sales: Special discounts are available on quantity purchases by corporations, associations, and others. For details, contact the publisher at the address below.

**Publisher's Cataloging-in-Publication data**
Cortney, Bryce
Aunt Lulu: Book One

ISBN 9781638291510 (Paperback)
ISBN 9781638291527 (Hardback)
ISBN 9781638291534 (ePub e-book)

Library of Congress Control Number: 2022905311

www.austinmacauley.com/us

First Published 2023
Austin Macauley Publishers LLC
40 Wall Street, 33rd Floor, Suite 3302
New York, NY 10005
USA

mailto:mail-usa@austinmacauley.com
+1 (646) 5125767

I thank all of those individuals, institutions and organizations that, in some way or another, have influenced the way in which I approached the structural development of this book. I am grateful to those that are of importance in my life, those that have stimulated my thoughts and encouraged me to write about issues that others prefer to conceal or prefer not to talk about. In particular, I thank those that I know personally, those that are no longer with us, and those that through their personal or professional greatness have changed my way of thinking, and a special thanks to those whom gave their time to edit the manuscript.

# Table of Contents

# Introduction

It is not unusual that people excuse their personal or professional failures with a hard childhood; perhaps they come from a broken home, perhaps they have not had the benefit of stability and parental love, convinced that these are reasons for their absence of success—what a pitiful baggage to have you accompany throughout life. Aunt Lulu, the lady that I was asked to call mum— the character that is central to my personal experience—had created a similar family environment some sixty years ago after she married my father, providing me with a shitty childhood, smothering me with an ill-conceived educational structure on which to orientate myself as a teeny, exposing me to soft abuse, mental torture to the point that I had felt abandoned by my father. Evolutionary psychologists generally agree that there are two major categories of behavior, in particular, inherited behavioral traits that are very difficult to change, and to some degree this is very true. However, behavioral psychologists also agree that as individuals, we do have the power to modify learned behavior.

This story deals with the son's struggle to maintain a relationship with his father throughout his youth, and the fight to remain connected with him during his life as an adult. Focused on our fading relationship, I began to realize the things that influenced my personal behavior, and at some point, I realized that the current circumstances could not be considered in isolation, I had to grasp the underlying reason for my personal crisis, eventually realizing that I was compelled to go back to the source so that I was able to understand the truth, extending my reflection to conditions and situations other than my father's behavior toward me, beginning to ponder our lives from the beginning.

So, I began to write about my early childhood, how I was left alone to deal with the ordeal—indeed, the anguish when my father left his first wife for another woman, when my father married a lady that I was asked to call mum— the lady that blamed me because she was unable to have her own children; the way she exposed me to her torture, her mental games. The time when grandma passed away, there was nobody with whom I was able to share my sorrow, there wasn't anybody to tell me that it is ok to cry, nobody explained how to handle grief.

Describing the people around us at that time and how they influenced our being, how they affected my general development throughout my youth, right up to my coming of age. As a child, reflecting on my decision to explore Australia; how my discovery of apartheid in Cape Town during the early seventies changed my view about humanity; the thirty-five years of life in rural Australia and how this time has shaped my life as an adult; being thrown out of my job during the Australian Domestic Pilots dispute in 1989; losing one of my buddies as he failed to correctly line up his B-747 during his approach to Guam's International Airport during the night of 6 August 1997.

Bryce Cortney, 17 February 2021

# Early Childhood

Perhaps ten months old, not yet able to walk, still being dragged around in a pusher, I dare to recall a scene that is still firmly registered in my memory; me sitting up in this pram, its top raised to around forty-five degree providing me with shade, it must have been summer time, I was able to see my mum standing in the sun together with another lady, lightly dressed, holding the pram handle with one hand, the two of them talking.

At that moment, I was occupied examining our house, looking at all the details: the ground floor was constructed of large gray stones; on the left, a stone frame that housed a heavy wooden door, stained in mahogany, the upper quarter of the door consisted of two leadlight panels framed in a heavy timber, below the door, recessed by about a half meter, the door hinged on the right side of the frame, and on the right side of the wall a large shiny brass panel with doorbells installed for each apartment.

To the right of the door, there were two window openings constructed of stone, the wooden window frames painted in white, two wings each with a division of the glass on the upper third of the window.

Above the window and the door opening, stones of equal shape and size arranged in an arch-like manner to support the building structure above.

The distribution of the windows and their construction on the first, second and the third floor were identical, except that they were not rounded at the top as they were on the ground floor, they were square and the windows framed by a stone mantle all around, unlike the ground floor, the facade was built from red brick.

In the middle of each of them there was stone ornament sculptured by hand, decorating the top of the window, except for the windows in the center, they featured an angel-like face shaped from stone. Still, today I can clearly recall the picture of our house, despite the fact that I have not seen it again since my early childhood.

Mum already had a child when she met my dad, William is his name and he is a couple of years older than me. From time to time, during the last few years when dad and I were reminiscing about past times, he was telling me stories about my brother William and me, the naughty stuff that we apparently got up to during my early childhood, the trouble we got ourselves into from time to time, and the worry that we caused mum and dad occasionally, but I have no remembrance of most of those occasions; in fact, I only recall the time when William and I were mucking around in a small tent during a storm on the camping grounds of Hyères in the South of France. Apparently, our tent was set up not far from the beach; my brother and I disappeared one night during a heavy storm and mum and dad had to look for us for over an hour, apparently, dad was nearly out of his brain, very angry.

On the way home from that particular camping trip, we stopped in the French Naval Base in Toulon; on a smaller boat, we were able to take a guided tour of the harbor. One of the moments stayed imprinted in my memory, a rather large aircraft carrier lying a couple of hundred meters out on anchor; our excursion boat got up to it and drove alongside it for quite some time, perhaps not further than forty meters away. I was fascinated and scared at the same time, hanging on to mum like grim death, she replied with her enchanting warm-hearted smile and the gentle squeezing of my hand that always made me feel safe and loved.

I never learned the truth about my brother, I am aware that he was with us on some occasions, but we never actually lived together as a family, I don't have any recollection at all about us sitting around the dinner table; though at that time, we lived in a very small apartment, I never shared my room with William; other than the camping trip, we never played together like siblings do, we never had the opportunity to quarrel over anything at all, in fact neither of us knew anything about the other.

I am certain that William didn't share his early childhood with me, I suspect that he was living with his aunt and uncle in the village where my mum was born, just like he did when I eventually met him during my later childhood. For some reason, this is an issue that we never discussed at home, not then, nor later in my life, it was never an issue to be talked about in our family.

I suppose that if I had asked, I would have received an answer; maybe I was afraid to ask for an explanation, afraid to learn the truth. I might have found out that my dad, for some reason or another, didn't want William to live with us in a family situation, or was it mum that refused to have my brother in the family home; rather unlikely, but I will never know.

I was perhaps two years of age; I recall that I was sitting at the Berettas' kitchen table—the caretakers that occupied the apartment on the ground floor—mum was taking care of a wound on Mrs. Beretta's arm, washing it out with a solution of cold chamomile tea and applying a clean bandage; mum was a qualified nurse, not officially working at that time, but always prepared to help others in need. I was observing mum, how she cared for this elderly lady; at the same time, I was fascinated by this rather large chestnut tree, it was very old and tall, covering much of the backyard, accessible through a glass door from the kitchen; it provided shade to most of the garden. I can still see its leaves being moved about by the breeze, but the most vivid memory from that particular occasion that I recall was the serenity that prevailed in the room.

In principle, mum was a softly spoken person, calm and collected, a personality that had the ability to influence others around her, but she could also be imposing, witty and humorous.

Much of the family life that I recall from that period took place in the kitchen, many years later; as an adult I was able to explain to my dad in some detail, the layout, that the floor was covered with red-brown octagonal shaped tiles, the wooden larder, painted white, fitted with two glass doors on the top part, the breadbox with the wooden roller door, the corner bench in the far corner behind the table, the kitchen sink with its drainboard, the gas stove and a work bench on the other side, near the balcony door.

Above the kitchen sink was a gas-operated hot water service, it had a small boiler, heated by a gas burner which lit automatically when the hot water tap was opened heating the water as it passed through; we had no bathroom, the toilet was out in the stairwell, the kitchen sink was the place where people took care of their body hygiene, filled with warm water was the place were mum used to bath and wash me.

I could never understand why my parents separated and got divorced around five years after I was born; being a little prejudiced, I considered my mum as the best, during my early childhood, when she was still living with dad and I she was always there for me, nurturing me through all my little difficulties, comforting me if after my countless mishaps on the tricycle or when I called out for her after a nightmare in the middle of the night, mum was there to protect me. I was perhaps three years of age, dad was convinced that kids had to eat what was on the table—mum had prepared lentils that evening—I hated them, I was even prepared to induce vomiting at the table, but mum, just in time recognized the reality and managed to turn around dad's order.

During that period, it wasn't unusual for women with family to stay at home, looking after the children and the household, making sure that lunch was on the table at midday, assuring that the beer was cold and the slippers ready when their husband returned from work, unfortunately a reality for many women at the time. My mum wasn't working as a nurse either during my early childhood and my father didn't share any of the chauvinistic ideas and attitudes that many of his contemporaries were practicing, attempting to safeguard this way of life, he involved mum in his business ventures.

After his apprenticeship as a furniture maker, dad maintained his occupation, perusing a Bachelor of commercial studies before getting married. At some point after his studies, he opened a small joinery shop, employing one fellow; they were specializing in the building of high-class coffins, dad was responsible for the construction and the quality, and mum took care of the finances, the accounting and all marketing aspects—the direct contact with the customer. My mum was also a very courageous woman; somehow dad got involved with some people that were running a large print factory; he desperately wanted to get involved in this business, but he needed money to participate, he got himself a job with the state public transport department, driving buses and trams for a while and mum had taken over the running of the joinery.

A couple of months later, dad started another business venture, washing machines had become a fashionable household gadget and dad had recognized that for most people they were not affordable, he bought ten AEG machines with a roller mechanism to squeeze the excess water out of the washed clothe, and began to hire them out, delivering the machines today, picked them up the next, making money, providing a service to those that couldn't afford to buy a machine. Dad provided the idea and Mum took over the running of this business as well; as I recall, the machines were delivered in a motorized tricycle, I don't know if dad had bought this vehicle, or if he had it modified, the rear part was in principle an Italian-made Vespa with a loading bridge at the front, perhaps one meter fifty by one meter fifty with side flaps and two wheels underneath, controlled through the handlebar.

I have fond memories from that time, I was dragged all over the place by mum, from the joinery to the funeral directors and back again, and on occasion, I was taken along by dad when dad made a delivery/pick-up tour with the Vespa.

During the same period, dad bought a 1948 Saurer, top speed 60km/h, a bus that was considered compatible for the mountains of Switzerland; his fascination wasn't the design of the vehicle, nor its technical specifications, he was interested in the 30 passenger seats that could be turned into money, just like a contemporary tour operator, he organized theme trips within Switzerland, some of them designed as day trips, other concepts included a weekend with accommodation and dining included; one that comes to mind was the daffodil trip on which occasion I was dad's "co-driver," a journey to a particular district of the French Jura, in an area where the meadows and hills were covered with daffodils during spring time, at that time it was also customary for the wedding party to take a tour after the church service, stop for lunch, and then continue the tour back to the place where the dinner celebration was to follow. Again, dad's idea and mum's job to realize the day-to-day organization of these events, as well as taking care of everything else that she was responsible for.

Organization and structure were a fundamental part of dad's life; before he got involved in the print factory he was driving buses and trams for the city public transport department, on the side, together with mum he was operating an unusual conglomeration of small business—the manufacturing of high class coffins, the hiring of washing machines and the tour operation, all of them fundamentally different by nature—each of them requiring a totally different approach with the customer, each demanding a different Colloquial language approach; modest, sorrowful, sympathetic and humble if someone from the funeral parlor called, efficient friendly and flexible for the washing machine hiring business, jovial, happy and adaptable for the tour operation, and neutral in the event that dad's boss called.

Mum managed all of this from our home, with one telephone line; unable to anticipate the need of the caller when the phone rang, I would love to know how she determined the mood of her answering the call; I forgot to ask her when she was still alive, and now I can merely guess.

I will never understand why dad divorced my mum when I was about five years of age, my memories of my early childhood let me believe that she was a wonderful person, this coming from me, it's perhaps a little bias, but she was beautiful. Much later in life I got to understand from dad mum had done a great job managing his crazy business conglomerate, that they made lots of money which eventually enabled them to buy a thirty percent share of the print factory that my father wanted so desperately. How could dad possibly let go of a woman like my mum, tearing apart a family structure that worked so well, at least from a child's point of view. What didn't mum have that other woman had that came into dad's life after her? I am very much aware that I am being presumptuous, even arrogant by saying that mum had everything and much more compared to the two of his ladies that I got to know later in my life as well.

At various phases throughout my life as an adult, dad was reminding me of the time; when I was a kid, I was telling him, "I will do things differently when I grow up, I will not make the mistakes that you made, and when I get married, I will not get divorced." I am sure that my views and intentions at the time were well meant, immature but sincere, what arrogance toward my father.

There are certainly a lot of gaps in the memories of my early childhood, but I assert, there are specific events that I do recall vividly—in some detail as if it had happened yesterday.

Many of those stories that I claim to be the way that I am describing them I was able to verify through my father in his late life; sure, he was not able to confirm that my mum, on this particular summer day was standing in front of the house with another lady, holding my pram with one hand; he was merely able to acknowledge my description of the house, the home that I have never seen again since that time.


## Celina

I grew up in a family where religion was of no importance at all. To be more specific, my natural mum was religious, she prayed with me every evening before turning of the light after she told me a bedtime story; usually it had some religious connotation. Unfortunately, dad got separated and divorced from my mum when I was six years of age; he re-married a lady that I used to call Celina, but I had little to do with her, the only thing that I remember clearly about Celina is that she took me shopping on a regular basis, once a week; we always went to this particular department store in town where I got lost in the toy department, drooling over the huge selection of Dinky Toy cars in particular. Usually, Celina left me in this department for about an hour or so that she could do her own thing, checking out the things that she was interested in. When she was ready to move on, she came back to the toy department, usually loaded with different bags and stuff, and she asked me if I had seen something that I liked; then I was allowed to choose one or two toy cars; her generosity caused a steady ascent in my ownership of Dinky Toy cars.

I don't recall that this lady had any influence on me, positive nor negative, I even don't remember what I called her; Mum, Aunt or anything similar, she did nothing that was of any consequence in my life, nothing that shaped or harmed me in any way. The sad thing is; the only thing that I remember her for is Dinky Toys, a baby by the name of Peter, and that on most evenings during the week she was out with dad, in the cinema, the opera or some other event, she surely wasn't replacing my mum.

Before the two of them left the house for their night out on the town, Celina would get my dinner ready; a local sausage called Cervolat, a piece of cheese, either Gruyere or Emmentaler, a couple of peace's of bread—all carefully placed on the table top without a plate or any other serving vessel—and to top it off she squirted some Tommy's mayonnaise out of the tube directly on the table surface, it was the sort of food that you could easily scoff with your fingers, and an uncomplicated manner of cleaning up was assured; a kitchen cloth dampened with a little warm water and a squirt of detergent wiped the table clean in no time, without any effort at all.

I don't think that my dad was ever aware of this minimalist culinary ritual; it didn't bother me either despite the fact that I had never seen my mum nor my grandma doing this, they always took grate care with the serving of the food, each component was presented in an appropriate vessel, or platter, nicely arranged with lots of care.

Because dad and his lady were out at least four to five evenings each week, sometimes at business gatherings but mostly amusing themselves, I spend a lot of time alone. From time to time when I was alone at home I would get up to some mischief, but mostly I was engaged with one of my favorite toy STOKYS; a construction kit consisting of different metal parts with pre-drilled holes which could easily be screwed together, plates and bars shaped in particular ways, plastic plates, rods, nuts and bolts, transition belts and chains, wheels with and without rubber tires, all sorts of cogwheels, electrical motors, transformers and other stuff from which you can construct anything you care for, from a simple crane to a complex model car with a working gear box.

Each year, for my birthday dad would buy me different extension kits which allowed a wonderful development of technical knowledge, as I could build projects with high levels of complexity which I loved and appreciated.

Very often I would simply listen to a radio play which was transmitted on the UKW frequency modulation.

From time to time when I was all by myself in the evening I thought about my mum, and my brother William, wondering what they were doing, if they too thought of me occasionally, and asking myself when we would see each other again next. I loathed this kind of thought because often it would set me in a melancholic mood, but I knew that I had to do something to make this horrible feeling go away quickly, so I got stuck in some interesting activities; stuffing around with some of the gadgets that dad had horded for me; a mechanical blinker from an old car, all sorts of small electrical motors, valves and switches, mechanical instruments and other interesting stuff, most of which he got from his maintenance department.

The only thing that I had to be aware off was to make sure that the lights were turned off before dad and Celina got back home, but usually this was not a problem, I got tired before midnight, around the time when the two of them returned.

## The Birth of Peter

About one year before dad got separated from Celina, she gave birth to a lovely baby boy whom was named Peter. In the lead-up to his birth, lots of details were discussed in the family; the brand of the pram—a symbol of status at the time—something my father loathed, the color of the baby ware which was to be especially created in anticipation of this baby, the style of the bassinette and its curtain were carefully chosen as well as other things and gadgets that apparently were of the utmost importance for the arrival of baby Peter.

At the time I did not realize that other than my dad nobody was paying any attention to me, nobody asked me how I was doing, how I was feeling, whether I was looking forward to this baby, everybody around me appeared to be preoccupied with the preparation of baby's arrival. Frankly speaking, I was very much looking forward to my brother, finally I would have a pal, a

companion with whom I could play and share things with, but I did not mention this to anyone; I had the feeling that it wouldn't be of interest to others, that nobody cared about me, and yet, I wasn't the sort of kid that felt insulted very quickly, nor would I get into a sulky mood over things, I just wished that Celina and dad had involved me a little to provide me with a feeling of secureness.

## William

My brother William whom I missed very much was living with my mum somewhere in Bern. Once, perhaps twice each year I was allowed to visit him and mum for a weekend, hence the birth of baby Peter had become an important event in my life to which I was very much looking forward to. Because Celina was working in my dad's business, once baby Peter was born, he spent most of his time during his first year of his life with a neighboring family, the only time that I could be with him was at the weekend, and then our activity together was limited to; me changing his nappy and preparing his bottle early on a Sunday morning. Strolls with the pram were not part of the activity that I was entrusted with for some reason or another. Sadly, the heating of his liquid breakfast and the changing of his nappies is the only memory that I have from Peter.

## Dad's Second Divorce

I was twelve when dad got divorced again from his second wife Celina. On this particular morning, dad explained to me that Celina, together with my brother Peter were leaving us. He did not explain in detail why this was so, I was simply confronted with the fact, he was the kind of person whom communicated in such a way that people that he spoke to understood what it was all about, what he was meaning, omitting any superfluous words from the conversation. I guess I would not have understood anyway if dad had elaborated on his decision, but I clearly recall that I was sad to know that I would lose my baby brother, as for Celina—I felt no emotion at all.

A little later that morning my father explained to me that he had made arrangements with my grandma. A couple of hours later he drove me to Villeneuve, a village in the district of Aigles, at the plain of the river Rhone, north east of the Lake Geneva. In this region people speak French; I was to stay with my grandparents for a while until my dad had sorted out his life and reoriented himself.

Grandma was around seventy at the time, her general health was not brilliant, her mother tongue was French and she spoke no German, I gathered that it would not have been easy at her age to take the responsibility of a soon to be teenager. As far as I was aware, at that time I was a pleasant kid to be with, not too complicated either and easy to get along with, but this was merely my opinion, Grandma might not have shared this view with me.

For one year I stayed in Villeneuve, going to school just like the other kids from there, learning in the same class as did the locals of my age. Mr. Denerea was his name; the class teacher whom coached me with a lot of patience so that I was able to achieve somewhat similar academic results as did the main stream of the class. It wasn't just the Grammar that was difficult to learn; suddenly every subject required the knowledge of the French language, even simple things like geography and mathematics. The names of the towns around the globe no longer were the same; they needed to be pronounced differently whilst their geographical location remained, as for the numeric system I now had to translate from German to French before I could cite aloud a string of mathematical rules in front of the class. It seemed to me that now I had to work twice as hard as everybody else, first I was required to translate each task from French to German so that I could understand what was required from me, then translate the answer back into French so that the teacher was able to realize my answer.

Very soon I understood that I needed to learn the French language quickly in order to survive, and after a while I began to think in the French language. This made things much simpler for everybody, I realized that with this change the learning at school had become easier, and the spoken language began to be fluent.

No doubt, the time that I spend in Villeneuve with my grandparents left its mark on me in a very positive manner. Not realizing this at the time, I learned to deal with different emotions, I got to realize that it is ok to cry and to be angry, I learned that it was not only good but indeed of great importance to question things; not to merely accept what is said, given or done in a particular situation, I realized how to handle difficulties in life, I began to understand that I was able to find something positive in most things; no matter how bad or uncomfortable the situation appeared to be. This was also the time when I began to understand that there are opportunities in life; I did miss my dad very

24

much but realized that now I got to know grandma and her husband in a different way.

It took my father about a year to sort out his life, to get rid of Celina, and to re-establish himself. It was probably not easy for him to handle all of this and to run his business at the same time. As I learnt when I was an adult, Celina had completely cleaned out the house, there was literally nothing left, no furniture, no carpets, no nick knacks, no curtains, the kitchen was totally empty, not even a plate, nor a cup or a glass was left. The only thing that remained was the kitchen sink and the stove; they were bolted down firmly. All my toys had disappeared as well; she simply left nothing when she moved out.

One of dad's natural abilities was to provide his staff with bits of information, proposing ideas in such a clever manner that in the end they had worked out the kind of solution that he was expecting, and they thought that the developed ideas were their own; dad was the kind of person that knew how to organize people, he had the ability to get things moving; understanding his capabilities, I don't believe that it took dad nearly a whole year to organize the few material things that were missing in the house, there must have been another reason that it took dad so long to get organized.

On that Friday afternoon dad called grandma to let her know that he was picking me up the next day, around lunch time. I had mixed feelings when grandma told me that it was time for me to go back home, I was sad not being able to enjoy the walks along the lake with her, the walks to Chateaux Chillon on the lake Geneva which had become my playground where I was able to chase my secret dreams, the bus rides from Villeneuve to Montreux where I always made sure to get a seat at the very front; so that I could observe the driver maneuvering this large vehicle along the narrow roads along the lake promenade, with which ease he drove into the bus stops as if he was in charge of a tricycle, the trips to les Diablerets, or les Rochers-de-Naye which we reached with a little train departing from Montreux.

I was also going to miss the little glass of vermouth, an herbal liqueur that grandma gave me before the Sunday roast was served at lunch time. This tradition was continued by my parents, they allowed me to sample a little alcohol here and there, as it was thought to be appropriate.

Because of this experience, at an early age I had become aware of the distinct tastes of different alcoholic beverages, and from time to time I learned about the effects that alcohol has on one's behavior.

The lake, the harbor, the boat dock and its surrounds were for me the most fascinating places in Villeneuve, but there was something else that drew my attention nearly every day after school; with a couple of minutes detour, a couple of hundred meters on the other side of the rail crossing, there was an old car yard, a place where these wonderful wrecks rusted away quietly.

Some of them had already been cannibalized in part, or almost completely, but it was fascinating to crawl all over them, to sit in them, to pretend that I was driving them, to pull apart the smaller, manageable parts like mechanical indicators, different mechanical instruments like the oil pressure, speed, electrical and other indicators, switches and other parts that I was able to remove with the few basic tools that I borrowed from grandpa's workshop.

My interest was not limited to those small components, motors and anything fitted to them intrigued me also, but they were far too heavy from me to handle, nor did I have the appropriate tools, nor the strength to pull them apart.

The pulling apart of those components had nothing to do with destruction; I was merely keen to know how things work, and to see if I could put them back together afterward. Getting to understand how some technical component of a car or a machine was simple in those days, computer chip boards and digital instruments were not yet invented, everything was of mechanical nature, and the electrical stuff consisted of wires coated with different colored plastic, connecters, simple relays, bulbs and switches.

Particularly with the mechanical gadgets you could easily get to understand the principle of cause and effect in a practical manner, for which I had an immense fascination, to see what happens as a result when you change the position of a component; a bit like the child that is testing the parent's patience, not consciously realizing exactly what he or she is doing, but despite this getting to understand the principle.

Grandma would have been outraged if she knew why I was coming late to lunch, she had to make sure that grandpa could begin his midday meal on time at twelve noon, exactly when the news broadcast started on the radio. Me being totally preoccupied at the car yard, I seldom realized that it was time to go home before the nearby church bells would announce the midday, but by that stage it was inevitably too late and it was clear that my grandparents were waiting to begin with lunch, which cause tension between the two of them, and I would be seriously reminded once more to be punctual in the future.

Realizing that I would miss my grandparents, the few school mates that I had, the village and all the outings that I enjoyed with grandma, I also knew that it would be nice to see my old school friends and mates again, to go back to Basel, the town on the Rhein that was familiar to me, and to be with my dad again was a good reason to be happy to go home.

I felt that dad was glad to see me when he arrived in Villeneuve the next day, he did not want to spend a lot of time there because the trip back was going to take about five or more hours, there was no freeway throughout Switzerland in those days. At the time dad had a 1961 Chevrolet Impala cabriolet with a fuel injected 283-cid V8 motor and a manual gearbox with overdrive. The color of the lacquer was red, just like the leather upholstery, the interior side panels and the dashboard. The soft roof was made from a white, water proof fabric. This car was absolutely stunning, it turned heads wherever we went with it, and frankly speaking I enjoyed being seen in this car, in particular when occasionally dad picked me up after school on a Saturday morning; at the time it was the only car of its kind in town, perhaps even in Switzerland, and my mates were a little envious, causing me to secretly smirk.

## Coming Home

On the way back we talked a lot about the things that I learned at school, how I got on with my grandparents, the things that we did together, the places that I got to see, and the things that I discovered. Dad was also talking about the future; that now I had to focus on the school, making sure that I would integrate myself well and to get back into a good rhythm of learning so that I could realize all my dreams. I knew that this was very important to him—to become someone, to be someone, to be respected, to do things in life that are meaningful.

Making lots of money, migrating to America, driving a Ferrari or a Maserati sports car, and to become a pilot formed part of my dreams at the time.

Our conversation did not include baby Peter which surprised me, after all, he was my brother and I was curious to know how he was doing, if he was already walking, if he had begun to talk, and I would have liked to know if he would still recognize me if we had met. All of these open questions troubled me, I plucked up enough courage to ask dad about Peter, not knowing how he felt about the fact that he was no longer with us as a family. Dad explained that he was doing well, that the court had decided that he was not allowed to have contact with him for some reason or another; that we should get used to this situation and that we had to try to forget him. I perceived this answer as pathetic and upsetting, but coming from my dad I knew that I had to take it seriously and that I had to accept it. I never understood dad's explanation to my question until much later when I was in my twenties; he told me that Peter was not his child, and that back then this was the reason for the divorce. If dad had explained the truth to me at the time, I would not have understood truly the meaning of it, but it might have been easier for me to handle the feeling of pain and sorrow.

During the drive home there were also periods where we didn't talk, dad was no doubt focused on his driving, occasionally he was cursing some driver for reasons that were not always clear to me either. Dad was also a person that didn't talk for the sake of talking; he was a very cool person, he thought carefully, considering different aspects pertaining to the subject before he commented about something.

He was a person close to nature; often he would point out something to me; "take a look at this, take a look at that," with enthusiasm he was able to describe the beauty of something, elaborating on the details, and where appropriate he would explain the correlation of something in relation to other things. As a child, he was working on a farm during the school holiday—this was probably the source for his interest and the curiosity for all that nature has to offer, he was intrigued by it, and he had the ability to infect others with enthusiasm for nature.

Particularly during autumn, when I am taking a walk through the forest, admiring the beauty of the different colors of the foliage, some of which are still in their full summer beauty—firmly attached to the branches; others that have changed to different shades of green, yellow, red and brown, some that are still desperately clinging to their branches, and others are falling—covering the ground of the forest, the smell that is caused by the different stages of decomposition of the leaves.

I recall this particular day when dad was explaining to me that during the autumn the shades of the different colored leaves is the result of night frost

causing the moisture in the leaf cells to freeze and to expand, destroying the vital green pigment chlorophyll that is stored in the leaves. The tree realizes that this would be fatal for its future, and begins to rescue the Chlorophyll by sending it back through the branches to the stem where it is protected from cold winter temperatures, saved for the next season. The different pigments, previously covered by the Chlorophyll remain, and the ferment substances begin to discolor the leaves.

As soon as the Chlorophyll is saved, a cork layer is developed between the leaf and the twigs, and so the leaf is starved from nutrition and falls off. The most fascinating aspect of this story is the falling leaves that apparently add weight on the earth surface, and as a result during autumn time the earth is turning faster as a result.

Whenever I am admiring the beauty of the foliage during autumn time I am reminded of my father, the odd tears rolling down my cheeks remind me how much I miss him.

On the way home, I was thinking about our house in Basel, wondering how my mates were doing, curious to know if we still had the same interests as then, imagine what it would be like to be back at school; hoping that I would be allowed to go in the same class with the same principal teacher as I was before, and in particular I was looking forward to be back home; having dad to myself, not having to share him with someone that had no time for me.

As we approached our final destination, I started to feel a little squeamish in the tummy, after nearly one year I came back to my roots, recognizing the different landmarks—the river Rhein, the bridges that enabled the people from Gross-Basel to cross to Klein-Basel, the industrial side of town, and the chimneys from the pharmaceutical industry. I recalled the excruciating stench that escaped these chimneys during the week when the factories were operating.

Then we drove passed one of the factories that produced my favorite mayonnaise and mustard, on particular days of the week, what appeared to me a very specific smell would escape through their chimney. I don't know what kind of process in the food manufacturing industry could create such an unpleasant odor, considering that this factory was processing merely materials derived from plants and dehydrated eggs, sunflower oil, vinegar, mustard, salt, and sugar.

If I would associate the fragrance that this factory produced from time to time with the product that was being made, I would not be able to enjoy my favorite Mayonnaise anymore.

Finally, we came to the bridge that crosses the Wiese; the source of this river is between the Feldberg and Grafenmatt in the Black Forest region in Germany, about 57 km north east from my home Kleinhüningen where the river finally flows into the river Rhein just at the start of the harbor area.

This river was of great significance to me, it passed by our house, during the summer time when she did not carry as much water; I spend a lot of my free time exploring the borders, the swimming holes, the sectors underneath the bridges and other areas of fascination.

Just at the final right hand turn on the bridge our house became visible, what a feeling, my excitement was probably visible to dad, I was simply happy to be home again; I could barely wait to find out what had changed since I left.

In our house, everything had changed with the exception of fixtures that could not be moved; the facilities in the bathrooms, the kitchen stove and sink and the laundry were recognizable. My room which I visited first had become a new look; entering the room, on the right-hand side stood my two-door wardrobe which my dad made during his apprenticeship as a joiner-furniture maker; a beautifully hand-crafted piece of furniture that was finished with French-Polish, which my father expected that I took good care of it.

The interior of the wardrobe was empty; dad explained that we would go shopping for clothes next week. In the corner on the right was a brand new bed, covered with a brand new colorful bedspread, perched on top was a stuffed elephant which I had named spontaneously Jumbo, to the left there was a new writing desk with its chair, neatly arranged, on top I found an ink pen, plotting paper, different stationery items, pencils—plain as well as colored—a pencil sharpener in the form of the Eiffel Tower, a erasing rubber, a couple of rulers, different protractors used for technical drawing and my high-quality Kern Compasses set which my dad had already used during his school time which I treasured very much.

To the left of my desk stood a lovely book case; well stocked with my old schoolbooks as well as books of general interest—some of them I had before I left—and some of them were new. The window was covered with a white cotton curtain, covered with a lovely outer curtain tied into a neat bundle on each side of the wall.

In the corner behind the door dad had constructed something like a wardrobe; it consisted of a solid wooden top on which he had hang a large curtain on a rail, and behind that there were some shelves. The idea of this construction was that I could tidy up my room quickly after playing with my toys—by stuffing everything in the corner and pull the curtain.

Dad explained to me that Celina had taken all my toys with her, literally everything, and this made me really angry, but as I opened the curtain I got a huge surprise; dad had bought a set of STOKYS with some additional components as well as an electric motor and a transformer to go with it, there was again some LEGO, a garage made from wood; at the base you could drive the Dinky Toys Cars in a little workshop, next to it was a car-wash, an office, and on the side there was a ramp on which the cars could be driven to the car park situated on the top of the garage, simply a wonderful toy.

In this area I also found some gadgets which I could take apart, to find out how they are working which I thought that it was wonderful that dad had carefully thought about all the things that were important to me.

The next area to be discovered was the living room; it was furnished in an unostentatious and uncluttered manner, on the perfectly polished parquet floor laid a plain, blue carpet with its fringes perfectly combed out, near the window side of the room a lovely lounge sweet consisting of two single, one double and one three sitters, covered with velvet material a little lighter blue then the carpet, a beautiful coffee table in the middle and placed against the wall opposite the door was a buffet build in solid walnut wood—French-polished. The buffet was decorated with a lamp build with a brass base, finished with a beautifully crafted shade. The only other decorative but functional thing in the room was a standard lamp similar in design to that on the buffet, like an ornament she stood on the floor and provided the room with a warm ambiance at night. The windows were enrobed with a lovely white cotton curtain decorated with a blue velvet drape covering the curtain railing and the sides.

Dad's room was not yet set up; a bed was positioned in the right-hand corner, a device with a large rod to hang his clothes stood on the side and a couple of boxes were on the floor on which he arranged his underwear, and there were no curtains either.

The other rooms in the house had not been refurnished at the time; dad explained that he would do this at a later stage. Plants and flowers were nowhere to be seen in the house. I remember, before I had left, we had lots of plants all over the place, and there were always fresh flowers in the house. It didn't matter either, the important parts of the house were functional, and there would have been nobody that would have known to take care of the plants either.

The kitchen was a surprise, the sink, the workbench and stove were still on the right-hand side when you entered the door. In the same line, near the window was a lovely kitchen table with four chairs and to the left side stood a rather large kitchen larder with lots of doors and drawers as it was usual in those days. In one compartment we had plates, bowls, cups and glasses for four, and in one of the drawers there was a cutlery set for four, a ladle, a couple of wooden cooking spoons, a whisk and a greater for the cheese.

It was clear that dad had been shopping, some rice, and lots of dried pasta; some spaghetti, lots of Hunkeler Noodles which were made in Basel until 1965, and some Hörnli—small curved pasta which are hollow inside. In another larder compartment I found canned food; baked beans, lentils, green beans, Ravioli in tomato sauce, peas with carrots, tomato puree, strawberry jam, and in the next compartment dad had stowed oil, vinegar, a tube of Mayonnaise and one tube of mild mustard, salt and pepper. A loaf of bread was stowed in a special breadbox on the larder. Some onions and a few bulbs of garlic were the only fresh food to be found.

Next to the larder stood our new Bosch refrigerator—the latest scream at the time. Mind you, not every family had one of those; many could simply not afford such an acquisition. In it were a couple of Cervolat, a Citerio Salami, a block of butter, a large piece of tarty Gruyere and a medium sized piece of mild Emmentaler cheese. It was clear that dad's culinary repertoire was going to be uncomplicated, but this was not important to me either, it felt simply great to be back home, having my dad to myself.

# The Year of the Bachelor

## Back to School

For dad it was important that I would become independent as quickly as possible, despite my mere thirteen years of age. I wasn't his only responsibility, he was directly liable for the multimillion investment of the business infrastructure, he was accountable to the bank that invested its money, he was responsible for some one hundred and twenty employees, and then there was me. The very moment I returned from grandma's place, dad taught me to be as unattached as possible, I had to make sure that; I put the dirty clothes in the right spot so that our part-time housekeeper could arrange for them to be washed, ironed and to be put back in my cupboard, I had to clean my shoes every day, that I took care of my personal hygiene, that I organized myself in such a manner that I kept my school, my music, sports and other schedules without having to be reminded. Dad taught me to take responsibility for myself, to be well organized and if I didn't, he was there for me, to support and to correct my errors in a very positive manner; dad could be very assertive, but he never yelled or screamed at me, he was mostly cool and composed, knowing that this is the best way to achieve good behavior.

Dad took time to check my homework meticulously every day, making sure that it was completed and that I had understood the subject matter, ensuring that I met the academic objectives. He also made sure that I had done the things for which he empowered me to be self-responsible.

The distance to my school was about one kilometer, on foot it took me around 15 to 20 minutes, pending on how often I got distracted along the way. The first possible distraction was the footpath on the bridge that led over the river Wiese, one had to check if there was something of any importance that was carried down-river on the water surface, the second possible distraction was the showcase of the local cinema on the corner, there were always photos on display of interesting scenes of the movie that was currently being screened, depicting the lovely looking actresses from that particular era, then there was the shoemaker; through the shop window you could watch him work; sometimes I could waste five or more minutes of my time because it was fascinating to see what he was doing, and then came the last time-waster just before the old school house—the bike shop. Displayed in the shop window was always the latest scream, racing as well as so called half racing bikes. The half racing bike interested me in particular, its handlebar was short and straight, and joint to the pedal rod the bike had two chain rings which you could select as you were riding the bike, at the rear, a six-gear selector was installed, providing you with a twelve-gear option. These bikes were also beautifully styled and the paintwork was simply stunning.

Often, I stood there slobbering over these bikes, wishing that I could have one as well, but dad was of a different opinion, he didn't think that I needed one just yet. Finally, when I approached the school on that particular morning I had a kind of squeamish feeling in my tummy, wondering what it would be like to meet my class mates that I had not seen for a year, end then it happened; finally I stomped on to a small group of them in the school yard near the bike parking area. We greeted each other as if we had never been separated, without wasting a lot of words, I was happy to be back.

I stood before the auditorium door, looking into the room toward the far corner near the window, and there he was sitting at his desk, the older, solid build, gray haired gentlemen Mr. Ragaz—my principal teacher who had his roots in the canton Graubünden. He was a down to earth gentleman, very close to nature, extremely knowledgeable about a lot of things; I felt that he was a teacher by heart, he loved his students, with great care he guided us through the curriculum; through his ability to fascinate others he managed to focus our interest on subjects that were considered difficult and dry. With a warm hug he welcomed me back to the class, wishing me a wonderful new start.

Mr. Ragaz was aware of the difficult time that dad and I had been going through but he never mentioned anything about this to me, he was clearly glad to see me back. Before he began with the first lecture that morning, he officially welcomed me back in front of the whole class; what a great honor this was, all my class mates focused on me, stood up, clapping and cheering at the same time which gave me the feeling of being important and appreciated.

The school desk I shared with a fellow by the name of Hans-Peter, he was considerably taller than I, very quiet, introvert, and he was a tambour in one of Basel's Carnival Cliques, for which many of us admired him. Hans Peter and I weren't the closest of friends but we got on well with each other, together we worked well on school projects, finding solutions to given tasks, shared ideas and ambitions, but we never talked about our home life. In terms of character we complemented each other very well, however, in the school band we were soft enemies, both of us were very competitive kids—he was a tambour and I was a drummer; believe me there is a difference, each one of us wanted to be the better musician, his skills on the snare drum were further advanced, he was mostly the one that was chosen by the music teacher for the performance of marching music whereas my skills were more orientated toward Jazz— unfortunately Jazz did not belong to the school repertoire.

Sure, everybody in the class was a mate but actual friends I had few. Other than Hans-Peter, my true friend, there was Hermann and Ernest; both of them very committed footballers; they were successful players in the junior league of FC Basel, and because of their commitment to the sport we didn't get to see each other very often outside the school, and then there was Paul; a rather tall fellow, very quiet and very intelligent. Some of my class mates were teasing him because he was a member of the Mormons. For me Paul was an interesting fellow; I remember, from time to time during our breaks he explained to some of us what Mormons are all about. I don't recall all the details of these conversations but I remember that the book of the Mormons is a citation of events similar to the bible as we know it from the Catholic or Protestant believes. I understood from Paul that their way of living is different to my life; although I was not particular aware of it; I was growing up in a capitalistic environment where material goods were important, religion was not. In contrast, Paul grew up in a very religious environment which was perhaps a little different from our experiences, and this became apparent through his impeccable behavior.

Why did some of my class mates behave in this way, ridiculing Paul because he was growing up with a religion different to main stream, a religion that Paul did not choose; it was a gift from his parents; was it a lack of intelligence or mere ignorance that cause this despicable behavior from some of my class mates?

I am not sure, but I do know that at that time we were old enough to know better than this.

At that time the official religious teaching in the common Swiss society was limited to Christianity, the Catholic and the Protestant believe in particular, and the two were clearly segregated. We were able to share the same classroom at the schools, but the religious instruction was taught in different locations, and it seemed that the system aimed to ensure that the difference was noticeable to all concerned.

The Jewish believe, and that of the Mormons were frowned upon by many blue-collar workers, Islam, Hinduism, Chinese traditional, Buddhism, Primal-indigenous, African traditional and Diasporic, Sikhism, Juche, to mention just a few of some 4,300 religions of this world weren't considered at all; most of us weren't even aware of the diversity of religions.

If Mr. Ragaz our principal teacher had known that Paul was being teased by some of his class mates, they would have been in deep trouble, he had very specific behavioral expectations from his pupil, and he did not tolerate any form of discrimination.

Around that time, we did learn and debate the struggle of the US-American human rights advocate Martin Luther King, whom was fighting for the abolition of the racial segregation which is known as the Apartheid in Africa; a system that I was to experience first-hand a little later in my life as I passed through Cape Town, South Africa on my way to Australia.

Without actually realizing it at the time, as a child I learned an awful lot about religion, racism and the white supremacy. Although my educational influence that I got from my dad did not include going to church on Sundays, nor was religion presented as a way of life. As I learned later, dad didn't have a problem with religion as such; he had a problem with the churches ground crew.

Despite this, the underlying principles of my education had very much to do with religion; I was taught the difference between good and bad, what was acceptable behavior and what was non-acceptable, I learned to respect others, to be polite but also to stand up for my rights and to defend them if necessary, to live and to let live, to help those in trouble or in need, to respect life in general, to respect animals, to care for mother earth and anything she is providing for us—all of which has something to do with religion.

I never knew what it was like to go to church with the exception of the day of my confirmation at the age of fifteen. We didn't talk about religion at home; I was taught to liv religion.

## My Friend Ernest

Ernest was another pal that played an important part in my life, he was a year older than me, he went to a different school, red headed with freckles, a kid from my immediate neighborhood; he was the youngest of four in his family. A couple of times per week, after I had accomplished my homework dad allowed me to invite a friend to our house.

Invariably I invited Ernest for those occasions, neither of us were interested in football, which was one of the reasons why we got on well with each other; mostly we got stuck into a STOKYS project, building something that was not listed in the instruction manual, figuring out how we can construct a gear box, a truck with its own motor, a crane whose hook could be moved up and down and its arm was operated with an electric motor—or similar stuff. For hours we would seriously amuse ourselves with the design and the construction of machines and the like.

We didn't just tinker about and create things, Ernest and I often talked about the United States of America, in particular the buildings in New-York; how it was possible to construct the skyscrapers so tall without them tumbling over, we speculated what it would be like to live in the States. Around that time, in our neighborhood there were a lot of folk that admired the Americans, saying that it was a great country long before Donald Trump came along, it was said that a lot of good things come from there, and we had at least one of those in our family—the red 1961 Chevrolet Impala cabriolet; then there was the significant military involvement in the Alliance that was responsible for the liberation during the Second World War, Henry Ford and Harley Davidson, the Gyrator Washing Machine, the Hoover vacuum cleaner and other household gadgets, the Wurlitzer Jukebox, Frank Sinatra, Luis Armstrong and Benny Goodman, King Kong and Walt Disney, McDonnell Douglas, Lockheed Martin and Boeing, the Submarine, Antibiotics, Radio and Television, Rocketry and Nuclear Power, the Cold War; all of the American inventions as well as other things that were considered more or less significant, and this was the foundation that impressed and stimulated our conversation about America. A lot of information we got from books; the country's history, its agricultural industry, the vast areas for grazing land and the growing of wheat, potatoes and other produce, the manufacturing industry, the diversity of cultures within the fifty states, the different landscapes ranging from North Dakota down to the border of Mexico, from San Francisco across to New-York, the Ku Klux Klan and the accent with which the Americans speak was fascinating.

There were others around us that didn't share our enthusiasm with us, for some reason or another which we didn't understand.

Both, Ernest and I were certain to one day go to America to find out what it would be like to live there.

By going to the USA, we weren't thinking about a visit as a tourist, in our fantasy we were actually contemplating to immigrate to the States, without truly understanding the notion of immigration.

It wasn't just the States that captured our fantasy; we also became interested in the vastness of Australia. I don't recall how we got hold of this material but I remember that we had gathered several picture books, informing ourselves about the country's history; how the first Europeans, the Dutch explorer Captain Willem Janszoon, landed in Australia in 1606, how in 1688 the British explorer William Dampier explored the west coast, and finally when in 1770 Captain James Cook landed at Botany Bay on the HMS Endeavour; as he proceeded to map the eastern coast and claimed it for Great Britain, how in 1788 the first British settlement was established in Sydney by Captain Arthur Phillip which was the start of the British penal colony, made up of mostly prisoners, the discovery of gold in the southeast region of Victoria—causing prospectors to flock to the area during the Victoria Gold Rush.

How in 1880 the folk hero Ned Kelly, the Robin Hood of Australia, was executed for murder, how the Commonwealth of Australia was formed in 1901, how the Australian woman were guaranteed the right to vote in 1902, the founding of the capital city Canberra in 1911, the signing of the Treaty of Versailles and the joining of the League of Nations in 1919, the founding of Qantas Airlines in 1920, how in 1932 the construction of the Sydney Harbor Bridge was completed, how the construction of the Sydney Opera house was started in 1959, and the fact that Kangaroos are native to Australia were factors that lead to the development an enormous curiosity, and strong desire to visit the country one day.

One of the aspects about Australia that drew my particular attention was the aviation industry, the way it was described in one of the books resembled the adventures times of the engine driver Casey Jones, one of my childhood heroes, as he was driving for the Illinois Central Railroad in the States, only in this case the author depicted the adventures of the Australian sky.

The Australian government sponsored race from Great Britain to Australia which was won by the brothers Keith and Ross Smith in 1919 with a Vickers Vim, Bert Hinkler that flew solo from Croydon Airport to Darwin with a Avro Avian in 1928, Charles Kingsford Smith and Charles Ulm that conducted the first trans-Tasman flight from Richmond NSW to Christchurch New Zealand in 1928, Maude Bonney, the first woman that flew solo in a Klemm KI 32 from Archerfield QLD to Cape Town in 1937, were some of the pioneer stories that characterized a great impression on my little person.

I specifically recall the time when I read the history about the fabulous achievement of Maude Bonney; growing up at time where our mum's responsibility in society had begun to change from being the caretaker of the house, the guardian of the children and the husband; it was now generally acceptable, even essential for women to be carrying out a job outside the home.

At that time, apprenticeships in the so-called soft areas were open to females, whereas trades like metalworkers were accessible to men only. This doesn't mean that nursing is a soft job, on the contrary, women as well as men that practice this job confirm that nursing is mentally as well as physically a tough occupation, but the point is that in the fifties and sixties there weren't any male nursing staff to be seen in hospitals, this profession was reserved for women.

Similarly, the local railroad company didn't employ female train drivers, nor did Swissair have any ladies sitting in the cockpit, and yet it wasn't unusual to come across a female doctor.

That's why people got shocked when they came across a situation that didn't fit the preconceived idea; there weren't any lady Truckee's, or mechanics, painters, plumbers, nor pilots, and if you would have seen one you would have been so surprised that you would have had difficulties to shut your mouth again.

The story of Maude Bonney had startled me because her achievement was far beyond that of what one expected from a female at that time, but because I was unaffected by the thoughts of preconceived ideas of others, I was delighted to recognize that woman can accomplish the same things as man.

As a child it is simple and uncomplicated to forge plans to immigrate to the States, or indeed anywhere else in the world, I didn't think about all the bureaucratic hurdles that would have to be overcome, the conditions that had to be fulfilled to realize such a dream didn't interest me either, I could simply decide in my fantasy how I would do this, and it worked. Now I realize how important it is to be able to think in a pragmatic manner without setting yourself limits or borders which can negatively influence the outcome of your thoughts and wishes.

I guess I was lucky that my dad thought and encouraged me to become a creative person, to question what others are saying or doing, validating opinions and statements of others without being scared or indeed embarrassed to hold an opinion other than mainstream, he provided me with the necessary mental tools as well as stimulating discussions which contributed strongly to my positive development during my childhood.

## Dad and Me

Dad and I, the bachelor period, age 13 to nearly 14, one of the happiest periods during my childhood was the time that dad and I lived alone, without a lady in the house, just him and me, almost like a couple of bachelors that shared the same household.

This is not meant to be a derogatory comment toward ladies, however the past couple of years of family life had been rather uneventful for myself; Celina, my stepmother might have been a pleasant lady that my father loved but to me she was no mother, I never observed any emotion from her, I don't recall that she ever talked to me about anything other than the trivial instructional messages that are essential in the daily life, she never gave me the feeling of being of any importance at all, she never bothered to give me a hug; I merely remember her for the toys that she bought for me, that she was out on most evenings amusing herself with dad, and her culinary skills that she surprised me with in the evenings before going out.

Deep down, my intuitive feelings told me that this situation could not be forever, that it was not normal for a young, good-looking fellow like my dad to remain a bachelor, that at some stage he would meet another lady, and that it was inevitable that she would move in with us. At that time, I understood that I had to enjoy every moment that I had with my father—and I did.

Despite the fact that dad had set clear borders which had to be respected and maintained, I always found guidance and support through my father during difficult periods, I was taught to make decisions and learned to contemplate the consequences from them, where necessary I was corrected with a fair degree of firmness without being brutalized, I was taught to be responsible, I was given time to develop mentally without compromising the need to be a child. In particular I enjoyed all the things that dad and I did together, the trips into the countryside, to France, the camping weekends, the pub crawls, the long walks along the river side, and the activities at the pontoon club—simply everything; I was very happy and at the same time enjoyed a lot of freedom.

During the summer whenever dad was free for the weekend, Saturday noon he was waiting for me outside the school, the red Chevy Cabriolet packed with camping gear in its rather large boot consisted of a reasonably large tent, a table with four small banks that could be folded into a suitcase like parcel, a small gas cooker, a woven Willow basket filled with white Bakelite plates and cups, cutlery, and a couple air matrices and blankets; we were heading to this idyllic place St. Ursanne, on the river Doubs which was situated in the French part of the Swiss Jura. The river has its origin in the East part of France in the commune of Mouthhel in the Doub's department in the Jura Mountains near the French-Swiss border, flowing down through the North-West part of Switzerland through the historic village St. Ursanne—our camping destination.

On a couple of acres of grazing-land, bordering the river we had the permission of the farmer to set up our camp about ten meters from the water. Between our tent and the rivers shoreline there was a narrow strip of woodland which cooled down the hot air somewhat, providing us with a fresh breeze of air and a little shade during hot days.

The field was not particularly level, during the week the farmer had some cattle on it to graze, and consequently there was cow dung to be found here and there, but this was nothing to be bothered about, providing one didn't accidentally step in one of them that had been freshly dropped by its owner. In the far corner there was a little wooden hut, within there was an earth closet which was shared by the campers. Each user had to provide their own toilet paper. Water wasn't available either, the stuff simply plopped a couple of meters downward, and to combat the sometimes-unpleasant odor that was rising from the depth we carried a tin of baking soda with us, sprinkling some of this white powder down the whole had the same effect as splashing around with a deodorant.

Setting up the tent was a job for two. First, dad laid out the tent on the ground, I started to join the aluminum rods that provided the support for the roof pitch, I had to hold in place the supporting rods whilst dad secured the rope on the pegs which stabilized the frame of the tent.

The table and bunks had to be unfolded and put into place, the air matrices had to be filled with air with a hand pump, the sleeping bags and blankets had to be prepared, the portable gas light in its position, ready for the night, the portable chill-box with our food and beverage provisions put in the right spot, and the crockery basket was set in its place.

Usually, there were another four or five couples camping on this two-acre parcel; they too were there to enjoy a peaceful weekend; the atmosphere was friendly but everybody did their own thing. During all the years that we went to St. Ursanne I was the only child among the campers, I didn't have any pals, I had to organize my own fun which wasn't difficult at all for me. Sometimes our camp neighbor, one of my dad's colleagues who also spend most weekends at St. Ursanne with his wife took me fishing in the river. Not that I was particularly interested in fishing, but I was always glad when he asked me if I wanted to join him.

He was wearing a rubber outfit which incorporated boots and trouser in one peace, with this he was able to move about most parts in the river. He would piggy back me to a little island or large rocks in the middle of the river, from there I could watch him doing his thing, and at the same time I observed the way the water was flowing around the rocks, the whorls and the turmoil that were created around the stones and other obstacles in the water which fascinated me.

On most such occasions I stayed with the old man for at least four or five hours, amusing myself, but much of the time I spend thinking about all sorts of things, pondering over the nature by which I was surrounded; the crystal clear water rushing by, the sun that was providing the light, the shade thrown from the woods on the side of the river, constantly changing as time passed, the cool breeze rushing past me, the different sounds created by the water flowing by, the rustling sound that came from the shoreline, caused by the wind that moved the leaves making a soft, muffled crackling sound, and the occasional comment from my fishing partner, but I was also pondering over school, my music and different projects that I was involved in, sometimes wondering what my mum, my brother or grandma were doing now.

Mr. Baumann, as I called him, used to catch four or five trout during a stint of fishing, sometimes there were around twenty-six centimeters from nose to tail weighing about tree hundred grams, from time to time he managed to hook a large one which was a meal for two.

The fish was always cleaned before we went back to the camp. I didn't like this very much, though I watched how Mr. Bauman cut the trout belly open from the anus, up toward the head, with his finger he then removed all the intestines, and finally he washed the fish on the river shore. Back at the camp he always gave dad a couple of trout with the comment that I was helping him which I thought that it was a nice gesture, knowing very well that I was of no help at all to Mr. Bauman.

More often than not, the Baumans and us would prepare the meal together, Mrs. making a potato salad with a rich mayonnaise dressing, Mr. would season the trout, wrap it in aluminum foil and place them carefully in the glowing charcoal.

Dad's contribution to this feast was usually a nice piece of meat from the grill, a green salad with a simple dressing, and a variety of French cheese which he usually got from the neighboring Alsace Region. It was my job to make sure that the table was set nicely, and that the men had a cold beer, which we kept in a shallow, rocky part of the river which provided sufficient protection so that the glass bottles would not be washed away by the current.

Cooking on the open fire was very fundamental which demanded a bit of effort, providing the kindling and the wood was my job; most of the time there was enough usable material to be gathered in the narrow wood strip alongside the river, only occasionally I had to go up into the forest above the access road where there was a larger volume of fire wood laying on the ground. Starting with the kindling, the actual building up of the different sized bits of wood was my dad's job.

Often these reef and beef Barbeques took place in the evening, sitting around the open fire when the sun was going down, at a time when mother nature created an incredible mood with the rays of sunshine changing their color, the different shadows that were thrown by the trees, the ever changing colors of the glowing open fire, the varying sculptures that rose from the smoke, the crackling of the fire, the sound of the troubled water that emerged from the background, and the aromas from the fresh trout braising in the foil and the smell of the slightly caramelizing outer part of the beef being grilled were sensational.

The evenings we shared together with the Bauman's were always interesting, all sorts of subjects were talked about, often there were differences of opinion which were heavily debated and defended without insulting each other.

Just about anything except religion would be discussed, and the subjects did not always interest me either but often I followed the conversation very closely because the content and the way it was presented was fascinating; at the same time I was secretly hoping that dad would win the debate.

Sunday mornings was the time for dad to enjoy a little solitude, deeply entranced in a book, with his Parisienne Blue and perhaps a coffee with condensed milk on the side he would spend the morning reading, and I was mucking around on the rivers shore. A couple of hundred meters from our camp there was a small wooden barge floating in the river; it was tied to a tree on the shoreline with a reasonably thick chain. I managed to pull the barge close enough to the shore so that I could board it, and with a long sturdy stick I was able to maneuver myself a few meters away from the shoreline, up river and then drift down again. I could do this over and over again for hours, and at the same time the clear, shallow water allowed me to explore the bottom of the shoreline.

At the camp, lunch on Sunday was always uncomplicated, knowing that late afternoon before driving back home, we would make a little detour to the Hôtel de la Couronne in St. Ursanne.

Around noon I would walk about one kilometer further downstream to the local bakery to buy some fresh bread, back at the camp we would enjoy the fresh bread with butter, cheese and a tomato salad.

From time to time the Bauman's son Rolf, a fellow in his early twenties joint his parents at the camp. Like his father, he was the proud owner of a 1959 Harley-Davidson, painted black with some white trim, the steering fork, the engine cover and other parts were chrome plated, the twin leather saddle, the side pouches and the side-walls of the tires were white.

Rolf was like a big brother to me; he would often invite me for a ride on his Harley; I guess he thought that I would appreciate some company of someone that was a little closer to my age group. We would follow the path beside the river for about a half hour or so until we got to this little pub on the shore, sitting in the garden, chatting about things. Rolf was a biology student and his interest in nature was impressive, with an astonishing enthusiasm he would explain to me the natural marvels by which we were surrounded; I absorbed everything in detail, I had the feeling that I was the little brother that he never had, and I looked up to him with great admiration, lapping up his company.

Around four in the afternoon it was time to clear the camp, I helped dad to dismantle the tent, to let the air out from the matrices and to neatly fold them, together with the sleeping bags and blankets, to put away the crockery, the cutlery and the glasses, making sure that they were clean, and to get it all ready so that dad could stow everything in the boot of the car. Usually by five in the afternoon, after the final walk-around; making sure that we had not forgotten anything but also to ensure that there was no rubbish laying around, we were ready to leave the place.

The Bauman's and their son Rolf joint us on our detour to the Couronne at St. Ursanne on most Sunday's. For dad and me it was mostly the last opportunity, until the following weekend to get to some decent food that we could eat with pleasure, because during the weekdays our cuisine created by dad was very basic, commensurate with his cooking skills; baked beans with tomato sauce, lentils, ravioli on tomato sauce, and corned beef, the entire selection out of a can, alternatively he served a soup created by Knorr or Maggi, usually served with a Weenies sausage, forming part of the lunch repertoire, and in the evening our menu was a composition of carefully chosen uncooked food; different cheese, a selection of small goods, mayonnaise, mustard, bread and butter were part of the creation.

The preparation of the evening meal was clearly straight forward whereas lunch was a little more complex. Dad placed some peeled and crushed garlic in the pan and glazed it with some fresh butter before the content of a particular can was poured in with it and gently stirred with a wooden spoon so that it would not cling to the bottom of the pan—this simple variation turned the ordinary content of a can into a magic meal.

The food that we chose at the Couronne was mostly the same during all the years that we went there after the camping weekend. Invariably the hors-d'oeuvre was a fresh trout or perch fillets pan-fried in butter, served with tossed almonds and a lemon wedge, whereas the main meal remained always the same—a rather large, fresh oven roasted chicken—in those days a luxurious meal fit for a king; the meat was very juicy and tender, the skin crispy, and it was served with canned baby carrots, peas and crispy French fries lightly salted.

Dad always ordered a whole chicken for the two of us, it arrived on a rather large silver platter which the waitress placed carefully on the réchaud on the side-table from which she then served our food. The chicken was always presented whole, and then the waitress, sometimes the hostess ore the host of the pub disjointed the bird in front of us with great skill and portioned the food on preheated plates. The French-fries were served separate, also on a silver platter with a doily under the fries so that any excess frying oil would be absorbed by the paper, the waitress would regularly pass by the table, and if necessary, brought more of them around, fresh from the kitchen, until we had eaten enough.

After we had devoured the chicken and its accompaniments, after we had eaten as many French-fries as we possibly could, there was no more space for dessert, and if, then we would order a meringue glace: a couple of large scoops of vanilla ice cream sandwiched in by two meringue shells, smothered with lots of whipped cream and a strawberry or a mint leave on top as a garnish.

During the meal it was mostly quiet around the table; I think everybody was silent because they wanted to reflect on the relaxing time that we spent at the camp as well as giving a little thought on the things to come next week.

Before the bill arrived at the table dad would discretely order a bottle of Absinthe; a liqueur of slightly green color, made from vermouth, anis and fennel, different infusions derived from herbs and the plant Artemisia Absinthium which formed the basis of the distillates which had alcohol content between 45 and 85 % Vol—deadly stuff, only suitable for those whom had been inaugurated.

Originally, Absinthe came from the Val de Travers in the canton Neuenburg Switzerland, and it was produced as healing liquid, liquor well known and adored by country folk, particular in the French speaking part of Switzerland.

In 1915 Absinthe was prohibited by many European countries, in the USA and in most cantons within Switzerland as a result of reoccurring Absinthe poisoning. At the time it was thought that dependency on Absinthe was inevitable, and that massive health problems would occur as a result of its consumption. Apparently, it was the substance named Thujon which was derived from a plant which gave the Absinthe its unusual taste. However, farming folk continued to distil and sell this stuff secretly. That is why dad had to place his order discretely, the making, that alone the sale of this liquid was still punishable by law.

The purchase of the Absinthe was not apparent on the bill; it was paid separately, without a receipt. On the way out from the dining room, down the stairs on the left was a door, when you opened it, immediately to the right on a small table, the host had placed the bottle that you ordered wrapped in a brown paper bag, he had placed it there just before you were ready to go. Just as discretely as the publican put the bottle there, the customer took it in his possession.

I didn't know at the time, but much later in life I learned from my dad that a bottle of Absinthe lasted him just one week, often he had none left when he picked up the next one on the weekend, he had become dependent on this stuff for a period of some three years but was able to quit the habit without external support.

## On Probation

I was just about fourteen years of age, sharing was no problem to me, I was used to it; when my mum was still with dad, I wasn't even aware of the fact that I was sharing my dad with her, and the second time when he was married to stepmother Celina—the sharing was no problem to me either. With the experience of sharing behind me I should have been well prepared for whatever was to come.

The day dad introduced me to Louise; a young, rather short and solid lady whom I had seen regularly before when I went shopping in the supermarket adjacent to dad's business, there she was serving customers at the small goods department, I had the impression that she was pleasant and friendly.

Dad introduced Louise to me as the lady whom was going to take care of a couple of things in our household and that she would prepare some meals for dad and I from time to time. Everybody called her Lulu, the short form of her classical French name Louise, she seemed very young, she could have been my older sister, and she was still living with her parents in another part of Basel.

At the beginning her visits to our house was now and again, perhaps once a week, and then her presence became gradually more frequent, spaced over several months, providing me with plenty of time to get used to the new situation. At first, I was not aware about the things to come, but was able to recognize some changes that were very pleasant and easy to accept; I realized that our menu plan was gradually improving; more often dad and I could reheat meals during the weekdays, meals that Aunty Lulu as I was asked to called her had prepared, packaged, labelled and placed in the chiller for us on the weekend, and I noted that dad appeared to be happy again.

Aunty Lulu came from a worker's family who migrated from Alsace France to Switzerland during the second world war, her dad was working for the local Electricity Company as a semi-skilled electrician, her mother had been engaged in a printing house, her sister Tabea was working in one of Basel's Pharma factories as a laboratory assistant, and Aunty Lulu had just recently completed her apprenticeship as a sales lady in the meat department in one of Switzerland's largest supermarkets.

Her mum was a tough lady, she appeared somewhat discontented with herself, even bitter, I think she was unable to digest all that had happened to the family during the war, and she had probably great difficulties to get used to the chronic monetary pressure, not being able to afford anything other than the things that were absolutely required to survive.

Soon after I got to know Aunt Lulu, I was introduced to her father whom at a later stage I called Grandpa Robert; he was a very jolly person; he appeared always happy, very caring, he was funny, very humorous and always ready for a prank—a person that I learned to love very dearly. Grandpa Robert was also a little overweight, I was told that in his younger years he was very athletic, among other things he played football, but now, apart from his work, his activities were reduced to reading books, taking care of the chores that Grandma Robert had assigned for him, and to cook for the family on Sundays.

Like her father, Aunty Lulu adored food, everything that she knew about cooking at that time she had learned from her father, it wasn't unusual to see the two of them stuffing around in magazines and contemporary cook books, drooling over some recipe for which they couldn't afford the main ingredient, the primary cuts of veal, lamb, beef and pork, mushrooms as well as some of the exquisite spices and oils, but this was about to change, my dad enjoyed good food and wasn't opposed to a food budget increase, he was providing the necessary cash to Aunt so that she could enchant us with different delicacies on the weekend.

During our bachelor period, dad and I had become accustomed to canned food which we enhanced with lots of butter, crushed garlic and diced onions during the reheating phase, Gruyere and Emmentaler cheese, different kinds of small goods carefully arranged on a wooden cutting board, Thomy's mayonnaise and mustard, fresh bread, butter and jam, and now we were introduced to a cuisine whose extent of fresh ingredient went beyond onions and garlic, a cuisine that omitted canned food, a cuisine whose preparation methods were a little more complex than glazing onions and garlic in butter, a cuisine whose scope for creativity and variety was almost endless.

Suddenly, we were acquainted with different kinds of ingredients and how they could be combined to complement each other; the types of meat, the vegetables, cereal and pulses as well as spices and fresh herbs that had become part of Aunt's recipes had completely changed the spectrum of flavors and textures that dad and I had been used to, and the presentation of the meals had become more sophisticated.

I understand today that dad couldn't have chosen a better way to introduce his girlfriend to me, at first, a couple of times per week she was in our house, charmed us with culinary treats that we had only experienced in restaurants before, and besides this, she appeared to be a pleasant person to be with, I quickly learned to associate Aunt Lulus presence in our house with good food and I began to look forward to the day that Aunt Lulu came to the house.

Although I don't believe that this gradual introduction was deliberate, I think that it merely happened this way coincidently.

Besides the culinary adventures that Aunt Lulu introduced to dad and I, gradually she established lots of other thingamajigs and useful staff in the house, things that a couple of bachelors that live on their own wouldn't do or bother about.

I guess she looked for the little things that may not be apparent to a man, she gradually introduced some plants and fresh flowers, placed some decorative bling bling's around, organized new curtains, gradually turning the house into a home; having Aunt Lulu around was very pleasant; her presence enriched my life and no doubt that of my father.

This phase of introduction, the trial-period as I call it today was an opportunity for dad, me and Aunt Lulu to find out more about each other, to see if we were compatible as an ensemble, to find out if a life together as a family was feasible, but I don't have any illusions about it, my opinion was not decisive in this decision-making process, despite the fact that dad had asked me on a couple of occasions what I thought about Aunt Lulu.

To me it was clear that the time was approaching where Aunt Lulu would come into our lives; I could only see positive and pleasant changes since she had been visiting us on a regular basis; I had no negative prejudgment or wicket preconceived ideas, nor did I see her as competition in terms of me and my dad.

As this experimental period continued for about six months or so, Aunt Lulu's visits became more frequent, she began to stay with us over the weekend, gradually taking up the position of the lady of the house.

That was the time when she began to involve me in the kitchen, helping her with the preparation of meals, beginning with the simple tasks; peeling vegetables and fruits, Later she taught me some fundamental knife skills, I learned how to cut fruits and vegetables into different shapes, suitable for different preparation methods, I was helping to wash and dry the cooking utensils as she worked her way through the different phases of the preparation, at the same time I was able to watch how she was going about the different tasks of the preparation and the cooking. She appeared to be very competent, organized and structured in everything that she did in the kitchen.

However, I don't think that she would have been successful as a teacher, she had no patience and her teaching method was lousy, her instruction was abrupt and not very precise, but it didn't matter, I was curious to find out how she magically turned the raw ingredient into a delightful meal, and I was a fast learner, able to understand what she meant very quickly.

Gradually, Aunt had taught me about the importance of the hygiene rules required during the preparation of food, how to organize the work in a domestic kitchen, Aunt taught me a lot about the handling and stowage of fresh, dry, chilled and frozen food as she had learned in a professional environment during her apprenticeship in the food trade area, and I picked up a lot of preparation and cooking skills from her, and this at the age of fourteen.

## Grandma and Grandpa Robert

I think it was before my fourteenth birthday when dad told me that Aunt Lulu was going to shift in with us; I had no particular feelings about this, I didn't feel that it was particularly great, nor did I think it was a bad thing, at least, up until now I had plenty of time to adapt and to get used to Aunt. But when dad explained that I had to stay with Aunt Lulu's parents for a little while until they had organized themselves, I didn't understand the world anymore. I don't recall my reaction at the time, I merely remember that I was very disappointed, keeping my emotions to myself, just as I did when my mum left our home, I closed myself off from others, keeping my inner thoughts within as if they were a great secret, I had almost instantly lost my happy go lucky way of going through life, I had thoughts of wanting to leave home and join my mum in Bern, I began to have feelings of hate toward Aunt.

I simply couldn't understand why I had to move out, even if it was only for a short time—whatever that meant. After all, I had learned to be fairly independent and capable to take care of myself; I certainly would not have bothered anyone.

To this day I don't know if it was my dad that took this decision or if it was Aunt Lulu, but I am certain that it had something to do with her; perhaps dad thought that they needed lots of privacy when Aunt moved in—maybe it was Aunt's wish. What peeved me off the most was the fact that nobody bothered to provide me with a reason; even if he had told me fibs, I wouldn't have cared, but I expected some kind of plausible explanation from my father, a chance to defend my position, perhaps an opportunity to convince him that I was capable to handle the situation, it felt as if dad was abandoning me.

Unfortunately, I never took the opportunity to ask dad later in life, and now that he has passed away it is too late, I will never know the truth.

Generally, my father treated me like an adult, talking truthfully, straight forward, uncomplicated, but in this particular case he didn't even dare to tell me white little lies, he merely put me before the fact that I was to stay with grandma and grandpa Robert.

To understand my father's behavior better, I know that as a rule, children were not consulted at that time, and frankly speaking I now must take the opportunity to put myself the question; have I always been truthful and straight forward with my own son in delicate, very personal situations? I guess not.

Some days later Aunt had been kind enough to pack my bag, it felt as if she couldn't wait to get rid of me, I would have been capable to get the packing done myself, I remember clearly, I was very angry, boiling inside, but I didn't want her to realize this, I kept my cool. Selfish as kids are, the fact that the two of them needed some private time did not occur to me at all.

Together we drove to Aunt's parents place, about fifteen minutes by car. Their home was in a working-class area, in a very old three-story house on the second floor; though each of the houses was individually build, they were hugging each other side on side, all of them constructed much in the same manner, other than the house number there weren't a lot of features by which you could differentiate them.

As we pulled up in front of the house, I had a meticulous look at what was to be my new home, at least for a while; between the house and the footpath there was a cast iron door and fence on either side about one meter eighty high, the ground floor was constructed from solid, large stones which had been carefully worked into oblong blocks, the first and the second story were built with un-rendered red bricks with the exception of the window casing and the mantles which were also made from natural stone, above each window the stone masons had placed beautifully shaped figurines reminding me of angel faces, a bit like the house that we lived in when I was a baby.

As I got through the gate into the front yard, I noted the narrow garden bed on either side of the coble stone path that was leading to the stone steps up to the entrance, the garden was designed very simple, there were some decorative plants, colorful flowers and a couple of young Chestnut trees, not taller than a couple of meters. The heavy wooden front door, set back into the building, fitted with cast iron guards over the glass, a heavy brass hand knocker in the middle of the door, a beautifully crafted door handle made from solid brass, with two glass panels about half way up from the middle of the door which were furbished with frosted glass; part of its design included small star shaped openings which were not frosted, through which you could see into the hallway, and build into the wall, on the right side of the entrance recess were the electrical door bells arranged on a brass plate with the names of each family displayed to the left.

I rang the bell to Grandpa Roberts and the door was opened very quickly, although the house was very old, positioned in a working man's neighborhood, to my surprise, the front door could be opened with an electric buzzer from each of the three apartments. The wooden stairs leading up to the middle floor was making a terrible squeaky sound, on the left side, before turning onto the second step leading to Grandpa's apartment, there was a small toilet room which was to be shared with the downstairs neighbor, because common toilet paper was not part of the budget, the old dunny was furbished with newspaper sheets cut to size, held together with a piece of string.

Once we had reached the first floor, on the left there was the door to the apartment. Both, the door and the side panels on the right and left side were fitted with wooden panels from the bottom to about one meter in height, the rest was fitted with a milky glass through which you couldn't see, beautifully decorated with an etched floral pattern. We were expected, Aunt Lulu's father opened the door, he greeted us in his jolly manner and asked us to come in. Aunt's mother was in the kitchen, she was somewhat taller than Grandpa Robert, overweight, her hair permed and short, snow white, she had a serious look on her face, clearly the difficult past had left its marks and characterized her facial expression.

As you would expect in an old city house, the kitchen was not very large, on the left-hand side there was an old four burner gas stove, a small workbench and a kitchen table surrounded by four chairs, on the right side there was a cast iron sink with an old brass tap for the cold water, above it was a gas boiler which produced hot water. At the far end there was a glass door leading to the balcony. Opposite the kitchen was the living room furnished in a traditional way; a dining table, six matching chairs, an old sofa, a buffet as it was fashionable in the thirty's, a grandfather clock that announced the time every quarter, half and on the full hour, so loud that you could not follow a normal conversation, and a TV in the corner. Then there was Grandma and Grandpa Roberts room which I never got to see from the inside.

My room was also very basic; it had a bed, a wardrobe for my clothes, a cupboard in which the family's winter clothes were kept, and at the far end there was a glass door that led to the balcony. The apartment was very old, relatively small, it had wooden floors which were polished with some kind of wax on a weekly bases, the walls could have done well with a fresh coat of paint in the kitchen, the kitchen tiles that surrounded the sink and cooking area looked as if they had been stuck to the wall a hundred years ago, the kitchen floor was covered with a linoleum that was cracked on the surface in several spots, and the wallpaper in the two rooms looked like it should have been renewed years ago, everything was old and tatty but very clean. The balcony was rather large, the view quite interesting to me; one could see the old houses in the neighborhood, their yards, one could look into the apartments on the other side, and if you wanted to, you could observe what people across the backyard were doing.

Getting to know grandma and grandpa Robert was strait forward, both of them were quite uncomplicated, to me it was clear that they expected me to behave and to do what I was told, to go to school as usual and to get my homework done, to help around the house, and I understood that my dad wanted me to obey and to be cooperative. I had no difficulties with neither of them, their behavior toward me was always correct, Grandma Robert made sure that my clothes were clean and tidy, she made sure that I had a snack to take to school; she generally cared for my wellbeing. Grandpa Robert and I had a good relationship; he was amusing and could be very funny and humorous, he was very clever, he was well educated and was able to explain things in a clear manner that could be understood by all.

Saturdays after pay day I had to accompany Grandma and Grandpa Robert for the shopping, we used to go to one of the town's large supermarkets. There was no doubt about whom was the boss in the house, Grandma seemed to have assumed the responsibility for the selection of the groceries, the fruits and the vegetables but Grandpa always chose the meat. He would have discussions with the butcher, wanting to see different pieces of a particular cut of meat, making sure that the animal from which the meat derived was not too old, that the grain of the meat was not too large, and that the fat content was just the way he wanted it, it had to be just right because he was the one that was going to prepare the Sunday roast for midday, just in time for dad, Aunt Lulu, her sister and brother-in-law to arrive.

Sometimes I accompanied Grandpa Robert to the cellar, a place of great interest. In those days the cellar wasn't just the place where you kept your supplies over the summer; it was the family larder where much of the provision for the winter time was stored—potatoes, carrots, red and white cabbage, bulb celery, parsnip, leek and onions were buried in dry sand—in this way they kept for several months, though showing slight deterioration in quality over time, there were a couple of hundred preserving glasses filled with green beans, whole tomatoes, small carrots, peas, plumbs, apricots and pears, apple pieces and sliced rhubarb, apricot, plumb, raspberry, blackberry and strawberry jam—all produce and fruit from the garden.

There were also oven-dried green beans—a typical Swiss specialty—sauerkraut stored in large earthenware pots, a couple of large pots of lard, some smaller earthen ware pots filled with rosehip jam and a few other things. On this early Sunday morning Grandpa gathered the things that he needed for the lunch menu, and I helped him to take the shopping up into the kitchen. It was a privilege to be able to help Grandpa with some of the preparation, to see how he was absorbed by what he was doing, totally focused.

On those days I was particularly content; I was close to Grandpa Robert whom I got to like very much, I also knew that I would get to see dad and perhaps be able to spend a little time with him, and I was looking forward to Aunt Lulu's brother-in-law, Heinz, a person that I very much admired and liked, and if I was very lucky, dad would take us for a little spin in his red Chevrolet Cabriolet after lunch.

## The Sunday Roast

I had always appreciated dad's cheese fondue for which he had assumed the preparation for in our house, but other than that his culinary skills were limited to the reheated canned food embellished with a little butter and crushed garlic, small goods and cheese carefully placed on a wooden board. However, in contrast, I remember clearly those moments when I was allowed to be with Grandpa Robert, watching how he was preparing the Sunday pot roast.

Grandpa Robert was born in Strassburg, Alsace where as a youngster he had learned to cook from his mother who was working as a house keeper, cooking for an influential family. His repertoire comprised "Beckeoffe"—different vegetables and meats, sometimes left overs placed in a stone-ware pot, covered with puff pastry, then placed in an oven to bake, "Surkrut"—sauerkraut cooked with some Alsace Riesling, served with steamed potatoes, cooked with smoked bacon and different pork sausages, "Kugelhopf"—a specific yeast dough either sweet with almonds or savory with smoked bacon pieces, baked in a specifically shaped, corrugated baking dish, "Kalbskopf"—calf's head poached in a red wine sauce, "Schmorbrote"—the pot roast that he used to prepare on Sundays were some of the specialties that he used to prepare during the time that I was living with the family.

The dish that I liked the most from grandpa's culinary repertoire was the Sunday Pot-roast with lots of sauce, served with broad noodles tossed in butter.

Because this was my favorite dish from Grandpa's culinary assortment, this recipe was the one that fascinated me the most; I adored watching him during the preparation, asking him about every step of the process, wanting to know why and how he did what he was doing.

Grandpa laid the raw, pork pot-roast on his large wooden chopping board, showed me how the butcher had very skillfully rolled the meat into a thick roll and then tied it in a particular manner with butcher's twine so that it wouldn't lose its shape during the roasting process, and then went on to explain that it was important to buy a piece of meat that was not too dark, that the color is an indication for the age of the animal, that the flavor of older animals is stronger and that the meat would be tougher, that the meat had to be nicely coated with a thin layer of fat on the outside, and the muscles needed to be slightly marbled with fat which would keep the meat juicy during the roasting process. He also pointed out that the meat needed to be cut against the grain, that cutting it linear would make it tough to eat.

Then he pierced the meat with a sharp paring knife all over, in these openings he pushed crushed cloves of peeled garlic, rubbed some mustard, salt and pepper into the meat and left it on the side to marinate for a bit.

In the meantime, he prepared what he called the "mirepoix" which consisted of carrot, bulb celery, onion, garlic, leek, thyme, bay leaves and cloves, these vegetables all cut coarsely in pieces about two centimeters thick, this was set aside for a later process.

After the leg of pork has had about twenty minutes to marinate, some oil, either vegetable or olive oil was added to the bottom of a cast-iron pan.

The ready to sear temperature had been achieved when the oil started to spit and crackle after Grandpa splashed just a little cold water on the hot oil; one had to be very careful, the hot oil could burn your skin, Grandpa cautioned.

Then he laid the rolled meat carefully into the hot oil, turning it from time to time, ensuring that all sides were seared to a light brown color, building up a very slight crust, then he removed the meat and put it aside in a dish.

Now he added the mirepoix to the cast iron pan, on a moderate heat he turned the vegetables so that they also got to be light brown on the outside, the leek, thyme, rosemary, bay leave and cloves he added last minute so that they would not get burned as these components were smaller and more delicate compared to the root vegetables, toward the end of this process he added a little tomato paste and left it to take color with the rest of the ingredient.

Then he deglazed the caramelized mirepoix with plenty of white wine, keeping the gas flame on high until most of this liquid had been reduced at which point he added some cold water, brought this to the simmering point, and then added the seared pork together with the juice that had been leaking out from the meat back to the pan. Other herbs and spices were now added to the pot as well, but I don't really know what they were, I guess this might have been Grandpa's secret. I merely recall; a touch of this, a pinch of that and a couple of strings of Saffron.

Grandpa called the searing of the meat, and the "roasting" of the mirepoix the process of caramelization. He was adamant that this was of the utmost importance, as this enhances the flavor of the dish and gives a lovely, rich and golden-brown color to the sauce.

The cast iron pot was now covered and the content left to simmer very gently for about an hour and a half, pending on the size of the meat. About at the halfway point of the braising process, Grandpa opened the lid slightly in order to speed up the process of the reduction of the sauce.

Once the meat had reached the perfect degree of doneness, the pot roast was removed from the pan, placed into a deep serving dish, covered with a hot, slightly dampened cloth. This ensures that the meat can relax for a moment before being served, and it leaves you sufficient time to complete the sauce.

The already reduced liquid was now strained, the mirepoix removed and set aside together with the meat, the strained sauce was now pored back in the cast iron pot and reduced further until Grandpa thought that it was at the right consistency, adjusting flavor with salt and freshly ground pepper if he deemed that it was necessary. He didn't have any artificial flavor or viscosity enhancing products at all, the consistency and the flavor of his sauces were achieved through the addition of fresh, natural herbs and spices, and the mere reduction of the liquid, and to complete his creation he added quite some lumps of fresh butter which he worked into the sauce through continuous whisking; this gave the sauce a glossy appearance and a stunning fine taste.

In the meantime, he prepared some pealed pearl onions which he had lightly caramelized in a little olive oil and butter and put them aside.

Grandma was taking care of the buttered noodles during the time that Grandpa was slicing the meat, placing it carefully on a slant, kind of overlapping like the tiles on a roof into the serving dish, laying the mirepoix to the one side of the platter, spooning the caramelized onions over the sliced meat and to complete this creation, he poured a little of his divine sauce over the top—the rest was served in a sauce boat.

When it was time to take once place at the Sunday lunch table, I made sure that I could sit next to Heinz, I had no chance to sit next to my father, he was requested to take his chair next to Grandpa Robert. With great pride Grandpa brought his culinary creation to the table, and Grandma served everybody with meat, the veggies and the sauce, making sure that Grandpa got the end bit of the pot roast, which was considered the best part—reserved for the creator— Grandpa Robert, the noodles were passed around the table for everybody to help themselves.

Sitting next to Heinz, I made sure that I explained to him in great detail how Grandpa made the pot roast, not really knowing if he appreciated my continuous chatting next to him, but he seemed interested and I had the feeling that he was glad that someone around the table was bothering with him.

Heinz did not consume any alcohol, he was a teetotaler and for some reason I was not offered a little sip of whine when Heinz was with us, but this was of no significance, the time spend with Heinz was far more important to me.

Living with Grandma and Grandpa Robert was not unpleasant; I went to the same school as I did before when I was at dad's place; only now I had to take a tram to get there and back, which was rather strange, every time when I stepped into the tram to go home, I felt anger in my tummy, knowing that I should have been riding in the opposite direction. I had to get used to other people and a different environment, but home life was simple, occasionally I could feel some tension between Grandma and Grandpa but this never lasted for very long and it had no consequences for me.

Although I missed a proper bathroom in the apartment; with a tub, shower, toilet and hand basin would have been nice, being able to wash myself and brushing my teeth in the kitchen sink as a teenager was not so groovy, the toilet situated outside the apartment on the middle floor, shared by everybody in the house wasn't my biggest problem either, but I truly loathe the days when the glossy pages from an old telephone book were provided in place of the standard newspaper, that was disgusting, I wouldn't recommend it at all, particularly when you understand that the next hand basin available to wash your hands was again the kitchen sink.

During this period I had learned to take a little distance from my family, not to take everything so bloody serious, not to become so emotional as I did from time to time, I began not to blindly trust anymore, I had become more critical, questioning just about everything that people did for me, if indeed it was sincere or if there was some bizarre reason for doing what they did, and I had become less communicative, keeping a lot of thoughts that normally I would have entrusted someone close to myself.

Then there came the moment where my behavior began to trouble me, rather it had become a problem for the adults around me as they began to realize that I had shut myself off; I don't know if this behavior was the result of growing up, perhaps it was the outcome of my complex family situation, or indeed the effects of both, but somehow I knew that if I would survive this, I could master anything that stood before me.

## Charity

After my stint at Grandma and Grandpa Robert, I was allowed to return home, still not understanding why I had to leave in the first place, but I couldn't change this any way, I had become to accept it as just another shitty phase in my youth.

During my absence dad and Aunt Lulu had completed the re-furbishing of the house and garden, it looked lovely, in deed it was just perfect, but somehow the house didn't have the same feeling of warmth and security that it had before I left, for some reason it didn't feel like my home anymore.

A lot of things had changed in my life, although I loved my dad, I was disappointed in his behavior, I had lost the trust that I had in him, Aunt Lulu I began to perceive as an intrusion to the bachelor period that I enjoyed so much with dad.

Of course, I cannot be certain, but I believe that if I had not been sent away from home to stay with Grandma and Grandpa Robert for a few months, I would have accepted the moving in of Aunt without any difficulties.

Despite the fact that my ego was a little bruised from the events that took place during the past month, I made sure that I didn't make live more difficult for myself as it actually was, I tried to continue in the same way as I did before my little mental detour, not knowing that things were to change soon.

In the mean-time Aunt had given up her job at the supermarket; now she counted to the staff of dad's business, taking care of a small department, instructing and checking the output of eight employees. I don't know how these employees reacted when Aunt took over the position, not understanding the technical matter of the job, a person considerably younger than anybody in the team, and now she was responsible for them and the quality of their production.

The first few weeks of being back home were more or less uneventful, gradually Aunt would delegate more and more chores to me; getting the basic preparation for the lunch menu organized as soon as I got home from school— peeling onions, garlic, potatoes or other vegetables, so that she could start cooking as soon as she arrived, washing, drying and putting away the pots, pans and the dishes, cleaning the stove and sink, and sweep the floor were part of my jobs.

On Saturdays after school, I had to begin with the cleaning of the house; sweeping and mopping all the stone floors, damp wiping the wooden surfaces, dusting, vacuuming the carpets and brushing their fringes, making sure that they were all aligned properly, cleaning the bathrooms; toilets, bath, shower, sinks, mirrors and the floor, come to think of it, Aunt expected a lot from a fourteen-year-old teeny whose chief pursuit was to produce academic achievements.

During the time before Aunt moved in, dad also expected me to help with the household, he had given me chores that had to be done, I had absolutely no problem with helping around the house, in the contrary it was always fun to help and to support dad, but this time it was different—the instruction now came from Aunt.

Why should it be different if Aunt instructed me what was to be done in and around the house? An instruction is merely an informative message for someone to do something, why did I suddenly have a problem with this?

I had decided that Aunt was the reason for me having to stay with her parents for some months, for having been temporarily sent away from my home, although I couldn't possibly know if this was the truth, but I wanted to believe it and this influenced my fundamental attitude toward Aunt.

During the first few weeks, Aunt's behavior toward me appeared to be normal, as it was during the trial period, but after a while her directions sounded like a command rather than a request, an approach to which I wasn't used to from my dad, not only did I perceive her directions as an order, I also noticed that the tone of her voice had changed, it sounded as if she was yelling at me and at the same time her facial expression had become serious, hard, almost rancorous. I don't know how close to the truth my description of Aunt's behavior toward me is, and how much of it was my mere perception about it, the fact remains that I had a distinct feeling that something had changed, that for some reason Aunt didn't like me very much.

It wasn't the fact that I had to help with the maintenance of the household that bothered me, it was the manner in which the instruction to do a particular chore was presented by Aunt.

I began to despise Aunt, asking myself what had happen to this pleasant lady that I was introduced to about a year ago whom seemed to like me at the time, did I do something that changed her behavior toward me, perhaps, the lady that I met then wasn't nice at all—I don't know.

I don't recall that my dad was ever present when Aunt instructed me about the chores, I was convinced that he couldn't have realized how she was treating me, and at the same time I knew that he would have fully supported Aunt.

I wouldn't have gotten any support from him anyway, hence there was no point in telling him how I was feeling—at least these were my thoughts as a kid.

Before Aunt had moved in with us, dad spend a lot of time in the business, but somehow he always found a little time for me, and I knew that if I needed him, he was there for me, helping me to resolve my problems and concerns, it didn't matter what or how trivial it might have been, he was there for me, but now I began to feel that my dad was abandoning me, beside his business he was more and more engaged with Aunt Lulu, he seemed to have little time left for me.

I began to slowly shut down the open communication that I was used to, fending off emotions, ignoring them, deliberately keeping as much as possible to myself; I had abandoned the openness that I once had toward the family and those around me.

The teenage phase that had begun didn't help either; I guess I was becoming a little difficult to handle, perhaps somewhat unpleasant. Not that I refused to cooperate, but I began to be moody, my behavior and facial expression made clear to others that I despised having to do as I was told, particularly when Aunt demanded something from me.

Gradually I could feel that the screws were tightening; Aunt had become very strict, she would make sure that I had completed all the chores that she had given me to take care of, she had become inflexible and finicky, not accepting if any of my chores weren't done to the standard that she had expected, she would criticize what she would call sloppy work and demand that it would be done again until she was satisfied.

## Aunt's Expectations

During the time that I was banished at Grandma and Grandpa Robert's, my father had our family home renovated, respecting the old, traditional peculiarities and style of the early 1900s, its period of construction, and yet the kitchen and the bathrooms and the laundry had been refitted to meet the latest comforts and trend, with the exception of a couple of antique pieces that dad inherited, the entire house was featuring furniture from the 1950s, in some of the rooms green Italian Marble had been laid, decorated with wool carpets woven from the finest British Marino wool scattered here and there, the upper area of the house was fitted with the original timber floors, throughout the house the curtains were designed to complement the intended purpose and mood of each room; some privacy curtains were made from white silk, and yet others from cotton whereas the blackout curtains were tailored from the finest velvet in particular colors to complement the desired atmosphere of the area, Bradbury and Bradbury wall paper as this was contemporary during that period, ceiling, wall and table light fittings had been chosen to fulfil their intended purpose and function, some were made from solid brass and beveled glass chandeliers, complemented with some designer fittings, providing just the right amount of soft or vigorous brightness for each occasion, the garden had been cleaned up and reworked and some fresh shrubs, flowers and ornamental trees planted, and the iron picket fence had been sanded and repainted in a British Racing Green; our house had become the architectural splendor of our street, reflecting gracefulness, elegance and beauty, unprecedented in our immediate area at that time.

The exterior of our house had become sensationally beautiful, the interior was breath-taking; I didn't realize this at the time, but retrospectively I suspect that its beauty was a reflection of my fathers' feelings for Aunt Lulu, his new lady. The changes to the property were impressive but not necessarily because I thought so as a kid, but mostly because other people were of that opinion and they said so.

However, I soon began to experience our home in a way that was fundamentally different from those that were mere spectators whose opinion was founded by looking in from the outside, they didn't get to see what was really happening in our home, they merely saw the beautiful things. Just the way it should be, Aunt had begun to assume her new role, the lady of the house, probably struggling to come to terms with her new position in life, possibly quarrelling with her inner-self to become comfortable with her newly acquired social status.

As a child, Aunt lived in Colmar during WWII until the Alsace region was annexed to the Third Reich, the time when Gauleiter R. Wagner the head of the civil administration directly under Hitler's order took over the responsibility for their territory around 1941, it was at that time that the family had to take refuge in the north west of France where they remained for a couple of years, living in poverty like most others did during this time. Just before the Allied invasion of the Normandie began in the early hours of the morning of June 6, 1944, Aunt's family was evacuated by the French, eventually finding shelter and protection in Basel, Switzerland.

The level of education that Aunt achieved was in line with what most other working-class kids were able to attain, she completed the fundamental primary and secondary grades and finished an apprenticeship as a sales person; Aunt had to do without a lot of things that were basic and normal for other kids at that time, her family was struggling with poverty, and now she lived in one of the most prestigious homes in the street, she was now known as the Director's Mistress, the fellow that owned the printing factory down the road, and now Aunt had to live up to these apparent high standing social expectations, most of which were probably created in her own imagination.

Through my father's business as well as private associates Aunt now got to meet and know people from different socioeconomic backgrounds, people that had enjoyed an impeccable upbringing as well as a higher education, people that had lots of money, people that were merely very clever, as well as "ordinary" people, though not yet married; most staff from dad's business addressed Aunt as "Missis Director" which was usual during that particular period, a gesture that she adored. Aunt might have had suffered from delusions of grandeur but I don't think that in her entourage there was anybody that would have accompanied her to handle her new role either.

From a kid's perspective, if there was anything at all that Aunt was in control of; she knew how to manage a household, our home was neat, well looked after, at any time it was groomed and dressed to the nines but this didn't happen on its own; very quickly I understood that the days of uncomplicated, male orientated housekeeping was over, the new lady of the house was caring meticulously for the ménage, and I was to play an integrate part of this pampering. Though we now had a superbly renovated and refurbished home, but gradually our house was losing its serenity that it was radiating before it had been renovated, it began to lose its warmth that it had during our bachelor period, or earlier still the soul, the atmosphere of spirituality that it ones emitted at the time when my mum was still with us; instead, I was able to feel how the mood was slowly changing—the little gadgets and touches of physical beauty that Aunt had placed throughout the house, the little things that emphasized or highlighted a particular place in a delicate manner began to disappear into the background.

I was now beginning to see another side to Aunt, suddenly I was able to feel a chilly breeze that was gently wafting through the entire house, I was now able to witness how my parents' words of wisdom and comfort were being evicted, replaced by Aunt's behavior of ignorance blended with a language of vulgarity.

*On Saturdays, the British Marino Wool carpets in the living areas had to be Vacuumed and mollycoddled, that is to say*; I had to pass over with the brush several times, ensuring that no crumbs or other small pieces of matter remained at the base of the woven part, that the fringes at the end were combed straight, and that there was no dirt underneath the carpet. Aunt would check these points in a very meticulous manner. If she could find some dirt underneath the carpet, she would insist that I had put it there deliberately, that I had swept the dirt from the surrounding areas underneath because I was too lazy to pick it up, which was simply not true, but to fend myself in this situation wasn't a good strategy. At the beginning I tried to tell her that it was not true, but it was best to accept her opinion, because Aunt was always right.

*Every couple of days after school I had to sweep the wooden floors,* and this was frequently a problem, on most occasions Aunt could find a little dust in some corner which she would show me with pleasure, commenting that I had not swept at all. When I maintained that I had swept I was told not to tell fibs, and she explained that she had eyes at the back of her head, that she would see and know everything. What could I possibly say to this kind of statement, coming from an apparent mature person? Even though I was only a kid, in my opinion Aunt had started to lose her credibility. What arrogance, to think that a fourteen-year-old kid would truly believe that she sees and knows everything.

*I had to clean the bathrooms thoroughly once per week*, more often than not I wouldn't do this according Aunt's standard, the interior part of the toilets were never scrubbed to Aunt's expectation, on most occasions Aunt could detect some stubborn lime residue on the sloped part at the back where the rinse water slides into the bowl, the wall tiles invariably showed streaky parts which were identified as soap residue in some areas, the hand basins still had dirt at the back of the faucet where it meets with the basin.

Aunt would demonstrate this with an old toothbrush, she would then show me with some pride, the floors were seldom swept properly, and the wet mopping had left some unclean traces around the corners. Unlike today, I didn't have a multitude of cleaning products available either, for the hand basin, the shower, the tub and the tiles I had a product called "Potz," to remove the lime from the toilet Aunt had prepared a blend of vinegar essence and lemon juice, and for the wall and floor tiles we had a liquid detergent, apparently designed for this purpose, on most occasions I had to redo the bathrooms.

*At the time I thought that Aunt was vastly exaggerating*, quietly I got angry, hoping that Aunt wouldn't recognize the rage that I was fighting with inside me, but maybe I wasn't overly eager to hide my emotions, I have a feeling that I rather enjoyed these moments when Aunt raised her voice, reprimanding me that I should not get cheeky; after all I was the one that did a sloppy job. Her standard of house-keeping were high, and what she expected form a teeny was perhaps not reasonable, and what I had to endure under her care and command I loathed, but I am glad about what I learned during this time of my life; I have learned how to clean a bathroom, how to take care of a carpet, and how to take care of myself.

*The kitchen had to be scrubbed daily after lunch as well as after dinner time*—work areas, oven top and floor, and this once per week thoroughly as well; food scraps had to be totally removed from dishes and the cutlery by rinsing them first, washed, if needed scrubbed in lightly, soapy hot water, ensuring that there was no visible grease or any other foreign substance left, thoroughly rinsed with fresh, hot water, ensuring that there was no soapy residue left so that the natural sheen from the China, steel and glass ware was clearly visible, and in the end polished dry with a clean, dry soft cloth.

Cooking pots and pans and utensils had to be freed from food scraps, if necessary—food matter that was slightly baked on to the stainless steel—difficult to dissolve stuff had to be gently teased out with the assistance of a scraper or broad based spatula, ensuring that the steel didn't get damaged, then the pot was thoroughly cleaned with a soapy steel wool pad and then rinsed, ensuring that all soap residue had been removed, the entire process carried out on a soft cloth to avoid any kind of scratching on the pot, or indeed on the surface on which the pot is being cleaned.

After lunch there wasn't sufficient time to clean the stove and oven thoroughly, but after the evening meal I had to take apart every component that could be removed, if necessary, soaking the parts that was covered with stubbornly baked on grime, ensuring that the luster of the enamel was perfect.

*On a weekly bases, usually every Friday, dusting was on the list of chores*; the surfaces of all furniture, ensuring that flourishes, embellishments and edges of the wood were free of dust, making sure that all the nick knacks displayed on the furniture had been removed before hand, that they too were free of any dust, all door and window frames, ensuring that the spaces between the heating elements which were hidden behind the curtains were cleaned, light fittings, picture frames and anything else on which the dust could have settled during the week. Aunt would pass over an area with a white cloth to see if I had done this job properly. As could be expected, on most occasions she would find some area that had not been dusted to her expectation.

*The cleaning of the windows* I had to do as needed, but usually once every couple of months all of the downstairs, and the following month the upstairs windows were taken care off, a job that I hated, because of the large number of them the cleaning was spaced over several days. We didn't have window cleaner as we know it today; first the glass was washed with warm water and left to dry. Then I had to form a kind of soft ball from old newspaper, dipped into a solution of about fifty percent warm water and fifty percent vinegar, then the glass was cleaned by gentle rubbing until it was dry and free of any dirt. It was important that this job was done when the sun was not shining directly onto the glass.

If I didn't follow this principle, I was unable to see if the glass was clean and free of streaks, but despite my effort and the fact that I had strictly obeyed this rule, I could never achieve a satisfactory result, mostly Aunt got mad, and sometimes reminding me that I wasn't stupid, that I was merely too lazy to do a proper job.

*Occasionally, Aunt would praise me* for a job well done, even though I had not done the job at all. This behavior was confusing to me; I did not understand what was going on and at the same time Aunt's peculiar behavior eroded her credibility even further.

*My room had to be Tidy* at the end of every day, just as it was the case before Aunt Lulu moved in with us. Knowing that sometimes my attempt to tidy was half-hearted, giving Aunt reason to grumble. Even on the occasions when I had made a great effort to tidy, and things looked well-organized in my room, Aunt found something to beef about which led me to conclude that it didn't matter how much or how little effort I put into the tidying, I would be grumbled at anyway.

*Arranging the bed in the morning* was self-evident, the expected standard was high, and it had to be completed before I was leaving for school. Before taking my breakfast, the linen had to be aired, then the bed sheets neatly tightened over the matrices, the top sheet and the blanket nicely folded back; the length of the fold had to be the same on both sides, the pillow had to be shaken so that it had a fluffed-up appearance, and the bedspread had to be placed evenly over the bed, hanging equally all around. Of course, not every day these requirements were accomplished, often causing unnecessary stress and a tense atmosphere between Aunt and myself.

One day Aunt discovered that my bedspread was torn on one side, this made her very angry, she accused me of having done this on purpose, she argued that I did not like its design. Frankly speaking, I don't know why I should have done such a stupid thing, I had nothing against the bedcover, I never even thought about its design or indeed how it was fitting into my room. None the less, I had to accept the accusation; Aunt was always right.

*Usually, when I got home from school there was a note on the kitchen table*, to peel the potatoes that Aunt had placed in the sink earlier that morning. I did, but this time it wasn't to the standard that Aunt was expecting. As she told me in her very loud, abusive manner, I had produced too much waste, there was far too much peal, the eyes from the sprouts had not been removed and the potatoes had not been washed properly, she ridiculed me and said that only an idiot could do such a bad job. I was deeply hurt, not because I did a shitty job, because of the way she was talking to me, and the fact that she thought that I was an idiot.

*Aunt had found some holes in some of my socks* and explained that she could not understand how this could possibly happen. As usual, with great vigor she questioned me about the "how's" and the "whys" about these socks, for what seemed to be a very long time. My head was spinning, I was searching for a plausible answer that she might be able to accept, but as usual I couldn't think of anything that could have pleased Aunt, I was waiting for her to tell me that she knew how it happened, and I was relieved when she did, as I expected; Aunt made it easy for me, I merely had to admit to her accusation—it was the fastest way to get my peace.

*Aunt had a good eye for shoes that weren't cleaned properly.* Today, as an adult I can accept the importance of clean shoes, and frankly speaking I am grateful for all the things that Aunt taught me, I learned how to be clean and tidy, to be structured and organized, to learn new things, to work hard, to respect others and the environment, to be disciplined, I even learned some fundamentals about cooking, I am grateful for anything else that I learned from Aunt, but I object to the humiliating approach that she took, the yelling, the screaming and the mental torture that she exposed me to from time to time.

*Wrong items in the shopping basket;* On a regular basis Aunt asked me to accompany her with the shopping of groceries, in a very short time I had learned a lot about the different foodstuffs, dry goods, herbs and spices, canned food commodities, convenience items, dairy items, meat, small-goods, fresh produce and other products. Food was her thing, she was very knowledgeable about it, she loved handling food, Aunt prepared and cooked with passion.

During these shopping sessions, among other things, Aunt would show me what I had to look for when I was gathering fruits or vegetables from the display boxes, they had to be free from blemishes or bruises, the size and shape had to be correct, she showed me how to feel and smell for the degree of ripeness, she showed me how to handle the butcher; Aunt never took the mincemeat that was displayed in the chilled glass counter; she would ask the butcher to mince a piece without fat in front of her so she could be sure about the quality that she was getting, and the butcher did oblige.

It was fascinating to learn the elements that were important to her during the shopping, I appreciate this experience very much, I still apply this knowledge today.

When Aunt send me shopping, I always had a list of the items to be bought, and where necessary I had made myself a little note of instruction, sometimes I came home with something that she was not happy with in terms of the quality, or from time to time something was missing in the shopping basket because it wasn't available in the shop.

I recall clearly one-time Aunt shouted, accusing me not to have bought lentils because I didn't like them, indeed I didn't like lentils, but honestly, I had forgotten them, an answer that she could not accept.

The missing screwdriver—Dad had a rather large workshop in the cellar, for the tools there was a large wooden template mounted on the wall, each tool had its specific spot, and at a glance you could identify if one of them was not in its place.

On this day dad asked me if I know where this particular screwdriver was, to which I answered no. Immediately Aunt interfered, stating that I probably had taken it to school to swap it for something else, insisting that she knew everything, that she knew how these things work, that this was the truth.

How miserable can you treat a kid, I was accused of something that I did not do, I wasn't responsible for the disappearance of this screwdriver, and yet I had no chance, I had to accept her calling me a liar, and to my detriment my father didn't intervene in Aunt's charade, he appeared to have accepted and supported her way of handling the situation.

More and more I closed myself off from the family, gradually I stopped talking about things, I merely said what was necessary, I hated the situation that I was in, to the point that Aunt had to ask me to put a little smile on my face, but I couldn't see a reason to change my attitude.

*When I really broke something, I was scared;* I had reached the point where I began to hide such mishaps because I hated to be yelled at, but mostly Aunt found out anyway, sometimes much later which made her even madder, and her interrogation was even fiercer.

*Chopping onions;* Coming home from school, as it was often the case, there was a note which instructed me to peel and finely dice twelve large onions and four cloves of garlic, Aunt wanted to make an onion soup. I began to peal the first onion and realized that the juice that escapes through the pealing process was extremely sharp, it began to burn in my eyes immediately.

I persisted with this job and began to peal the second onion, then realizing that I had to find a solution to this problem. I don't know why some onions burn more than others, but they all caused an instant, excruciating feeling of discomfort, I couldn't see properly anymore, and the tears kept flowing down my cheeks continually.

My solution to the problem was very pragmatic; I got the diving mask and snorkel from my room, placed them over my head as if I was in the water, and continued to peel the onions. For some reason, some of the onions burning vapor managed to get into the diving mask, which made me truly mad; to the point that I began to curse at the top of my voice, using words that you wouldn't expect a fourteen-year-old kid to know. I honestly can't remember where I had learned all these words, but as the devil wanted it to be, Aunt walked in just at this very moment. Needless to mention that she had blown her stack; huffing and puffing like mad, threatening with the devil if she would ever hear these kinds of words from me again.

I was truly scared of this lady, hoping that she wouldn't bash the brains out of my skull. A few moments later she showed me that if I placed the onions in some cold water, the vapor that occurred through the pealing would not get into my eyes.

That was a moment where I did not feel hate toward Aunt, because I knew that I had done wrong, that it was not ok to use cursing words like this, I understood that she got mad with me.

I also appreciated that after her outburst she corrected me, and showed me how to avoid this unpleasant experience.

I am of the opinion that kids need to be clearly shown the barriers in an age-appropriate manner, that parents must be firm, but not unkind with their kids. Yelling, screaming, verbal or physical force do not lead to good behavior, in the contrary it nurtures more of the same; which I think is the opposite of what I believe most parents want to achieve. Then, from the perspective as a teeny I felt that Aunt's expectations from me were unreasonable, I felt deprived of at least some of my childhood, there was nobody among my buddies at school, nor anybody in the neighborhood that I was aware off that had as many chores to do as me.

In fact, most of the youngsters that I knew at the time had little to no chores to accomplish at home; they appeared to be busy doing their own thing, perusing their hobbies and sport activities when I was mostly involved with the things that Aunt had delegated to me which generated feelings of abuse and hate toward Aunt; often I felt that I was robbed of valuable time that I would have liked to spend for my hobbies. Considering this teenage view today from an adult's perspective; I am of the opinion that indeed, Aunt had expected to much from me at that time, that perhaps half of the chores that she made me responsible for might have been appropriate.

Today, I do recognize and appreciate much of what I learned from Aunt; the running of an household, how to apply cleaning methods and materials to the different surfaces on furniture, flooring materials, stone and wet areas, how to handle diverse home products and chemicals in the household in general, I learned how to operate a washing machine with its varying programs for different types of fabric, I acquired the skill of ironing, I learned a lot about intelligent shopping of food products, Aunt's respect for food products and produce, together with and immense pleasure for cooking is the reason for my passion as a hobby cook—all of which I am grateful for today.

However, it was Aunt's behavior toward me that overshadowed all the good things that I have learned from her, the arrogant manner in which she approached me, her presumptuous behavior, apparently knowing everything, her special way of insulting me, and the mental torture that she inflicted upon me I will never forget.

*Not everything in my life was wicked at that time.* Since the moving in of Aunt there were also lots of good things happening that were appreciated by dad and I; it seemed that my father was happy again, the household was in great shape, our culinary repertoire had grown beyond canned ravioli enhanced with butter and crushed garlic, and finally we got that dog that I had been wanting for a long time, but unfortunately, the negative things that I was experiencing at home were far greater than the positive ones.

## What was Aunt Lulu All About?

As a kid, I didn't ask myself the question why Aunt acted the way she did, I merely realized that I didn't like the way she was treating me, and later during my childhood I was able to observe how she treated others in the same manner, with the exception of a few.

I know that one should never presume, but I allow myself to suspect that Aunt's ego was in mighty need to impress others, particularly with material things, she used to enjoy immensely telling people around her what we possessed, she adored everything that was perceived as high class and expensive.

We had the Chevrolet Cabriolet, but dad didn't want to drive it every day, so he bought a Volvo Amazon 121, red in color, the body of the car were similar to a fifties American build vehicle and yet there were lots of contemporary aspects in its finish; dad and I loved this little family car, I thought that it was nippy to drive around town but Aunt loathed it, she was of the opinion that it was too lively, even vulgar, kind of ordinary and that it made her nervous to sit in it. The Volvo wasn't one of the cheapest cars you could buy at the time but after all it was affordable for some—I dare to assume that Aunt was too snobbish to be seen with this vehicle.

About six months later dad sold the Volvo, I guess he wanted to please his lady, perhaps he was sick and tired of her constant nagging about this car, and a couple of days after the Volvo had gone, dad came home with a 1959 Jaguar Mark 1, classic gray paintwork, a large British saloon car, with a 3.8 Liter motor that boasted 220 bhp, it was capable of a top speed of 193 km/h, it could accelerate from 0-97 km/h in only 11,9 seconds, its fuel consumption was 14.9 l/100 km, it featured an engine start button and an overdrive, leather seats and wooden panels all around; sitting in this car was like taking a seat in a luxury leather lounge chair, this car was fit for an aristocrat, there were very few of these cars to be seen on the roads of Switzerland at that time presumably because only the rich could afford it; this was a car fit for Aunt, when she sat in it you could have thought she was Hyacinth Bucket. *Keeping up appearances*, the British sitcom creation; those of you that are familiar with this comedy will be able to better visualize Aunt's behavior, and if you haven't had the pleasure, I recommend that you check it out on the Internet.

Aunt was also very proud of her knowledge that she thought to have just about everything and anything, although she had left school at age fourteen, the way she carried on you would have thought that she had studied medicine, law and philosophy, all at the same time, it was pathetic as well as amusing to see how she appeared to inflate herself, taking on a pompous appearance, together with the appropriate posture and facial expression to suit the situation when she was talking with people, often it became embarrassing when she slobbered her knowledge in her very loud voice around herself so that everybody around her was able to hear it, even those that would rather not have taken part in her verbal parade.

Aunt came from a very poor working-class background, other than a bicycle and a few clothes in an old, tatty suitcase she had nothing when she came to live with my dad, and she wasn't highly educated either. I am not sneering at Aunt's misfortune, I merely loathed the way she was treating me and others, I am not qualified, nor do I want to make presumptuous statements about her behavior, I am solely constructing a hypothesis based on my childhood memories which might explain the reason for Aunt's code of conduct.

I am also aware of the fact that some of us were lucky to be born in a rich country like Switzerland, fortunate to have more then we need to survive, perhaps we had the chance to have grown up in a wealthy family, whilst others did not have the same fortune, they have to be content with considerably less or even nothing, perhaps their education was poor, or they couldn't go to school at all, and some are condemned to live in absolute poverty.

At the same time, I understand that I am not responsible for the poverty of others as I am not accountable for the richness of some. It isn't my fault; I don't have to have feelings of guilt or pity. If you are born as a farmer's daughter or son in the backwoods of Ethiopia, your chances to become the countries Prime minister are most probably very slim. But if you are born into a working-class family in a developed country, you can become almost everything you desire to be, providing you have the necessary intelligence, the motivation and the opportunity to do whatever it takes.

Having said that I am not responsible for the misfortune or the poverty of others doesn't mean that I do not care about those that have to live with this kind of sorrow, to show sympathy and to waffle on with compassionate words isn't the solution either; each one of us is accountable for what happens on this earth, be it a humanitarian or an environmental matter, each one of us must feel compelled to support these issues in an appropriate manner, as best we can.

Aunt's desire to be "somebody" was immense; when she was with other people, her behavior was hideous, almost scary, desperately she tried to convince that she was highly educated, knowing everything better, and Aunt desperately wanted others to respect her social status—after all, she was the Director's Lady.

Admittedly, I very much enjoyed being seen in my dad's Chevrolet Cabriolet or indeed in the Jaguar by my colleagues; honestly it felt great, I was very proud, but never presumptuous; my dad would have put an end to this kind of behavior very abruptly, that's why I couldn't understand that dad tolerated Aunt's obtrusive behavior. He must have seen it to, or was he so thrilled about her looks and her appearance that he chose not to notice.

It wasn't just her behavior that bothered me, she was also very loud when she talked, probably so that she was sure to be heard, and she could be very aggressive if things didn't go her way.

Very often, when Aunt was reprimanding or interrogating me about something that I was supposed to have done, she had an incredibly dirty smirk on her face. On these occasions I felt great disappointment, even anger because often she accused me of something that wasn't true, it was almost as if she was laughing at me with great satisfaction, as if she enjoyed seeing me squirming of fear; my hate toward her was growing fast, I thought that everybody had abandoned me; it appeared that no one protected me anymore—I hated Aunt's presumptuous behavior.

## Aunt's Childhood

*Aunt's childhood experience;* having grown up during the second world war must have been very tough for her and the parents, fleeing their home in France with her family was probably traumatic, and the time that Aunt spend at the Convent as a young woman wasn't pleasant either, all of which contributed to her personality and without a doubt characterized her being.

Realizing that this kind of childhood experience leaves a person with lots of scars; despite all of the unkind adventures, I don't understand why Aunt was so tough, so bitter and presumptuous, I would have thought that with this kind of background; having felt pain, stress, grief and fear, that she should have been able to feel and show understanding, warmth and compassion toward others; instead Aunt had become presumptuous, her behavior toward others seemed arrogant and superior, and it appeared that she had learned to hate, to torment and to afflict mental pain upon those that had little or no choice to be inundated by Aunt, either because they worked for her, or like me; I lived with her.

Aunt was very different; she was very tough with others, she appeared to be a person filled with anger, she had no problem in letting others feel this negative emotion, she was very egocentric, she had this great need to be someone of immense importance, she had to be always right, she was very loud, almost boisterous when she was talking, she made sure that she drew lots of attention toward her, and she seemed to enjoy watching others in mental pain when she was questioning or interrogating them—she was the kind of person that you would rather not meet.

I cannot understand that a grown-up person can get enjoyment from the pain of others; did Aunt really perceive pleasure when she interrogated me? Was it not obvious to her that I was suffering, that I was extremely uncomfortable? Or was she simply ignorant to all of this?

I dare to believe that she was very much aware of what she was doing.

What could possibly motivate Aunt to reconstruct some kind of story that was plausible to her, when something happened at the house for which I was supposed to be responsible for. She then described the events as she had constructed in her mind in great detail, and was expecting that I would admit to whatever she had just invented.

Did she really believe that she was right in her assumption; did she not consider that her assumption may not be correct, and if this was so, what would I think about her, did she not realize that I might lose respect for her?

I allow myself to believe that you can only behave in this manner if you believe that you are clever, and the other person is stupid.

What right did Aunt have to treat a child in this manner?

Parent through blood or step-parent, if you assume the accountability for a child, you must accept the responsibility to show respect toward it, to nurture the elements that are necessary for its development, to support and to guide the child, to clearly show the barriers and the guidelines of the expected behavior, to reprimand bad and to praise good behavior—all of which Aunt was not capable of.

## The Convent

During one of the conversations that we had long after my teenage, Aunt was telling dad and I the story about her youth. I knew that she grew up in a very poor working-class environment, her parents experienced a difficult time during the German occupation of France, they were suffering from the memories of terrible things that they had experienced and seen, there was not always enough to eat, and they had been exposed to danger and abuse from German soldiers. Though Aunt and her sister were still little at that time, from the way in which she was explaining things it was apparent that these memories were haunting her.

After the family fled to Switzerland toward the end of the second world war, life had become less strenuous, they were soon allocated an apartment in Basel, clothes and foot ware was given to them to begin with, basic food items were provided through the Swiss government, the two kids were sent to the local school, and eventually the parents found a job which allowed them to survive without any Government assistance. Gradually, over a period of time the parents were able to buy some furniture for their apartment. Apparently, the beds and some basic household items had been provided by the local social department.

During the time that the two girls were growing up there was always sufficient food in the house, but still not enough money to take care of all the things that they would have liked; for a long time, meat was affordable only at the pay days; Grandma was able to get a pork cutlet for Grandpa and she shared a grilled sausage with the kids.

Some of the girls' clothing was provided through the local school-committee who took care of the poor in the district, the shoes that they provided the girls were obviously second hand and old fashioned, and because of this the girls were often laughed at and bullied by other kids.

Once the oldest of the girls began with her apprenticeship things started to look up for the family.

Tabea was absolving an apprenticeship as a laboratory assistant in the local pharmacy industry, earning around eighty Swiss Francs per month, from which she had to give sixty to her mother. With this extra income they bought a black and white TV which was considerate luxury at the time.

Apparently, her mum was very strict with the girls, but particularly with Aunt Lulu, she would not hesitate to apply force if she thought that it was necessary. Aunt didn't elaborate any further on the subject and we didn't ask about any of these details either, dad and I were simply listening.

Aunt completed the compulsory four primary, and the four secondary school years, subsequent to the basic education it was normal that kits that came from a higher socioeconomic background carried on with further studies at the Gymnasium, to achieve the Matriculation status at the age of eighteen, and from there the path was open to the Universities. However, for most kids at that time, particularly for those whose parents didn't have the money to send them to the University, or simply kids that hadn't achieved the necessary academic result, an apprenticeship in a trade area was usual.

Aunt told us that her parents did not have the money to prepare her for the University entry examination, nor was she to learn a trade; she was expected to find a job as an unskilled person so that she could help the family situation financially straight away, but frankly speaking, in my opinion Aunt didn't have the necessary intelligence for a higher education either.

This begs the question about justice; how can a family with two children, apparently with a similar degree of intelligence, with the same educational background decide that one can do an apprenticeship but not the other. What criteria did her parents apply? Was it because Tabea was the older girl, or was it because she was tall and skinny, perhaps better looking, whereas Aunt Lulu was short and overweight—just like her mother? Was the decision taken on the basis of academic achievement? Did the parents consider the personal strength of the two girls; which of them would rebel against the decision not to be able to sign up for an apprenticeship, which one of them would be more likely to succeed, or was it merely a matter of personal preference?

I know that I am presumptuous, but I dare to conclude that Aunt's parents decided on the basis of preference.

Aunt's parents never had a chance with their plan, for some reason Aunt's secondary school principal assisted her, he had been able to organize a one-year pre-apprenticeship training in a Convent near Paris where the girls were coached in various aspects of house-keeping.

At the Convent, all of the apprentice girls came from a poor family background, some of them had the benefit of having had some French lessons during their secondary school time but none of them could speak the language fluently. As a rule, for the apprentices it was prohibited to speak any other languages, only French was allowed. This made the communication for young girls a little difficult, but in this way the learning of the language was probably accelerated.

Although the primary reason for being at the Convent was to be instructed in the different elements of house-keeping which was usual for many girls to do at that age, considered as being part of their education. At that time, a house-keeping course would also have been possible in one of the colleges in any of the four language zones of Switzerland, where the syllabus included the theory as well as the practical aspects of cleaning, with the different agents, all of them natural products like; Savon de Marseille, Vinegar, lemon juice, Bicarbonate of Soda, Salt, Baking powder, brewed Coffee grains, Vanilla, and one of the more bizarre products, dry Bread-crust, as well as the associated methods were taught.

All elements of clothes making and their maintenance, the use of templates for the cutting of different textiles, sawing, and knitting also formed part of the learning program.

The subject with the broadest scope was undoubtedly dedicated to food; the various categories of food stuffs, their composition and origin, their usage, menu planning for the private home, the basic preparation and the different cooking methods were attended to. The pickling, smoking and the preservation of foodstuffs, baking, the preparation of dessert and bread making formed also part of the course.

The colleges in Switzerland that offered the house-keeping course were fundamentally different from the pre-apprenticeship at the Convent in France. In the Swiss colleges the Syllabus was documented, with clearly stated learning objectives, regular practical and written tests were carried out to determine the students learning progress, and a final examination was necessary to establish a degree of pass or fail.

The course was not free of charge either; once the students had passed their entry examination and were selected for the course, a substantial fee had to be paid before the girls could begin with the first semester. The costs were composed of subscription, board and lodging, and a tuition fee. Incidentals like toiletries, external visits to subject related industries and other incidentals were charged for separately.

Anyone enrolled in one of those Colleges had to come from a particular financial background; they certainly didn't come from poor families, whereas kids that were accepted into the Convent in France as a pre-apprenticeship participant were generally poor, in a few cases they were send there from well to do families that wanted their kid to have a very tough school experience.

As I understood from Aunt, the students of house-keeping were primarily accepted into the Convent under the pretense to be absolving a pre-apprenticeship, but the reality was completely different, these kids were there to work hard and to take care of the cleaning, gardening, washing and cooking for the nuns and the paying students. The apprentices did not have to pay any fees, but they didn't get any pay for their twelve-hour days seven days per week either and it was said that their labor was paying for their board and other costs that they incurred.

Clearly, because the nuns were speaking French only, the kids learned the colloquial language very quickly, grammar was taught in a class room situation but it was of less importance, the main emphasis was placed on the house-keeping, physically working hard during ten to twelve hours per day, cleaning, preparing food, providing a room service for the nuns and the students, doing the laundry for everybody, helping in the garden as well as doing other chores. From the way Aunt was telling us this story, it sounded very much like slavery. A sign of appreciation, a smile, a thank you or an acknowledgement of a job well done did not belong to the nun's vocabulary, in the contrary, mental and physical abuse were no exception, smacking a kid in the face, pulling them on the ears or by their hair, to strike the kids on their naked butt with a thin bamboo rod in front of others were the forms of punishment or as the nuns called it, the corrective measures, and this occurred every day, several times.

The Convent accommodated around eighty catholic nuns and some one hundred female students as well as about sixty girls that absolved their pre-apprenticeship internship at the Convent, these girls came from different non-French speaking European countries, primarily with the aim to learn the French language and the aspects of house-keeping; under the strict guidance of the teaching nuns these girls were responsible for the cleaning of the entire Convent facility, making the beds of the students, the preparation and the cooking of the food for the nuns, the students and their own group, taking care of every bodies laundry as well as some chores in the garden.

Life at the Convent was hard, "reveille" (the wakeup call) was at 05:00, enough time was given to the apprentices to get themselves organized so that the Breakfast for the nuns and the students could be served by 06:00, and at 07:00 they were allocated to different duties with different tasks, some had to spend the day in the kitchen; peeling and preparing vegetables and fruit that were predominantly produced in the Convents gardens, getting the meat dishes ready for the midday and the evening service, making pasta dishes, helping in the house own bakery with the making of the bread and the dessert.

For the production of around 480 meals for the day, not counting the breakfast, there weren't any peeling, cutting, shredding, dicing or slicing machines available, everything had to be cut by hand and the cooking was done on old, large wood-fired commercial stoves.

The only mechanical aid in the bakery was a dough mixer, no other machines for the making of the different kinds of pastry, and no electric equipment either; eggs, cream and other products required for batters and dessert mixtures were beaten by hand, as were the special doughs and pastries.

The washing of the kitchen utensils was also done by hand; they didn't have a commercial pot-washer.

A commercial dish-washer was not available either; all crockery, cutlery, glass ware as well as the serving dishes had to be washed by hand.

One of the Convents matrons was in charge of this big kitchen, apparently, she was the fully trained professional in the area of cooking as well as in the bakery and pastry department, Aunt was explaining that she was very tough with her staff and the apprentices.

Apparently, to peal the seventy or so Kilogram of potatoes for lunch there were three of the trainee girls sitting in a circle around the pile to be peeled, together with one of the teaching nuns assigned to the kitchen, the nun began to cite a specific prayer which the girls were supposed to know off by heart, then she stopped suddenly, asking at random one of the girls to continue with the prayer, and if they weren't able to take off where the nun had stopped they got punished in some way. One of the favorite disciplinary action that the nun in charge of the kitchen was that the person being punished was send to work in the laundry the next day, and in the evening being send to bed without dinner, on a regular basis Aunt received this kind of reward for not being able to take up the prayer where the previous one had stopped, and at the same time to be told that in any case, she was fat enough to endure a night without getting any dinner, a charming comment from one of god's ground crew.

Those that were assigned to the laundry duties had a particularly hard job. There weren't any machines for washing, no spin dryers to remove the access water after the washing process, no dryers and no hot water heater either.

Before the washing process could begin, under the strict guidance from one of the housekeeping supervisory nuns, the girls had to get the fire underneath the washtubs going, nurturing it, making sure that the cold water was heated to about sixty degrees before adding the soap and the clothes to the hot water. The actual washing process lasted over an hour; a wooden stick about one meter long, with a diameter of around five centimeters, fitted to this stick was an upside-down bowl-shaped metal peace with holes in it, around eighteen centimeters in diameter at the base was used to continually pound the clothes in the hot, soapy water until the dirt was thought to be removed from the clothes.

This job was particularly hard because the girls had to ensure that sufficient wood was on site to keep the fire going, working near the glowing fire, pounding the cloth over the hot and steamy water was an extreme sweaty matter.

During the washing process the supervisory nun was carefully checking the girls make sure that the water temperature was maintained, ensuring that the pounding of the clothes was done with a regular rhythm, and the cleanliness of the clothes was examined very closely.

After the washing process, the clothes were removed from the hot tub and rinsed in cold water until all the soap had been completely washed out.

To remove the excess water after the rinsing process each piece of clothing was held by the ends, twisting them in a counter action, squeezing out the water, and then placing the clothes in large woven baskets, ready to hang for drying.

Pending on the season, the clothes were hung to dry, fastened with wooden pegs on large lines, either outside or in the back part of the washhouse.

If the level of cleanliness did not match the nun's criteria, the washing process of the particular batch had to be started all over. A refreshing shower after this strenuous, sweaty job the girls could not look forward to, although a communal shower was available in the bathroom, but they had to content to wash themselves on the hand basins, with cold water only.

The caressing dragon from the housekeeping, was the nickname the girls gave the nun responsible for this particular department. Apparently, she was particularly tough; the inner courtyard of the main building featured a wide path in the form of a cross, covered with natural, large stone pavers, along the path there was a low hedge like barrier consisting of ornamental plants including different types of lavender, and in the center of each cross path there was a lush green lawn which was cut by the gardener on a regular basis with a hand mower, but the girls were responsible for the trimming of the edges, by hand, with a pair of sharp scissors.

The cloister on the ground floor of the four main buildings was paved with marble, the dirt that collected in the joints and gaps of the uneven material had to be removed regularly, the girls on their knees, brushing the edges and the nooks and crannies with a small wire brush, gathering the dirt with a small hand brush and pan, carefully inspected by the dragon during her walk-about, and she would not hesitate to induce the necessary corrective action with the assistance of her rather long, thin cane rod which was particularly painful if she got you on the backside or indeed if you had to hold out your hand upside down in a stretched out position.

The wide stone steps leading up to the first, the second and the third floor of the main buildings had to be scrubbed with a hard bristled hand brush, then wiped dry with a heavy cloth, and if someone walked up or down during the time of cleaning, leaving their boot-prints on the stairs, they simply had to wipe over it again, and again, and again, the dragon didn't want to hear about how many nuns or students were trampling up and down whilst the girls were cleaning it, some of them perhaps deliberately leaving their dirt where they had already cleaned, the stairs had to be clean, and this in a particular time.

For the tiled floor in the corridors a normal mop and bucket was used for the daily cleaning, and this was done during times when the nuns were occupied with their daily activities and the students in their classrooms, but the edges where the floor tiles meet with the wall buffer and the corners in particular had to be scrubbed with a small gadget a little larger than a tooth brush, on their knees.

In the bathrooms, there were two of them on each of the floors, to the one side had some twenty individual cast iron troughs without mirrors, toilet compartments without doors on the opposite side, fitted with bundles of old newspapers, old tiles on the floor, white tiles from the floor right up to the ceiling, cold water only, the showers were in a separate facility; just like in the public pools today, in the middle of the room wooden benches to deposit your clothes, along the wall showerheads, perhaps forty or so and no warm water either, the girls were allowed to shower once per month, the daily hygiene care was taking place in the wash room. The dragon placed particular value on the washrooms, ensuring that they were thoroughly cleaned after being used every day; these areas were often used as a training ground for girls that needed reprimanding, with their own toothbrush, coated with a little bicarbonate soda they had to rigorously clean the toilet bowls under the strict supervision of the dragon herself.

Disposable hygiene pads for ladies were not available in those days, rags from old bed linen were used, handled with a great deal of discretion, they had to be washed separately from the other laundry.

The student's dormitories swept, dusted and the beds made in such a manner that they all look like a carefully wrapped gift, the matrices which were placed on a metal frame were clearly visible as you walked into the room, mattress cover, bed sheet and blanket all had to be tucked in symmetrically, ensuring that the overlapping part of the folded material had an equal distance from the edge, creases and plaits were unacceptable, and the pillows had to be fluffed up, as you would expect it to be in a first class hotel. If the beds weren't made to standard, the dragon would strip them so that the girls could try again until she was satisfied.

The abbey which was not connected to the mother house, though reachable through a long hallway, the girls had nothing to do in this area, for the early morning Sunday church service they were accompanied to the end of the corridor that led to the church, there, all lined up along the wall, under the care of one of the nuns they were allowed to follow the church service before they had to return to their chores. Aunt was not able to tell us why they weren't allowed in the abbey, though she suspected that the nuns didn't want them to see the priests that were responsible for the service.

For some reason, the nuns took care of their own chambers, but their shared bathrooms, the common reception and sitting rooms, corridors and other facilities were also maintained by the apprentices.

At different times during the day, as different jobs had been completed by the girls, together with their supervisory nun they had to attend common prayer session that would last around fifteen minutes, molding the girls, getting them acquainted in the finer point of respect and the acceptance of the lords wishes and to accept the commands of the nuns in particular, to be humble, un-presuming, respectful and to embrace their mental and physical abuse, in the name of God.

The learning of the French language was the primary reason why Aunt and the other girls in her group took on this apprenticeship. Indeed, they learned a great deal about French, but their experience was limited to the colloquial language used in a house keeping environment and some words that are customary during prayers, the theory classes that had been described on the application form as being a key component of this educative "apprenticeship" year with particular focus on all aspects of the French language, was mostly cancelled, replaced with some additional chores or prayer sessions; hence the learning of the rules of the written language was very humble indeed.

Some of the stories that Aunt was telling us about her experience at the convent were very compelling, captivating my full attention, at least in part some of the details appeared very comprehensive and detailed – almost unbelievable, but I don't see any reason why she wouldn't have talked about the truth.

At the convent, though under extremely difficult circumstances, Aunt was exposed to lots of skills that would have been very useful throughout her life, she got to know much about the preparation of a meal, she learned a great deal about hygiene, cleaning and general housekeeping, she experienced many aspects of life in a convent, an organized and structured organization, she got a glimpse of how the catholic religion influenced the daily life of the convents members and those that were associated with it, she learned something about hard work and discipline; all of which might have influenced her life in a positive manner.

However, as I gathered from her recount, Aunt and the other girls in her apprenticeship group were exposed to conditions and behavior that wasn't particularly kind, nor pleasant, looks of hatred could often be observed in some of the nun's eyes, sarcasm toward the girls was apparently applied with pleasure by others, hostility and mental torture could be experienced every day, and some of the supervisory nuns seemed to be pleased, perhaps delighted if they were able to inflict corporal punishment to some of the girls, and this was taking place during the late forties to early fifties, not long after the end of WWII, a time when most people must have been acutely aware of the effects of getting hurt, both mentally and physically, even worse; all of this had happened in a convent, an establishment with the mission to teach others about the all mighty, in a house where god's message should be listened to, lived and passed on to others—how wicked.

I refused to believe that the management of this particular convent set out deliberately to mistreat, indeed to abuse anybody within their custody, I would have thought that the objective of members of the clergy ordinated for religious duties was to care, to nurture, to provide an environment conducive for the development of those within their care. What was it that went wrong? Was the Prioress, Mother Superior not aware of how her staff was treating some of the apprentice girls? Aunt had explained that those that mistreated them belonged to the Rassophores and the Stavrophores, many of them appeared frustrated and grim in their behavior, whereas the Novices had a different attitude all together. Whatever happened to some of those old established nuns, were they so ingrained, was their discontent so deep-rooted that they took pleasure in mistreating some of the young girls that were entrusted in their care?

I recall clearly, at the time, when Aunt was telling dad and I about her tragic experiences at the convent I felt great sympathy for what had happened, endeavoring to imagine how this would have characterized her life, causing deep traces in her mind, but it didn't occur to me that I had observed very much the same kind of behavior when I was a kid, the hostility that I felt from time to time, the mental torture that I had to endure when Aunt was questioning me about some mishap for which I had to take the responsibility for, regardless of the facts, the yelling and screaming that I had to endure when Aunt was angry, the look of pleasure that I thought to have seen in her eyes when she was cross examining me, it didn't occur to me that despite the fact that Aunt had experienced mistreatment, abuse, mental and physical torture, she didn't reject this kind of behavior, in the contrary, she appeared to have embraced it to apply it on others, me being one of them.

## Aunt Lulu's Wedding

Just recently, I dug out the old family photos that Aunt gave me a few years ago, sorting through them I came across two photos depicting Aunt's wedding, the only two that remain with her in any of them; I had the urge to check out how this dysfunctional family looked like back then. Although I never asked Aunt specifically, I assume that the day of her wedding must have been one of the most beautiful ones in her life. Both of the photos, almost like the perfect postcards featuring the wedding party; Aunt and Dad being the main actors, surrounded by some of the towns beautiful people, a composite of my father's entourage of important characters in his life, Aunt's mum, dad and her sisters Tabea and Madelaine, a couple of close friends, my cousin Céline, my grandma and I.

These memorabilia were carefully staged and shot in Rue du Temple, Saint-Louis, France, in front of the Protestant Church who is remnant from the Romanesque architecture style of medieval Europe, characterized by semi-circular arches dating back to the 11$^{th}$ century. Calved into the main door of the church, as I was about to respectfully enter the Nave (the area where the congregation sits) I noted the words "Gottes Zeit ist die allerbeste Zeit," a saying that accompanied my life until right now, a notion that I never forgot, particularly in difficult times, a concept that from time to time gave me the strength to go on with stealth, rather than emotion in my private life—"God's time is the best time," sometimes it is worth the wait for something until the time is right.

At first glance, the two photos, rather the staged content looks stunning, the grouping of the people; everybody looking in the direction of the photographer, everybody immaculately groomed, beautifully dressed appropriate to the occasion and the season, with the church in the background, the shadows thrown by the sun could not have been placed better, the gentle breeze that blew from the west didn't bother the trees in the background either, nor did it affect anybody's hairdo, it simply appears to be perfect until I noted the young boy on the far left.

If I didn't know that this kid was me, I would have wondered why this child was invited to this wonderful occasion, standing next to my cousin Céline at a distance sufficient to indicate that I didn't truly belong to this party, straight like a soldier, very serious looking, sad, pitiful, indeed pathetic, obviously shaped by my youth, the expression on my face not only reflected the realization that I had now lost my father definitively to Aunt Lulu, the fact that Aunt had become very tough, often unreasonable, nor did she behave like a mother which obviously bothered me as well.

As I considered the pictures very closely, for a short moment I was able to recall some of the day's events, other than the believe to have lost my father to Aunt permanently, I also realized that not everything about that day was horrible for me personally, on the contrary, with a retrospective view, the day was filled with lots of beautiful and funny stuff; the moment when Tabea's husband, a fellow that was known to be a little clumsy, accidentally stepped on Aunt's wedding gown as she was about to board the bus; the way Aunt looked at Heinz as if she was going to bite and gobble him up.

The fabulous lunch that we were able to savor at one of the best restaurants in the regent, the afternoon mystery tour in the old FBW (a 30-seater bus that was built in the '50s by a Swiss company in Oerlikon, Zürich) when suddenly we got into heavy rain, unfortunately the sliding soft roof wasn't totally watertight, the rainwater began to drip on Aunt and a couple of other guests, the scrumptious buffet style dinner where only the finest of French specialties were presented, composed of pâtes, terrines, fresh seafood trucked up from the south of France, special local cold cuts, composite salads, the best cuts from the Charolais beef prepared to traditional dishes—Boeuf Bourguignonne,

Boeuf Wellington, Côte de Boeuf rôtie, Gigot Agneau rôtie pré-salé, a type of lamb that is raised in salt marsh meadows in the area of Mont Saint-Michel in the Normandy, France, accompanied with a variety of fresh vegetables, Gratin Potatoes, a large cheese and dessert selection, my grandma that was hugging the Cognac bottle, amusing herself with a big, fat cigar, fogging in some of the table neighbors, Aunt's sister Tabea had clearly consumed too much alcohol—bumbling about the dance floor—her husband, a member of the blue cross, utterly embarrassed about his wife, me—stuffing around on the drums during the band's break.

Having said that, the day was filled with lots of beautiful and funny stuff—funny from an unhappy adolescent's point of view whom at the time secretly enjoyed the misfortune of others that he didn't particularly care for, gleeful about the things Aunt had to endure on the most beautiful day of her life.

# The Tender Age of Fourteen

It was now nearly one year since Aunt had moved in with us and I had reached the tender age of fourteen, the beginning of pickles all over the face, tons of Brylcreem in my hair, trying to hold back the Elvis hairstyle that had become fashionable at the time, although my hair grew naturally sideways, pared on the left hand side, it was now combed straight back with force—held into position with this greasy stuff called Brylcreem that left its dark marks on the pillow which prompted Aunt to complain about it. I don't know why I put myself through this torture, having to listen to Aunt's grumbling every day, but it looked just great to me, but above all, the girls loved it.

There were enormous changes going on in my body which I didn't understand, it felt like gremlins were locked in me somewhere, creating total chaos over which I had no control.

The teenage had started to shake up the chemical cocktail in the body that is necessary to make the transition from child to adulthood. I had become very moody, even sensitive, if I was asked or told something I got to be a little aggressive, I was not afraid anymore to show that I was unhappy, I began to contradict Aunt when I felt that we had reached a situation of conflict, like Aunt, I had learned to raise my voice a little and demonstrated assertiveness, I progressively started to feel the oats.

I also had become very moody to the point where Aunt reminded me regularly not to pull such a gob when I was spoken to. What she meant was that my facial expression together with my negative behavior were a clear indication that I was not happy, and she was right, I now had gotten the courage to show my emotion.

Unfortunately, my performance at school started to show signs of failure, to the point where my principal teacher contacted my dad, trying to find out the cause of this change, as well as wanting to help in some way if he could.

Dad was trying to discuss this matter with me, wanting to know the reason for my sudden bad school performance, but I couldn't get myself to be honest with him, rather I did not tell him part of my problem. Honestly speaking, at the time I was convinced that Aunt was the cause of all my problems; in my mind I had condemned her for this. Of course, this was not fair, she was certainly my biggest challenge, but the other reason was the biological warfare that caused havoc in my life, turning everything upside-down.

Although I was known as a serious but happy kid, my behavior had become introvert, I had closed myself off from others, keeping my worries, my irritation and resentments to myself; I had lost the confidence to share these problems, over the past twelve months, I had learned that if you open yourself up to others, you expose yourself to criticism that you may not be willing or able to handle.

I appreciated that dad was aware of my teenage difficulties, where possible he was supporting me, trying to ease my trouble but he seemed to ignore, or perhaps he was not aware of the grave difficulties that I was having with Aunt, dad and I never talked about that particular problem, I dint think that there was any point in addressing the issue; I knew that dad would have supported his lady, believing that she was doing a great job, that the problem was me. Though I don't think that he was aware that she was so vicious toward me.

Dad was very clear in his words that he was not prepared to accept my lousy school performance; he was expecting me to fully embrace my education at school, he was going to check my homework every day.

Because dad did not always have the time to do this, he organized a law student to support me with my homework during three evenings per week.

The student that came to our house was a slim, tall and hansom looking young fellow, he was very quiet, and polite; he obviously came from a good home, George was his name. From the beginning I learned that he was here to guide me through my homework, as a tutor he was very firm and structured in his approach, and he had the ability to motivate me. I very much enjoyed the sessions with him, he coached me to the point where I had fun again with learning, he was a bit like the big brother that made sure that I was well taken care off.

At the end of each week my tutor had to provide dad with a report about my academic progress, within a very short time it became apparent that I was going to make it, just like dad expected me to. Because I was a little less available for Aunt, because she had less opportunity to control me, and the fact that now I had a big brother who supported me, I began to recover from my depressive behavior. I had also realized how important school was to me, how much I loved to absorb this stuff, I had found my yearning for the general knowledge as well as for mathematics and whatever elements that belongs to this subject again.

Thinking back, the turn-around wasn't very difficult either; George provided a solid structure, he facilitated a positive learning environment, and he refocused my attention on the fundamentals—a recipe that leads to success.

I didn't see much of dad, when I got up in the morning on most of the days he was already gone to work and at mid-day when he came home for lunch it was only for a short time to have his lunch. On most week days Aunt left a note for me so that I could begin with the basic preparation of a simple hot meal which she would continue with and finish of when she got there. At the lunch table it was mostly dad and Aunt that talked about business, the time spend with me was scarce; a brief how do you do, how is school, and what are the subject matters that are you dealing with currently.

As a matter of routine, before going back to school for the afternoon classes, the dishes had to be washed, dried and put away, the floor swept and washed with the mop. Although I would have preferred to utilize this time to do something for myself, I didn't mind doing it, this chore was always strait forward, it didn't take too much time, and Aunt didn't have the time to check if I had done it properly either.

## Mum or Dad—The Choice

I was at the house, just finished my homework, searching through my music library for some interesting stuff to practice on the trumpet, I just got a hold of the note book of the American funeral march melody written for the Brass section, a kind of a Jazz version, "just a closer walk with thee" when the phone rang; it was dad, he was still in the office, he asked me to come over, he wanted to see me. There was nothing unusual about that; dad would call me over once or twice a week, but this time our meeting was somewhat peculiar, he asked me to take a seat, his facial expression was cold, dead serious, I knew that something was not ok and I began to worry about what it might be that bothered my father, but as usual, I didn't have much time to brood about it, dad got straight to the point.

Without beating around the bush, he asked me if I was happy to live with him and Aunt, he stated that if I would prefer to go and stay with my mum, that that he would understand and that this would be ok with him.

I recall, my head was spinning, everything was happening so fast, although dad told me that I didn't need to answer him immediately, that I should take my time to make the decision that was going to be right for me, and that I didn't have to consider him at all in my decision.

I didn't hesitate with an answer either, I told dad that I wanted to stay with him.

I am astonished about the speed at which I had considered so many issues and circumstances, I also recall that I didn't want to hurt dad's feelings, that was important to me but I don't think that it was the only determining factor for my decision; on the one hand I tried to find an event that might have been the cause of this confrontation, and my emotional thought said yes, I would much prefer to stay with my mum because I had come to hate Aunt, but then my intellectual thought decided that staying with dad was more beneficial to me.

Although the emotional attachment to mum was still very strong, and as I suspect now that this attachment was so profound because I wasn't living with her, because I knew that this was something that I couldn't have, and I knew that living with my mum wasn't so easy either, I was very much aware that my brother William was in a boarding house, that he hadn't actually lived with mum, he only got to visit her once a month or so for the weekend; a future to which I didn't want to look forward to.

The thought process described here was conscious; my description is merely an assumption of how it may have taken place at the time, reaching a decision based on past experience and knowledge.

For quite some time after I was regularly brooding over this particular conversation with dad, wondering how this question came about, trying to establish what had happen during the weeks, perhaps months prior that might have triggered this event, speculating as to whom came to this conclusion that the question had to be put; did my father recognize the agony that I was going through, the fact that I had difficulties to accept Aunt that led him to the point that he confronted me, giving me the opportunity to make a choice? Or did Aunt decide that the question should be put because she recognized that I was unhappy, or did she realize that she was not equipped nor fit to handle me, or perhaps she had concluded that she would prefer not to be responsible for me anymore?

Retrospectively, having considered all relevant aspects that I am aware of, I allow myself to be of the opinion that this discussion was initiated by Aunt, because I am also aware of the fact that my dad was fighting for my custody at the time that he got divorced from my mum, he would not have wanted me to live with her; he had a clear vision for my future.

## The Blue Cross Brass Band

The feeling of neglect together with the idea that Dad and Aunt consumed too much alcohol were reason enough for me to get involved with the Blue Cross band in 1964, I was playing drums and learning the trumpet at the same time. I had joined this organization, without the knowledge of dad and Aunt, primarily I wanted to demonstrate to my parents the revolt that I felt toward alcohol. Like the members of the Salvation Armey, the folk from the Blue Cross practice teetotalism, but their activities don't have any religious aim. To get involved in the Blue Cross band was very important for me at that time.

My trumpet teacher Heinz, Doctor Heinz, was an intelligent, very quiet, reserved kind of fellow who had a tremendous amount of patience with his music students. Not only was he brilliant in the way he taught us youngsters the different playing techniques, he also had the ability to Inspire us for classical pieces that were written for the trumpet, at a stage when we would have preferred to get involved in Jazz music. I guess like many other youngsters at the time, secretly it was my ambition to be able to play the trumpet like Lois Armstrong some time down the track.

I knew Heinz also as a private person; he was the brother-in-law of Aunt— my stepmother. Outside our meeting sessions at the Blue Crosse Conservatory, I saw Heinz at family gatherings for the Sunday lunch or some other private occasions.

It was pitiful to see how most of the family members ridiculed him for reasons unknown to me. Perhaps the cause for this was his appearance; he was bold headed, a little solid, round faced, he wore glasses with reasonably thick lenses, and within the family atmosphere he only talked when someone spoke to him. Behind his back, the family had nick named him "Muggeli," whatever that was supposed to mean. I guess the fact that he was the only person at these family gatherings that did not drink any alcohol made him very different from the others, everybody else did consume, and often plenty of it.

At these family gatherings I always made sure that I could sit near Heinz, to be with him, so that I could talk to him, to demonstrate to the rest of the family that it was ok to seriously be bothered with Heinz, to me he was a kind hearted, very intelligent person from which one could learn a lot, he was also a brilliant music teacher, he was a Doctor of Chemistry engaged in the Pharmaceutical Industry as well as lecturing at the University of Basel, Switzerland.

Heinz and I never talked about his reason for having joined the Blue Cross; I had learned that his father was an alcoholic and that Heinz experienced considerable difficulties during his growing up time because of it. In contrast to Heinz's father, my father was definitely not an alcoholic; he merely consumed a lot at different times.

## Dad's Printing Factory

By this stage of my teeny life most of the week day evenings had become very pleasant for me. Both, dad and Aunt where very involved in the business, the two of them worked hard and long hours, often they worked until after 20:00 h or later, it wasn't unusual at all if I didn't get to see them at all in the evenings, almost like the time when he was married to Celina.

The good thing about all this was that dad's business was virtually across the road from the house, I could see the office building from one side of our home. In many ways this was very comforting, I knew that dad was nearby, I could usually get hold of him very quickly if I needed to.

Late afternoon when I came home from school, I always called in at dad's office to let them know that I was back, but not very often I found him there, usually he was somewhere in the production area, talking to staff, making sure that they had all that was needed to get the job done, or I would find him with one of the maintenance fellows checking out some technical problem. After the official reporting to dad—as I thought of it at the time—in a nice and positive way, I began my walk around through the factory, not aimlessly, nor was it a matter of showing off as the bosses son; not being aware of this at the time, my walk-around was structured which was without a doubt behavioral influence from my dad; I would start in the office by greeting those that were available, ignoring others that were obviously occupied with something or another, then I moved to the part of the business for which I felt passion and fascination—the different production areas.

There were several aspects that interested me in particular; on the ground floor there were several brand-new keyboard-based composing machines that had an output-capacity of 16 fonts in the sizes from 4 to 72 points, used for typesetting of newspaper text and other complex printing jobs. This method of composing newspaper text and other complex printing tasks was a substantial improvement from the previous process where the composer stood in front of a huge battery like setup with lots of boxes filled with metal plates of different points, each plate being a different letter from the alphabet, numbers, characters and space plates, having to choose each one to place them in the correct order of the text in a type frame. This frame could then be placed in the printing machine, ready to process.

It was ok to watch these fellows working but usually they were very concentrated with what they were doing and couldn't be disturbed, although, from time to time when someone was fiddling about with the mechanics of the machine, I was able to have a brief chat and ask some questions.

Dad's business was set up for the offset lithography, the so-called offset printing process, specializing in the printing of books and magazines.

The biggest of the printing machines was located in the basement, it consisted of various in-line towers that made up the total entity of the machine, and it was about fifty meters in length. The machine was designed for black and white as well as for color printing; at the beginning of this inline system was the huge paper roll weighing around one ton, the material to be printed was produced onto different cylinder templates and then transferred onto the paper with different printing cylinders which were distributed over the production line.

Down in the basement where big mama as I called the inline offset printing machine was installed, I always had a great time; not only could you hear the loud humming of this machine; you could almost feel it in your bones the moment you walked into this facility.

I had developed sufficient social skills to know when I could approach the fellows and when not, I had learned to observe their activities, their facial expressions and even the intensity of the mood, but as a general rule I knew that I always had to ask the chief printer if it was ok to snoop around.

It was intriguing to watch how the fellows were constantly monitoring the different elements of the inline towers, making little adjustments here and there to make sure that the quality of the print was the way it should be, and sometimes during the time that the machines were getting prepared for the next print process I was allowed to crawl all over them, up and down the steps walking along the narrow walkways that were fitted to and between the towers.

*I enjoyed being with the people* that worked for dad, not all of them were nice, like everywhere, some of them I didn't particularly like for reasons that I cannot explain, others still were all right but not necessarily the kind that you would want to spend a lot of time with, and then there were those very special ones that I adored, each one of them different in his or her own way, interesting to talk to, people that I felt very comfortable with, people that seemed to love me for what I was, not because I was the bosses son, and people that were very serious but just great and yet others very funny.

In my mind I had classified them without being aware of it; I had a clear opinion about whom I liked and whom I liked less or not at all.

In each department I had one or more of my favorite people, but particularly in the sorting and packing department was *Mrs. Manz,* a little, round shaped lady that spoke the dialect from Bern which was like music to my ears, her voice reminded me of my mum; she had something smutty to say every time she saw me, sometimes her comments were bordering on disgusting, but she understood how to get people to laugh.

*Our electro engineer Mr. Pfannenschmied,* the little professor with his glasses sitting on his nose, moving his head into a downward position so that he could look at you above the glasses frame when he was talking to you, he was short-sighted, listening to what he was saying when dad and he were pondering over a technical matter on one of the machines whom had very complex electronic systems.

Mr. Pfannenschmied was an electro engineer; he had his own engineering studio somewhere in town, he was called whenever our in-house technicians couldn't solve an electro technical problem.

*The Print master Mr. Busterla,* a rather short and stubby person, appeared somewhat arrogant, often grumpy, but he understood his business. I didn't get to chat with him very often, mostly when I came across him, he appeared to be busy. I had classified his personality as being a little difficult, and was wondering how my dad would get on with him, particularly because I knew that dad didn't appreciate arrogant people, but it seemed to work ok between the two of them.

*Mr. Schnurrenberger*, this was his nickname because he was talking a lot. I don't recall his true name but I know that dad got him a job as an all-rounder in the print shop. I always made sure that I greeted him especially; taking a moment to talk to him, asking him questions about what he was doing at the time, knowing that he appreciated it.

Schnurrenberger was a very intelligent fellow, previous to his engagement ad dad's printing works he had been engaged as a financial comptroller in a large company, and for some reason he had lost his job. This had traumatized him to the point where he suffered a so-called nervous breakdown, these days we might call it a burn-out. Although I don't understand any of these notions, I have never seen the broken nerves from a person that suffered the breakdown, nor have I seen any signs of burn by people that experienced a burn-out. Jokes aside, this fellow was off work for over one year, he had become mentally a little impaired, he was hard to understand when he talked, and if you looked at him carefully it became apparent that something wasn't the way it should have been.

Sometime you could hear someone singing aloud a song in English somewhere in the facility, without seeing the person you could be sure that it was Schnurrenberger, it didn't matter, he was very well integrated in the company, knew a lot about our business, and I think he was appreciative of his job.

*Mr. Mueller*, the head of the graphic design team, in principle a nice person, could be very arrogant, knew everything, needed to show that he was the boss in his department, he would talk a lot but not let others, his posture was interesting; arms crossed behind his head, nose slightly up in the air, I wondered how dad could possibly get on with him, apparently, he was brilliant in his job.

Then there was *Rosita*, the beautiful, young lady from Udine, Italy, a town North-East of Venice. She was working in the assembly and packing department, had a short-term work permit valid only for a few months; as I recall she came to Switzerland under the umbrella of the seasonal workers. Dad and Aunt had provided a room on the ground floor, at the back of our house for Rosita until such time that she could find something of her own somewhere in the vicinity. At the beginning Rosita didn't speak a word of

German, the only way I could communicate with her was with a bit of French, some hand signs and lots of hearty laughter.

*Lena the Austrian lady*, she was working in the office, had a short-term work permit just like Rosita. Dad and Aunt had also provided a room at our house for Lena until such time that she could find her own apartment. Like any other healthy teenager, one evening before Lena had come to the house, I decided to take a look at her room which was upstairs, just down the hallway, a couple of doors from my dwelling. For a moment I thought that lightening had struck me, her bed was not made, there were clothes laying all over the floor, her writing table was also full with make-up products; cotton pads and other similar stuff, and there was a small bowl with what looked like dried up egg yolk with a brush firmly stuck in it, it wasn't put there yesterday either.

I secretly wished that Aunt could see this discussing mess, but I could not tell her about it because I know that I wasn't to go in Lena's room in the first place. Some weeks later, one evening I had the fortune to meet her as she was coming out of her room to go to the bathroom across the floor. Frankly speaking I got a shock at first; her face was totally covered with a thick coat of yellow stuff which was most probably a beauty mask that she had made up from egg yolk.

I remember when Lena moved in with us, despite the fact that she was about ten years older than me, I thought that she was very pretty, in my reckless teeny fantasy I appreciated that our bedroom doors weren't very far away, it wasn't by accident that I bumped into her one evening, when I discovered that she had a beauty mask all over her face, that was the moment my sentiments for her had ended abruptly.

*The chief accountant Mr. Blumenstein*, a very intelligent fellow who was very calm and collected. When I did get to see him, like most of the white collars, he was always very formal, polite but reserved, with his head high up in the air, slightly arrogant. Mr. Blumenstein had a reputation of chasing the ladies, it was said that it was his specialty to seduce them, enjoy them for a little while and then to go on to the next one which created a bit of gossip among the staff.

I was not brought up in a religious way, but you don't have to be religious to understand something about behavior that is morally intact, or to know what is correct and what is not. Despite my knowing that Mr. Blumenstein's behavior was unhealthy and totally unacceptable, secretly I felt a little admiration for him, rather for his adventures.

*Aunt, her role in the business*, since the time that Aunt had taken over the responsibility of the dispatch room, I tended not to spend a lot of time in this area, it was merely a matter of self-interest that caused me to see Aunt first, making sure that I greeted her and asked for permission for my walk-around, because there were a couple of people that had been working there ever since I remember.

Monika, a young German lady whom commuted from Freiburg in Breisgau in Germany to Basel everyday by train, as the oldest from a family of six she supported her parents, brothers and sisters whom lived in a very old house in the inner city. Before Aunt had moved in with us, from time to time I was allowed to spend the weekend at Monica's place in Freiburg, over a period a close friendship had developed between us, an amity between child and adult that allowed us to talk about things as if we were brother and sister, I was able to tell her some of my little secrets, and sometimes she confided how terrible Aunt's attitude toward the staff was, and how this was having an effect on the working morale of the dispatch department.

People like Monika were called Frontaliers, already in the 50s there were a lot of folk from Switzerland's neighboring countries that lived relatively close to our border that commuted from their home to the place of work and back every day of the week, in the case of Monica the distance from her home to Basel was around 70 kilometers which took around an hour and the same for the return journey, a travel time of around two and a half hours each day.

The social impact of the Frontaliers in those days was different compared to the implications that exist now; Switzerland was in need of labor, particularly in the lower earning segment like manufacturing, construction and the service industry, and these gaps were filled by people from the neighboring areas of France, Germany, Austria and Italy, earning considerably more in Switzerland as they were able to in their own countries. Unlike today, the financial burden on our social system as a direct result of the so called Frontaliers was negligible then. After my walk around at the plant I crossed over the road to our house. On three of five schooldays my tutor came to the house, I recall very clearly the calmness with which he taught mathematics; the numbers, quantities, measurements ant the relationship between them, he had the ability to explain the details in a manner that must have been clear to anybody. He complemented the very structured approach to any task that dad had taught me, to the point where after a while I could almost anticipate his next move in the lessons that he instructed.

On the days when dad and Aunt were working late, or if indeed they had planned some other activity which inhibited them to be at home, Aunt would come across from the plant to get me organized for the evening. Sometimes there was something in the fridge that could be reheated as my evening meal, sometimes Aunt send me across to the supermarket to get the little things that were missing in the larder. Particularly during the summertime, I enjoyed the simple things that didn't involve any preparation; Gruyere Cheese, Cervelat, or assorted small goods, pickled gherkin, bread, butter and the most important accompaniments, Thomy Mayonnaise and Mustard. Still today I very much enjoy this kind of food, particularly during the warm weather.

### Aunt's "Wähe"

During the summer, when Aunt had the time, she would prepare a "Wähe" (Wäie) which is in principle a sheet cake. For this purpose, the baking sheet can be oblong or round, depending on the size to be produced, the sheet including its side wall was covered with a short-crust pastry about three millimeters thick and the edges of the pastry that were overhanging the sheet rim was kind of twisted into a fancy pattern.

Then she would pierce the bottom of the pastry all over with a fork, apparently to avoid bubbles from forming during the baking process. On top of the pastry, she then evenly distributed finely ground hazelnuts which would prevent the pastry from absorbing the moisture of the cut fruits that formed the basis of the "Wähe" and they enhanced the flavor at the same time.

Although the topping could also be made from savory items like onions, cheese, vegetable or indeed meat products, during the summer months Aunt would create this dish with fresh, seasonal fruits; Apricots, plumbs, rhubarb, prunes, cherries, pears were the usual choices, where as apple was mostly reserved for the cooler parts of the year. Pending on the kind of fruit, it was washed in cold water, pealed, de-stoned, and the pith removed. The cherries were left whole but de-stoned, the strings were removed from the rhubarb, cut into pieces about one centimeter long, apple and pear cut into wedges and the stone fruit was merely halved.

Then the fruit was nicely arranged on top of the pastry; stone fruit like apricots were layered in a circle, beginning on the outside of the pastry with the cut side of the fruit facing up, building up until the entire pastry was covered. The same procedure took place for apple and pear, whereas cherries and rhubarb were loosely distributed on the pastry.

Usually, Aunt completed this creation with baked vanilla custard. For this purpose, she took a vanilla bean, crushed it open, placed it in some fresh cream and heated it just under the boiling point, and left the vanilla in there so that a flavor transfer into the cream could take place, until the cream had cooled down.

For a thirty-centimeter diameter cake sheet she mixed three to four egg yolks and some sugar, and then added the vanilla flavored cream to it. This mixture was then poured over the fruit just before the "Wähe" was pushed into the preheated oven at a temperature of around 150° Celsius.

Needless to mention that the vanilla cream custard was the first job in the making of this dish, to ensure that the egg yolks would not curdle, hence the cooling down of the cream before they were added was essential. The initial baking temperature of 150° Celsius is of the utmost importance; this temperature must be maintained for the first twenty minutes or so, until the custard has set properly. After that you can increase the temperature to around 180° which will help you to get the pastry crust just perfect and the top has the chance to get a little glazy as well. The fruit—"Wähe" how we called it in our dialect "wäie"—could then be enjoyed warm, or cold the next day, if there was any left over.

With it, Aunt would serve crème fraîche very lightly whipped. I didn't believe everything that Aunt told me, but everything that she emphasized about cooking or cooking methods you could believe without questioning. Once I had learned to make a "Wähe" without the supervision of Aunt, on one occasion I didn't observe the initial baking temperature because I thought that I could speed up the process a little, and sure enough when we got to taste it, we realized that the vanilla custard had curdled, a bit like scrambled egg. Aunt was quick to tell me that I had not observed the initial baking temperature.

From this day on, I never doubted her authority as a cook, I had realized that she was the master of this subject; her authority was not to be questioned.

# A Question of Trust

The evenings that I spend alone at home became more and more frequent, but I had learned to see the positive in this situation and enjoyed the feeling of being alone, having the freedom to be able to do what I wanted. Mostly I perused one of my hobbies, but more and more the radio became important in my life, primarily because of the music and a little later I found my fascination in the national radio channel that broadcasted radio plays.

For some reason or another, from the moment Aunt moved in with us all rooms in the house, with the exception of the visitor's rooms, the kitchen, and my bathroom were locked when dad and Aunt were not at home, I could never understand the reasoning for this.

I merely gathered that it had something to do with trust—for some reason Aunt had no trust in me.

I cannot imagine that there might have been something behind those locked doors that I wasn't supposed to know or see, the fact that the doors were locked didn't bother me except that I didn't have access to a radio, this was yet another reason that caused me to further alienate myself from my parents.

On those occasions where I knew that I would be alone for the evening I asked dad if I could borrow the radio that was in his office; though modern at the time, this small stationary model still operated with bulb like glass tubes filled with gas, containing electrodes, and the choice of radio stations was fairly limited.

Dad never refused my request, and so I started to develop a fascination for radio, I was free to choose the type of music that I was interested in, for these moments I was not forced to listen to something that didn't interest me.

Since the time that Aunt had moved in with us she selected the radio stations that broadcast the then popular hits vocalized by Elvis Presley, The Beatles, Tom Jones, Engelbart Humperdinck, Frank Sinatra, Roy Black, Lolita, Freddy Quinn, Edith Piaf, Connie Francis, Peter Kraus, and many other popular artists which I didn't mind at all, but after each song there was this dreadful burst of advertising of household products which I absolutely hated; riming words accompanied by some music, very loud and artificial in its presentation, which in an intrusive manner gave the impression that everybody had to have one of those; whatever it might have been, and others left you with the impression that you were a nobody if you didn't get it as well.

Before this pop period, when dad was at home I was used to hear the news and perhaps the occasional report, and then the radio was turned off, in the evenings after dinner, as well as on Sunday mornings dad would start up his Philips record player and put one of his Vinyl's from his carefully stowed collection—Tchaikovsky, Debussy, Stravinsky, Verdi, Puccini, Rossini, Di Stefano were his favorite composers and Maria Callas, Joan Sutherland, Mario Lanza, Franco Corelli, Ettore Bstianini, some of the vocalists that he adored the most.

I had learned to appreciate Opera as well, some of the arias I knew of by heart, I grew up with the musical material of Maria Callas and Mario Lanza, and later I developed a fascination for Luciano Pavarotti, José Carreras, Plácido Domingo, Andrea Bocelli—artists that accompanied me throughout my life.

However, increasingly I became fascinated with Jazz. At that time, without the knowledge or the approval of dad and Aunt, Jazz was for some reason or another frowned upon in my family, though I know that dad appreciated artists like Luis Armstrong. On certain nights I was listening to a French Radio station that began their two-hour Jazz broadcast just after the 22:00 hour news. Luis Armstrong, Charlie Parker, Duke Ellington, Count Basie, Oscar Peterson, Benny Goodman, Dave Brubeck, Woody Herman, Jon Coltrane, the Dutch Swing College Band, Lionel Hampton, Stan Getz, Gene Krupa, Buddy Rich and other great bands and musicians were regularly featured to my delight.

I got to appreciate the different styles of Jazz; Avant-Garde; a style of music combined regular rhythm with improvisation, Big-Band Jazz, Contemporary, Cool, Crossover, Dixieland, Trade and other forms of Jazz. But in particular I appreciated the Big-Band arrangements; I was fascinated by the precise interaction between Buddy Rich and the rest of the band, but also intrigued by the sound that Avant-Garde teams produced the swing of the Ellington band or the vast scale of tones that Mils Davis was achieving with his Trumpet.

I also explored the available channels and found out that there were radio plays as well that walk some enthusiasm in me, I became fascinated by the fact that the play could capture and retain my attention during a whole hour, merely because the story was usually exciting, enhanced through the changing modulation and expression of the actor's voices enriched through deliberate pausing between sentences or words, whenever possible I tried not to miss them.

On a regular basis I was also practicing my trumpet playing, working on the piece of music that my teacher Heinz asked me to improve upon. So that I wouldn't disturb the neighborhood too much, dad had organized an insulated corner in the cellar where I had sufficient space for the drums as well. Actually, the space was large enough for a small band to practice. Much of the drumming practice, particular the pieces played on the snare I would do on the rubber practice pad, but the real stuff I played on my Rogers set which consisted of the 22-inch base, one 13-inch Tom, one 16-inch floor Tom, a Dynasonic Snare, the 16-inch Hi-Hat, one 20-inch Ride, and two 18-inch Crash Cymbals.

To me, the drums were a fantastic instrument; I played the kind of stuff that I was given to practice, always aiming to play the rhythm as it was prescribed, observing the range of volume indicated in the piece.

Often, when dad and Aunt weren't in the house in the evening, I went to the cellar, laid a Gene Krupa or a Buddy Rich record on the disk, and with a reasonably high volume I tried to imitate their drumming.

Compared with the musical and the technical skills that Gene Krupa and Buddy Rich had, the sounds that I produced where rather modest, but I certainly had a lot of fun doing it. I don't think that I realized as a kid what effect these wild drumming sessions had on me, I was only aware of the fact that I was having fun, but today I believe that it also had a therapeutic cause, at the end I always felt as if I had gained a mental strength that I didn't have before.

On some of these lone evenings I perused my other hobbies. Dad had bought me a lovely Balsa Wood kit from which I was able to build a Police boat from the bottom up on the scale 1:87, this required a lot of skill and a lot of patience. With most of the skills that I needed for the project, dad was supporting me; he would demonstrate and explain so that I was able to work independently.

Even as a kid I understood that there was no point in beginning with the boat building if I was in a bad mood, it was not pleasant to be around me if I wasn't in a good state of mind.

I had the ability to become furious and when I got to this state of mind, I was capable to smash and to break things with an incredible force.

Today I conclude that it is a fact that I never got into this state of fury when dad or Aunt or anybody else were around, it only happened to me when I was alone, as if I had given myself permission to get mad, subconsciously understanding that this would help me to overcome some of the frustrations that were apparent in my life.

On other occasions of these lone evenings, I would amuse myself with the electronics kit, with the components you could build a simple radio, more or less complex circuit boards for different projects, blinkers and other interesting stuff, not unlike the model building, it was essential to be concentrated on the task, calm and collected, working in accordance with a plan, which required me to work in a logical sequence.

## Moments of Insanity

There were also moments of insanity; I adored the smell of Amsterdamer tobacco, I couldn't get near enough to those that smoked it, as claimed by the advertising campaign at the time, fellows that smoked this particular tobacco were real men, a notion that probably made some kind of impression on me, so I bought a pipe and the tobacco from a school mate; like a grownup fellow, I stuffed the pipe with Amsterdamer, pushed down the tobacco reasonably firm, just like I had observed a pipe smoker doing it, lit it and started to inhale this stuff that I had pulled through the mouth piece, being careful that not too much smoke got into my lungs, keeping it there for a short moment, trying hard not to cough, and then releasing it slowly, in a controlled manner by gently squeezing my lips together as if I was playing the trumpet, with my head slightly tilted upward, just like I had observed some of those connoisseurs that obviously got enormous enjoyment from smoking the pipe—the only thing that was missing was an audience that would admire my sophisticated behavior.

The smell was heavenly, the taste bitter and dreadful, and within ten minutes or so I couldn't get quick enough to the toilet to throw up, and with this the thoughts of being sophisticated had vanished down the hole as well.

I was convinced that if I opened up all the windows, the smell of the tobacco would have left the house by the time dad and Aunt would come home. I was mistaken, I pretended to be sleeping when they returned, I could hear every word they were saying and became a little concerned about the next day, having to face up to my little excursion into the adult world, having to explain where I got the pipe and tobacco from, and how I could possibly think of doing such a stupid thing.

Indeed, the next day I had to listen to both, dad who was lecturing me clearly, but he kept it brief, and Aunt who went on and on about it, it seemed for ages; wanting to know why I did this.

It was the "why" questions that I hated the most.

Why did you smoke—"because I wanted to know what it would be like." But this was not enough for Aunt; she had to put the next why question; "why did you want to know what it would be like." And so, it could sometimes go on and on.

She didn't understand that a kid's answer could be simple and uncomplicated, she had the feeling that I should analyze everything in depth and provide her with an answer accordingly, and she couldn't accept that kids don't function this way, nor did she realize that there isn't always a plausible answer to something that you did, and sometimes you do something stupid because you didn't think or consider the possible consequences

Aunt's questioning technique haunted me all my life, even until this day. Again, and again she drove me to incandescence because she couldn't let go, she had to put the "why" question over and over again, even if you had provided her with an answer several times explaining something in different ways in the hope that she would finally understand.

On most of those occasions Aunt was not satisfied with the answer that was given to her, and consequently she would then tell you the reason for your action of behavior, she would allege that her account of the matter was the truth, and then I knew that I had lost the game, and I was aware that now I had two options; I stuck to the truth, knowing that Aunt could not accept it and as a result I had to put up with the abuse and punishments, alternatively I was able to abandon the truth, accepting her allegation and still enjoying abuse and punishment, the difference between the two options I never understood, but I assume that the sentence was similar if not the same, I only learned that the second choice was unfair but I got released from Aunt's torture faster.

## My Fifteenth Birthday

Later that year, for my fifteenth birthday dad surprised me with a Ghetto-blaster. It appeared to be the biggest and most complex portable that I had ever seen in the local shops before, it was a Blaupunkt Derby Commander portable radio, it featured Longwave, Middle wave, Shortwave, UKW, and other functions that I had never heard of before, and you could operate it with 240 volts as well as with batteries. This unit was the latest scream, designed and furbished with the latest technology; it was stuffed full with transistors.

Now I had more listening options, as well as the normal channels that you get on a radio, at night I was able to receive private radio operators from all over the world; although spoken in different languages some of the wireless messages I could understand, some of them were encoded or scrambled, most of the others I didn't grasp, they were merely fascinating to listen to for a while.

At the time the cold war was at its peak, not that I understood its meaning, nor its impact on our society, I merely understood from the bits of information that floated around that people were concerned and scared about it.

I was hoping to find a radio channel that would reveal something about this mysterious war that you couldn't see. You could feel the mystery when you listened to radio messages, as if you were eaves dropping into something that you weren't supposed to hear, it was mysterious and cool. Of course, those broadcasts that dealt with such matters were spoken in a language that I would not have understood, and the messages were probably encoded.

From time to time I picked up some discussion about politics in dad's office, ideas and opinions were stated but I didn't understand the context of the debate, nor did anybody bother to explain it to me, I was merely an observing outsider. Even privately, dad might make some comment about a political issue, but he never elaborated upon it, and for some reason I never asked any questions about politics either. The subject that was frequently discussed and feared was Russia and its communism, a subject that intrigued me totally; all I ever heard and understood from these conversations that communism was something very dangerous, frightful, horrible, even gruesome, it sounded like the devil in person, but nobody ever explained why communism was so scary—they merely stated that it was.

Even as a kid I was very curious about everything and anything that apparently couldn't be explained became a fascination, and so I spend a little more time at night to listen to wireless broadcast, hoping to pick up something that might explain what communism was all about.

Unfortunately, it wasn't until later when I was doing my high school diploma that I came across *George Orwell's book Animal Farm,* apparently one of his finest works, which deals with a political fable, based on the events of Russia's Bolshevik revolution and the betrayal of the cause by Joseph Stalin. This book revealed some of the mystique of communism to me, and it inspired me to learn more about it, a little later in my life.

Around the age of fifteen I had completed my eighth year of school, and the time had come to decide the academic future. Some of my school mates decided to get into a trade, others had ambitions to peruse medicine, law, science, engineering and other fields of studies, and I was determined to become an airline pilot. Those of us that had decided to go for a higher education had to absolve an entrance examination to get a seat at one of the colleges that prepared its students for the university. Most of us from my class that had decided to peruse the higher studies succeeded with the exam and got a place to study.

I had passed the examination at a reasonably high level and would have very much liked to join my colleagues at the Gymnasium situated near the cathedral, an institution that enjoyed a great reputation, but for some reason dad had decided differently; he was of the opinion that I was capable to absolve the first year in French, and he was able to get me a place at the Gimnase, lycée Cantonale de Neuchâtel.

I don't think that the French language was the primary or indeed the only reason for this decision, I very much suspect that it had something to do with the young lady that I got to see more frequently, I am sure that if I hadn't been sent to the boarding school in Neuchâtel, this might have been my first teenage love, but it wasn't to be.

In those days' kindergarten and the first four years of primary school were coeducational, during the secondary school years we were segregated, and most high schools practiced segregation as well, most unconsidered, just at a time where I began to become interested in girls.

I never understood why educators at that time insisted on segregation, and I am not convinced either that we were more able to focus on our studies. Most of my schoolmates had brothers and sisters, I had a step brother whom I was able to see once or twice a year, we never had a chance to become close, and so I missed out on this healthy sibling interaction from which I believe I could have learned a lot of important social interaction skills. Other than Aunt and some of the grown-up ladies that I knew through dad's business, I had no understanding of the social interaction with females, particularly not with young ones, a social disadvantage which is not to be underestimated. Though

I was able to spend a little time with my cousin Celine from time to time, mostly under the suspicious eyes of Aunt.

## Boarding School at the Age of Sixteen

To go to boarding school at the age of 16 was tough, just like Prime Minister Malcolm Fraser, in 1971, in an address to the people of Australia he stated "life wasn't meant to be easy" a statement that proved prophetic for the country, it was not easy to be a boarding college student either, I guess the idea was to keep the teenage youngsters busy with studies and physical education and lots of minor exams, so that we were truly tired at the end of the day, which helped to keep us in a straight line. Generally, we didn't have too much energy, nor the time to get up to pranks. Other than studying, the library, sport and the music evenings there was nothing else that we could do, we didn't even get the chance to secretly smoke a cigarette, nor was it possible to sneak out undetected at any time of the day or night.

Honestly speaking, we didn't know what a joint was either, nor were we aware of the drug scene that had begun to make its début with teenage school kids in Germany at that time; we were innocent from that point of view, and I am sure glad for this because I don't know how I would have reacted to all this stuff that promised a lot of freedom and a good time, I don't know if I would have been able to resist.

Most of us in this particular intake came from the German speaking areas of Switzerland, French was the second language for us, some of us had already reached a reasonably high level which made it easier to follow the lectures, easier to get the home work done, in my case the stint at my grandma's place provided me with a healthy advantage. None the less, I had to work hard to keep up in class; I put a lot of effort into my homework to get good notes.

The science subjects were very demanding because you needed to learn the subject specific technical terminology, whereas mathematics was reasonably straight forward and you could generally achieve good notes. In contrast, the French classes were for me extremely demanding; the spoken part of this subject was ok, my accent was pretty good, my vocabulary was constantly growing, but the written part was disastrous, I had difficulties understanding the Grammar, on average I achieved bad grades in this subject which affected my overall result, making it kind of ok but it wasn't good enough.

I was very lucky that I was the only one in the college at the time that was pretty well in command of the drums; my technique was deemed to be at a very high level, the resident college music teacher thought that I had a lot of talent for big band arrangements, and this at the age of sixteen.

For that one year at the college, I was celebrated as the drummer boy and I felt very comfortable with this reputation, enjoying a bit of recognition from my mates, but I hadn't forgotten my dream, to become an airline pilot, and accordingly I continued to focus on the school subjects.

On most evenings the college band was practicing in the music hall for an hour or so, sometimes we could stuff around with improvisations, but mostly we had to play material with all seriousness, because music was an elective subject which was commented in the semester note book, but not evaluated.

Once per month we could apply for weekend leave which had to be acknowledged by the parents and approved by the principle, but for some reason I got to go home for one weekend only during my entire year that I spend at the college with the exception of the official holiday time. Mostly for reasons that I never fully understood my coming home was not convenient for Dad and Aunt, although I was given an explanation which didn't make much sense at the time.

I felt abandoned and hurt; more and more I felt alienated from the family, but I accepted and made the best of this situation, I enjoyed the college environment, I was not exposed to Aunt's iron fist, didn't have to listen to her continues nagging, I didn't have to fear her presumptuous stories and the never-ending questioning when something had gone wrong, not being part of this was very comforting to me.

Of course, I was engaged in constructing different scenarios in my mind about my family's behavior toward me but I wasn't preoccupied with these thoughts, I didn't brood about it either, the speculation about having being abandoned didn't fit my perception that I had about my father, I preferred to believe that dad had become aware of the awful relationship that I had with Aunt, that he wanted to protect me from her manipulative behavior, a notion that was not confirmed, but strengthened much later in my adult life.

I don't remember much about the one weekend that I was allowed at home, dad and Aunt picked me up on the Saturday morning, we had eaten fresh fish in one of the restaurants on the lake, the following day we went for a little tour in the Alsace regent, and later that afternoon I was brought back to the college, but I don't recall any of the details, I only recall that Aunt was reasonably pleasant to me.

The day my grandma passed away I was at the college, the only reason why I knew that she died was because this particular morning, to my surprise, I was called to the lobby by the principal; dad and Aunt were there to greet me, I was told that Grandma from Villeneuve had passed away.

In the college dining room, we spent a short moment together, talking about what happened and then the two of them left for Villeneuve to bury Grandma, without me.

I remember I felt very touched by Grandma's death. After all I had spent a year with her not so long ago, and I was disappointed and angry because nobody bothered to ask me how I felt, nor was I invited to take part at the funeral.

Although we never spoke about it, I had the feeling that death was a taboo subject in our house as this was the case in our society in general at that time, particularly among city folk, death was something that only adults could talk about, that kids weren't supposed to get involved in any of the activities surrounding death, that they should be spared the emotional burden.

In my opinion this was a lot of crap; as a kid I was able to take part in the celebration of birth on a number of occasions, I couldn't understand why I was not allowed to take part in the burial of my grandma, whom assumed that I couldn't handle this, why was I not allowed to cry for my grandma at her grave?

I will never know because dad and I never talked about this, even later during my adult life, I don't think he felt comfortable with the subject.

## The Day Grandma Passed Away

The passing away of my grandma was at a period when people in the countryside of Switzerland were still able to die at home. Those that were leaving this world were looked after and comforted by the family members, the house doctor would call on occasion to provide the necessary medical and moral assistance, and this was not foreign to kids either, not only were they tolerated, they were part of the process and so got to understand that death was a natural occurrence. Of course, there were other cases as well; the dying that needed particular care that could only be provided in a hospital environment, and there were those cases where the family didn't have the opportunity to suitably care for their loved ones, or those that simply didn't want to accompany the dying to the end.

In those days, the funeral consisted of two parts, the first being the sad part, filled with sorrow, mournful for the person that departed, and the second was rather reflective, generally over a few drinks and some nibbles.

A few years before the passing away of my grandma in Villeneuve, I was barely six years of age when my mum took me to her mother's funeral in Wiedlisbach, Switzerland. I never had the chance to get to know Grandma Anna well, I don't recall much about the little time that I spend with her either, but I remember her as a lovely, very quiet person that took care of the house and the kitchen, and that she prepared this wonderful local food whenever we were there for a short Sunday visit.

I don't know the cause of Grandma's death, I only remember that her body was on show in the middle of the living room, the coffin had been placed on two stools so that Grandma was laying at around seventy centimeters above the floor, I guess so that she was reasonably close to those that were mourning around her, and for those that wanted to say the last good bye before the undertaker placed the lid on the coffin.

The coffin was made from mahogany wood; lacquered, constructed as a so called "body shape"—narrow at the head end, then broadening in the area of the shoulders, and from there narrowing down to the feet, the base of the box had four elaborate brass handles, two on each side, on the left as well as on the right side there were carvings of Jesus with his disciples depicting the last supper, together with other decorative carvings.

The lid to the coffin was standing upright against the wall; it was built from three tears, all of them decorated with delicately carved ornaments, and the top tear being flat, decorated with a simple branch carved into it.

In her white dress Grandma laid in her beautiful coffin which was lined with white lace, she held a small bunch of flowers in her hand, her face looking almost angelic, and her tummy was very huge, as if she was pregnant. I still remember, from a distance, near Grandpa's big lounge chair I observed all that was going on that morning, but I couldn't get my eyes of the coffin, it was so beautiful, one could have gotten the impression that it was more important than Grandma, and on the other hand you could have thought that a person like Grandma deserves only the best to travel in for the last journey.

Still today, particularly during the season when the elder blossoms in the garden, I am reminded of the particular smell in the room where Grandmas body laid – a blend of elder and death filled the surroundings.

I also remember that it was a little scary, no one was talking to me how I was doing, nor did anybody bother to explain to me what was happening – I was simply left there to take part, it didn't occur to anyone that this little kid could do with some support. A little scary it was, somehow, I knew that Grandma would not wake up again; somehow, I understood that she was not coming back, but at no point in time did I feel traumatized, it all seemed very natural.

My mum, the person responsible for me on this occasion, although she was no doubt preoccupied with all sorts of little duties, taking care of the visiting mourners as well as coming to terms with her own grief, would have done well to take a little time for me, the little kid that had to try and work out everything for myself, a little explanation here and there, and a touch of comforting would have been well placed. I don't mean this to be disrespectful to my dear mum; it may merely serve as a reminder to others, just in case you find yourself in such a situation.

A little later that morning, I remember I was outside the house with a lot of the other people that were there when the undertaker arrived with his black, wooden coach, drawn by two black horses, him sitting high up on the driver's bench, wearing a black suit and a hi-hat perched on his head. He stopped, descended from the driver seat and secured the vehicle and the horses. A little while later Grandmas Coffin was brought out, carried by four men, Grandpa walking very close behind them.

The coach was fully glazed so that you could see every detail on the inside, then through the back-double door the coffin was placed into the coach's glass compartment, the sides of the coffin were then decorated with lots of flowers, surrounding Grandma for her last journey.

With Grandpa, Uncle Willy and mum and me immediately behind the coach, the funeral assembly walked down the hill, to the main road, through the first of the gates of the fortress which surrounded the old part of the village, through to the second gate, on to the cemetery which must have been a two-kilometer walk.

First there was a short service at the cemeteries church, and then the coffin was carried to the open ground where Grandma was going to be buried. I was among the people that stood around the grave when the coffin was lowered into the ground, and then my mum helped me to pick up some dirt; together we threw it on the coffin, the dirt hitting the coffin made a terrible sound, kind of hollow, and I wondered if Grandma would be aware of all that was going on now, and I recall that I didn't want to be there when the soil was going to be put back in the hole, covering Grandma.

I didn't know at that time why I was doing this, but it felt good, it was a bit like the last physical contact with Grandma before she left.

After the cemetery the entire assembly, including the priest walked back to the village where we called in at one of the pubs. I guess it must have been prearranged, a roast with mashed potatoes and vegetables were served and there was plenty of wine and beer for everybody; there were times when you didn't think that we were at a funeral party, it was a bit like the final part of an Irish wake, an important part of the grieving process. I recall some of the scenes very specifically, people were drinking, laughing and appeared to have a good time. Sure, I didn't understand what was happening at the time because no one bothered to accompany me emotionally; my mum holding my hand occasionally or brushing her fingers through my hair which probably gave me some comfort without words, but it didn't explain what was going on.

I don't think that children have to be exposed to everything and anything, but I am convinced that they can handle the truth about life; be it the death of a family member, or a grave illness that someone has to deal with, or the death of a pet, providing we explain things in an age-appropriate manner, and that we accompany the child morally along the way.

Looking back, nobody explained anything to me, I knew that grandma was not the way she was before, I could see that she was sleeping in a box in the middle of the living room but I didn't know why, I could see that her tummy was now huge, nor did I understand why she was holding a little bunch of flowers in her sleep, when the fellow in the black suit put the lid on grandmas box I knew that I would not see her again, when grandmas box was lowered into this hole in the earth, it became clear that she would never come back to us.

As a little kid I had gathered all of these impressions and I had to try to interpret this puzzle to understand what had happened and what this was all about.

The experience of Grandmas funeral in Wiedlisbach, did not have any negative effects on me, not then and not now, despite the fact that I was left to work out what had happened, sure, the experience would have been even richer had someone bothered to let me into the truth, despite this it was an experience that enriched my life, I wouldn't want to have missed it. It was this kind of farewell that I expected to be able to take part in when Grandma in Villeneuve passed away, I recall, I was very angry because this was denied to me, till now I have not been able to forgive my folks for this.

## Summer Break

The college summer break lasted for six weeks. Dad and Aunt picked me up on the Saturday morning, in his red Chevrolet Cabriolet, it was the spunkiest car that was parked outside the college that morning, and I enjoyed the attention that my departure caused among the other kids.

The first week I spend at home, although both, Aunt and dad were working, we went out for dinner a couple of times, the rest of the week I spend catching up with some friends that had not gone on leave, stuffing around with my favored technical toys, and on the weekend, we went camping in St-Ursanne on the river Doubs.

This particular week at home had shown me that Dad, Aunt and I had grown apart from each other a little further, my folk's behavior toward me was a little more distant, as if they were beginning to respect this young fellow opposite them whom had become taller, my voice had begun to change, and my appearance and behavior toward my folks was self-conscious, confident and assertive, it was clear that this fellow had done plenty of growing up in the time that he was away.

The next four and a half weeks I spend on a farm above Muttenz, not very far from home, perhaps twelve kilometers. As a teenager dad spend his summer breaks at the same farm, except that during my time the old farmer's son and his wife were in charge, as it was traditionally the case, they had taken over from their parents. I don't think that a lot of things had changed since the time my father was here, most of the work was still done by hand, the old Hürlimann tractor that dad used to drive as a youngster was still going strong, in the spirit of progress a grass cutting and a hay bailing machine were purchased since.

The old farmer's son who was now running the farm with his wife was around the mid-forties, their two sons and two daughters between eighteen and twenty-two, and the old man was still working as well, although I think that he was primarily supporting the younger generation, and in particular he was taking care of the horses, his wife, a lady in her seventies, together with the young fellow's wife was taking care of the vegetable garden and the kitchen.

The girls had to work primarily in and around the house but during the various phases of the harvest they too had to help, like the men they were asked to handle the same tasks as did the men, despite the fact that the work was physically very demanding.

For some reason I never got close to the two of them, Monika the older and Brigitte the younger of the two, both of them very reserved, shaped from their Catholic upbringing at home and the segregation at school as well as in church had molded their behavior, I had the feeling that the two of them had been taught to be weary of young city boys.

The youngest son was also very reserved, other than work I had little contact with him during my stay at the farm, I think we were totally different people, and the age gap was probably a factor as well.

However, the oldest of the two sons, John, could have been my big brother; from the very beginning we got on very well, he made me feel welcome, he took me under his wings, showing me the ropes, guiding me with whatever we had to do on the farm, giving me little tips about what was expected from me, and how I should behave in general, it was great to get all of this support from the person that was the oldest son of the farmer as well as his right hand, the fellow that was going to take over the operation in a few years to come.

John was also a biker in the Swiss Armey, he was required to take his motorbike home when he was off-duty in the military service, and when he took up his annual military refresher, he had to make sure that he turned up with his well-maintained Condor A250, a Swiss build machine from the fifties.

The days at the farm were very structured; I had to get up early enough to wash myself, brush my teeth, comb my hair and get dressed so that I was ready for duty in the cow stable before 06:00.

Normally, during the summer time the cows are kept out in the fields to graze and rest overnight, but for some reason or another at that time they were kept in the barn for the night; Mr. Haefeli Senior, together with his oldest son John were organizing the milking of the forty cows, half of them were held on the right side and the other half on the left, and through the middle was a walkway with a drainage trench on either side. The cows were all standing in line, for the milking process their heads were locked in a wooden bail which could be opened or closed from a central point on each side. This was essential to keep the animals disciplined and standing up during the milking.

One of the two went from cow to cow, washing the cows teats with warm water containing a little disinfectant, the other followed and lowered from the ceiling the flexible rubber hose system with the four teat cups and placed them on the cow's teats. In this manner all forty cows could be milked within an hour or so. During my dad's time at the farm, the cows were still milked by hand.

At the same time the second son, Hans was cleaning out the straw from each of the cows compartments, and I was positioned on the walkway in the middle with a pitchfork and a wheelbarrow, picking up the soiled straw that the younger son Hans had mucked out, then I wheeled the filled barrow out in the yard to the so called crap collector, in principle a very large, square or oblong concrete tank, about three meters deep, on top of it was a solid wooden roast on which the soiled straw were neatly piled up. The wooden roast was constructed in such a manner that any liquid contained in the solids could drain into the holding tank. This liquid was generally left to brew in the container until it was pumped into a liquid manure tank, and then dispersed in the fields as a natural fertilizer.

The application of this natural fertilizer is still being applied today, like then, you can smell it a mile off, and when you do, you will know that the farmer is out there taking care of his fields. At that time, perhaps with some exceptions, people weren't concerned, nor were they talking about biological farming or organically grown products, nor were there products and produce labelled with "Bio"—to the best of my knowledge anything that is covered under the term food chain, meat, seafood, cereal, pulses, fruits and vegetables, herbs and spices were produced biologically, I never heard any of the Haefeli's talk about herbicide and pesticide's, nor did I ever observe any chemicals anywhere on the farm, no machines or gadgets that would have been able to distribute this dreadful stuff on the fields or trees; they merely produced organically grown products without making a lot of noise about it.

Once the solids had been removed from the barn, with a wooden board about forty centimeters wide, mounted on a wooden handle I had to scrape the crap and the wet stuff from the cows down the trench, starting at the rear, moving to the front. During this process it was inevitable that the gumboots became very grotty, and the smell wasn't that great either, but I got used to this as well—it was more pleasant than getting yelled at by Aunt.

When I think about it, it is a sad statement to make, it is pathetic to think that a sixteen-year-old kid prefers to clean out cows' crap, rather than spending time with his stepmother; not a very kind thing to say, but it is a declaration of the state that the relationship between us had reached at that time.

After the cows had been milked John and I would accompany them to the paddock; the lead cow in the very front, guiding the heard in the right direction, us making sure that they would not stray from the path and we made sure that the gate to the paddock was closed properly once the cattle had past the gate.

The largest room in the house was the kitchen, from the door you had to climb four steps down to reach the old stone floor, the room sparsely filled with smoke from the wood stove, the odor of fried bacon and Rösti absolutely glorious, in the middle of the room was this huge wooden table with banks constructed from wood on either side, and at the head there was a chair, reserved for Mr. Haefeli Senior—the boss.

The kitchen was a very important part of the farm; against the back wall was a very large cast iron stove, over two meters in length, the left-hand part consisted of a large fire box, on the right were two large ovens, and on the top plate there were six large holes, each covered with several cast iron rings which could be removed to place a pot or a frying pan of corresponding size in the ring, so that the pots and pans were somewhat lowered into the stove and hence exposed to the open fire underneath.

The other side of the stove top was merely a solid cast surface which was used to keep the food on a lower heat, or to keep it hot before serving it. A hot water tank was also connected with the stove; in fact, the only source of hot water in the house, a bath tub, a shower or indeed hot water from the hand basin taps did not exist.

The breakfast table was always laid out with the same components every morning, with the exception of the home-made jam. Mrs. Haefeli made the most delicious Rösti, made from precooked, grated potatoes, diced onion, finely cut pieces of smoked bacon, fried with lard on the wood stove. The Rösti, about forty centimeters in diameter was put on the table directly in the frying pan, and the second one was already kept warm on the stove, ready to be served.

Then there was the home-made bread which was more like a German type whole meal, with a dense texture and a lightly sour taste, made from sourdough whose culture was kept cool in the larder for the next bake-off.

Homemade jam was also on the table, usually Cherries or Rose Hip, cheese and butter made by the local dairy. The cheese was a true local, he was more on the mild side, with a diameter of around twenty-two centimeters, about six high, weighing about 2.5 kilograms.

Straight from the cow, a very large jug of milk, slightly heated, and coffee was also placed on the table, most of us around the table would first eat the Rösti, then perhaps bread, butter and jam, cheese and to wash it down a bowl of milk coffee.

The drinking bowls were rather large—a base diameter of around six centimeters, the top diameter about twelve, and the height about four-point five—some of them put pieces of bread in them and would then ladle the bread coffee to the mouth with a spoon, a most peculiar, sloppy consistency to which I could never get accustomed to.

After breakfast, still sitting around the table, Mr. Haefeli, the boss held a briefing, discussing and delegated the jobs that had to be done for the day; on this particular morning it was John's task to mount the grass cutting attachment to the tractor, and to cut the grass at a particular paddock. The cut grass was left to dry in the sun until after midday, and in the mean time I was given the job to clean out the piggery with Hans, a facility that provided space for about sixty pigs which were held in several holding pens, together with the concrete fodder troughs they had to be mucked out and scrubbed with water every day. Then we redistributed clean straw in the holding pens and fed the pigs, usually with swill which consisted of any leftovers that we received from the local pubs in old forty liter milk churns, and a mash made from home produced grain. Not getting attached to these animals was very difficult, it seemed as they appreciated the fact that we cleaned out their housing, with their damp snout, sniffing, wiggling their tails and grunting at the same time, through their long, white eyelashes they were looking directly into my eyes as if they were saying thank you—a very touching experience indeed.

The girls were responsible for the cleaning of the milk churns, with the tractor and trailer they had to transport the milk to the local dairy in the village on the days when Hans was busy with other things, at the same time they came back with butter and cheese which the dairy produced.

Because the farmers didn't wear a watch when they were working, for centuries it has been customary for the village church bell to sound quarter to twelve, to let the folk that were working on the field know that it was now time to get back to the farm to have lunch, still today the village church calls the beginning, the different breaks in-between and the end of the working day as a matter of tradition, but most of us are unaware of its purpose.

During the summer time, unless it was raining, lunch was taken under the old chestnut tree on the far end of the court yard, the tree providing sufficient shade and usually a breeze of cool air; there was a large wooden table with benches on either side, bread, butter, Cervelat, Thomy mustard, cheese from the local dairy, tomatoes, onion rings and greens, all fresh from the garden, together with a dressing were served. Fresh from the barrel there was apple juice, slightly alcoholic, cold water from the fountain in the middle of the court yard and tea were available.

I would have appreciated a break after lunch, something like a little siesta, but there was no chance of this, we had to get on with work as long as the weather was kind to us; John attached the large hay-wagon to the tractor, loaded the pitch-forks and the grass-rakes, secured them, and we hopped on to drive to the field where he had cut the grass earlier that morning.

First, we arranged the cut grass with the rake in straight lines about two meters apart from each other along the field, then we got back to where we had started the lines and dissipated the grass a little so that it could dry quicker. This process was repeated a couple of times until the grass were well dried by the sun. Once dried, with the rake the rows were pulled together into small heaps, picked up with the pitch-fork and loaded onto the bridge of the hay-wagon. The chassis of the trailer was made of metal with large rubber tires, and the bridge, about one meter above the ground was a heavy wooden construction with foldable front and rear guards. Getting as much hay as possible on the fork, and then onto the wagon bridge was relatively simple at the beginning, but as the layers of hay got higher, it became very difficult, almost impossible for a little fellow like me to continue. Physical strength was a factor too, I wasn't the strong, well developed body builder, I was merely a city kid that wasn't particularly interested in sport at the time.

During those moments I had the feeling that John and his siblings were making fun of me, teasing me in a nice manner, but never to the point where I felt hurt, it was more a kind of kidding. Though the girls were a couple of years

119

older than me, sometimes it was a bit embarrassing to see that they were in command of more strength than me, they were able to endure more heavy work, they were true farm kids.

Depending on the weather, on some days we worked until late in the evening, particularly when there was the possibility of a summer thunderstorm, we had to ensure that the hay was collected and stowed away before it got wet, under no circumstances where we allowed to put damp hay in the barn; it would have started to ferment, creating an enormous source of heat, and it could have started to burn.

Like on other farms, the hay barn was positioned above the stables. The hay wagon was backed up into the shed, with a grabbing device on a crane system the loose hay was taken from the wagon, transported to the top where a couple of us distributed and piled up the hay on the barn floor.

The sides of the hay barn were constructed in such a manner that the air could flow freely, making sure that a fermentation process could be avoided, the roof was constructed in such a manner that it was overhanging the timber walls of the hay loft by about two meters which prevented the rain from coming into the barn. It was a lot of hard work to get the hey up there in the first place, but it simplified the job when it was time to feed the animals, through a shoot in the stable ceiling it could be thrown down directly where it was needed, and it served as insulation during the winter months, keeping the animals below warm.

Something that never changed was the time that the cows were milked, the cleaning of the stables, taking them out to the paddock and back again for milking in the evening, and the general care of the other animals on the farm, no matter what, the most valuable assets of the farm were pampered and well taken care of.

The farm was producing a range of products; milk, veal and pork meat all year around, fresh grass during the spring, summer and autumn, hay for the winter months, different types of grain and cereal produced for the milling market and some of it put aside as fodder for the pigs, sugar beet which was sold to the refineries in the area, potatoes that were sold to the local cooperative, and a wide variety of vegetables in a separate garden for the family. As I learned, a particular crop was never planted in the same area, Mr. Haefeli had a crop rotation plan displayed in the kitchen which indicated which product was going to be planted in which area the following season, apparently a method that ensures that the soil remains fertile.

During the summer period the family had eaten a lot of seasonal vegetables, salad in particular, and items like leek, bulb celeriac, potatoes, carrots, parsnip, cabbage, onion, garlic were stowed in the cellar—covered with dry sand so that it could keep more or less fresh far into the winter.

White cabbage was also cut into small strips, salted and then stowed in large earthen ware pots as sour kraut which was to be eaten during the winter months. Green beans were also consumed fresh, but some of them were dried in the oven at a moderate heat until they had shriveled up and had become free from moisture. This was also a great winter dish which is served with steamed potatoes and smoked pork items like bacon.

Tomatoes, zucchini, apples, pears and prunes were blanched, put into large glasses, sealed, sterilized and kept in the cellar for the winter.

Gooseberries, raspberries and blueberries were generally made into jam. The old Mr. Haefeli also had some beehives near the border of the nearby forest, he was the only one in the family who understood how to take care of them, but the honey we didn't get to taste very often, perhaps once in a month on a Sunday for breakfast.

The Haefeli's also were in possession of a number of acres of forest which produced sufficient fire wood for the farm, but also the necessary building materials that were needed from time to time for the repair work on the barn and the fences.

For the potato harvest the Haefeli's had a machine which was attached to the tractor. The tractor drove along the furrows whilst the machine behind was digging into the ground, picking up the potatoes, they were transported above the soil through a flexible wire system.

The most difficult part of this process was to ensure that the forged, slightly rounded blade was adjusted to the right depth; to ensure that the machine would pick up all the potatoes in the ground without damaging them. Unlike the modern machines of today, this equipment merely saved the process of digging up the potatoes from the ground, once they had been dug up, we had to walk along the furrows to pick them up manually and put them straight into Hessian sacks, the good ones in one, and the ones that were either too small or badly deformed in a separate sack, then the sacks were loaded onto the trailer to take back to the barn.

At the same time, we had to pick up the large stones that were brought up to the surface by the machine, they would be piled up at certain intervals alongside the furrow, to be picked up at a later stage and brought back to the farm yard.

In those days few people were aware of ergonomics, they did not know how to best perform certain tasks in such a manner that the body muscles and tendons, in particular the back area would be kept in a healthy state. Nobody told me either how to best pick potatoes from the ground; I merely observed the others and did just like them, bending over from the hips, rather than lowering the body through the knees. After a few hours of constant bending over, my muscles in the back and lumber area made themselves known, letting me know that they were there—despite this I tried to keep up with the others.

The Haefeli's were a very religious family, down to earth people that I could have accepted as my own; during the time that I was there I never felt any tension among them, the atmosphere was very familiar and enjoyable, I had wished that my own home could be just like this.

On some evenings everybody disappeared into their own quarters after work, and yet on others we all gathered in the living room, ready to listen to a radio play broadcast by Radio Beromünster. The furnishing in the living room was simple, uncluttered; there was an old side board, a large table with its chairs, the center of the room featured a rather large tiled stove which served as heating for this area, and placed against one of the walls there was a chest of drawers with an old radio placed on it which could only be operated by either Mrs. or Mr. Haefeli. We pulled the chairs into the middle of the floor, creating a half circle in front of the radio, in the center of the circle there was a large woven basked filled with about fifty kilogram of fresh, green beans, some medium sized bowls and paring knifes for each one of us to grab; everybody began to de-string the fresh beans, taking particular care not to cut the top and the bottom of the bean to low, thus avoiding unnecessary waste, which was periodically checked by Mrs. Haefeli, there was no such thing as a free ticket to the radio play; everyone was expected to contribute something to this evening of entertainment.

Whatever chores that had to be done, I never felt any pressure from anyone, I simply got involved with what had to be done, nor did anybody beef if one wasn't as fast as others, the family made you feel at ease, as if you were part of them, it was simply well worth the effort, only to be able to listen to the radio play.

The next day, the cleaned beans were blanched, bottled and sterilized, and then stored in the larder for the winter.

The larder wasn't merely a piece of furniture filled with food stuffs, it was a separate room in the cellar, about twenty square meters in size, fitted with lots of wooden shelves and rods that were fixed to the ceiling to hang things from.

The cellar was built into rock, the rock floor was covered with fine gravel, the ceiling was insulated with a double wooden floor with some kind of insulation in-between, and the whole area was well ventilated through a couple of shafts that were dug into the rock, keeping the room at a constant temperature of around five degrees Celsius. I had only ever seen the larder when I was helping the ladies to carry the sterilized goodies.

On other evenings, when I was not to tired, I would grab the old bicycle that I tinkered together from old parts in the shed with the help of John, with this scrappy looking racing bike which had only three gears I went for a little tour; sometimes, when I got away early enough, I drove down to Muttenz, then on to Basel so that I could spy on our house, to see if there was something going on that I should have been aware of. It was kind of thrilling; I had never done something like this before, to take off without dad or Aunt knowing where I was going, it felt exciting because I was cheating on Aunt, doing something that she wasn't aware of.

Sometimes during the evenings John would ask me if I would come for a spin on his military motorcycle. Of course, I never said no, I was always prepared for an adventure; mostly we would take of just before sunset, from the farm yard we would be driving on the gravel road down to the main path that led to the village and from there we would be heading toward the forest situated at the back of the farm. Driving through the forest on a motor cycle at this time of the evening, almost in darkness, yet through the leaves on the horizon you could still recognize some glowing light beams from the setting sun, a mysterious mood started to develop, almost to the point where it got to be a little scary, but exuberating at the same time.

Other than the mystery ride through the forest on the motor cycle, I very much appreciated the fact that John took some of his time to share with me;

after all at my age we didn't have too much common with each other, it was like being out with my big brother.

Sometimes, John and I got up to no good, on occasion we went out to spy on those couples that didn't appear to have a home, those that drove out into the country side to find a quiet spot, perhaps a lane that was abandoned at night, or indeed somewhere in the forest where they could park their vehicle, where they had a feeling of privacy and security.

Every time I am listening to Tina Turner, I recall the time when John and I were spying on the couples in the forest of Muttenz; at that time Tina was not yet popular in Switzerland, she was touring with the Turner band, being the opening act of the Rolling Stones concerts, the connection between her and the spying excursions didn't exist then either; it wasn't until 1989 when this connection became reality for me, because on the album Foreign Affairs that was released that year, the song *"steamy windows"* was featured—now it makes me smile every time I hear it.

The first of August is the official national day of the Swiss people, the day of remembrance of the coming into being of the confederation. In the year 1291 three representatives of the three regions; Uri, Schwyz and Unterwalden met at the Rütliwiese (a mountainous meadow about 480 meter above sea level, located in the canton of Uri, in the municipality of Seelisberg, above the lake of Lucerne, called Rütli), to swear an oath of a defense alliance against the neighboring Austria.

Over time, other regions or cantons as thy are called today, joint this annual ritual. Still, today the national day celebration begins at the Rütliwiese, where one member of the federal council holds a speech on that day.

In some places of Switzerland, the national day is celebrated in a more contemplative manner, in particular in the Swiss highlands, large fires that can be seen over a far distance, even in the lower parts, fires are lit to symbolize the unity and the togetherness.

In addition to the public speeches presented by the prominent, or the local politicians, marquees are set up and furbished with trestles, benches, a catering facility, a band-stand and a dance floor for the public's entertainment.

Large wood stacks arranged in a particular manner so that their fire can be seen from far away are set up, usually by the local municipality, they are then lit at the twilight, creating an eerie but very exciting spirit that can change people's mood very easily.

Once the fire is reduced to the glowing charcoal, folks gathered around the fire can now grill their goodies over the fire place, usually some kind of sausage like Bratwurst, Schüblig or Cervelat, a steak, vegetarian items, or in deed anything else that you care to grill.

Generally, the local municipality provides a firework display by dark which lightens up the sky with the most wonderful displays in different colors, the banging and the crackling of the ignited fireworks combined with the kind of whistling when they are launched into the sky, at the same time creating a hazy atmosphere with the smell of gunpowder in the air. The igniting of fireworks is not limited to the municipality, anybody that cares to have a little fun with these things can buy and ignite them for this occasion.

Most of the kids carry the traditional round harmonica like build lanterns, when you pulled the top away from the bottom, you ended up with a cylindrical shaped lantern; in the Swiss colors, red with the white cross, all lit up by a candle which was fixed at the bottom, on the top of the lantern there is a wire which is then hooked onto a stick; the candlelight that penetrated the red and white colored paper lit up the immediate surrounding of the lantern, provided an unearthly, wonderful sight.

Until that time, I had experienced part of the first of August celebration only a couple of times, I had never seen the full program from beginning to the end. For some reason or another on most of those occasions we were not in Switzerland, nor was it a subject that was talked about at school or among my mates.

All of this was going to change on the first of August 1964 when I was at the Haefeli's farm; after the cows and the other animals had been fed, the stable mucked out, the fresh straw scattered about for the comfort of the animals, and our own tummies filled, most of the family members retired to the living room, it appeared as if nobody was interested in the celebration of the National day. I found out later that John and Hans got all dressed up and headed to the village to celebrate on their own. John was talking about this night a couple of days later, and then I understood why he could not take me with him, the places where he went to would not have been age appropriate for me.

It was the first time in my life that I was free to choose what I was going to do on a National day evening celebration; I was curious to find how other people would spend their time, knowing that I could not take part in any of their activities because I had no money to spend, and I didn't have clothes that might have been worthy of this occasion, I wore a pair of clean shorts, a T-shirt and a pair of socks and shoes, I quietly grabbed my racing bike and discretely left the farm yard.

It wasn't just a ride to I don't know where, I knew what I wanted; to take part in the fireworks that were launched from a barge which was tethered on the river Rhein in the vicinity of the main bridge that joint the two sides of Basel, my home town.

As I approached the bridge I could see that there were a lot of people standing around on the footpath adjacent to the river, the road was blocked off so that cars could not enter this area; it looked like you couldn't get onto the bridge anymore, there were already lots of spectators on it, along the river lane marquees with wooden trestles and benches had been put up, they were fitted out like pubs where drinks were offered, quite a number of grill stands had already started to sizzle the different traditional sausages that were on offer, the odor of the glowing charcoal, together with the smell of the sizzling sausages created a wonderful, smoky atmosphere.

During the previous century the cast iron street lanterns were gas operated and had to be lit individually by hand every evening, and extinguished the next morning, today they still stand in a row, alternating with the old chestnut trees, together embracing the avenue along the river Rhein, only now the light source has been changed to electricity.

The lanterns were throwing their soft light onto the river where through the ripples of the flowing water it was being reflected as a distorted picture.

Further out in the river you could see the distorted silhouette of the lights that were reflecting from the houses on the other side of the shoreline.

I would have appreciated one of those grilled sausages, but I had no money on me; it didn't matter, I wasn't hungry, it was merely the desire and the fact that I knew that I couldn't have one of those that bothered me a little for a short moment.

I was very much hoping that no one in the crowd would recognize me, or worse still, if Dad and Aunt would have been there, I would have had a lot to explain and my fun would have ended abruptly.

There was no place for a traditional wood fire in the city, and it didn't matter either because the fire-works that started around 10:00 were very elaborate and lasted for about a half an hour. During this time, you could hear loud banging which resulted from the little explosions that took place when the fire-work tubes were ignited, catapulting the smaller parcels of gunpowder which ignited high up in the air, providing a colorful display of sparks that lit up the skyline of the city, blended with the smoke and the smell from the igniting gunpowder.

Although I had wished that I could have enjoyed this atmosphere in the company of my dad, I was content to have been there, to have been a part of it, I no longer had to be curious about how our National Day was celebrated in my city, I was now able to talk about it from my own experience.

Admittedly, I felt a little sad seeing all the mums and dads that were there with their kids of all ages, having a ball, and I could not understand that my dad could not be with me on such a wonderful occasion. Surely, he wasn't working that evening; he must have been somewhere, having a good time with Aunt. The question if he had forgotten that he had a son was bothering me a little, or was he so besotted or indeed intoxicated by Aunt?

The thought of me having children was very far away, not at all present in me, I was far to selfish for this, just like it should be at that age and I had a lot of ambitions that were very important in my life, and I was determined to get out there and get them all. Regardless, I do remember that I had promised myself never to behave like my father, if ever I had a child, I would not repeat the same mistakes that my dad made—or at least the mistakes that I thought that he made.

With hindsight, my opinion about my dad's behavior was the judgment of a child, though age appropriate at that time, in the mean time I have come to realize this today, as a grownup person who has lived life at its fullest, having made if not the same, at least very similar mistakes which might have had equal consequences.

I am not the kind of person to lecture others about education, nor to give them advice about something or another, but if a parent would ask me; I would tell them to get very close to their child, don't just set the borders and expect the kid to obey, do not talk at them; talk to them in an age appropriate but meaningful manner, learn to listen to your child and ask yourself if your decisions that you take for them are fair, know when you have to comfort your child and when to let go, handle it in the way you would like to be treated, and above all, love and enjoy your children and have fun with them.

My working holidays on the farm were slowly coming to a close. I remember, when dad told me what he had planned for me during the summer break, I wasn't impressed at all, in fact I was very annoyed at him, but now that I had made this experience, I was so glad that he had organized this for me. Although I was looking forward to join my class mates at the lycée cantonal de Neuchâtel for the second semester, I knew that I could look back with fondness to the time at the farm; working for the Haefeli's from the point of view of a city kid was certainly hard at times, they were very strict but also very fair, they treated me like one of their own, hard but with a lot of affection and understanding.

The farm life itself I had also become very fond of, I had learned so much about the production of staple food; milk, grain, fruits, vegetable, honey and meat, in a very humble manner, I learned how to care for mother earth, how to respect nature, the preservation of food stuffs, I had learned that the eggs don't grow in a carton, I witnessed how fruit mesh is fermented and distilled to turn into alcoholic beverages, I had taken part in the making of apple cider, I had gathered potatoes from its soil, I picked fruits from their trees and I have seen how these produce were taken to the local farmers cooperative from where they were distributed to the different market places and stores, and I had grown very fond of all the farm animals, but the calf's I adored in particular.

I firmly believe that every child that has not been able to experience farm life as I was allowed to should be given this opportunity and the privilege to spend some time on the land, to better understand and appreciate the wonderful gift that Mother earth is providing for us.

The recollections from my working holiday on the farm remain firmly embedded in my memories; the sunrise which was getting to be a little later every day, often bright orange to gold in color rendering the lower laying clouds appear dark, gray in places and the clouds higher and closer to us were shining white with a touch of yellow, and the blue sky high above, the hush in the air together with dew that had set on the blades of grass, providing an eerie atmosphere, the liveliness in the stable, early in the morning, the cows somewhat impatiently waiting to be relieved from their milk filled udder, the smell of hay, mixed with the scent of the animals and their freshly dropped dung, the vapor caused by the difference of temperature being respired by the cows in the stable blended with the smell of partially fermented fodder that escaped from their four stomachs, the swishing of their tails and the occasional mooing, snorting, grunting and other noises caused by their feeding.

As the process of milking, feeding, and cleaning progressed, you could feel a particular calmness and satisfaction that seemed to go throughout the stable, entering the kitchen at breakfast time being hit by a waft of freshly brewed coffee, the smell of the bacon Rösti that had just been taken from the stove, cuddling up close to the calves, feeding them from the bottle with fresh milk, the damp, earthy smell during the cutting of the grass, the scent of the burnt diesel and the lubricants as we drove out to the paddocks with the tractor, the sweet smell of the sun-dried hay, the not so pleasant smell of the piggery, the unpleasant odor of the swill, the way in which the pigs look at you through their beautifully styled eyelashes, and then, on many evenings when the gas molecules together with the dust particles were scattered around the sky, we could enjoy the most spectacular red sunsets.

Dad and Aunt came to pick me up from the Haefeli's on the Saturday morning, around ten, I was happy to see them, but also a little sorrowful having to leave this place. As I was packing my bag, there was a kind of de-briefing going on between Dad, Aunt and Mr. and Mrs. Haefeli to which I was not invited; unfortunately, I never found out anything about the content of this conversation, but I gathered that it couldn't have been bad, I never heard anything negative and Aunt wasn't commenting at all. On the other hand, Dad and Aunt had nothing positive to report either. As we left, I noticed that Mrs. Haefeli had a couple of tears in her eyes; I was very moved by this and was trying to hide my watery eyes, knowing that I would miss them.

Feedback is one of the most important tools available to educators, it is also a significant instrument in the management of staff and indeed in one's private life, with your partner and children.

What's the use of setting borders, stating expected behavior and measuring someone's performance or indeed their behavior, if you are not prepared or able to provide them with feedback?

Having noted, analyzed and assessed performance and behavior, it is of the utmost importance that appraisal takes place.

Feedback does not have to be a longwinded or a complicated session of performance review, it has to be done at an appropriate time and location but it can also be a spontaneous measure; feedback must be relevant, objective, as brief as possible, conveyed in an unemotional manner unless emotion is specifically appropriate.

The manner in which you provide feedback depends on the circumstances; feedback to a staff member usually does contain complex technical as well as behavioral performance subjects, feedback to your partner is normally limited to delicate behavioral matters which you would like him or her to be aware of, feedback to a kid covers a wide spectrum of behavioral matter which needs to be conveyed very carefully, with lots of thoughtfulness.

When we do provide feedback, we must ensure that the content is factual, we have to address the things that are not good or not acceptable and provide a reason, where appropriate we should suggest realistic corrective measures and set goals that can be realized, and we should always close the feedback session with a positive observation or comment.

The debriefing between dad, Aunt and Mr. and Mrs. Haefeli to which I was not invited had undoubtedly something to do with my behavior during the stay at the farm.

However, I didn't get any feedback.

At that time, I was not aware of the word feedback, nor did I know the importance of it, but I was wondering why no comments were made, I wanted to know what the Haefeli's thought of me, it was important, but all I got was silence. I don't think that I was traumatized by this utter lack of communication but I am convinced that it left its mark.

We should learn to trust our children; understand that they can handle the truth, let them know what they did wrong, and equally important, let them know what you expect from them, let them know what they are doing well, and don't be surprised when shit happens because you didn't talk to your kids.

The weekend at home was occupied with getting myself prepared for college, Aunt had organized my clean clothes that I was taking with me, something that she did well, we had dinner at one of dad's favorite pubs in the neighboring St. Luis, Alsace, and on Sunday, on the way to college we enjoyed a fresh fish "friture" which is served with boiled potatoes tossed in butter, homemade mayonnaise and tartar sauce. To be more specific for those that do not know what a "friture" is, you could describe it as fish and chips without the chips. However, I wouldn't want to explain this to a Frenchman in this way; he or she would feel insulted by this statement. This wasn't exactly a low-calorie meal; the fish fried in oil, the potatoes tossed in lots of butter, the mayonnaise and the tartar sauce, both consisting of at least 85 percent oil, but it was a simple dish, very fashionable at the time and delicious to eat.

Around four in the afternoon, dad and Aunt dropped me off at the college, and they accompanied me into the lobby, we headed straight to the big notice board to the right, opposite the reception. Before the summer break we hadn't been given the end of semester results because they had not been completely evaluated. Though each of the kids had a good feel for the final result because of the periodical written and verbal tests that we had to undergo on a regular basis for each subject, we were keen to learn the facts.

I was reasonably confident that my result would be good, but until this could be verified, I was a little stressed. We stood in front of this board, looking for my name; Dad was the first one to find it, the posted result was an above average, he smiled, pressed my hand very firmly and said "well done my son." Aunt didn't say anything; she simply stood there with us; she didn't show any emotion either.

This was an important moment in my college life, to be confirmed as a high achiever; dad's feedback was brief, but very positive, Aunt's lack of words was also feedback but it had a negative impact on me, I will never know if her answer was merely ignorance on her part, or if she simply didn't care.

## Second Semester at Boarding School

The second semester at the Lycée Cantonale de Neuchâtel had started, it took me and my college mates a week or so to settle back into this particular routine; getting used to the organization again after the holiday, to get accustomed to teachers and tutors that we didn't know from the first semester, finding out how they ticked and getting to know what they expected from us.

I was doing well in the area of all the social sciences and mathematics in particular, achieving very good test results which demonstrated that I felt comfortable with the subject matter.

Linguistics was still a bit of a problem; in both, with the spoken English assessments I was shining, but the French language was a headache despite all my efforts, in the day to day classroom situation I was functioning ok, I was continuously building up my vocabulary, the spoken French was well developed, the pronunciation was authentic and my speech fluid, I understood most things that the teachers were conveying, but grammatically I was a total looser; for me to compose a reasonable essay that the teachers could actually read was almost impossible, frequently I was called by teachers, asking me to explain what I had written, because they were not able to read my compact

French spelling. Compact because I scribbled letters so close together that they had become illegible, on purpose, because I was never sure about the grammatical rules, because of my inability to get the French grammar under control, from a very good student I was reduced to a good student which annoyed me.

This challenge has accompanied me throughout my life, even to this day I am not in command of the French grammar. Although for the bigger part of my life I had no application for the French language at all, it wasn't until I returned to Switzerland some years ago that I had the opportunity to use the language again.

For the first week of the autumn break dad had organized for me to do an entrance examination test at the gymnasium at the Münsterplatz in Basel, with the aim to complete semester three and four which form part of the preparation for the Maturity examination, the prerequisite for the admission to any University in Switzerland.

To pass the Maturity examination with honors at the end of 1967 was my target. To gain entry into the Swiss Aviation College (SLS—Schweizerische Luftfahrt Schule) a Maturity pass was required, or indeed a pass from another institution of equivalent value.

In the event that for some reason or another I would not gain entry to the SLS, I was then able to apply for most courses of study at most federal universities, or alternatively I could still decide to get into a trade area, but this wasn't an option for me, I knew what I wanted to study, what I wanted to do in my life.

Academically, the time spend at the lycée cantonal de Neuchâtel was tough, particularly because the classroom instruction was in French, with the exception of the English classes, and if we were caught speaking German on the college grounds we were reprimanded.

In my opinion, the college was well managed, the principle and his staff demonstrated great commitment and good attributes; they were strict, their decisions appeared to be fair to all, most of them were accessible if you had a problem or if you were concerned about something, and some of them had a great sense of humor.

The general code of conduct was clearly communicated, we knew what was expected from us, and the consequences for not adhering to the rules were clearly spelled out, our days were filled with a good balance of school, private study time, sport, music, and sufficient private time, the food was good basic Bourgeoisie style—almost like home cooked, and the general atmosphere in the college was great—I was proud to be part of it.

Maybe what I enjoyed most of all, was the fact that I was away from Aunt, I dint have to endure the injustice with which I felt that she was treating me, I didn't feel the constant pressure of having to do things her way. The fact that the college time in Neuchâtel was coming to an end made me unhappy, I asked myself how I would handle Aunt.

In the past, Aunt had often accused me of defying, secretive, uncommunicative, and that I was a liar, and this was bothering me.

I realized that I had changed a lot during the year at the college; I had learned that I didn't have to be scared of people like Aunt, I had begun to realize my worth as a young human being, I had gained a lot of self-confidence during my college time.

At the same time, I was also aware that hard confrontation with Aunt was not an option either, my dad would never have accepted this; eventually I decided for the smart alternative behavior toward Aunt; try to be as pleasant as possible, try to accomplish the things that she demands, walk away from one-to-one confrontations, brush aside any negative behavior on her part, keep out of her way, avoid contact where possible.

I had decided to persist with my strategy; that I was smarter than her, and that sometime in the near future I would gain this battle and I would walk away from all of this—for a kid, a rather arrogant decision to reach. I don't recall the underlying thought processes at the time, how I decided what my behavior should be like when I returned home, but later in my life, from my own child I learned how this might have worked. Our son was around one year old when I observed some interesting behavior; during a visit at the children's doctor, he was clinging to his mother, observing what the fellow in the white apron was doing, he was checking out if he was ok or not, at the same time he would also check out our faces, probably to ascertain our thoughts about this situation, and I am convinced that he could also feel vibes; once he thought that this fellow was ok, he opened up and the doctor could check him out.

At least that is how I observed this particular situation. My good friend George, the children's doctor agreed with the observation that I made between him and our son, he perceived this particular situation in the same manner. This taught me a lot about children's behavior; they observe a lot more then we believe, intuitively they seem to understand if someone, or indeed a situation is ok or not and accordingly adjust their behavior. Although as a sixteen-year-old teenager, the decision-making process was of a more conscience nature compared to that of a one-year-old, but it's clear to me that I knew precisely how to behave so that I would survive.

The autumn break was about to begin, I could feel a certain nervousness because I was going home to take part in the entrance examination test at the gymnasium in Basel, the pressure was beginning to mount, I knew what was at stake; if I didn't achieve a pass, my dream to become an airline pilot could be over. At that time, I didn't want to consider other options, I hadn't thought of an alternative profession that I might be perusing, I was so convinced that I would accomplish my aim. The entrance examination was distributed over two days, and it consisted of written as well as verbal testing in most subjects. The written part was conducted in a classroom environment with around twenty or so kids in one room at the time; in the front there was a supervisory staff whom would answer questions where appropriate, he made sure that none of the kids were communicating with each other, that nobody would spy for answers by his neighbor, or indeed in hidden notes, and if you were caught spying you were immediately disqualified from the entire examination. For the verbal part there were two examiners, sitting opposite me, when I got into the room, I was shown to a chair without armrest which was positioned a couple of meters away from the two. They introduced themselves and explained the procedure of the verbal testing briefly. Sitting there opposite the two examiners I had the feeling that they were also interested in my behavior, curious to know how I was handling the situation with the chair without armrests, but this didn't bother me, I was focused on the subject matter whilst the two of them, randomly, fired questions at me for about an hour about this particular subject; the first impression was one of being interrogated, but after a couple of minutes I forgot all about how uncomfortable the seating arrangement was. Thinking about this situation now, the examiners wanted to learn more about one's person through the observation of the body language, which would have provided them with some information about my personality.

Dad phoned me at the college one evening, and told me about the examination result; I passed in all subjects with an above average result, and that my place for semester three and four was secured. From his voice I recognized that he was very proud of my achievement, he encouraged me to keep up the good performance. I was over the moon, I was sure to manage the two upcoming semesters, and to come through the final examination at the end of next year, eligible to take the next step, the entry examination for the SLS (Schweizerische Luftfahrt Schule) as a pilot candidate.

The second semester at the Lycée Cantonale de Neuchâtel was equally as tough as the first one, except that we had the advantage to be familiar with the daily sequence of events, we knew the rules, and we had gotten to know all the college staff. I was fairly methodical in my learning approach, I didn't merely learn subject matter off by heart, I had learned that you must understand what it is that you are learning, to know how it works or how elements interact with each other, to know the consequences of an action, or indeed an inaction; I am sure that this kind of approach was my success to achievement. I worked very hard in all subjects, wanting to achieve good marks, and I had success with my learning approach with the exception of the French Grammar, despite the extra hard effort, the result was only a marginal improvement over the semester, the relationship between effort and achievement were off balance; I had to be satisfied with a half note betterment.

## Christmas Holiday

For the Xmas break I was at home, dad and Aunt had invited Grandma and Grandpa Robert, Aunt's sister Tabea with her husband Heinz, her sister Madelaine and my cousin Celine for Christmas eve, it was dad's turn to captivate the family's attention with his culinary skills which were limited either to Ravioli, Bake Beans, Lentils Corn beef, out of the can, or small-good, cheese and fresh bread, nicely arranged in a very appetizing fashion, his other specialty, as I found out years later was Rösti, overbaked with cheese and tomato slices, or indeed, the Cheese Fondue for which dad was famous for within the family circle.

Aunt had decorated the house impeccably like I have never seen before; a broad wreath made from thin pine branches, wrapped around a wooden frame that dad had constructed especially for this occasion to enrobe the outside of the house door, beautifully decorated with golden glass ball ornaments which were attached to the branches with tiny red ribbons, in the center of the front door, fittingly there was a round pine wreath left just plain, undecorated, on either side of the path leading from the street gate to the front door, there were four large cast iron lamps fitted with light green glass and grand looking lit candles were showing the way to the house.

It was the year where people were skiing down the narrow lanes of the old part of town, there was snow everywhere, just like in the picture book, now we only had to patiently wait for Santa Claus to arrive with our presents.

As you walked into the front door, in the hallway which was a rather large area about sixty square meters in size, the light was dimmed, in the middle of the two staircases—one on the left, the other on the right—leading to the upstairs rooms, Aunt had set up a display featuring a miniature barn constructed of wood, containing the cradle with a baby representing Jesus, Mary and Joseph, the three Kings, the animals, and other figures that were visiting the holy child, all presenting the story of Christmas as we know it in our Christian faith.

All the figures were carved from wood, in the barn there was real straw to be seen, the inside of the display was discretely lit with tiny, concealed 12 Volt lamps, and the surround of the barn was decorated with white candles, creating an atmosphere that looked real, admiring this display, you couldn't help but to believe that the story of Jesus was true.

Our guests we received in the Fumoir, a large room that dad had installed as a multi-purpose area, it featured a very large bookcase on the one end of the room, a writing desk, an antique grandfather clock, a small buffet that matched the clock, or the other way around, four large leather couches, each of them seating four, four matching coffee tables and one very impressive leather armchair, reserved for the master of the house. On the side, the dark green marble encased fireplace was decorated very softly, a medium sized white candle which reflected its glimmering in the mirror behind it, and a couple of small pine twigs appeared to be sufficient to render a feeling of Christmas.

As our guests walked into the front door, I observed the facial expression of Grandma and Grandpa Robert in particular, I had never seen them so rapturous, they were obviously, honestly touched by the warm reception and the mood that the house diffused.

Everybody made themselves comfortable in the Fumoir with a glass of chilled Gewürztraminer d'Alsace, except for Heinz and myself, Aunt had bought some grape juice which dad served in the same type of glass as the Traminer. I think that Grandpa Robert was particularly happy that the evening started in the Fumoir, it was the only place in the house where smoking was allowed, except in the garden and on the balcony upstairs, but those places weren't particularly inviting this time of the year.

The moment where the Christmas gifts were handed out was not handled in the same way in all families, as I recall; among Protestants it was customary to distribute the parcels before the dinner was served; in this way the adults were assured that they could enjoy the Christmas delicacies in peace, and so it was in our house, Grandpa Robert announced that the living room was now ready to receive Santa Claus; my dad, slightly disguised, wearing a red jacket decorated with a fluffy white material around the edges and a matching cap.

Grandpa opened the double doors of the living room; a fire was burning in the fire place; its mantle was decorated very simply with a red candle. Then there was the large Christmas tree standing next to it; very tastefully decorated with colored glass ball ornaments in gold, green, red, and purple, real pine cones, candle holders with small, white candles, the flickering candlelight reflecting in the glass balls, on the very top of the tree there was a golden colored glass angel; as if he was majestically overlooking the scene, and at the same time there was the smell of the freshly cut pine, blended with the scent of the burning candles. Everybody was astonished, the room was amazing, it had something sacred, holy, something blessed, almost saintly about it.

Placed underneath the Christmas tree were carefully wrapped parcels, each had a name tag so that Santa Clause was able to read out the name before he handed them to its rightful owner, the parcels were carefully enrobed in lovely Christmas paper with motives representing the festive season, decorated with beautiful ribbons, it had to be just perfect, as if the wrapping was equally important as the content.

I don't recall how Santa Clause surprised all the family members, like a selfish teenager I merely recall the presents that he had given me; a professional book about meteorology as it was required for my course at the SLS, a Jeppesen VFR airway manual for Switzerland and Jeppesen CR3 circular aviation hand held calculator, an instrument to calculate just about anything that you need to, from fuel converter to complex navigation tasks, a bit like a sliding ruler—only this was round—the gifts were truly representative of my ambition, failing the upcoming tests were no longer an option.

After the presents had been distributed by Santa Clause and everybody had a chance to open their gifts, dad removed his disguise and announced that dinner was now being served in the dining area.

Just like the hallway, the Fumoir and the living room, the dining area was equally beautifully decorated in a very simplistic manner, the table in particular; the white cloth covered the wood top, the chairs around the table were aligned like soldiers, the cutlery set was laid down for each person, the glasses lined up as if they had been adjusted with the use of a tape measure, and in the middle of it all was a candle holder with a large, white, burning candle. Everything had its specific purpose and place, as you would expect to see it in a high-class restaurant—simply stunning to look at.

With everybody seated in their proper place on the table, Aunt announced the menu for the occasion.

She explained that the hors d'oeuvre was kept light on purpose to compensate for the main dish which she didn't want to reveal just yet. This little cold buffet as Aunt named it consisted of; Scottish smoked salmon served with toast and butter, Bündnerfleisch (air dried beef from the Grison, a canton in Switzerland), Prosciutto (a raw, air dried ham from Parma, Italy), a pâté en croûte, a pâté de canard, red peppers grilled with olive oil, pickled artichoke hearts and a couple of compound salads.

To me it sounded more like a hors d'oeuvre riche, and as usual Aunt had excelled with her presentation skills, the only thing that was left to say was simply wow that's just great.

At the same time there was this heavenly scent of the burning candles, the odor of the fresh pine twigs, blended with the smell of the Christmas Cookies that Aunt had baked that afternoon.

*Meiländerli*, made from flour, butter, egg, sugar, a pinch of salt, lemon and zeste de citron; *Brunsli*, a Christmas specialty from my home town Basel, prepared from flour, butter, ground almonds, cinnamon, sugar, and chocolate; *Zimtstern*, consisting of casting sugar, egg white, ground almonds, cinnamon, a pinch of salt, and a little flour; *Chräbeli*, a crunchy specialty from Baden, the canton Aargau, created from castor sugar, flour, whole eggs, kirsch and aniseed, they all formed part of the Christmas cookie collection.

Nearly an hour and a half had lapsed after the light hors d'oeuvre had been served when Aunt announced the course to follow. It wasn't particularly a dish that was served traditionally for Christmas Eve, for this occasion you would have expected something like a filled calf's breast, a roast duck or turkey, perhaps a roast leg of lamb, or a Fondue Chinese style, but certainly not a Cheese Fondue, but this was very appropriate for our family, a meal that is conducive to the social gathering around the table, for people that adore cheese. Heinz was again the exception, because he did not consume alcohol, Aunt had prepared a steak from the grill with seasonal vegetables which I considered very thoughtful of her, and he appreciated the special effort and attention that Aunt had made.

## Dad's Cheese Fondue

The Cheese Fondue, dad prepared in the kitchen, he had split the cheese into two Caclotte so that it was more comfortable to eat on our large dining table. For those that are familiar with the recipe and the preparation method of a cheese fondue I don't have to elaborate, but I will explain the process so that it can be understood by all.

You need a Caclotte which is a fire-resistant stoneware pan with one handle, specifically made for the preparation of a cheese fondue. In this pan you melt a little butter on a low heat and at the same time a pealed clove of garlic is impaled on a fork and rubbed at the bottom as well as the sides of the pan, so that the garlic flavor is transmitted to the melted butter. Once the butter has reached the so called noisette stage which you can clearly identify, the garlic is removed and it is now that you add the white wine to the pan. The noisette stage of the butter you will be able to recognize visually as well as sensorially, the butter has turned to a light brown color and its smell will be nutty. The white wine is now added to the pan. Depending on the budget, you can use a less expensive Fendant du Vallais made from the Chasselas grape, or indeed a similar white wine; keeping in mind that the quality of the wine does influence the taste of the fondue.

Now it is time that you add the coarse grated cheese. Mind you, not any cheese. Dad always used fifty percent Gruyère and fifty percent Emmentaler cheese which he used to sample before buying it at the local deli shop.

The Gruyère should be aged at least eight to twelve months to ensure a vigorous taste whilst the Emmentaler is more or less on the mild side. The Emmentaler cheese renders the fondue somewhat stringy and gooey; you can change this characteristic simply by increasing the ratio of the Gruyere if you wish.

The next step in the fondue creating process is of the utmost importance. A little Kirsch which is a spirit distilled from cherries is added to the mixture, and at the same time you need to gently stir the bottom of the pan with a wooden cooking spoon, ensuring that the fondue does not stick to the bottom. During the gentle stirring which takes around twenty minutes until the mixture is ready to eat, my dad observed the development progress of the fondue mixture very carefully, at the same time he took the opportunity to assure himself that the quality of the white wine and the Kirsch that he had chosen was appropriate for the occasion.

It is important to understand that the quality test cannot be determined with a sip of the wine, nor the Kirsch; it takes at least a couple of glasses and a shot or two to be sure.

Whilst dad was occupied with creating the fondue and the wine and Kirsch tasting, Aunt was allowed to set the table, get the dessert ready, and cut the bread. The bread was always chosen by dad, it was made from processed wheat, the texture of the dough was fairly robust, and it had a sturdy crust. It has to be cut in such a manner that each bread cube; approximately 2.5 X 2.5 X 2.5 cm has a crusty side ensuring that the fondue fork can get a good grip in the crust so that it does not get lost in the cheese mixture during the stirring. The bread cubes are placed in a basket, covered with a cloth so that they do not dry out, and presented on the table.

When dad considered the fondue to be ready, the Caclotte was carefully placed on the table top cooker in the middle of the dining room table. The heating source is an open flame derived from a kerosene burner; it should be adjusted in such a manner that the fondue mixture is just lightly seething on the surface. The fondue can now be enjoyed; the bread cube is speared on a special two-pronged fork, dipped into the fondue, scraping the side and the bottom of the Caclotte so that the mixture does not cling to the pot. Once the bread cube is nicely coated with the cheese mixture you need to turn the fork slowly but continuously until the cheese mixture clings to the bread, at the same time it has been able to cool down a little—ready to eat. Guide the fork into your mouth, position your teeth in such a manner that you can scrape the bread fondue cube off, without the teeth touching the fork itself.

As the fondue mixture begins to be less and less in the pan its consistency will get thicker and the mood around the table more and more relaxed, even jolly. It is also part of the fondue tradition that in the event that a participant loses a bread cube in the cheese mixture during the eating, he or she has to buy a drink of some sort, usually a bottle of wine or a shot of Kirsch—all considered part of the fun.

Now it is important that you continue stirring and wiping the pan with the bread cubes. You should also lower the flame gradually to avoid the burning of the fondue. Toward the very end, when there is very little cheese left in the Caclotte you turn off the flame altogether. If you have done it correctly you will find a small bit of fondue at the bottom of the pot which is lightly caramelized but not burnt. This is considered the titbit of the fondue which is usually reserved for the creator of the dish, dad. Generally, the same white wine and Kirsch that was used to create the fondue with, is served at the table— the Kirsch in a shot glass. In our house, like in most true Swiss families, the children were allowed to take part in this wonderful winter tradition. Despite the fact that we consumed a little alcohol, most of the kids turned out to be fine, upstanding citizens.

As usual, the fondue was appreciated and praised, dad accepting the compliments in his straightforward but humble manner. To complete the festive delicacies of the evening, Aunt announced the gâteau glacé meringue a la Chantilly; a meringue cake filled with vanilla ice, decorated with lots of whipped cream, a lovely, refreshing dessert, relatively light, followed by the homemade cookies, coffee and different liqueurs, Martell XO Cognac and dad's favorite, a Vieil Armagnac Baron G. Legrand 1930 Armagnac, a Cognac like brandy produced in the province of Gascoigne South West of France, also appreciated by Grandpa Robert.

For me, this Christmas was without a doubt the best one sense my childhood, I was supporting Aunt where ever I could, the two of us got on well with each other, together we had fun making this Christmas a good one for the entire family, and my thoughts were "why could our relationship not be just like this all the time?"

# The Beginning of Tertiary Education

The new start at the Gymnasium in my home town Basel at 1967, at the age of seventeen; during the first semester I got more and more involved with my studies, adapting to the new environment, learning to get my way around the facility, finding out how the new tutors and lectures were ticking, what was important to them and learning about their style of instruction.

Getting to know the other kids that were participating at the Gymnasium, particularly those that shared the same classroom, and finding the ones that I felt comfortable with.

The Gymnasium took only boys, coeducation was introduced in '68, the year after I had completed my preliminary studies, at times I wished that I could have taken part in the class of 1968.

We quickly found out that we were expected to learn more independently, at the Lycée Cantonale de Neuchâtel we were handled very gently in comparison, here we had to spend more time in the library and other designated areas after the lectures and readings to solidify what we had learned, and some project work had to be achieved in small teams. To establish our learning progress, regular written and verbal tests in all subjects were realized. Some of my class mates hated these tests, others approached them with abeyance, and yet others like me, I loved the tests; I had learned to handle the pressure, not to pay any attention to those symptoms, and I appreciated the feedback, knowing how I was doing, knowing if I was on track.

Apart from the compulsory subjects we had to choose one foreign language. Given the fact that I had spent one year at the Lycée Cantonale de Neuchâtel where the spoken and the written language was French it would have made good sense for me to choose French as an elective, but I didn't, I would not have reached a pass level in this subject because I didn't master the grammar, and so I chose English. On the one hand I wanted to consolidate and broaden my English language skills, I understood that the English grammar is considerably simpler—I was convinced that I would achieve a good pass or better.

Aunt's expectations about my contribution at home had not changed, she now had set even higher quality standards, she behaved like a grouchy old lady out of a horror movie, demanding certain jobs to be reworked, in a manner that was formulated to be scary. But I had learned not to be scared of her anymore, from time to time I was able to fake more home studies than I actually had, and that was when she got really angry with me.

Maybe I was suffering from paranoia at the time, but I was convinced that she might have been envious of the fact that I enjoyed a better education than her, and I wasn't sure that she appreciated when I was achieving high marks, I felt that she would have preferred that I was a low achiever so that she might have better been able to manipulate me.

My thoughts about Aunt might have been exaggerated, at least in part, but she was very unpredictable in her behavior, I was never sure when she was going to be nice, and when she would be atrocious and cruel.

From 07:00 until 18:00, sometimes till later in the evening I was out, busy at the school, the lunch break was too short for me to come home, leaving very little time to spend time with dad and Aunt during the week days.

On most evenings dad and Aunt weren't home anyway, actually I don't recall that we spend any time at all as a family during the week days, and I am sure that not all of their outings had to do with business either. The peculiarity of this situation also had its advantages; I was able to do my homework without any interruption from Aunt, I could peruse my hobbies, on Wednesdays I was attending my trumpet lessons with Mr. Heinz at the Blue Cross hall, like most of my colleagues, at night I wasn't allowed out, I was convinced that Aunt didn't want me to get involved with girls. There were times when my house key was taken away from me when Dad and Aunt went out in the evening, a decision that Aunt had taken at some point, a ruling that I never understood. Our house didn't just have a second story, it had a ground floor as well, even if the front door was locked, I had every opportunity to get out from the French door that was fitted to most rooms' downstairs. In any case, the girls that I was interested in were not allowed out at night either, their upbringing was just as strict as mine, for the time being I had to be content with the short periods that we were able to spend with the girls on the way to and from the Gymnasium and the occasional lunch break.

Because I had dad's support with my school work, and because I was increasingly avoiding the contact with Aunt, closing her off from as much as was possible, Aunt found it increasingly difficult to control my life.

## The Summer Break of 1967

For the summer break of 1967 (I turned 18 at the end of that year) dad had plans to spend a couple of weeks in Spain, usually Aunt and him had stayed in an apartment on the beach in Sant Feliu de Guixols, and this year I was to travel with them; I was registered at the Club Med, somewhere on a rugged beach between San Feliu and the French border with the intention to do a diving course and to get the certification.

Dad being very meticulous with his cars had checked and prepared the car as he always did before we embarked on a trip; the fat naps on the different joints underneath the car were topped up with grease, the engine oil changed, all nuts and bolts of the steering mechanism checked, the contactors in the distributor head been changed and re-tuned, spark plugs renewed, radiator fluid topped up and checked for possible leeks, the electrical system checked including lights and blinkers, the batterie topped up with distilled water, tires including the spare checked, all little spare parts that could be needed during the trip neatly packed away, the fuel tank topped up and a couple of cherry cans with spare fuel, ready to stow the luggage.

We didn't use suit cases, Dad thought that they take up a lot of unnecessary space in the boot, everything was carefully packed by Aunt, in carry bags similar to those that are issued by the Swiss Armey, they were then taken to the car for dad to stow away, making sure that his tool case and the spares were loaded last, in immediate reach in the event of a breakdown.

By the time we were ready to leave, after we made one last check in and around the house making sure that we had not forgotten anything, even I managed to get into a holiday mood; much of my good spirit had to do with the fact that Aunt was in great vain; she appeared to radiate happiness in a way that I had never seen from her before, she was very talkative, nice, pleasant, she didn't have anything to beef about, she involved me in conversation—"did you see this, did you see that," I almost felt comfortable around her, I tried to forget the things that I hated about her, I asked myself why she couldn't always be in this kind of mood—my life would be simply a ball.

Dad had planned the route that we were going to drive some weeks ago, on the charts he had marked with a pensile the particular points of interest along the way. His travel plan wasn't simply a list of places that we had to drive to and through, he could also spontaneously decide on deviations.

In principle the itinerary started with the first leg from Basel to Lyon, Valance, to Montélimar. We had made several stops before we reached Montélimar, Aunt wanted to have a look at the street markets that you find all over the place, and of course to get some of the famous Nougat de Montélimar.

From there the track took us to Orange, then we took a South Westerly direction to Nîmes and on to Montpellier where we stayed for the night, about ten kilometers before the township, in one of the "Les Routier" places where truckers and travelling representatives were staying overnight. There were few tourists to be seen on the parking lot, in particular it was interesting to note that there weren't any Germans, despite the fact that they were a lot of cars with German number plates to be seen on the road. I believe that the reason for this was that the average German tourist could not speak French, or at least not well enough to feel comfortable, hence they tended to pass through France, directly to their final destination; Spain.

"Les Routier" were to be found all over France on the major highways where the truckers were en-route, you could recognize them from the distance, places on the side of the road with mostly semitrailers and other long-range trucks parked on the side as well as private cars.

The facility itself was fairly basic; you could take a room for the night, some merely wanted to eat and use the large bathrooms to freshen themselves up, there was a large Bar where you could get a drink and a little snack, and there was the restaurant, patronized by truckers, commercial travelers and few tourists.

The dining area was fitted out with long tables and chairs, each seating around twelve people. As we asked if there was room for three persons, the waiter pointed to the tables, we were free to sit wherever there was space for three, and so we were among truckers and others that chose to eat there, very uncomplicated and pleasant. One of the fellows on the same table wanted to know where we came from, when he found out that we are Swiss and French speaking as well, we were warmly accepted on the table which wasn't self-evident in those days, many French people were skeptical about the Germans, or indeed German speaking folk, a remnant from World War two.

In this place there was no menu card, on a large black board in the front of the room you could see what was going to be served on this particular evening. The concept of "Les Routier" in my time was simple; with few exceptions the food was local, it was seasonal, it was prepared Bourgeoise style—simple, uncomplicated, and reasonably priced.

The blackboard illustrated the soup of the day, the hors-d'oeuvre riche, les plats du jour and the cheese.

On the table, the waitress had placed a carafe of white and a carafe of red wine, a large bowl of pumpkin soup which you could serve yourself, fresh bread and butter.

The hors-d'œuvre riche was served next; a large earthenware dish with a lovely terrine, a variety of fresh and composite salads, a platter of air-dried meat, a platter of cooked and salted ham, bread and butter was always topped up by the waiter.

Les plats du jour, the main courses of the day on offer where gigot d'agneau rôti, jarret de porc braiser and boeuf Bourguignon, served with fresh vegetables of the day and gratin potatoes. Every one of us chose a different main course, the gigot and the jarret were each served on a heavy white China platter, the Bourguignon and the gratin in an earthen ware dish, and the vegetables in a bowl. The presentation was not fancy at all, in fact very simple but the wonderful aroma that wafted from each dish was very stimulating.

To complete this festal dinner, a large platter of different cheeses was brought to the table which we enjoyed with yet another glass of red.

There is a lot to be said for a glass of wine or two, the conversation about all sorts of things was flowing freely between the three of us; we chatted about everything and anything, dad tried very hard not to talk about business, rather we focused on what we had seen on the way thus far on this trip, and of course the wonderful dining experience.

I think it was during this trip with dad and Aunt that I began to realize how important food was to Aunt. As I understood, during her childhood there had been times where not enough food was on the table because of the war, and this might have been the reason for her close affiliation with food.

Before we left in the direction of Narbonne the next day, we visited the Cathédrale Saint-Pierre and some other architectural attractions that were created during the 18th Century, from the time of the French revolution.

After Montpellier we headed down to Sète the seaport town also known as the Venice of the district Languedoc. Once we had arrived at our destination, we took a little detour to Carcassonne, a provincial town about sixty kilometers West of Narbonne; dad wanted to visit the Château Comtal, the Burg Queribus and the Canal du Midi, the 260km water connection between Toulouse and the see, he thought that sometime soon he would like to explore this route on a barge.

Further down the track, in the 13th Century Perpignan was the capital city of the Kingdom Mallorca; in the city center you can clearly see the architectural influence from Catalan, the Kings palace and the Cathedral.

From Perpignan we drove straight through to Sant Feliu, dad wanted to get to our final destination by late afternoon.

We had gotten through the check-in formalities, began to unpack the car, ready to move our luggage to the fourth floor where our apartment was situated, featuring; three bedrooms, two bathrooms, a large living area, a small kitchen, furbished in a simple manner, uncluttered, and a large balcony facing the see.

Dad moved one of the bags aside, and suddenly I saw something yellow, something that I had not seen at our house before; soon it became evident that dad had bought me a rubber dinghy and oars, it wasn't just any dinghy, it was of very high quality, as you might find in the Navy. I was able to make this statement because I understood something about rubber dinghies; I had checked them out for some time before. Dad and Aunt whom had planned this surprise some time ago were clearly touched to see me so excited.

This trip had been full of pleasant surprises; to my amazement, Aunt was very pleasant to be with, she was nice to me, involved me in conversation as if this was a normal day to day occurrence, she showed emotion during the visitation of the point of interest on our journey, expressed great interest in the different styles of architecture, and she was raving about the food markets that we had visited, and to top it off, I got a rubber dinghy, something that was on my wish-list for some time.

During the week we spend a lot of time as a family, the early morning breakfast; I got fresh bread from the local bakery, butter, jam, a selection of cheese, local small goods and tomatoes were part of it. On some days we left early to check out the points of interest in the area, but mostly we took off to the beech to enjoy the swimming, driving the dinghy and sun-baking.

At that time, it was said that you have not had a holiday unless you came back dark-skinned—burned from the sun. People weren't aware of the dangers and the risks of excessive sun-bathing; I had the impression that it was important for many people to return from their leave with a dark skin, to demonstrate that they could afford to spend time down south.

Lunch was usually kept fairly simple, it comprised of grilled fish, fresh salads, olives and bread followed by a little siesta at the apartment or under the shade of the beech umbrella, and the afternoon was again spent in and on the water. For a seventeen-year-old, the beech had other attractions to offer as well, there were lots of interesting young ladies, most of them were either Spanish or French speaking. I was very much aware that Aunt would watch out for me on the beach, making sure that I would not get up to too much mischief, but the beach was large and there were always plenty of people around, she couldn't possibly see everything, I assumed that she too wanted to enjoy herself, or simply relax, and so I took the opportunity to have a wonderful time.

The way we spend our evenings was very much predictable; after a shower we got dressed to go out for a drink somewhere along the beach promenade, talked about the day, sometimes we got into rather serious conversations about life, we observed and commented on the people around us; the impression that they left on others, about their behavior, and other observations that we made, but most of all we had fun and got along well; I don't recall that we had a quarrel during this trip.

During this particular time dad took as to Barcelona for the day. I clearly recall the moment when dad had parked and secured the car, I was standing there on the footpath, watching the people walking in all directions talking Spanish, a language that I barely understood, the old trucks, buses, cars, and bikes driving past, throwing out a huge amount of smoke from the exhaust system, most of which were clearly the result of old, not so well maintained engines, the stench from the traffic was horrendous, and the noise ear deafening, and yet, it was an intriguing display of different colors, smells, and sounds which I had never experienced in this way before.

From the harbor where we had parked the car, we took a bus, heading to the Sagrada Familia, still under construction—a church of immense magnitude and beauty.

In 1874 the bookshop keeper and author Joseph Mario Bocabella from Barcelona had this idea to build a large church financed through donations, and hence he founded a society for this reason. The terrain was bought in 1882, the architect Del Vilar was engaged to design the building, and in 1883 he began with the construction. However, because of unsolvable differences with the members of the society, probably in relation to the concept, the architect abandoned the project, the then very young architect Del Vilar took over the task of planning and continued the construction.

At the time that we visited the Sagrada Familia it was a huge construction site: there were parts that might have been completed but the scaffolding on the interior reminded visitors of the fact that the project was nowhere near completion, many parts on the outside of this monument were still fitted with scaffolding high up. The four Apostle Towers weren't finished, it wasn't until 1976 that the first of them was completed. In some areas high up near the front facade we were able to explore some of the gangways which formed part of the scaffolding, being able to see the work of the stone mason's close-up. It is anticipated that the project will be completed by 2026; the anniversary of Antoni Gaudies death, by then it will have taken 144 years to complete this great monument.

I don't have to pretend to be the grand connoisseur of history and architecture, but the project Sagrada Familia which is supposed to be one of the most exotic buildings of the world, as I was allowed to experience it as a teenager in 1967 has left an impression of fascination with me until today, and if I am fortunate enough, I will be allowed to witness its anticipated completion.

From the Sagrada Familia we walked in the direction of the Placa de Catalunya, the very large open area, featuring huge fountains, greenery, lovely flower gardens and monuments, a place for locals and tourists to feed the pigeons, to relax, ant to marvel the busy surrounds. From there we walked in a Southerly direction onto La Rambla de Sant Josep, one of Barcelona's great and famous avenues, the center is lined with trees on both sides, along the footbath you come across clusters of tables and chairs forming part of the bistros, cafés, restaurants establishments situated on either side of the Rambla, and there are lots of interesting shops and notable buildings that invite to be admired.

The Rambla, Today, I feel Goosebumps all over, and a shiver runs through my body, realizing that I was sitting there in one of the boulevards cafés with my dad and Aunt, enjoying a cool drink with probably thousands of other people that lived, worked and strolled through this area, knowing that on 18 August 2017, 16 people lost their lives and 100 or so were injured as the terror attack unfolded.

A horrific reality for which there can be no reason on earth, nor can this be justified on the grounds of religious differences, a terrible criminal act committed by radicalized extremists. We should all pray to the one that is right for each one of us, that this kind of traitorous crime is not repeated.

The walk from the Placa de Catalunya to the restaurant Los Caracoles, one of Barcelona's most famous eating places in town would normally take around thirteen minutes, but because we were so fascinated by the diversity of places, people and not least the ambiance of the Rambla that this short walk took about three hours, and I am sure that Aunt could have spent more time going in and out of the different shops, had we not had a dinner appointment.

From the Rambla we turn left into Carrer dels Escudellers and walked to the corner of Carrer Nou de Sant Francesc. The terrain was somewhat rugged, consisting of large stone plates placed on the ground a bit like coble stone, the three to five story high buildings on either side were build close together, the streetlights, creating a mysterious atmosphere, and in the far distance we could see the reflection of the fire coming from the old cast iron outdoor grill which was built into the corner of Los Caracoles. As we walked toward the restaurant, one of the cooks was basting the chickens that were fixed on the spits, the sizzling sound from the fat hitting the fire, the glow of the dancing flames and the wonderful smell of fresh roasted chickens created an inviting atmosphere. Along the way, on both sides of the alley there were small shops fitted with metal roller doors some of which were closed at that time.

If you stood before this narrow alley in a foreign city at knight time, lined with buildings that are not so sophisticated, nor well looked after, pondering if you really want to go through here, you probably wouldn't do it, unless you knew that you are about to reach one of Barcelona's most famous restaurants. The main entrance consists of an old door, glazed with led light. The layout of the restaurant is very complex, made up of several smaller and larger dining areas downstairs as well as upstairs, and each one of them had a different décor, different light fittings, the walls were overloaded with old paintings and pictures from famous people that had dined here at some time or another, the place was very cluttered, but it was this blend of almost chaotic interior décor, the multilingual chitchat, together with the hustle of the open kitchen and the different food fragrances that filled the rooms that created an incredible ambiance. We were very lucky, the waiter took as to a table that was situated only a couple of meters from the open kitchen that was built into a slightly different level, perhaps half a meter lower in reference to the dining room, it felt like we were sitting in a theatre where you can watch the cooks from above.

If you tried very hard to design a crazy interior decor you probably would not be able to come up with something like the dining area that we sat in. The lower part of the windows were covered with acid etched glass, the top consisted of colorful LED light design, the floor was made from stone, above the kitchen there was a large painting, the top of the kitchen exhaust canapé was decorated with different pictures and lots of nick knacks, the hanging lights were Tiffany style, the old, probably original timbers were exposed on the ceiling, from there small twigs with leaves were hanging, the counter before the open kitchen was covered with old, very colorful patterned tiles, the side pillar painted white, covered with old photographs, on the front of the pillar stood tall an old grandfather clock from the last century; it was with amazement that we sat there looking at this astonishing sight.

Los Caracoles is in the hands of the same family since 1835 and I don't think that the food concept has changed in the past fifty years, the restaurant still prepares traditional dishes like snails prepared in different ways, hence the name Caracoles; baked fish on a bed of white beans, fresh seafood of the day—perhaps simply sautéed in butter with a touch of garlic, paella, a bouillabaisse if I might call it that, or simply a Catalan seafood soup, chicken from the charcoal grill, different grilled meats, tampas and fresh vegetables.

If you expect to find your food to be presented in an innovative, contemporary way as you would experience in a splendid high-class establishment with Gault Millau awarded points, then you are sitting in the wrong restaurant. However, if you want to experience a stunning down to earth atmosphere, if you enjoy the multilingual chitchat from the surrounding customers, the sometime loud but very convincing voices of the waiters, and if you appreciate the hustle of the open kitchen and the different food fragrances that waft across the dining area, and if you love fresh food prepared in a very basic manner with a natural taste, then you are in for a fabulous dining experience that you will never forget.

Sitting virtually in the kitchen of this great restaurant was for Aunt in particular an unbelievable adventure, being able to watch the cooks how they prepared dozens of different dishes at the same time on this very old wood fired cast iron stove.

I observed; to increase the heat in the frying pan, the cooks would remove the cast iron rings that were designed for this purpose and placed the pan directly over the open fire, and to lower the heat, they removed the pan, placed the cast iron rings back in the hole.

From where we sat you could feel the heat of the wood stove, and from the other side of the room a breeze of cool air was blowing across our direction, generated by the air-condition system.

I think Aunt's eyes and mind were more often in this open kitchen than with dad and I, with great enthusiasm she commented from time to time what the cook was doing, I am sure she would have loved to know every little secret herb or spice that was added to the different dishes. It didn't matter that Aunt was focused more on the kitchen, it was marvelous to see her having a ball; clearly cooking was her passion, whereas dad and I were more focused on the eating part of this spectacle, that's not to say that Aunt didn't enjoy eating, on the contrary, she adored eating, her few extra pounds demonstrated this, or at least that is what I thought at the time; it wasn't until much later in life that I learned that her weight had very little to do with her food intake.

## Club Med

After I stayed a week with dad and Aunt in Sant Feliu, I went to the Club Med in the vicinity of the Andaluse fishing village of Cadaqués, about 90 km North East of San Feliu; dad and Aunt had driven me there, they wanted to see where I would spend the next couple of weeks.

The club was settled on a rugged hill in the middle of nowhere, the check-in was fast and uncomplicated, after a very short wait I was taken to my bungalow; there were no conventional rooms that you might expect in a hotel, all over the hill there were small huts constructed from building blocks that weren't roughcast nor painted, covered with a tin roof, the door you couldn't lock, on the interior there were two very small rooms with just enough space to put a sleeping bag on a matrices placed directly on the stone floor, and there was a very small bathroom, with a toilet, a shower with cold water only, and a hand basin. The bungalow I shared with another fellow whom I didn't get to meet for the first few days.

The Club was like a small village on the see with little houses suitable for mums and dads with kids, bungalows for youngsters like me, indoor and outdoor restaurants where fresh food was cooked every day, offering a vast variety so that everybody could find something that he liked, the red and white table wine was also included in the deal, fruit juices and fresh fruits were available all day long, there was a night club, a large arena with a stage where the rock band was performing every night, there was an office area where you could get assistance if you needed it, a small medical center and everything else that you might need as a holiday maker.

Then there was a large range of water sports and other activities that the guests could get involved with, sailing, snorkeling and scuba diving were the most popular among youngsters like me. Around half of the guests in the club were parents with kids ranging from two to teenage, the other half were young women and men, some of them couples and lots of others like me, students and young tradies that were hanging loose, looking for sport activities and adventure. It was also a marvelous place for families with kids, the children were occupied the whole day with age-appropriate water sport, games and other activities, organized and controlled by young Club staff, giving the parents an opportunity to do their own thing.

I soon found out that everybody was here for a reason; most of us were enrolled in one of the courses the Club offered, I was here to learn scuba diving and to get my basic certification which would then allow me to dive anywhere in the world. However, the social activities were not to be underestimated either; there were lots of opportunities to meet someone that you liked, someone to spend your free time with, to have lunch and dinner together, to go to the concert with, to share anything at all with them.

I was about to experience life like never before, boys were looking to connect with girls of similar ages and the other way around, some searching for friendships, others for adventure, you had to be either stupid, extremely unsympathetic or totally insensitive not to find a mate at the Club.

If you believe that the Club life was just drugs, sex and rock and roll like as it was not unusual in some areas in the sixties, then you are mistaken. Rock and Roll we all knew, drugs we hadn't heard of where I came from, nor the youngsters that I cared to hang around with, and sex was something that was almost sacrilege, something to be cherished, we weren't in a hurry to have it, which doesn't mean that we didn't want it either.

I believe this rather modest behavior had to do with the fact that at that time co-education was not practiced in the secondary schools as well as in some of the colleges, and many of us enjoyed a very strict education at home which did not allow that boys and girls spend time together without any supervision which caused many of us to be a little shy, even reserved as far as this is concerned.

Now, in this situation we were confronted with the art of getting to know someone from the opposite sex, but most of us didn't know how or where to begin because it was a part of education that was missing in our vocabulary—nobody had ever bothered to teach us how this works.

Sure, we had made observations in our surroundings, and picked up a few behavioral hints here and there but they weren't very helpful either.

Frankly speaking, I don't know what our parents were thinking of at the time, they were so concerned about our education, with focus on academic subjects and socially acceptable behavior, but the part about the normal behavior among teenagers of the opposite sex was simply omitted, indeed ignored, we were totally left to our own devices, and yet it would have been very simple if our parents would have tackled this subject matter in an uncomplicated, very natural manner that we would have understood.

## The Diving Accident

On this particular morning of the second week of our diving course we drove out on the old wooden barge, a crew of four, two diving instructors and about twelve learners. The weather was superb, the sea was a little agitated, and about a mile out from the coast, in around forty meters of depth the anchor was set very near an old fishing boat that sank during the thirties. On the way there we had already put or wet suits on, and now that we had reached our destination the equipment check began; making sure that the weight belt was set correctly, the mask had a good fit, the oxygen bottle full, the regulator working properly, and that the depth indicator was in good working order.

The instructor discussed the dive plan with us in detail, we were to descent to forty meters to reach the wreck, spend around thirty minutes down there exploring, he told us clearly that we were to remain on the outside of the sunken ship, under no circumstances were we to enter the hull or the interior of the infrastructure, and that we were to stay in predetermined groups, well in sight of the instructor. He also explained the decompression procedures on the way back, how we would proceed with the prescribed stops that was necessary for this particular dive configuration, in order to avoid the so-called bend.

The dive instructors weren't mucking around with learners that did not take things seriously, safety was of the utmost importance, if anyone appeared to be a danger to the group, they were dismissed from the course. During the descent of this particular dive, I was very close to the instructor, we were at around thirty-four meters when I began to realize that I had a problem; as we continued our descent, I had the feeling that I didn't get enough oxygen into my lungs, and I began to hyper ventilate. I knew that I had sufficient oxygen in my bottle, and the regulator was working properly, it wasn't a technical hitch—the problem was me.

I tried very hard to take control of my breathing, but the intervals at which I was gasping for air had increased, to the point where I signaled to my instructor that I was going up, I had almost reached the point of panic, I went straight up without the specified depth and time of stops during the ascent to allow nitrogen "off-gassing" before continuing with the ascent, to avoid the "bend," nor did I manage the recommended safety stop at 15 feet. I was very lucky that the dive boat was not far from the point where I hit the surface, immediately I pulled of my mouth peace and began to gasp for fresh air for quite a while before I was able to swim across to the boat without any assistance from the crew, I didn't suffer any of the typical consequences that such an ascent can cause.

During the debriefing, I explained to the instructor what had happen to me. It was clear that under the circumstances during the dive the instructor was aware that I had a hyper ventilating problem; he had indicated to me that I should breathe slowly, but he could not accompany me during the ascent, his responsibility was with the other eleven divers.

After this event I didn't dive for a couple of days, I was slightly traumatized from this experience. I was very fortunate; I was able to talk about my diving incident with one of the instructors and a couple of diving mates, talking about the same thing over and over again, which was a therapeutic measure to assist me getting over the trauma. I am not sure if the diving instructors were aware of the trauma counselling process as we know it today, or if they merely did what seemed to be natural, whatever; talking about the events that took place helped me to overcome being scared.

For the past sixteen years there was always someone there to tell me what to do, what not to do, how to do it, when to do it, where to do it, and suddenly there was nobody on my side to guide me, to direct me, not only could I take my own decisions, all of a sudden, I was in charge of my life, and at that moment I realized a tremendous amount of self-confidence. No doubt, the strong influence, the firm guidance from my dad, the grandparents, the teachers and other people of notable reference to me, and to some extend the impact of Aunt's educational methods, even if her way was often questionable in my opinion, they had all contributed to my success. The fact that any of those people around me had something to do with this did not occur to me; it was solely my achievement and felt immensely great.

## Dad's Strategy

Dad's strategy for the SLS; One of dad's colleagues from the Air force was an instructor at the SLS in Kloten, he mentioned to dad that the entrance examination to the SLS (Schweizerische Luftfahrt Schule) as a pilot candidate was extremely tough, the academic level demanded was at a very high level, that it was unusual for eighteen-year-olds to gain entry, apparently most candidates accepted were either people that had absolved the military pilot cadet school, or they had a technical, engineering education.

Dad and I discussed this at some length; me, the arrogant, full of self-confident little shit that I was at the time was convinced that I would be among those that would gain entry as an eighteen-year-old without any problem, so dad proposed a strategy; to complete the Private Pilot's license first. This course of study could be started at the age of seventeen, ironically one year before youngsters were allowed to apply for a learner permit to drive a motor car.

The proposal that dad made was that he would pay for the school, the practical training, and any other costs associated with this course of study, and I had to cover my living costs for that year, which I could easily achieve with a part-time job.

The best location for this training would have been Zurich, the Flight Academy MFZ offered the course of study, and they were situated directly at the principal airport. However, me being a smart fellow, I proposed the location Bern-Belp; their hourly flying rates were a little cheaper compared to Zurich, the curriculum was equivalent, the school's reputation was very good, but my personal expenses would be considerably lower, providing that my mum whom lived in Bern, not far from the airport, would let me stay at her place.

If dad could accept my proposal, I would also be able to enjoy the company of my mum, and get to know her better.

When my parents separated I was around six years young, at that age you don't understand what is going on, you simply realize that your mum is gone, you don't know why she is not here anymore, you wonder if she had given up loving you, you don't really know what it is that you are missing about your mum, you don't know if she was a good person or not, you just remember the intensity of her look, how she cuddled you, how she loved you unconditionally, you don't remember why you love your mum, you just know that you miss her.

Whatever reasons my dad had for leaving mum, for me, to this day she was my mum; a gentle, loving and caring person whom I loved very dearly, and now I had a chance to do some catching up.

My dad agreed, I was going to Bern for a year to get my Private Pilot rating, in the preparation for the SLS in Zurich, providing that mum would agree, I contacted her to see if she was able and prepared to take me in as a border for the coming year, it wasn't self-evident that mum would agree, she was re-married with a man ten years her junior, a hard-working son of a farming family, in some way he was a little strange and very money conscious, but ok. I didn't expect an answer from mum straight away, I was aware that she had to consult her husband first.

As I was talking to her on the phone, I realized that she did not consult her husband about my possible coming to Bern, she merely informed him of the fact, she was so excited about my enquiry, for her it was obvious that I was welcome in her home.

The phone call I made when Aunt was not around, I didn't want her to hear the conversation, I didn't want to provide her with anything at all that she might have misinterpreted or twisted to confront me with. Aunt might not have had anything negative to comment at all, but I had become so suspicious of her reaction, my thoughts were perhaps exaggerated or in deed unreasonable.

## Snooping Around the Flight Academy, Bern-Belp

After the summer break of 1967, dad had made an appointment at the Flight Academy in Bern-Belp, him being a dedicated flight lieutenant at the

Swiss Air force, he wanted to know the structure of the course, the academic content, the teaching staff, the type of aircraft that was used for which purpose of the practical training as well as other school relevant information, he wanted to get to know the people of the Flight Academy Bern.

The day of our appointment was a Monday mid-morning; it was as if they had consulted the meteorological office to arrange this meeting—a wonderful, clear day.

We were met by the director of the Academy whom showed us around the facility before the meeting with staff members to discuss the details of the training.

The airport facility at Bern-Belp was somewhat humble; an old building with a tin roof, the Tower was located at the front, facing the tarmac. Actually, there was no Tower; it was merely an area in the main part of the building where the aviation communications equipment was installed. In the same area the director of the Academy shared this rather large, open-space office with the airport manager and other airport staff, a bit like a multipurpose room, which appeared to provide a very pleasant atmosphere.

Under the same roof, adjacent to the main office there were several rooms, some larger than others, most of them furbished as class rooms, with teaching aids hanging on each side of the blackboard; illustrating different cockpit configurations of a number of aircraft, showing the different arrangements of electrical, hydraulics, mechanical, navigation and radio communications equipment, switches and indicators, and in one of the rooms at the back of the facility there was the pièce de resistance—the link trainer, then the equivalent of today's motion flight simulator.

The building was very old, the class rooms simple, but the visual teaching aids indicated a sense of excitement, stuffed with intriguing learning material—I couldn't wait to be part of all this.

The director whom showed us around was also involved as an instructor, teaching theoretical subjects as well as operating as a flying instructor at all levels. The way in which he guided dad and I through the facility reflected his commitment to the Academy and you could feel the fascination that he had for the subject matter; in great detail he would explain how things are and how they work.

I was a little disappointed that the link trainer was being used by a student at the time of our tour, but we were allowed to observe quietly how the flight path was being lodged on the rather large display table which represented an aeronautical chart, from which the instructor guided the exercise the student had to handle, giving him instructions on the two-way radio, just like the communication between an aircraft and the Tower.

From there he took as on the concrete tarmac which was reserved for the F-27 (Fokker Friendship) whom landed in Belp a couple of times each week, all other small aircraft were parked on the grass area, and some of them in the hangar which was also the area for aircraft maintenance. The Academy small aircraft fleet consisted of four Cessna-150 which were predominantly used for the basic part of the PP licenses, 3 Cessna-180, a four-seat sports aircraft, two Piper Cherokee, a high-performance sport aircraft seating three plus one, fully IFR equipped; the Academy used the aircraft for the training of the IFR rating. And a couple of Piper twin Comanche, also fully IFR equipped. We were also told that all aircraft could be rented on an hourly basis as well, providing that the person was in charge of the appropriate current rating.

Back at the facility, one of the senior instructors joint us for a round the table meeting pertaining to the next step. The entry requirements including the medical examination were explained, the curriculum was discussed in some detail as well as the practical flying lessons minimum requirement.

It became clear to me that the actual flying was the smallest part of the training, the theory of flight, aerodynamics, weight and balance, the technical and mechanical knowledge, navigation, meteorology and radio operation were by far the bigger part of the curriculum.

Mr. Rindlisbacher, the senior instructor asked me if I had been already able to sit in the cockpit of one of their aircraft, as he found out that this wasn't possible during the time of our tour, he asked me to come along with him. We walked straight toward one of the Piper Cherokee that just got back from a training flight, the aircraft was about to be checked out and refueled. We walked around the aircraft, Mr. Rindlisbacher, explaining how the external safety check was done, making sure that the ailerons, the side rudder, the elevator were moving freely, that the flaps were locked firmly in place, the wheels and tires in good condition, no visual damage to the fuselage, the luggage hold locked, all inspection doors firmly closed, and that the propeller showed no signs of damage.

Then I was asked to climb into the cockpit on the left side, the captain's seat, and Mr. Rindlisbacher stepped in on the other side. First, he began to explain the fundamentals of the steering mechanism's; the pedals for the rudder movement left, right, and the steering of the nose wheel and the ground breaks, the yoke movements for the up and down direction, the right and left banking of the aircraft, and the flaps settings for take-off and landing. Then he went through the electrical switches for the navigation and other lights, the circuit breakers, the battery master switch, the fuel pumps, the fuel tank selector, the flaps setting and the aircraft trim for the take-off, he explained the throttle and air mixture setting, then he talked about the engine performance monitoring instruments and their function, he showed me the instruments that were used to navigate the aircraft.

Finally, Mr. Rindlisbacher handed me a check-list, explained the different phases of the flight—from the walk-around on the ground, which he had already demonstrated, pre-start-up, engine start, after engine start, engine test through the magnetos, the taxi clearance, before take-off, climb, cruise, approach, pre-landing, after landing, parking and shut down.

Then he asked me to call out the items listed on the pre-start-up section of the checklist, and he would action the request and read back at the same time, confirming his action, then we got to the engine start section and he actually started the engine, from there we got to the after-engine start. He now revealed that we were actually going for a short introduction flight, that I was to place my feet on the pedals without any action on my part, merely to feel what he was doing, how he was steering the aircraft on the ground, and then the same with the yoke, merely holding it very loosely to get a feel of how to direct the aircraft in an up, respectively down position, and how to bank to the right or left side.

On the two-way radio he requested permission for this particular VFR flight (Visual Flight Rules), and to taxi to Runway 32. We were cleared to taxi, apart from the meteo conditions and the QNH setting we were instructed to hold clear before Runway 32. Once we had arrived at the Runway holding position we went through the before take-off check on the list.

Then the message came through, HB-CST you are cleared to line-up, the pre take-off check had been completed, we checked to the left and to the right, ensuring that there was no other traffic around, particularly on the approach side, the breaks were released, Mr. Rindlisbacher added a little thrust and we rolled onto the centerline of the runway.

A moment later the Tower advised us—Hotel Bravo Charlie Sierra Tango you are cleared for take-off; full thrust, ensuring that the aircraft stayed on the centerline, yoke pushed slightly forward to hold the nose wheel firmly on the ground until the rotate speed of 75 knots was reached and then the gentle pulling back of the yoke, and we began to climb quite fast, pulling back the thrust a little, turning to 230°, a little later another left turn to 140°, levelling off at 1600ft above ground, set power at 100kts with around 1800 RPM, started the stopwatch abeam, 35 seconds plus wind we turned left to 050°, flaps to 10 degree, reduced power to 1200 RPM, booster pump on, carburetor heat on, set flaps to 20 degree, maintain a descent rate of 500ft/min, set flaps to 30 degree.

Banking the aircraft to the left onto the final 320°, received our landing clearance, we made very small directional as well as power adjustments and finally set the aircraft down after the threshold, applied the brakes very gently until we were able to leave the runway to the right. Instructor Rindlisbacher requested permission to taxi back to Runway 360; he wanted me to repeat this traffic pattern under his guidance. And so, we set off for the second round with me on the controls.

Dad was aware that I was going to get an introduction flight that day but he didn't tell me, it was a total surprise to me and without a doubt the best day in my teenage life thus far.

A couple of years back my half-brother William gave me a great book which illustrated the story about some American pilots who were testing the X15, a hypersonic rocket powered, the world's fastest Mach 6 aircraft at the Edwards Air force Base USA which made its first flight on 8 June 1959—Neil Armstrong was one of the pilots that flew this aircraft. A lot of details about flying were explained in this book, and I recall how I was fascinated by the cockpit illustrations, driving dad just about crazy, wanting to know the function of every switch, every handle and instrument, and now I had actually done it—I was flying an aircraft, how exhilarating it was.

On the way home there was only one subject for me to talk about and that was my flight with Instructor Rindlisbacher. I think dad was equally excited about my experience, he was asking me about every technical detail, wanting to know how we handled the procedures at the various flight stages, he wanted to know about the radio communication, and he was interested in the safety aspects that we had discussed, and occasionally, as a comparison he would comment on how a particular procedure functioned in the DH-112 Venom that he was flying in the Swiss Air Force.

Back home, Aunt wanted to know how our day was. I wasn't sure if she really wanted to know, or if she was merely interested in how dad's day had been. I had lost my objectivity when I was around Aunt, doubting the sincerity about every question that she posed, putting in doubt every friendly gesture, I had learned to analyze every nuance in her voice, I had become so much aware of her facial expressions and her body language, I realized that I hated her.

Despite all of this, I tried hard to be a little enthusiastic when I was telling her about my first flight, and how exuberating an experience it was.

Perhaps she was happy for me, I don't really know, maybe I had become totally unreasonable toward her, there were also positive things to be said about Aunt, unfortunately those things were in the minority, but she always provided me with clean clothes to ware, she made sure that I wasn't going out looking tatty, she was a great cook, and she took good care of my dad.

## End of Second Semester, the Maturity Examination

Semester two 1967, as in the previous semester, I spend most week evenings by myself, Aunt and Dad were either working late, or out on a business meeting, or amusing themselves somewhere around town, Aunt was usually keen to see a movie at the cinema, whereas dad's preference was the opera – to be part of one of a concerts presented by his favorite performer, dad and would sometimes travel to Milan, Rome, Paris, or London. I never got to enjoy an opera during this period, nor a film at the local cinema, my reward was a moment of peace from Aunt, allowing me to focus on my studies.

My availability to do chores for Aunt was now limited to Saturdays, and she made sure that there was plenty to be done; she always planned more work for than I was able to complete in the allocated time, more often than not I had to work an hour or so more to complete Aunt's list of chores.

The holiday in Spain was very pleasant, Aunt was particularly nice to me during this time, I could not understand why now that we were back home her behavior was again like before; deceitful at times, horrible, vulgar, and bitchy.

I quickly readjusted to her style, I had also learned to be horrible with Aunt, even calculating; pre-empting her reactions, I began to exploit her weakness without being embarrassed, deliberately working against her whenever it was appropriate, using every opportunity possible to disobey her, and all of this in a willful manner, and this made her even more vicious.

I knew that I had to focus on my studies so that I could pass the end of year examination, which would reward me with liberty, a life without the depressing feeling of being manipulated by Aunt. I was very much aware that by leaving home I would not be able to always do what I want, but would be able to take my own decision, it was going to be my responsibility to shape my own future, I was so much looking forward to rid myself of all this negative stuff that Aunt had forced upon me.

The two-day maturity examination at the end of 1967, the prerequisite for further studies at a university, or as in my case, the SLS. The examination was tough, but I knew the subject matter well, I had studied hard for this, I just turned 18. The examination results weren't posted until a couple of weeks later, the written result was sent home.

Dad had phoned the house and asked me to come to his office. He looked very serious when I got there, as if there was a problem. He asked me to sit down, handed me a large envelope and asked me to open it. Then I knew that this was the moment of truth, and I was agitated to open the envelope and yet I wanted to do it slowly, just like unwrapping a present, enjoying the moment. The thought that it might be negative news didn't even occur to me, outside of my fiascos through Aunt's cleaning assignments; the word failure did not exist in my vocabulary.

Immediately, I looked at the bottom line, not saying anything for quite some time, but I think that my facial expression exposed the result, I guess I must have been excited and yet very cool when I finally was able to show the result to dad; a pass with honors, just like my arrogant little self had expected it. That was one of the very few occasions where dad gave me a big hug, the man of few words telling me that he was very proud of me, a very emotional moment for both of us, a moment that created a bond between us without having realized it.

For both, dad and I it was clear that now there could be nothing to stop me from realizing my dream. At the same time, a little light of the tunnel suddenly began to shine very bright, not only was I heading fast toward the basic training of an airline pilot, I became also aware of a foreseeable future, free of Aunt's mental torture.

# Revenge—The Day I Left for Bern, January 1968

On the weekend, I had spent a few hours getting my stuff together, ready for packing, Aunt made sure that all my clothes were clean and neatly folded and I packed everything in a medium sized suitcase, together with some of my books that I wanted to take with me.

Then there was the drum set which I had dissembled and carefully stowed in their soft-bag, making sure that none of the components could get scratched during the transport, it wasn't just any kind of set, it was a "Rogers," and I was very proud to have it. The trumpet in its case and a few note books for practice.

Dad was going to drive me to the railway station in Basel, my one-way ticket was organized, I had arranged for my mum to meet me at the station in Bern in the afternoon, I was burning to go. Together with dad we stowed my luggage in the back of the car, I went back upstairs to say good bye to Aunt whom was looking out of the window in the hallway.

I gave her a little kiss on the cheeks, pretended to listen to the things that she had to say, turned around and walked away without looking back. I felt anger, frustration and great relieve at the same time, and I began to realize that I would never return to live in this house for as long as Aunt was here. When I got to the car I got in, closed the door and never looked back, I didn't wave to her either as we drove off, and this behavior was to haunt me as long as I had contact with Aunt.

It was my family home that I was leaving; I had very fond memories from the time when my mum was still living with dad, the bachelor period with my father was also very dear to me, and then were the thoughts about the dreadful time that I spend with Aunt, I was glad to leave.

The day my father passed away was the last time that I said good bye to Aunt as I left the family home, moments before that she reminded me of that time, back then when I left home to join my mum in Bern; how disappointed she was at that time, that I never looked back once I was at the car, and this after all that she had done for me.

Just about every time when Aunt and I had a fight, she mentioned this particular incident and began to ask me for the reason why. "Why did I do this, why did I do that, and why wasn't I...," and every time when she started with this subject, I reminded her of the fact that because of this kind of questioning which occurred regularly, several times each year over the past forty years, she had driven me to stay away from home, closing myself off from any communication with her.

Each time I asked her if we could not forget the "whys," to get on with life, and to enjoy the time that we still have together, but Aunt was not capable of forgetting, after a verbal fight there was always a time where we didn't see each other—usually for several months, then she would be ok again for a while, sometimes she was even pleasant, only to restart with the same drama again some four or five weeks later.

Still today I don't know why Aunt kept this fight alive all of these years; was she traumatized by the way I had left home, or did she truly believe that I was an ungrateful sod, not appreciating the wonderful job that she believed to have done in helping dad to raise me?

Had she forgotten how she treated me during these five years, the way she humiliated me, how she tried to mentally grind me into the ground, or was Aunt simply to unintelligent to realize how I might have felt?

Since adulthood I have endeavored to be fair toward Aunt, trying to acknowledge the good things that she did for me, recognizing how the positive had a sustaining impact on my life, and to be thankful for this, trying to push the negative experiences that I had with her into the background; Aunt took care of my dad, at least I had the impression that he was happy, Aunt took care of the household—the cooking, the laundry and some of the cleaning, Aunt was at the same time working in dad's business, Aunt taught me how to take care of myself—how to manage a household, doing my own laundry, ironing my own shirts, cooking my own meals, and she taught me how **not to** handle people.

An impact on my life had also the stuff that I hated about Aunt; as a kid, she never gave me a hug, mostly she was cold, very unlike a mother, and extremely authoritarian, she traumatized me, with her interrogative questioning technique she sometimes tried for me to admit something that was not true, watching me clenching for answers that I dint have, with her dirty smirk on her face; she appeared to be enjoying to see me scared and helpless, and she taught me how to hate.

The sad part about our quarrels was that after each fight there was a period of several months that passed before I tried to reconcile my problems with Aunt, a period I couldn't spend with dad.

The farewell at the railway station was tough, Dad providing me with the last-minute advice and reminders about specific things, at the same time looking deeply into my eyes and squeezing my hand firmly, as he always did in this kind of situation. Listening very carefully to what dad had to say, I couldn't help thinking that we wouldn't see each other for a while, and that I would miss him very much.

Mum was waiting for my arrival in Bern, it was mid-afternoon, the train had begun to slow down considerably, about to pull into the station, and I was standing at the window in my compartment, hoping that I would be able to get a glimpse of her before the train came to a holt.

I gathered my suitcase, the drum set and the hand luggage and got out as soon as I could, not easy with all the stuff that I had to. I didn't see mum straight away, a few minutes had passed until many of the travelers that were in the same train, together with the entourage that were on the platform to welcome them had slowly diminished, about fifty meters in the direction of the exit I now recognized my mum, about at the same time that she was able to see me.

There was great excitement, we hadn't seen each other for nearly one year, lots of hugs were exchanged, we could hardly talk because of the frenzy that had built up between us, and then I realized that mums' husband was standing there as well, the poor fellow must have felt neglected. Paul told me that he had taken the afternoon off from work, apparently, he suspected that I had a bit of luggage, that it would be less difficult to get home with by car. I didn't know Paul very well, I had only met him four or five times before; I knew that he was an engineer working for the local power company, one of the fellows that took care of the old water power plant "Matte" on the river Aare in Bern. I had a feeling of being welcomed by Paul, to my surprise he was excited that I had come to stay with them, he began to quiz me about my schooling at the flight academy, and he wanted to know in detail when this was all going to start.

## My Brother William

My brother William came home early that evening, he knew that I was coming to stay for a while, he too was looking forward to it, he is a couple of years older than me; he had completed an apprenticeship in the metal construction industry and was working in a responsible position in a local special equipment manufacturing firm. Although William and I were brothers, half-brothers to be more precise, we didn't know each other very well, we weren't aware about how the other one is ticking, now we had the chance to find out more about each other.

I soon realized that we were fundamentally different, he was apathetic, unconcerned at times and he consumed too much alcohol. At times, on a Saturday evening, when his girlfriend was working, we went out together; visiting pubs and clubs which featured bands until four on Sunday morning, just in time to walk across to the railway station restaurant which opened at five—we ordered a hearty breakfast and another beer.

This kind of outing was ok once in a while, my brother enjoyed topping up the alcohol level to the brim, sometimes getting pissed out of his brain, but this wasn't my world at all, I enjoyed a beer, a glass of wine or a Gin and Tonic in a while, in fact I detested these outings.

On occasion I tried to talk to William about his habit, trying to influence him a little, but he was of the opinion that he couldn't change it anyway; it was in the blood he thought. I knew that my brother had spent several years in a children's home because mum had to work full time before she remarried, she didn't have the time to care for him.

I realize that William resented this very much, he felt abandoned at the time, any kind of difficulty that came along in his life he pushed aside with the justification that he had been treated badly as a child. He also revealed to me that although he never got to know his father, he knew that he was an alcoholic, that he had inherited his drinking habits from him. I don't pretend to know much about genetics, nor inherited threats, but I have been reading some research publications in the hope that I would get to understand a little more about the subject matter.

In 2008, a study conducted by the NIAAA reviewed much of the research on alcohol use disorder and possible genetic contribution. The study concluded that genetic factors account for 40-60 percent of the variance among people who struggle with alcohol use disorder. Since then, some specific genes that contribute to alcohol use disorder have been found, and they correlate with the development of the reward centers in the brain.

The phenotypic expression of genes is complex, however. For example; a person may have one parent with blue eyes and one parent with brown eyes, so they have genes from both eye colors, but only one eye color will be expressed. *Strong genes* are the exception of the rule, and a gene responsible for the movement of gamma-amino butyric acid (GABA) in synapses between neurons appears to be a strong association with a higher risk of alcoholism. It is still unknown how precisely; this genetic sequence can ultimately influence the outcome for a person.

I know that there are other opinions as well, there are those that believe that "growing up in an environment influenced by addiction can also predispose a person to the condition," and others that firmly believe that the alcohol use disorder can be overcome with will power, and in the case of my brother, he never spends any time with his father, nor did he know him.

I do respect the scientific work and the different opinions that are derived from research in this area, but I do believe; if you have a strong desire to change your alcohol consumption habit, and if you set yourself realistic goals, you can overcome the problem. I don't know if alcoholism and the habit of smoking can be compared as an addiction, but I would have thought that the same principle applies if you want to stop one or the other. Perhaps this kind or argument is too simplistic.

It is now nearly five years back since I have stopped smoking, I was puffing about forty cigarettes a day, and this over a period of some forty years.

Still today, nearly every day I am looking either for my cigarettes or the lighter; at times I truly crave for a fag, sometimes I have to sniff on my wife's cigarette packet to satisfy my desire.

And yet, when I am in the vicinity of smokers, there are times when I enjoy the smell of the burning tobacco, and there are other times when I feel revolted by the odor; on many days I have to remind myself that I am a non-smoker, and it works for me.

I also have to admit that for the past ten years prior to having stopped; I have tried to give up smoking, the desire to stop smoking was particularly in vogue a couple of days before each New Year's Eve, listing all the non-desirables that I wanted to change when the church bells next door began to ring in the New Year. My wife and I sat in the kitchen this particular New Year's morning, sipping on our coffee, both of us secretly looking for a fag, reminding each other of the fact that we had agreed to stop smoking.

After a while, I got some newspaper, sticky tape and a pair of scissors; cutting the paper about eight centimeters wide, and about forty centimeters long, then folded the paper lengthways and cut it in the middle. From these to equally long pieces of Newspaper I tightly rolled two sticks that looked like cigarettes and held them together with sticky tape. Now that each of us had a "cigarette," I pretended to light them, pulling in the air through the newspaper, commenting about the lovely smell of the tobacco. The satisfaction of this pretend fag did not last very long, I think it wasn't much more than fifteen minutes later that I stood up, told my wife that I had to get something from the garage and left the house.

I had hidden a packet of cigarettes and a lighter in the boot of the car the day before, which probably was an indication of my seriousness to give up smoking, I opened the garage door and lit a cigarette, moments later, back upstairs, my wife asked me what I had been getting from the garage; I burst out laughing, showed her the cigarettes, and that was that; neither of us gave up smoking that particular year.

## The First Part-Time Job

My first part-time job as a student was at the small goods manufacturer Meinen in Bern, they had a couple of hundred employees, most of them occupied full time jobs, and some youngsters like me in particular were employed as part-timers. At that time jobs were announced in the local papers as well as by employees, spreading the news. I don't know how he was informed about this but it was mums husband Paul that told me that the local small goods company were looking for part-time staff, he also gave me some good tips about my application. I gathered my school certificates and the couple of written recommendations that I had from some of my teachers, knocked on the company's office door and presented myself as the young fellow that was keen to get himself a part-time job. I think the fact that I had the courage to call in unannounced and ask if they had a job for me impressed the lady, she told me to wait for a moment; she was going to talk to her boss.

The time to note my identity and the reason for wanting a job were quickly established, the boss was more interested in my reason for being in Bern, he was fascinated by the fact that I was going to do my Private Pilot's license with the view to become an airline pilot, wanting to know in some detail how this was going to happen, he was very happy to offer me a part-time job. Twice per week, starting at 06:00 working until 11:00 in the packing area which provided me with sufficient money to live without a problem. The job was perfect, it was physical work but not too hard either; it was tailored to my study schedule.

In the dispatch section, there were several packing stations, each with a raised desk where the caller announced the material that was to be gathered and packed into baskets, a bit like the priest in the church, calling out to his congregation. In each packing team there were four or five runners, for some reason all men that would go and get the different small goods products from the nearby supply cool room; returning with the products to the pack station where it was checked and packed by the lead person.

Often, I had to think of Aunt, she taught me a lot about small goods, that was her thing, she had done a three-year apprenticeship in this subject, she taught me the difference between a salami and a salami; an Italian style salami has different quality aspects compared with a Citerio, and this kind of knowledge was definitively a huge advantage in this job because I had already a fundamental understanding of the products.

It was cold in the packing area, around five degrees Celsius, a temperature necessary to ensure the continuation of the cooling chain between the manufacturing and the delivery to the retail shops was assured. Once an order was completed, the caller provided the necessary documentation and ordered the consignment to be loaded on the delivery truck. There was a certain hectic that prevailed in this department, everybody took their work serious, and there was a certain competitiveness among the teams, aiming at zero mistakes, zero complaints from the customers; I very much appreciated this kind of commitment from ordinary people, simply trying to do a great job. A wonderful, smoky smell of different small goods products was in the air enhancing the atmosphere.

When we finished the five-hour shift, the caller, our immediate superior always provided us with feedback, briefly talking about the things to better focus on, the things that we might do better the next day, but he also mentioned the positive things that occurred during the shift. The management style that this fellow applied was exemplary, although he was in charge of only a small group of unskilled staff; he understood what it means to lead people, his feedback had an effect far greater that he could imagine, we were prepared to give our everything for him, we were proud of our simple achievements and we had learned that as a group we were stronger than as individuals, this fellow had not studied rocket science; he was an ordinary staff member leading a group of four to five staff.

# Getting to Know Mum

My being in Bern was a good thing for my mum; finally she was able to be with her two sons, at least for a little while; as for my brother William this situation was likely to be indifferent, except that now him an I had a chance to get to know each other, the one that would have been affected the most from this addition to the family was Paul, when he got married to my mum, he was probably not counting with the second son of hers to shift in with them as well.

As for myself, I was uncomplicated, I needed a bed for a while, knowing that I could finally spend a little time with my mum and brother was comforting, although Paul was a little complicated as a person, he was a decent fellow, intelligent, not unpleasant to be with.

Though I was looking forward to be with mum and William, getting to know them better, it was important to realize that the main purpose of my being here was obtain the PP license, all requirements had been achieved; my seat at the flight academy was confirmed and the finance organized, I had a place to stay at, my source of income was secured, and the local trams and buses provided me with transport.

Not everything at mum's place was glorious either; from time to time it was unpleasant; often William's behavior toward Paul was unacceptable, he could not accept him as a father figure, he ignored the fact that he was in Paul's home, and that he was paying the bills and he was my mother's husband. I was of the opinion that if William was unhappy with the family situation, he could have moved out and get his own place.

I didn't like getting involved in William's fights with mum or Paul, but I thought that the two of them deserved a little gratitude for what they were doing for us youngsters, we had a roof over our heads, mum was trying hard to put on the table what was possible within her budgetary constraints, our laundry was taken care off and Paul tried very hard to provide us with little outings whenever he could.

Paul wasn't the kind of fellow that I would have chosen to be my best friend, but he was nice to mum, he respected her and he appeared to take good care of her.

We didn't spend much time as a family, everybody was busy doing their own thing, mum whom was also working tried hard to accommodate every body's time schedule, but it was rare that all of us were sitting around the dinner table at the same time.

On a regular basis William was getting presumptuous when mum had prepared a simple meal for dinner; he expected to see meat on the table every day, something mums budget did not allow for, it didn't occur to him that he could have given mum a little more boarding money, on such occasions he would spit the dummy, get up and leave the house to eat his dinner in a pub; I am sure that mum was very hurt by this kind of behavior, I know she would have loved to have a bigger budget available to please his desires.

With the start of my course at the flight academy I had less time to get involved in the family life, my days were very structured, during two mornings each week I was working at the smallgoods factory until 11: 00, home for lunch and in the afternoon, I had classes. The other days were taken up also by the school.

I came to Bern with very specific ideas and expectations; the main aim was to get my PP license but I also had certain thoughts and visions about the relationship with my brother whom I had missed since our separation some eleven years earlier when my parents divorced, I was curious about how we would get on with each other, the kind of interests that we might be able to share, what kind of things that we would be able to do together, what it would be like to be able to spend time with my brother. I didn't have preconceived ideas about all this, but none the less I had some expectations.

I was glad to spend time with William but I began to realize that we were fundamentally different, I had difficulties to accept his sometime despicable behavior toward mum and Paul, I despised his self-pity, his apathetical behavior, and I did not agree with the amount of alcohol that he was consuming either. But he is my brother, I tried to talk to him about his alcohol problem, but what I perceived to be a problem was no problem to my brother. I was of the opinion that he was on his way to become an alcoholic.

We often talked about the past, what was happening in our lives since we had been parted, and we came to realize that his life was probably more difficult; having been shunted around from his uncle's place to different children homes, and eventually back to mum, most of the time thus far William had spent outside of the family, in institutions.

William and I also talked about the future, more specifically my future; he never talked about his dreams, he didn't have any particular plans, nor did he have a vision; he appeared not to have any ambitions, and if he did—he didn't reveal them to me—he behaved as if he didn't care about anything.

I knew that I loved my brother very much, but he didn't fit my preconceived perception that I had shaped in my head over the past years, I didn't receive the moral support that I anticipated from him, he wasn't the big brother that I could look up to, the contrary was the truth—as the younger of the two of us I had to encourage him, but I learned to accept him unconditionally the way he is—he is my brother.

Part of my expectation with my coming to Bern was also to enjoy, and to get to know my mum that I had very much missed all these years during my childhood, now was the time.

As a child, how often did I quietly cry before going to sleep at night, hugging my soft toy elephant called Dumbo, thinking about Mum – with her warm smile that always had a soothing effect on me, her dark blue eyes that radiated love, the way she would look at me and console me when I was on one of my visits, and how heart breaking it was each time when the time had come for me to return to Aunt and dad.

The only thing that I hated about mum was; as a small child, she cleaned my chocolate covered face with her saliva, at the time I felt that this was yucky, despite the fact that I tried to combat this cleaning method of hers, she won the battle every time.

From the very time that I was able to talk, I recall that mum and I had a special way to communicate; if I asked her for something which required a yes or no response, I was able to read her answer merely by looking into her eyes, a ritual that I can never forget—we kept it throughout our lives.

What I found out during my stay with mum was different to what I expected; I loved her very much, there was no doubt about it, we had maintained a good understanding for each other despite the long separation, but something was missing, I didn't understand what it was.

If I ask myself which are the essential elements required for the emotional attachment between mother and child, I would reason that; mother and child are closely connected to each other during the pregnancy, not only is the child feeding from her, because of her the child has a chance to grow into this wonderful, small human creature—no doubt, during this time I was aware of her emotions—the happy as well as the sad ones, I got nourished from what she was eating, I was feeling her comfort as well as her discomfort, as well as being part of her I had become an individual, but all of this does not suffice, I believe that the interaction between mother and parent that occurs after birth is far more bonding than the period of the pregnancy.

I didn't find the closeness to my mum, I was missing the emotional feeling that I once had for her, as if I was secretly blaming mum for the separation with dad at the time, as if I wanted to punish her for the emotional hardship that I suffered during my childhood, I had feelings of being a victim of parental neglect, at the same time I felt abused by Aunt, but I knew that I was responsible for my own destiny, it was clear to me that I could not blame mum, dad or indeed Aunt for the past; I have my life in my own hand, I decide the direction that I will take, I can make my life different and great, but somewhere along the way I had lost the emotions that I once had toward my mum.

For my birthday my mum presented me with a book written by Robert G. Jackson, "never to be sick again" was its title, a gift that didn't make sense to me, although I did read it at the time, and I did understand the content, but it didn't make sense to me until some forty-seven years later. The book was fascinating to read, the author described how we as individuals can contribute a lot to our health, that with a positive attitude and the believe that we are responsible for our health our immune system can be strengthened, keeping away illness.

## The Flight Academy, Bern-Belp

The actual admission to the academy together with the introduction to our learning environment took a couple of days, we were introduced to the academic and the training staff, the theory training facilities were shown, the IFR (Instrument Flight Rules) motion simulator set-up, the aircraft maintenance area and its equipment, the tarmac area with its aircraft parking area, the runway and its taxi way system, the taxi and runway technical installations, the key personnel from the airport operations and the maintenance department were introduced, the general house rules and regulations explained, and finally the curriculum was presented in some detail.

The medical examination which was a prerequisite for the application of the learners permit I had done several months beforehand through a government appointed and certified doctor, the permit I had to present and the identification number was documented in the academies register.

Text books, manuals and accessories necessary for the training we were able to purchase from the academies shop, except the Jeppesen aviation manual for Switzerland which included all technical information, landing and departure relevant details of each airport facility as well as the Radio navigation systems and their relevant frequencies, the Meteorology book; specific for the aviation industry, and a CR hand held navigation computer which Dad had presented me with this past Christmas.

The theory of the course was clearly structured, with the initial phase intended for standard VFR private pilot license, followed by endorsements for night flight, an introduction to aerobatics, IFR, and twin engine;

*Communication*—the radio telephony license, one of the first things to accomplish through the Federal Office of Civil Aviation.

*Air Law*—local as well as international regulation Conventions, agreement and organizations.

*Aircraft general knowledge, airframe, systems, powerplant*—design, load and stress factors, airframe.

*Principles of flight*—aerodynamics, stability, control, limitations, propellers, flight mechanics.

*Instrumentation*—sensors and instruments, measurement of air data parameters, magnetic and flux valve compass, gyro instruments, navigation systems, flight control systems, trim-yaw damper, auto pilot, communication systems, alerting systems, maintenance and monitoring systems, and circuits.

*Weight and balance*—the center of gravity, the point over which the aircraft could be balanced, essential for the stability of the aircraft during each phase of the flight.

*Aircraft performance*—B class single and multi-engine.

*Flight planning and Monitoring*—all phases of VFR and IFR flight planning, inflight monitoring and in-flight re-planning.

*Meteorology*—the atmosphere, wind, thermodynamics, clouds and fog, participation, airmass and fronts, pressure systems, flight hazards and meteo information.

*General Navigation*—fundamentals of navigation, magnetism and compasses, charts dead reckoning, in-flight navigation.

*Radio Navigation*—radio aides, radar.

The philosophy of this kind of school is straight forward; either you know your subject or you don't, either you have understood a process or you haven't, either you can master a particular procedure or you don't, as long as you don't know it, as long as you can't do it, you don't get licensed. There are no maybes, no could be, or perhaps, it is black or white, and that's the way it should be.

The weekly contact with dad; I made sure that I called home at least once a week, usually on Sunday evenings when I could be reasonably sure that they were home, I was eager to provide dad with an update about school, to tell him in detail what I had learned during the past days and dad being a keen military pilot intensely listening to what I had to say, he was genuinely interested in the progress that I was making at the Academy. Sometime toward the end of our conversation he would ask if I wanted to talk to Aunt, though I wasn't particularly interested in a conversation with her, I tried to sound enthusiastic and indicated that "that would be nice."

I think that Aunt's enthusiasm to talk to me was as limited as was mine, more often than not she was too busy doing something or another and merely send her regards through dad—a situation that I was not unhappy with.

During the same year, my first car that I bought was a 1960 VW Beetle, second hand which I had bought from the savings, two thousand Swiss Frank's this fellow wanted for the car but I was able to negotiate the purchase price for one thousand eight hundred, I didn't particularly like its color, Reseda green, a light green, almost like the curtain of baby Peters cradle, but this didn't matter, the car was affordable, it provided me with freedom and I bought it without the knowledge of anybody in my family. There was good reason for my secrecy, I didn't have a driver's license, though I had discussed this with dad before I came to Berne, he was of the opinion that I should focus on my PPL first, but arrogant little me had different plans, I applied for a learner's permit and forged my father's signature which was required because I was still considered minor until I had reached the age of twenty-one. What irony—I was allowed to learn to fly an airplane, even perform some stuff without having an instructor by my side, and yet I was to be denied a learner permit for a motorcar, a hideous situation that I had to change.

The principles of driving a car I began to understand at an very early stage of my life, observing my father very closely whenever we were on the road together, and the practical part I practiced in dad's garage when they had gone out in the evening—hopping into the driver seat, adjusting its position in a forward direction, noting precisely its original location so that I was able to place it there when I had finished, pushing the clutch to the floor, moving the gear lever to neutral, making sure that the handbrake was pulled, and then starting the engine just like my father, releasing the key as soon as the motor started.

Then I began my exercises—very slowly driving the car back and forward, changing its original park position, being very careful not to bump into the other cars or indeed one of the pillars, making sure that the car was placed in the same position as it was before my excursion. The actual driving on the road I practiced with my own Beetle during periods where there weren't any cars on the road—something that you couldn't afford to do nowadays.

For several months I drove around without a driver's license in my pocket, I had started to take lessons about three months after I bought the car. Deliberately I had chosen a driving instructor from Giswiel, Canton Obwalden, about 95km from Bern so that nobody locally was able to find out that I didn't have a driver's license. As I recall, after twelve lessons I was scheduled for the driving test, on this particular day, as usual my driving instructor was waiting for me at the local railway station, I didn't see him as I pulled up at the parking lot in my green Beetle, but he had seen me—he didn't tell me this until after I had returned from my test with the examiner—a couple of days later my driving permit was in the mail, a story that I never revealed to my father.

William and I decided to visit dad and Aunt for the weekend, I had phoned dad to make sure that this was suitable, I don't know how other families handled this kind of situation, but ever since I remember, people including members of the family didn't just turn up at the family home, it was customary to make an appointment, a ritual that we maintained until the very end of my father's life.

On this particular Saturday morning we turned up with my Beetle, William in the driver's seat, pretending that he was the owner of the vehicle, at that time when he had lost his license, apparently because he was caught driving with lots of alcohol in his blood, but this didn't stop us from fooling around with cars, had I been aware of the facts at the time, I probably would not have allowed William to drive.

The fact that I had been away from home for some time by now had given me so much self confidence that my behavior toward Aunt had totally changed, I no longer feared her, I was able to stand next to her without any feelings of inferiority, I knew that she could not traumatize me anymore.

Much of the trauma that Aunt had subjected me to I had not forgotten but I had repressed them from my thoughts, rarely did I think about it and if it happened, I was quick to brush these thoughts aside.

No longer did I brood over what had happened, or indeed why Aunt treated me the way she did, I had stopped to speculate, my aim at that time wasn't to begin the process of healing, for this I was far too young; it was my objective to get on with life and to live and to achieve my dreams.

Still, I refrained from telling Aunt everything that was going on in my life, and if I did reveal something, I didn't care about what she might have thought, I respected her as my father's lady; not more, and not less, and I was correct, even nice to her, trying to forget the mental torture that she had exercised on me, I tried to focus on the good things that she taught me, I am sure that she also had become aware of my changed attitude toward her. It was only much later in my life, at a time where I had begun to take into consideration the reappraisal of the events that had traumatized my childhood that I began to wonder about Aunt's perception of that particular time.

By early August I had completed the mandatory navigation flights, accomplished and passed all prerequisites, the theory examination and the practical test, I had become the proud owner of the PPL, it was now time to focus on the next phase, it was my aim to complete the introduction course for aerobatics, the VFR night flight and prepare for the twin engine and the IFR endorsements in preparation of the schooling for the following year. During the same period, I had prepared my application for the entrance examination to the SLS.

## SLS Flight Academy, Zürich

January 1969, I moved to Zürich, I was lucky to get to share an historic attic apartment in the old town above the East bank of the Limmat, the river that flows from the end of the lake through the city of Zürich, it was a two bedroom apartment, my room was sparsely furnished with a single bed, a tatty two-door wardrobe—one of the doors could not be closed properly anymore—and a writing table with a chair, then there was a small lounge area which was to be shared, equally poor in its appearance, a couple of very old lounge chairs, a side board from the twenties and a floor lamp with a slightly torn lampshade, in the kitchen stood an old wooden table, the top covered with a colorful floral plastic cover, two old chairs, a larder, kitchen sink and a two-element table-top gas burner, and the tiny window that opened up, overlooking the roof tops of the West side of the building, and finally there was the piece de resistance—the bathroom.

There was a toilet to which the door didn't close properly anymore, and on the outside of that, hidden by a heavy curtain was a small sink with running hot and cold water, it replaced the bathtub or indeed the shower. The whole place was in desperate need of renovation, but the rent was incredibly affordable for its location, so the state of the place had become of no importance. A jazz club was occupying the ground floor, bands like the Piccadilly-Six used to play there regularly, an old, creaky stair leading up to the fourth level where the attic apartment was situated, the first, second and third floor was taken up by small apartments, and then, directly under the roof was my new home.

My mate Hans Peter that I had shared the classroom with the previous year made me aware that his sister whom was in her fourth year of law study was looking for a flat mate, I contacted Ursula, we met on a weekend and we agreed that both of us found the other sympathetic, trustworthy, suitable to be flat mates, despite the fact that she was actually looking for a female partner, I assumed that my mate had given me a decent reference.

The location of the apartment was in an area that wasn't considered the best place to bring up your children, in my days this wonderful maze of narrow alleys, some of them a little sleazy accommodated a pub on just about every corner, most of them were patronized by boozers and ladies of pleasure. I was determined to keep my new place confidential; I had installed a post office box near the airport, I was certain that dad and Aunt wouldn't have agreed with my new, exotic address, in fact I am certain that they would have been outraged—another story that I never revealed to my father, ever.

Shortly after the entrance examination I received the notification of acceptance for the next intake as a student pilot to the SLS, the initial practical training and IFR endorsement was achieved on the Italian build Piaggio P149, the standard trainer that was stationed for much of the time at the airfield Hausen am Albis near Zürich. The SLS was one of the most prestigious platforms in Europe for young trainee pilots, many of us came from an Airforce background, others were graduates from the ETH (Eidgenössiche Technische Hochschule) with a background of engineering, and some were already licensed private pilots with additional endorsements, most of the students well over their twenties.

In part, the subject matter taught was much the same as that instructed during my PPL training, however on a higher grade, the standards of achievement were set at an extremely high level, the course had an immense intensity and the personal commitment from each student was absolute. After the IFR and the multi engine ratings the focus was shifted on aircraft specific knowledge, airframe, hydraulics, landing gear, wheels, tires and brakes, flight controls, weight and balance, pneumatics and air-conditioning systems, anti-icing, fuel system, electrics, piston engines and turbines, oxygen system, radios for communication and navigation ADF, VOR, Doppler, cockpit procedure training, navigation procedures, flight planning and meteorology, navigation with the radio compass, VOR, ADF, ILS, VDF, approach by radar, the board weather radar system and its application, DME integrated with VOR, the secondary radar and the ATC transponder, integrated flight instrument system-course indicator, flight director indicator horizon, flight director control, monitoring and surveillance of instruments and sequential scanning, by early June 1970 I had completed my training, flying short haul routes on the F27 turboprop.

## The Salvos

I clearly recall, during a particular time of my teenage life I thought that the members of the Salvation army were very strange, I could not understand how these ladies and men in their funny looking outfits, with their ridiculous hats perched on their heads could even dear to enter the jazz club where I was working as a part time waiter during my studies in Zürich, and to dear to begin to impose themselves by singing their religious stuff during the bands break. This was a time in my life where I did not consume any liquor at all and could understand others that resented the consumption of alcohol. Yet I felt ashamed during these moments of interruption of our guest's conversation, ashamed not so much for myself but for the guests in the pub.

On the other hand, I also felt that it takes a lot of courage for a small group of people to march in a public place, to gather themselves in front of everybody, and to perform musical material with a content that could not appeal to all, particularly not to those gathered in a club consuming alcohol, and it wasn't as if the people in the pub had invited the Salvos. Frankly speaking, for this courage I admired the Salvation Army folk as much as I hated their presence.

In a way, the behavior of the Salvation Army members fascinated me so much that I felt the urge to find out more about them, I was curious to know what makes these people tic. My fascination for this group was probably triggered by the fact that some of the younger female members in particular were very good looking, many of them seemed to be glowing with natural love and charm.

As I observed the members of the group closer, I realized that the fellows displayed similar characteristics as did their lovely females' companions, regardless of their age, most of them seemed to be radiating a very natural charm, indeed holiness. I came to suspect that there had to be a reason for this apparent wholeness of these people, I needed to get to the bottom of this mystery.

One evening as I was working in the club after school, again a group of Salvation Army officers came to surprise our guest with a musical message during the time when The Piccadilly Six had taken a break. At the end of the performance one of the fellows collected monetary donations from those that were prepared to give freely as well as from others that probably felt obliged, others still gave nothing. At the same time one of the young ladies walked around the tables and handed out pamphlets relating to the faith of the Salvation Army. The group was about to leave the pub as I plucked up enough courage to ask the lady with the pamphlets how I could learn more about the faith of the Salvation Army.

She didn't seem to be surprised, she told me to come to the divisions headquarter, there I could inform myself about the Salvos regular church services, teachings of faith, youth events, as well as band and other activities. Frankly speaking, it wasn't the faith that I was interested in; it was merely the curiosity to know how these people function and what made them the way they are.

Over a period of a couple of months, during a couple of hours per week I took the opportunity to visit the Salvo's at the divisional headquarter in Zürich, where I was allowed to take part in information evenings, learning about the faith in Jesus Christ. When I mention the word Salvo's, I am not talking about them in a disrespectful manner; on the contrary, I have a lot of respect for them and support their endeavors. During this time, I got to meet a few of the Salvo's officers, some of them elderly, and others were young and a little more open to a discussion other than religion.

I learned that the faith of the Salvationists is often described as the mainstream of the Christian faith. The eleven doctrines form the basis of the believe and teaching of the Salvation Army, some of them I understand clearly, with others I have some difficulties in believing and the sharing of the same opinion.

As a protestant I am aware that there are different bibles: the new testament, the book of the psalms, the old testament, the book Moses, the King-James-Bible, the Koran, letter from Paulus, the gospel Matthews, the catholic bible, the three parts of the Tanach, which explains the traditional and the modus vivendi, the philosophy and cultures of the Jewish people, as well as others, I also know that religions different from mine are being practiced in this world, and I am of the opinion that all of them have their legitimacy in their own right.

The picture of god as it was taught to me by the Salvo's, I have difficulties to accept, but I do believe that there is a mightiness in our universe that is in charge of everything, something superior that controls and directs nature, and that we are part of this impingement.

The trinity (the father, the son, the holy spirit); Officer Claude, one of the elder in this particular Salvation Army group tried very hard to explain to me the notion of trinity, the more he was trying, the less sense I was able to make out of his illustration. Still today, I don't understand the notion of trinity, no one thus far has been able to enlighten me on the subject matter.

Ray Pritchard has written that "if you do not believe in the doctrine of Trinity, that is, if you have come to settle conclusion that the doctrine of Trinity is not true, you are not a Christian at all. You are in fact a heretic. Those words may sound harsh, but they represent the judgment of the Christian church across the centuries.

"What is the Trinity? Christians in every land unite in proclaiming that god eternally exists as Father, Son and the Holy Spirit. Those who deny that truth place themselves outside the pale of Christian orthodoxy.

"Having said that, I admit that no one fully understands it. It is a mystery and a paradox. Yet I believe it is true."

Pritchard says that he can think of at least three reasons for believing in the Trinity:

1) The bible teaches this doctrine.
2) Christians everywhere have always believed it.
3) No other explanation makes sense.

I don't want to comment on Pritchard's reasons for believing in the Trinity, I don't understand his reasoning either and I am of the opinion that it is very arrogant to state that anyone not believing something that they do not understand is a no believer.

Jesus Christ is Devine and human; so, I was told, and I understood that he was human, demonstrating Devine abilities.

Sin from the beginning of time; Officer Rebecca enlightened me on the subject of the Garden of Eden, and how the Sin was begun by Eve and Adam, and how they were expelled from this paradise.

The atoning work of Jesus; I understood that Jesus was on earth to recompense for the Sin of man.

Repentance for Salvation; as I gathered from Officer Claude, man has to show remorse for his Sin, that each person that turns to God in genuine repentance and faith will be saved.

Justification by faith; if the relationship between God and Man has been tarnished through Mans Sin, the teaching of justification conveys what has to happen between God and Man to sort out the problem between them, to re-establish the trust.

A continuing faith; Faith is a substance of things hoped for, evidence of things not seen, a prerequisite of hope and love, in a sense, faith is to believe in something and a requirement to possess other things, to trust in something, to believe, to have confidence, to hope and to show loyalty.

Holiness; Holiness is a work of gradual development, it is carried on under many hindrances, hence the frequent admonitions to watchfulness, prayer and perseverance.

Eternal reward or punishment; According to the biblical truth there are only two destinies for the immortal soul; heaven being the place of eternal bliss for all that receive Jesus Christ, and hell is the place for eternal torment reserved for those who fail to accept Jesus Christ. As for myself; the only thing on this earth that is eternal is death; the moment when we stop breathing, the time when the body begins its process of decay, the moment the mind has ceased to function, the moment where there is nothing but emptiness, nothing at all, just like a full anesthetic that lasts forever.

To provide man with a place for Christian fellowship where they can grow spiritually, to be spiritual leaders within their family, to encourage involvement in the serving of the local community, worship to God, allowing us to freely learn and explore the Christian faith and its principles in a conducive environment—this was Officer Claude's message to me.

Even though I have never read the bible entirely, I think that I have understood, in principle what Officer Claude and his colleagues have endeavored to teach me; the creation of earth; day and night, heaven, land and water, plants and animals of the sea, birds and man.

I don't know why this experience with the Salvo's had such an impact on me, I am astonished that I even remember it, that alone to write about it, for some reason or another I can still visualize these moments in some detail.

However, the bible to me is a wonderful story, teaching us about the modus vivendi, the good and the bad, the principles by which we should live, the totality of life. I don't mean this in a disrespectful manner; the teaching about the good and the bad, the fear of god, anxiety of repentance for our sins, the notion of god seeing and knowing everything, the devil and purgatory, all of these notions have kept most of us in a straight line for centuries – but over time, generation after generation, this believe has become diluted, and it seems that today for many Christians much of the believe is being pushed very much into the background, for many the smart mobile, the intelligent phone has become far more important, a tool that many couldn't imagine life without.

Having met the Salvo's, having been allowed to learn about their particular religious orientation and the activities that they get involved with have enriched my being, their influence caught up with me later in my life time and time again.

# Early 1971, Heading for Australia

The last day of the MS Achille Lauro, a passenger ship 193 meters long, 25 meters wide with 572 passengers and 408 crew on board when she was cruising 125 miles off the coast of Somalia on November 30, 1994, a fire started in the rear of the engine compartment which despite extensive efforts by the crew could not be brought under control, because the shutters were closed the fire was expanding rapidly, threatened to take hold of the entire ship. Eventually the captain was forced to evacuate all passengers and crew.

Subsequently the live savings boats were put into service. During this process three people died tragically, one of them as he stepped on the live boat, he suffered a heart attack.

Ships that were sailing in the vicinity had arrived on the scene to assist with the saving of passengers and crew, among them the marine boats USS Halliburton, USS Gettysburg and the Tanker Hawaiian.

In 1946 MS Achille Lauro was "sailing" for the Rotterdamsche Lloyd as Willem Ruys from the slip, and in January 1965 she started to operate for the Italian Lauro-Line. The ship became famous during 7 October 1985 when she was kidnapped whilst on a twelve-day Mediterranean cruise with an Italian and Portuguese crew from Alexandria to Port Said Northeast Egypt.

The abduction of the MS Achille Lauro was executed by four Palestine tourists whom threatened to kill passengers on board, starting with US citizens, in the event that Israel did not free some 50 prisoners of the terror labelled Palestine's, they were imminent to blow up the ship if someone endeavored the rescue of the passengers, the Captain was ordered by the terrorists to steer toward Port Tartus in Syria, but the Syria authorities failed to give permission to let the Lauro into the harbor, and so did the authorities of Cyprus who was the terrorists second choice, finally Achille Lauro steered toward Port Said. The terrorist was given a guarantee to clear the ship and disappear without any problems, providing they did not further harm anybody. Earlier, a US

American citizen was killed, the terrorists ordered some of the crew members to throw the body over board (the 69-year-old Leon Klinghoffer of Jewish descent)

The reason for my following news reports of the Achille Lauro that appeared from time to time on TV as well as in the printed media is simple; in the spring of 1971, I embarked this passenger ship in Genova together with around 900 other passengers and spend around six weeks on this grand lady.

At the tender age between thirteen and fourteen, my childhood friend Ernest and I were forging plans to immigrate either to the States, or indeed to Australia. This childhood dream started to take shape at the time when I was studying at the SLS to become an airline pilot. Together with one of my trainee colleagues Hans Peter whom was a year ahead of me we concluded the forging of my childhood plan, to visit Australia, we began to make tangible plans to prepare the journey. In principle, the idea was to take a year out after the completion of our pilots training, make our way to the continent down under, touring the country, trying to get some jobs here and there to supplement our lean budget, visiting as many places as possible without having any particular preference.

In particular I was fascinated by the history of this vast country, the history about Captain James Cook who reached the east coast of Australia in April 1770 when he and his newly discovered land New South Wales, the manner in which the Aborigines—the native inhabitants—treated, the way many of them were slaughtered upon his arrival, others driven into the center of the continent, and others still were made to slaves, a compelling story that haunts the Australian society still today, the rugged, unspoiled outback, the gold rush days that were focused on the areas of New South Wales and Victoria from 1851 into the 1860s, in particular in the areas of Beechworth, Castlemaine, Daylesford, Ballarat and Bendigo, the time when the first Chinese arrived as indentured laborers on the continent, the down to earth population that urbanized the coastal areas, a country of opportunity where dreams could still be realized.

## Boarding the Achille Lauro in Genova

After I had a little farewell celebration with dad and Aunt and some of my closest friends, I boarded the train to Genova via Milano at 10:00 in the morning, to arrive at the Port of Genova around 17:00. I booked a room in one of the smaller hotels in the city center where I was to stay the night.

Without our knowledge, the hotel management had taken care to assemble the singles from Switzerland that arrived that evening on the same dinner table; John, a fellow in his early twenties, just completed his masters in the science of mathematics, Willy, who had completed his apprenticeship as a piano maker, Jörg, he had a bachelor of psychology, Christine, a young French lady from the Alsace regent whom had recently completed a Bachelor program at the Ecole Hôtelière de Lausanne, and myself, as newly fletched commercial pilot found ourselves tossed together at the dinner table. Although our backgrounds were fundamentally different, all of us had enjoyed a good education, we were young, intelligent, open-minded, unencumbered without preconceived ideas about the future, and inquisitive for adventure; we were heading for the country down under, each of us with our own cocky dreams and ambitions in our baggage.

After the introduction around the table, I felt comfortable with the people around me, John, Willy, Jörg, Christine and I had very quickly developed a very close relationship, a true friendship, excepting each one of them unconditionally for what and whom they were, I don't recall any negative or subliminal comment or behavior toward each other at any time, it seemed that we were inseparable, as if we were made of the one composite.

As an airline pilot to be it might have been inevitable that I would make my way to Australia by aircraft, With Swissair from ZRH to LHR, with British from LHR to KUL, on to HKG and from there down to SYD would have been an option that was considerably cheaper compared with the sea journey that I chose.

The next day we were taken to the boarding area at the Port of Genova, for the first time I got a glimpse of this middle-aged lady, she laid there very graciously, ready to take some nine hundred passengers on board.

Just above the red antifouling line the hull was painted in a lovely sky-blue color, based on the bull eyes three decks could be identified in this part of the hull, from the main deck onward the exterior was painted white, only the two chimneys that rose high above the superstructure were painted in the same blue as the hull, each carrying a large white star on either side.

The main deck was taken up with economy cabins, the one assigned to me was forward on the port side; one of the few that had a couple of bull eyes on the side and one facing the front, my view was not limited to the side, I also had a lovely view to the bow of the ship.

Dining and entertainment areas were located on the second upper deck, with the exception of the forward area – this section contained the first-class passenger facilities which we weren't allowed to visit.

At the third upper deck rear area the pool for the economy class was situated, and again, the forward area was closed off for the first class.

The Bridge, the communications office, the chart room, other technical facilities and the captains' quarters were situated on the fourth upper deck.

The boarding was exciting, it took quite a while but I didn't mind the wait, slowly approaching this gigantic lady was like the kid standing in a rather long queue in front of the candy shop, watching the kids in front how they seem to take forever to make their choice, then dragging their feet to get the hell out of the shop to make space for others, but this long wait was also an opportunity to absorb a lot of details about the exterior of the ship, a moment to delight in the smell of the sea air which created a fantastic ambiance, a magic moment that I will never forget.

When we finally got on board, we were assigned to one of the stewards, he put aside our luggage that was going to the hold, he then showed us to our cabins which had been reserved for the Swiss entourage in consecutive order, immediately next to each other, by chance or deliberately, I don't know. My cabin was located on the main deck, Backboard, at the very front with one of the portholes facing to the left, the other to the front, the single cabin that I had booked was actually large enough for two, it appeared to be comfortable, it featured a 160cm wide bed, plenty of stowing space, a writing table and chair, and most importantly a compact but very comfortable bathroom which included a shower. My mates were a little jealous; John and Willy shared a cabin that was similar to mine, only that it had only one porthole and it featured a twin bank, Jörg had to share his cabin with another fellow and Christine shared a similar cabin with another lady, but it was a good feeling that our cabins were next to each other.

My culinary experience during the past twelve months was limited to simple, fast meals that I was able to prepare quickly on the two burner gas stove that we had at the flat, the range of food was limited to pasta with lots of cheese, sometime accompanied by a couple of fried eggs, on other occasions my evening meal consisted of a can of Ravioli or Baked Beans with bacon, the flavor highlighted with a touch of crushed garlic, and the occasional instant soup created by Knorr—the distinct commercial flavor ameliorated by adding plenty of fresh butter flakes—my culinary repertoire reminded me of my childhood, the time when I was alone with my father, and from time to time my flat mate had brought me something that her mum had prepared on the weekend, and now, finally I was able to take a seat in the dining room of the cruise ship Achille Lauro, enjoying Italian Cuisine.

Because the dining room on the Achille Lauro was limited in size, all meals, Breakfast lunch and dinner was served in two sessions, all economy passengers were allocated to one of the two, and the little Swiss team had one of those large, round tables to ourselves, in a way this was fabulous, the disadvantage was that we didn't get to share the meal time with other passengers from other countries, and yet, as far as I could gather, none of us had any prejudice against people from other nations, the contrary was true, we were yearning for adventure.

Breakfast was always buffet style, there was a remarkable choice of cold meat cuts, different kinds of cheese, most of them of Italian descent, a selection of fresh sliced fruit, cereal, butter, a variety of jam, fresh bread and Italian baked specialties, Omelets, scrambled eggs, Baked Beans, grilled sausages and bacon, fruit juice, coffee and tea, the service at the Buffet was supported by several cooks, all of them looking very professional in their whites, most of them spoke English with an Italian, Spanish or Portuguese accent, and they were most obliged if you needed something special.

The lunch and dinner concept was in principle the same a hot appetizer was offered, comprising; Cannelloni with different types of fillings, a slice of some kind of Pizza, filled, baked Peppers, Crostini with some kind of topping, Ravioli on tomato sauce, fried Calamari, Spaghetti Napoli or some other kind of Pasta, or indeed, a fresh vegetable soup, there were always two appetizers to choose from, they were served on individual plates or bowls respectively.

The main embraced Pasta, prepared in all kinds of different Italian styles, accompanied with a wide range of meat, seafood or vegetable sauces and toppings, Meatballs, tomato sauce and Pasta or Polenta, different types of Lasagna, Fish from the grill was a standard choice on Fridays, Ossobuco, from the pork, Piccata Milanese, Risotto with sautéed mushrooms, Italian style Chicken, similar to a Ragout with lots of tomato and olives, or indeed a simple Roast, are some of the dishes that I remember in particular. For the main course there was no choice, but it didn't matter; everything that was put on the table was simple, its preparation was authentic and presented in a very appetizing manner just as you would expect it from an Italian Bourgeoise cuisine. The main dishes were presented and served on large platters that were placed in the middle of the table for everybody to serve themselves.

The choice of dessert was modest, canned fruit salad, different cream-based desserts, Panna Cotta, Tortes, Fruit Tarts and Ice Cream were part of the repertoire.

During the entire trip I never craved for food other than what had been served, on each of the days during the six weeks that I spend on board the Achille Lauro my appetizer choice was Spaghetti Napoli with lots of grated Parmesan à discrétion, followed by whatever had been prepared on the day.

Around 14:00 we could hear the start-up of the diesel engines, one after the other, at the same time the gray smoke began to escape from the smokestacks, the boarding and supply bridges were removed, the ship was moved forward to loosen the rather thick steel cables that secured the vessel on the pier, cables one and three were then removed from the huge bollards anchored firmly in the dock, once sufficient slack had been achieved cables four, five and six were removed and finally cables two and four were removed and winched on board; it is in this sequence that I recall the de-docking procedure.

Simultaneously, on the Starboard side a couple of tugs connected to the Achille Lauro through steel cables had begun to gently move the ship away from the pier, so that the big lady could be maneuvered into the correct position to independently leave the harbor. There was hardly a vacant position along the railing, I think just about every passenger on board had taken up a place to watch the ship pulling away from the dock, waving Goodbye to either somebody, perhaps members of the family, friends or merely saying farewell to the continent, as did we, the Swiss-French connection, none of us had family or friends to wave to.

I said goodbye, not knowing when I would see my folk again, I had left my country without having had the opportunity to truly getting acquainted with it; during my childhood I travelled a lot with dad and aunt, mostly through the neighboring France, Spain, Great Brittan and Scotland, my knowledge about Switzerland was limited to its history, the few places that I had travelled to as a result of my childhood fate, and the consultation of the charts when I was planning a flight during my PPL training.

The harbor of Genova, indeed the coast line got smaller as the Achille Lauro slowly moved further away.

Later in the afternoon, over the PR system we were notified by the crew that we could expect to hear the ships siren within the coming hour which would indicate an emergency evacuation, and that in the preparation of this exercise we had to go to our cabin to study the plan that was displayed on the inside of each cabin door, large enough to be seen, even by someone suffering from long-sightedness, to grab our life jacket and then, the moment the Siren was sounding, to make our way to the relevant meeting point.

The emergency procedure instruction in my cabin, indeed in all cabins was very simple to understand, written in four languages including English, at a glance it was clear where the life jackets were stowed, the graphics were easy to follow, the same was true for the corridors, the emergency path was unmistakably, clearly labelled right up to the point of assembly.

From my cabin I simulated the evacuation plan well before the actual alarm, grabbing my life jacket, putting it over my head, tying the cords in front, leaving the cabin, holding on to the side rail on my right, counting the number of steps to the next cabin, noting the number of cabins that I had to pass before I had to take a right turn which was leading to the heavy emergency steel door, taking note about the large handle position, noting on which side the door was hinged, identifying the manner in which direction to turn the handle to open the door, realizing that the door was opening to the outside, noting the 15 cm high step over which I had to pass to reached the point of assembly.

At some point during the embarkation process, as I was standing in front of this grand lady, it had occurred to me that a moment of emergency was perhaps unlikely to become reality, but it was certainly not impossible, so I had embedded this escape route in my memory so that I could take it, regardless if there was no light, perhaps if the corridor was filled with smoke or at worst case if water had started to flood this level, it crossed my mind that if the latter was the case it would probably be a little late, it would probably not have been possible to open the emergency door outward.

My awareness of security was not limited to the way from my cabin to the assembly area; I made sure that I was aware of the emergency exits of all the other zones wherever I was, without being paranoid about it.

Having left Genova, we more or less followed the coastline until abeam Ile du Levant in the South of France, at which point we continued to cruise further to the South West toward the center of the Mediterranean See, leaving the Eastern tip of Menorca, Mallorca, and the Eastern tip of Caló des Mort on our Star Board side down to abeam the Southern tip of Spain at Morrón de los Genoverses where the course altered again, this time heading directly toward the passage of Gibraltar, the water stretch where the two continents nearly come to touch each other, a mere twenty kilometers separate the Southern point of Spain from the Northern part of Morocco on the West tip of Africa.

Already abeam Gibraltar I felt that the size of the waves began to increase, as we moved through the passage the prevalence of the water pounding on the bow had become more frequent and the water that was splashing up had become higher and more intense, blasting a fine mist of sea water around the ship.

Cruising through the Mediterranean was a gentle introduction to those that had never been to sea, getting used to move about in an environment where your liberty is severely limited, whatever I had been accustomed to before has changed the moment I stepped on the Achille Lauro; I was not sleeping in my own bed, as I laid there my body was being swayed about, I could feel the gentle vibration caused by the two enormous diesel motors, I was captured by the monotonous rumbling of the engines, I had become aware of the air stream caused by the ship moving along in the water and the scent of the salty sea air kept hanging around in the atmosphere, if you didn't get yourself ready in time to attend the breakfast session, it was over, you then had to content yourself with a packet of Chips that you could buy in the bar, and much the same was true for lunch and dinner, if you failed to be there on time, it was over.

Though very good, the food was not the same as I had been used to from home, had I not appreciated Italian style food I would have had a problem because that was what you got for the next six weeks.

I had to accept that the daily routine that I was accustomed to until now laid in the past; no longer did I attend the aviation college, no longer was I able to enjoy the sometimes emotionally charged debates with my mate that I shared the apartment with in Zürich, I couldn't take dad's dog for walkies along the river anymore, every day for as long as I cared I stayed up I got to see the same faces, providing the feeling is mutual, I was able to choose with whom I spend time with and whom I would rather not be together with.

The places where I could go to were limited to; my cabin, the dining room where I had an appointment with the same faces for every meal session, every day, the theatre where different movies were shown and from time to time we could enjoy a life band, the different lounges that offered different activities, some were equipped with different games of different levels of sophistication, others were thought for those that merely wanted to laze around in a pleasant surrounding; when I went to the library around the same time of the day I would mostly meet the same people snooping around for something to read, people that had already assumed a little more responsibility in life, the older ones and if you took note of what they had chosen to read you were able to discover something about their personality.

I could go to one of the bars, mostly I would find the same faces, in the fitness rooms I did come across those that genuinely wanted to either get or keep fit as well as those that thought that they would do their body a favor after a heavy night, then there were the sundecks with its pool, an area where the same folk reserved their deck chair on sunny days around the same time by depositing a personal item on the chair whilst they were in the dining room enjoying their breakfast, or you could simply stroll around the decks only to see much the same faces every time, and if I felt like talking to my family or one of my friends, the only form of communication available on board ship was a telegram, so I decided to renounce this kind of thought and got used to my new life style, embracing the assortment of the different activities, take part in the things that I found enjoyment in, I began to relax and focus on the delightful moments that life on board surprised me with.

The crossing of the Mediterranean was also an opportunity to get to know more about the characteristics of each individual from the Swiss / Alsace connection; to me Christine was the sister that I had often secretly wished for, John, Willy and Jörg the brothers that I never had, together we were just like the family that I had dreamed of as a kid, it seemed that jointly we were a sophisticated bunch, an indescribably beautiful compound sustained our relationship, among ourselves we could talk about anything at all in an honest, uncomplicated way without having to fear to be misunderstood, in collusion we were funny, even witty, ready to thieve horses, our alliance had molded us to an inseparable team within a very short time as if we had known each other ever since.

Particularly fascinating was to observe the different characters of each, to ponder over what events and experiences in life had molded their personality, the differences in opinion that each one of them carried in their baggage, presumably influenced through their professional background as well.

## The Five of Us

Willy came from a working class background, his arguments about some philosophical discussion weren't as structured as were those from Jörg whom grew up in a family of academics, I assume that the difference in the level of education, together with the professional conditions that characterized the fellow whom had learned to tune pianos, for most of the time he would have worked on his own, not requiring a dialog or consultation with anyone but the instrument he was about to tune, whereas Christine was different again.

She too came from a working class background, her scope of education in comparison with the bachelor of psychology was also very different, she would have been used to work in an environment that was buzzing with people and a multitude of different activities most of the time, having to take care of different things at the same time, John coming from a family of medical doctors had just completed his masters, taking up a fellowship at the Melbourne University to do his doctorate, meticulously structured with whatever he did and said, he would make sure that his veggies, starch and protein would be equally divided during his meal so that at the very end there was sufficient of each to finish the dinner, and there was myself with a working class background; as a pilot I would describe myself as a technically influenced fellow, very much process-orientated.

Despite the mighty dissimilarity in our family backgrounds and the vast educational differences we appeared to suit, indeed complement each other very nicely, though I suspect that had we met by chance at a different time in a different location, in a place where our movements had not been restrictive like on the Achille Lauro, we may not have become the close friends that we were.

The journey from Genova to the end of the Gibraltar passage took around four days, for much of the 86 hours I had spent with my buddies, getting to know them better, finding out more about our private lives, beginning to understand what makes them tick, revealing our dreams and ambitions to each other, high-spirited was our behavior, keeping late nights, rather early mornings, sleeping for a couple of hours before we met for breakfast again, but after a couple of days I tried hard to install some sanity to my alcohol consumption that had become routine, finding a healthy balance between spending time with my mates, hard play, allocating a healthy portion of relaxation, time to deal with some of my favorite books that I had taken with me, and making sure that I had sufficient sleep.

One of the books that I had taken on board the Achille Lauro with me was written by Pierre Taillard de Jardin, Philosopher, born 01 May 1881 in the French town of Clermont-Ferrand, he died 10 April 1955 in New York; he was a French Jesuit, (a monk in the religious community, members of the Catholic Church), he had studied anthropology, the science of the human, (Paleontology, the science of the living thing, the science of the historical, geological environment for which fossils and bodily remains are the subject of research)

## Pierre Taillard De Jardin

In 1925 Taillard handed his manuscript which described the ancestry of man to his superior in Paris. At a later meeting his senior explained to Taillard that Rome had denied him the right to publish his paper, that the church refused to accept Taillard's views about the evolution of man, that his perception of the subject matter did not coincide with theirs, that the clergy refused to accept new findings coming from the Science of nature, although Taillard was endeavoring to explain both notions, the biblical and the scientific one in unison, trying to harmonize them. Despite Taillard's indisputable scientific findings, the church was of the opinion that he was trying to undermine the biblical faith.

After this particular meeting with his superior, Taillard concluded that many theologians refused his notion because it didn't fit their perception; he argued that you can't solve the problems from the Science of nature with biblical solutions, in response the church requested Taillard to publish his articles in scientific trade journals, and not to conclude theological Inferences which would be in conflict with the opinion of the church.

Taillard questioned this order and asked the church if he wasn't allowed to think about his findings about the evolution of man, he begged the question if now he was not allowed to think anymore.

The biblical narrative about the creation of Adam and Eve in the book of Genesis, together with the concept of the sin committed by the two; in my opinion is a spiritual interpretation about the evolution of man, none the less a lovely story that provided man with a framework of laws and rules by which we are able to live. Taillard, together with the National Geological Survey of China during the excavations discovered a Homo erectus skull known as the Peking man from which he was able to establish the dating of this discovery as a result of this he was able to ascertain that our ancestry can be traced back to the primates—the order of them includes lemurs, monkeys, and apes.

Taillard's denial of the biblical story about Adam and Eve as it is written in the book of Genesis – endeavoring to bring in harmony the bibles view that of his indisputable scientific findings of the evolution of man was very courageous, a notion that I find particularly interesting as it better fits my personal perception of the creation of man. This is not intended to be an insult to those that believe in the traditional Christian model of the evolution of man or indeed particular religious views of other religions.

On countless occasions Tail lard's findings about man's evolution provided exuberant material of discussion around the table on board, very emotional on occasion particularly in Christina and Jörg whom had grown up as Catholics.


## The Passage of Gibraltar

Now that we had nearly reached the end of the Gibraltar passage, the larger and more frequent waves caused the ship to behave more lively in the water, no longer did she gently pierce her bow through the water, the bow had now reached a more spirited up and down movement, the rolling from left to right and back again as well as the pitch had increased in frequency and intensity, all of these vivid movements announced a squeamish sensation to my stomach, a feeling that I wasn't so comfortable with, it gave the impression of having consumed too much alcohol, and this discomfort increased as we got closer to the point where the Mediterranean meats up with the gigantic Atlantic.

From Genova to Gibraltar the Achille Lauro had covered 961 Nautical Miles in four days, that's and average speed of 12 knots.

As we finally took course for the Canary Islands the Achille Lauro was exposed to the rough water of the Atlantic, we approached a series of waves about 10 meters high, the ship began what seemed to be a never-ending repetition of Pitching coupled with heaving motion. The extreme combined motions of pitching and heaving resulted in the forward part of the ship plunging into the sea surface after it encountered a wave, the bow slammed hard onto the surface as if the ship was about to dive into the water at a steep angle, the entire ship was vibrating as if it were about to break apart, at the same time she was banking at an extreme angle on the Backboard, bouncing back to Starboard to an angle that was equally as extreme.

I was well aware that if you are stuck at sea in a heavy storm that it is not a good idea to orientate yourself on the horizon; apparently, gazing at a point on which you can orientate yourselves is not conducive to see sickness, it makes it worse.

For much of the time during which we tracked down the West coast of Africa, the bumpy ride in the Atlantic forced me to remain in my cabin, running between the bed and the toilet bowl. Lying in bed, facing forward, looking out of the front porthole seeing nothing but sky, then the roll to the Port side, the sky started to gradually disappear and now I could watch how the dark blue Atlantic came into the picture and when the ship had reached its lowest point I could see only water, the waves that had caused the ship to move about so heavily were about twelve meters high, one after the other hit the Bow, from time to time the Stern had been lifted out of the water sufficiently that you could hear high pitch sound of the prop turning considerably faster and at the same time a frightening shuttering went through the ship.

As we learned after the storm, part of the stabilizer system was not functioning, as a result we were exposed to extreme motion which only a proficient sailor could survive without being sick, though at the same time I was surprised to observe that most of the passengers were not affected by the rough weather.

I was astonished that my stomach didn't want to participate in this turbulent, wonderful show that nature provided and yet after my basic training I was taking some lessons in Aerobatics; the "Loop," which is a vertical circle entered from straight and erect level flight, "Immelmann"—a half looping followed by half a roll, the "Snap Roll," induced by a rapid pitch input followed by a rapid yaw input, were maneuvers that I was able to fly with a reasonable level of competency, perhaps I wouldn't have won a competition with my performance at the time, but it sure provided a valuable emotional and physical experience and it enriched my flying skills, however it didn't prepare my body for a six week sea journey through the Atlantic and the Pacific Ocean.

We were passing the island Santo Antao situated most Westerly of the Cabo Verde, the volcanic island groups of the North West coast of Africa, on the same degree of latitude as Saint-Luis, Senegal Port Side, and from there we tracked further in a South Easterly direction toward the island St. Helena, on to Cape Town, our first stop for this journey. For this second leg of our trip, from Gibraltar down to Cape Town we had travelled 5889 NM in 21 days, that's an average speed of 12 kts over the distance.

## Cape Town, and It's Apartheid

It was early morning, in the East the sun had just raised itself over the horizon as the Achille Lauro began its docking procedure at the Cape Town Warf, slowly getting close enough so that the ropes could be fastened at the bollards, a process that endured for nearly an hour. Many passengers had taken up position on the different decks of the Portside watching the spectacle, observing how this gigantic ship was approaching the land that probably most of us saw for the very first time, getting a first impression, breathing the early morning South African air, getting a glimpse of the place of which I had shaped a very particular image through information that I gathered from media reports and the diverse literature that we had read and discussed during my secondary school time in particular.

To me, the docking was interesting to watch, perhaps unlike other observers I was fascinated by the procedures that are inherent for this sequence of events that has to take place to secure a vessel to the dock, but suddenly my focus of interest had changed, the docking procedure had become insignificant, as I had scanned the dock line I saw two small toilet blocks which were probably intended to be used by the waterfront workers only, they were separated by about two meters and in front of each there was a large, white signboard mounted to a two meter high pole, with the black imprint; *BLACKS, COLOUREDS and ASIANS / ABANTSUNDU, KLEURLINGE EN ASIERS* and suitably for the other block *WHITES ONLY*.

Sure, at the secondary school we did read some stuff about South Africa, we also discussed the political system and debated how it might have been to live in such a society, I knew that the indigenous were forced to live separate to the white folk, but the moment I had discovered the toilet signage on the pier I realized that I had understood nothing about apartheid thus far, despite what I thought I knew I wasn't prepared for this, with my elbow I nudged Willy whom stood next to me on the railing, as if I was stunned I didn't say anything to him, I merely pointed in the direction of the sign, for a moment Willy had forgotten to close his mouth, he too alerted Jörg, Christine and John whom were on his side.

As a group, together with other folk from the ship we had booked a City Tour, for a few dollars each, a white, local tour guide accompanied us in the bus on this tour of discovery, surrounded by enormous curiosity and emotion as well as an odd feeling in my tummy I boarded the bus with my buddies, ensuring that I got a window seat because I wanted to capture this sorrowful sight as a future reference with my camera.

The instructions from our guide were loud and clear, after he had introduced himself to the group in his South African accent he bid us welcome to Cape Town and briefly told us what we could expect to experience during this four hour tour, explaining that we would drive through the City, have lunch at one of the oldest pubs in town, that we would get to see some of the outskirts, down to Camps Bay, and that we would make brief stops here and there, stressing that during these halts we were not allowed to wonder away from the group, a statement that wasn't very comforting to me.

From the Warf we drove in a North Westerly direction toward Green Point, down to Sea Point, past Bantry Bay, Clifton, on to Camps Bay where we made a brief stop on the beach side. I don't know if this was so on purpose, or if it was indeed ignorance on behalf of the Tour Operator, the bus had stopped in front of a rather large signboard on which I was able to read;

THE DIVISIONAL COUNCIL OF CAPE **WHITE AREA** by order Secretary / DIE AFDELINGSRAAD VAN DIE KAAP **BLANKE GEBIED**

And a few meters further down there was another sign:

**THIS BEACH IS FOR THE USE OF WHITE PERSONS ONLY.**

Distributed in regular intervals along the road side were wooden benches, painted in white and at the backrest, written in black you could read; **EUROPEANS / BLANKES** which meant that the native population was not allowed to take a seat to enjoy the lovely view of the beach and the sea.

I was astonished by what I had just seen, dumbfounded that something like this can actually still exist in the seventies, I began to realize that reading stuff from a textbook or a news report in some daily paper does not capture the true spirit of an incident, it doesn't provide you with the true picture, it can't exhibit the feelings and emotions that the event deserves, to understand what it means to live in apartheid you have to go there to see for yourself. I wasn't the only one trying to hide the tears that were rolling down my cheeks; many of us were deeply moved, and yet we had not personally experienced what it was like to be severely discriminated.

Preoccupied by these thoughts, we left the beach area and drove back toward Cape Town, signs of discrimination were to be seen on just about every street corner, the manner in which some of the indigenous folk looked at us as we drove passed was an indication of the relationship between black and white that prevailed in this place. The bus stopped at the corner of Buitengracht and Mechau streets, the guide reminded us to remain within the group, not to wander away from it, we were about to have lunch at one of Cape Town's oldest pubs, in 1964 the Firemen's Arms was established, its ambiance was that of an old English pub but for a long time it could only be patronized by white people—even at that time the pub was famous for its good food, beers and wines.

The menu was written with chalk on a blackboard, fried onion rings, pan-fried chicken livers, green salad and a soup were offered as starters, the mains consisted of crumbed Spicy Chicken with Rice, Bangers and Mash, Steak and Kidney Pie, Fish and Chips, Bacon and Eggs, Black Beans and Tomato, Steak and Egg served with green Peas and Chips, and the two dessert choices were a Chocolate Fudge Torte or Apple Crumble with Ice Cream.

The memories about food that I had from my travel through England weren't very exciting; I recall the steak and egg that I once ordered in a pub in London, the meat grilled to death, very well done, the egg was fried on both sides, it was more like a hard-boiled egg, it had nothing to do with a fried egg, the chips were not crisp, they were limp and soggy, and the peas were a frozen product, heated in boiling water, briefly strained and slapped on the plate together with a little chopped mint. With this kind of thought in mind I was very careful with what I was about to order, I ended up choosing something that I had enjoyed in England, fish and chips, having being told that fish was fresh and if the chips were a bit limp I wouldn't be upset, it kind of had to be this way.

I guess because I had travelled a lot with dad and Aunt, and the fact that Aunt was an excellent cook my expectations of food had become a little more sophisticated than the Steak and Egg that was served in some of the pubs at that time. The other thing that I hated about the British Pubs was the beer, served un-chilled—"warm," coming from Switzerland I appreciate a chilled beer.

After lunch we were assembled in front of the pub waiting for our bus, as I stood there with my mates my eyes crossed those of a native man on the other side of the road, he was watching our group, probably curious about what was going on; for a short moment we had stared into each other's eyes, I thought I could feel frustration and hate in his harsh, penetrating glare.

Under normal circumstances I would not have looked the other way, I would have challenged the other person visually, even in a provocative manner to find out whom is first to look away, probably it would not have been me, but in this case, under these circumstances it was appropriate to redirect my view and look away, an experience that touched me deeply.

As we were heading off, in the direction of the rural Durbanville, a province in the Western Cape, a rural suburb of Cape Town where wheat is cultivated, and in this region some of the oldest vine cultures have been growing—Diemersdal, Groot Phesantekraal, Meerendal, Nitida, Hillcrest and Altydgedacht are some of those wineries, that we learned about from driving past, unfortunately a visit was not possible for some reason or another.

On the way to Durbanville our bus was battling its way through the streets only sluggish, slow enough for us to see the things that perhaps we weren't supposed to see, driving past the post office I noted a large sign; *TELEGRAAFKANTOOR nie-blankes / TELEGRAPH OFFICE non-Europeans*, and a little further down the road at a taxi rank; *HUURMOTOR STAANPLEK VIR BLANKES / TAXI RANK FOR WHITES*, accordingly, the taxis were also appropriately labelled: **TAXI / WHITE PERSONS**, I didn't see any taxis that were designated for people other than white. As we moved further away from the center of Cape Town the bus had to stop at a crossing, on the roadside there was a very large sign that could be clearly read from as far as fifty or more meters away, I thought I had misread the message but it was true; *CAUTION BE AWARE OF NATIVES* was written on the sign.

On the way back from Durbanville we drove through Milnerton, on to the sea port.

The drive through Green Point, the lively beech of Sea Point, Bantry Bay, Clifton, the brief stop at the beach of Camps Bay, the lovely British atmosphere at the Firemen's Arms, the fish and chips made from fresh hake smothered in a lovely beer batter, fried golden brown together with the crisp chips, and the drive up to the vineyards of Durbanville, all of this was clouded by the rather sorrowful experience of the blatant signs of discrimination all over the place, a sight that has deeply embedded itself in my memory of my journey to Australia.

Realizing that my brief experience in Cape Town was inconclusive to make any kind of assessment, it was a mere fugitive glimpse at something that I didn't understand, I kept questioning why and how a country could reach such a state in the seventies, to understand the current situation in South Africa, one needs to understand the country before, during and after apartheid.

The first European settlers in South Africa were sponsored by the Dutch East India Company which controlled the Nederland's trade between India and East Asia.

Their settlement in the Cape in 1652 provided fresh food supplies for ships sailing to the East, but some twenty years later they wanted to start to grow the food themselves and began to move inland, they had decided to become permanent settlers and farmers of vegetables, wheat and grapes for wine.

In order to acquire land for farming the Dutch settlers attacked the **Khoisan;** a popular name for the original inhabitants of most of the territory now known as South Africa. This is not an ethnic designation, but a linguistic one. These are who the Dutch settlers first encountered.

The Dutch settlers also needed to farm the land and as the local Khoi resisted them, they imported slaves from West Africa and Malaysia.

This was the beginning of the mixed-race community in the Cape. After 1700, some Dutch settlers moved away from the Cape in search for more land and became known as *trekboers*. The trekboers invaded more land that belonged to the Khoi and San; they stole cattle and livestock for their sustenance. As the Khoi and the San resisted the Boers, they fought many wars but lost many because the Boers were equipped with guns.

Eventually they retreated to mountain areas such as the Kgalagadi desert whilst the Nama moved to present day Namibia. Many Khoi and the San also died from European diseases like smallpox. The few Khoi people that remained in the Cape region were forced to work for the Boers as slaves.

Many of the Boers became prosperous from the slave labor before slavery was abolished in 1834.

In 1806 the Cape became a British colony after the Dutch lost a war and by 1820 the British settlers had grown to around 10,000 in numbers. The British settlers were encouraged to become sheep farmers, they were to produce wool for the British textile industry.

As Britain passed laws against the slave trade between 1807 and 1833, the British farmers and missionaries called for an end to the Boer slave system, it was their intention to gain the Boer farmers labor force, the British decided to start paying workers and as a result most of the Khoi and African slaves left the Boer farms to go and work for the British.

To consolidate their power, the British decided to build schools, English was made the official language and laws were introduced that allowed to govern the Cape colony.

The Boers refused to accept the British influence and left the Cape colony around 14,000 Boers had left the Cape between 1835 and 1845 under the umbrella of the "Great Trek." In time these groups formed new colonies called the Orange Free State and the South African Republic or Transvaal.

As the Boers moved further inland, they came into contact with the Nguni who they could not easily defeat. For 30 years the Boers and Nguni fought wars for land with no clear victor. In 1812 and 1818 the British fought the Xhosa for land along the Fish and Kei rivers. The British fought the Xhosa again in 1820 and 1853, wanting to gain additional land from them, but the Xhosa had become more difficult to defeat because they now also had gotten hold of guns, as a result many Xhosa people remained independent until the 1880s.

Until the 1870s many African states with South African remained independent and in control of their land. However, the discovery of diamonds in 1867 and gold in 1885 changed the attitude of the British and soon they wanted the whole of South Africa for themselves, they were stealing the natural resources that belonged to the native people.

After the success of the Afrikaner National Party in the national elections at the beginning of 1948 a series of laws were drafted, South Africans were classified into one of the four racial categories; white, black, colored, meaning mixed race, and Asians or Indian, and in 1949 mixed marriages were outlawed.

In 1953, amenities were segregated by law. Increasingly the blacks of South Africa were segregated into townships and Bantustans, independent "homelands" for Africans, they were required to carry documentation to work in South Africa and needed to leave after they were done.

Colored's who were eligible to vote were systematically disenfranchised, Indians and other Asians were not allowed to vote at all.

Between the end of WWII and the declaration of the republic in 1961 the internal politics were dominated by the division between conservative republican Afrikaners and liberal monarchist British whites.

Apartheid, an Afrikaans word meaning "separateness" had greater support among Afrikaners and less among British South Africans, on the 3rd February 1960, the British Prime Minister Harold Macmillan held his famous speech where he made the statement about the **wind of** change, this was during his one-month visit of Cape Town, it had become apparent that some countries would have left the Commonwealth in protest of an unrepentant South Africa.

On 31 May 1961, South Africa became a republic after a vote which was limited to whites, narrowly winning by 52,9% of the votes, with this, its citizens in South Africa, they had to choose between the South African or the British passport.

The end of the country's harsh, institutionalized system of racial segregation apartheid came to an end in the early 1990s in a series of steps that led to the formation of a democratic government in 1994, it appears to me that the term Apartheid has been abolished but the system has remained.

Just recently, on the news I was watching a report which stated that as of December 2011 to the beginning of 2019 approximately 3,811 white South African farmers have been killed in attacks by Native people, my spontaneous thought was; isn't it despicable? Yes, it is unacceptable.

The report didn't talk about how many Native people that were killed during the same period by the white farmers, nor did it justify why the young black kid was murdered by the white farmer because he has stolen a couple of sunflowers from his fields either—also despicable and indeed unacceptable.

It is clear that the situation in South Africa has gotten out of hand some time ago, steeling, attacks, raids, forays and murdering on both sides are caused by and are characteristic of hopelessness, desperation, frustration and mutual hate.

However, murdering each other cannot be the answer to this very complex problem, that has its roots back in 1652 when the first European settlers, the Dutch East India Company came to South Africa to begin and to control Nederland's trade between India and East Asia, with the import of slaves from West Africa and Malaysia, later when the Cape in 1806 became a British colony, in 1948 when a series of laws were drafted to classify South Africans into one of the four racial categories; White, Black, Colored, meaning Mixed Race, and Asians or Indian, the outlawing of mixed marriages in 1949, the segregation of amenities by law in 1953, and the segregation of the blacks into townships and Bantustans—apartheid was born and well alive.

I know that my conclusion is the result of the limited observations that I made during the few hours that I spend in Cape Town, mixed with strong emotions about great human injustice, together with undisputable historical events that I was able to gather from books at a later time as well as my personal experience that I have obtained during my five-year stay in PNG (Papua New Guinea) who has a similar history, understanding that my conclusion is not based upon a scientific research, nevertheless, having considered the relevant facts in an unemotional, rational manner I conclude that the root cause of South Africa's problem is the fact that white man has stolen the black man's land and his natural resources, and if this wasn't enough, white man has endeavored to destroy the black man, both physically and perhaps worse still, mentally.

From what the media is reporting it appears that the South African government is doing little to nothing to resolve its racial differences, doing nothing and hoping that the problem might go away? I doubt it, I suspect that it will get worse before it can get better, and yet I would have thought that the leading party ANC (African National Congress) was made from the right composite to begin a dialogue that will guide the two extremes toward common ground, or have they forgotten the dreams of their courageous leader—the great Nelson Mandela who left us on 5 December 2013.

Around 18:00 hours of that evening, the Achille Lauro slowly pulled away from its berth, heading toward the Cape Point where the Atlantic and the Indian Ocean merge, where the current from the South Atlantic makes a left turn to head up the African coast in a Northerly direction, where the current from the South Indian Ocean moves in a Southerly direction to make a left turn to drift

East toward Australia. The journey from Cape Town across to Perth was estimated at 5085 NM which would take around 18 days.

I clearly recall this great feeling of belonging which had little to do with nationality, Christine whom was of French descent belonged to our group as did all the rest of us, we eat together at the same time, we amused ourselves, sometimes as a group, other times alone, each one of us was able to peruse our own interests and time out from the gang without being judged or misunderstood.

After a time, our little Swiss-French group was well integrated on the Achille Lauro, free to take part in all the activities on board, or at least so I thought at the time.

It is true that we eat the same food in the same dining room as all the other passengers whom where predominantly from Italian, Greek, and Yugoslavian descent, together we shared some of the activities and games that were staged for passengers, we went to see the same movies, we enjoyed the same night life and we shared the same sundecks, pools and reception rooms, but just like the others, we did not mingle with other nationalities on board at all, I think language was one of the key difficulties.

Retrospectively, I must confess that the five of us behaved in a presumptuous manner, we were a little arrogant toward the rest of the passengers, we felt that we were the chosen ones that had enjoyed a good education, we were about to be the academics, the managers and the airline pilot of the future.

Despite the impression that most of them were working-class people It didn't occur to us that some of these other passengers might also have enjoyed higher education, that they too were worthy of respect, regardless of their level of education. We simply didn't know because we didn't bother to find out— so much for our superior behavior and our level of intelligence at the time.

# Arriving in Australia in 1971

The third leg of this journey was coming to a close, North of our course we could see Rottenest Island, to the South the tip of Garden Island was visible, and about twenty Km ahead of us laid the mouth of Swan River—the entrance to Fremantle harbor—during the past 18 days we had covered around 5085 Nautical Miles between Cape Town and Perth, though this was merely our first port of call in Australia, the Achille Lauro spend a mere six hours on the dock to refuel, to take on board additional supplies and it was an opportunity for the passengers to have a short break on solid land, to take the first steps on Australian soil, to get a first impression of the country, to feel the emotions of the first moments of having reached down-under, cross-referencing the perceived imagination with the reality.

As we were allowed to disembark the temperature was 28 degrees Celsius, bloody hot at that time, particularly for a fellow coming out of Switzerland, the time on solid ground was limited to a couple of hours, just enough time to take a couple of sniffs of this glorious place that I had been waiting to see for some years.

Perth, the Swan River Colony was founded in 1829 Captain James Stirling in 1827 as he sailed to the Swan River in the HMS Success, he was of the opinion that this area would be suitable for a settlement, hence he persuaded the British government to found a colony. The place (Perth) was named after the birth place of Sir George Murray who was British Secretary of State for the Colonies when the city was founded in 1829.

I was a mere 1720 Nautical Miles away from my final destination, Melbourne, six days away from getting to know what the "Ozzie's" are all about, watching the business men getting about in town in their black shoes, long, white socks up to their knees, shorts and a wide brimmed hat, seeing my first Aussie-Rules football or indeed a cricket match at the MCG—large enough to hold 100,000 spectators—enjoying my first Aussie meat-pie learning not to have its sauce dribble all over the front of my shirt, to see the members of the Bowling clubs all in white, to learn some of the pronunciation of the Ozzie slang, to enjoy my first icy cold Fosters on the beach, learning to drive on the wrong side of the road, all of this was soon within reach, the fourth leg of this journey from Perth to Melbourne was going to take six days.

Leaving Perth we were heading into the West, keeping that course for several miles until we were clear of the West coast of Western Australia, than turning onto a Southerly direction, once clear of the States South coast the Achille Lauro changed course to an Easterly direction, heading into the Great Australian Bight, past South Australia, abeam the Victorian Town Warrnambool we entered the Bass-Straight, sailing across to Cape Otway, the most Southerly point West of Melbourne, with King Island on our Starboard-side, eventually turning toward Melbourne's Port Philip Bay. A mile or so before Victory Bight, with Point Lonsdale lighthouse to the Port and Fort Nepean on the Starboard side we could see the pilot boat from the Melbourne Port Authority waiting for the Achille Lauro, ready to accompany us through the notorious Victory Bight, through Port Philip Bay to the Port Melbourne Piers.

I knew that I was going to be picked up by Hans Peter, my old school buddy from the SLS, he had arrived in Australia a year before me; back then he was my mentor, and again now I was counting to be able to look up to him, with his assistance to become established in Melbourne. With his girlfriend he was living in South Yarra in an old Victorian style house that he had rented together with another fellow that was flying for Ansett Airlines.

Disembarking was a slow process, once we got of the Achille Lauro, we were escorted into the baggage hall, it was a bit like being in a cattle yard during an auction, to the one side the luggage was neatly arranged by the stevedore, we had to move along the wooden railings looking for and identifying our baggage, then moving further toward the immigration officers where our documents were thoroughly checked until a couple of hours later, we were able to get into the arrival area.

The farewell from the Swiss / Alsace team was emotional but we knew that we would meet again soon, once each of us was established, for now our focus was on the people that were receiving us, guiding us through the beginning of a new life, and I wasn't disappointed when I eventually noticed my mate in the crowd, I was glad to see him again and appreciated to be welcomed in by someone familiar, someone that I could trust.

I was to share a house with Peter, another Swiss fellow whom was managing a restaurant in St. Kilda; the house was located in Brighton, on the main road, just across a narrow strip of beech. Peter was in his forties, appeared not to be too straight, there was something crooked about him but I couldn't point a stick at it, it was merely a sentiment that I had about him from the moment we met, with his girlfriend he lived in this rather large house in this rather sophisticated surrounding. I think he was not unhappy that someone was moving in, sharing the rent, and some of the work in the garden. For ages I tried to work out how on earth Hans Peter got to know this fellow; together, the two of them were like day and night, totally unsuitable as colleagues, I couldn't work out what common interests they could possibly share, but I appreciated to have a point of reference that was more or less reliable.

## At the Swiss Butcher's

At the Swiss Butcher's, on a Saturday afternoon I met Edith, a Swiss lady, married with a couple of small children, her husband Marcel was working on his doctorate in chemistry at the University of Melbourne, I was invited there on a regular basis in my spare time, I enjoyed mucking around with the kids, talking to Edith about everything and anything in life, but I didn't get to see much of Marcel, he was usually busy with his studies.

One Sunday, she invited me to a church meeting; I had to bring along a flower which I borrowed from someone's garden along the way, I was asked to place the flower, a purple hibiscus, on the mediator's table at the front of the room, and eventually it was to be my turn, the lady that mediated the meeting took my purple hibiscus in her hand, held it up in the air and with closed eyes began to talk about the person that brought this particular flour along.

At first she was talking about things that might have been interpreted as being general, things that could have fitted many other young men in the room, but suddenly she became very specific: "This flower comes from a young man, just recently arrived in Australia on a boat, hid didn't have a pleasant journey from overseas, most of the time he was ill, I also see that this man had a very tough childhood, he was traumatized by one of the family members, but I also see that he will be ok, he will soon be able to begin his dream job in Melbourne."

This was scary stuff, nobody that I had gotten to know in this short time since I arrived in Australia could have possibly known about my background, Edith was the only one that knew about my pilot's career that I was planning to start, but about my background she didn't know, we never talked about it. I joint Edith at the "free church" a couple of times after this session, I was intrigued but at the same time also sceptic and a little scared, I was glad when my free time on Sundays got to be scarce and finally, I stopped going to these sessions, though Edith's family and I remained good friends.

Religions in today's Australia are as diverse as you will find in many other parts of the world, however; in 1901, the government passed an act limiting immigration to those European descent in what came to be known as the White Australia Policy) this policy was widely used to encapsulate a set of historic policies that aimed to forbid people of non-European ethnic origin, especially Asians (primarily Chinese) and Pacific Islanders from immigrating to Australia, effectively limiting the immigration of practitioners of different faiths, ensuring that Christianity remained the religion of the overwhelming majority of Australians for the foreseeable future and indeed to the present day.

The first census that was conducted in 1911 showed that 96% of those that responded identifying themselves as Christians (Australian Bureau of statistics 2006). The tensions that came with the first fleet continued into the 1960s, job advertised vacancies occasionally included supplementary information, prescribing "Protestants preferred" or "Catholics need not apply."

In accordance with the Constitution of the Commonwealth of Australia signed into law in 1900, section 116 of this act provides that; the Commonwealth shall not make any law for establishing the free exercise of any religion, and no religious observance, or for prohibiting the free exercise of any religion, and no religious test shall be required as a qualification of any office or public trust under the Commonwealth, a sobering reality, which permits the so-called "free churches" to operate freely in Australia, as they do in many other parts of the world.

## Ladybug

My first car that I bought in Melbourne was a 1960 Fiat 600 which I acquired in the second week of my arrival, I bought it from Peter, the Swiss fellow that I was sharing the house with at the time, he told me that he wanted to buy a new car, I could have his Fiat at a very good price, assuring me that it was mechanically in good condition. Despite the fact that I personally witnessed that the car was a little difficult to start in the morning, despite the fact that most of the interior side paneling was missing, the window winding mechanism on the left side was defect which was a bit of a problem when it rained, the handbrake was not functioning, you were able to pull it into the full brake position but it didn't hold the vehicle on the smallest of slopes during a handbrake start, the rear seat was torn to bits to the point where only the supporting springs were held together by the frame, the blinkers worked occasionally, and on the floor left-hand side, you could see the road in parts.

The paintwork told the little Fiat's story; it had been exposed to the harsh conditions of Australia for a long time, without anybody caring for this poor thing. I truly should have known better, despite the fact that I had serious doubts about Peter's honesty; his sales skills convinced me to by this car, it was simply crying out—please buy me. Peter was managing a well-known restaurant in St. Kilda at the time, but as I learned a little later, he was a professional salesman, perhaps he was selling second hand cars; he was the kind of fellow that could have sold his grandmother, twice to the same person, on the same day.

At three hundred dollars the car was clearly a snap, I was in need of a car, I didn't have a lot of money, and here it was standing right before me, I would have been stupid not to buy it.

During the entire three weeks, I enjoyed the liberty that this little Fiat had given me, being able to drive to the places that I needed to go to, swishing around town, learning to drive on the wrong side of the road, getting to know Melbourne reasonably well, practicing the special right turn also known as a hook turn. This hook turn enables you to make a right turn in the inner city for selected intersections, you can't miss it, they are clearly indicated, signs with a large hook pointing to the right "Right Turn from Left Only." These turns were introduced so that trams can pass through the intersection without being delayed by cars waiting to turn right.

To prepare yourself for one of these special turns, approach and enter the intersection from as near as possible to the left, with your blinker set to the right. Now you move forward as far as possible to the centerline of the road you want to entre, keeping clear of the pedestrian lane, remain in this position until the traffic light on the road you are wanting to enter changes to green, then you complete the procedure by turning into the road.

When I started to drive in Melbourne you could still observe many drivers sticking their right arm out of the window, then above the roof of the car pointing to the left, a habit with the oldies that were used to drive cars that didn't have modern blinkers, they merely had an arrow that popped out from the central door support on either side of the car which were difficult to be seen by cars behind you, or not at all by the traffic on the opposite side. Melbourne is the only city in the world that has a hook turn procedure within its traffic system—this is special indeed.

Soon after the fiasco with my Fiat whom I had gotten very close to, Peter asked me if I would be interested in a part-time job at the restaurant that he was managing in St. Kilda, he was of the opinion that if I can prove to the finance company that I was working, I could get a loan to buy a decent car. I was a little pissed off that he emphasized the word **decent** when he talked about the car, it was now clear that he was fully aware of the mechanical shortfalls of the Fiat, and despite this assured me at the time that the car was in good mechanical condition. I wasn't angry with Peter for very long, I realized that I needed him for a while until I got truly started in Australia.

I accepted his job offer, and a couple of weeks later, low and behold, I drove a brand-new light blue Chrysler Valiant station wagon out of the car yard. Just like Peter had told me, getting a loan for a car was uncomplicated, the sales people from the garage were merely interested to know that I had a job, in fact any job, the fact that Peter accompanied me to buy the car was important, through the excellent reference that he supported me with, the approval of the loan was straight forward, perhaps he felt a little guilty—or he was genuinely interested in my well-being.

At that time people in Australia bought big cars, there was plenty of space all over the place, the city streets as well as the country roads were considerably wider compared with those in Europe, the price of fuel was so cheap and nobody cared about polluting the air, one didn't even talk about the environment and the greenies were considered a mere nuisance, it was said that they didn't know what they were talking about.

During the same period the Australian Government began a country wide campaign against littering; it was customary to rid yourself from any garbage that you had in your car, take away packaging and other rubbish was simply tossed out of the car whilst you were driving, it wasn't thought to be a good idea to clean up the BBQ place that you just left, you left it all for someone else to clean up.

Hence the campaign "don't rubbish Australia," a campaign that was fought on most radio and TV stations, educating the resident about public hygiene, how to dispose of your garbage to keep our country clean. And it worked; the campaign was able to convince the vast majority, even those hogs with the most atrocious attitudes toward nature, the countryside had become visibly cleaner within a year or so. It is apparent that people then understood and accepted the message about "don't rubbish Australia," if you care, the same slogan can be applied anywhere in the world, "don't rubbish Zürich" could be equally as effective today.

## John Smith

Monday 8 March 1971, I began training at the old international Essendon Airport, to maintain my flying proficiency I was doing some IFR training on an old Link-trainer that was used by the Australian Air force during the Second World War, in principle it was very similar to the one that I trained in at the SLS in Zürich, but this simulator was so antiquated, it had been conceived about twenty years earlier, the mechanical elements dominated the electronics. I spend more hours getting to know how this antiquity was functioning than actually practicing the procedures.

In preparation of my application with TAA I wanted to make sure that I was fully up-to-date and fluid with the execution of all IFR procedures and the local peculiarities in particular. John Smith, the instructor that operated the Link-trainer, a fellow in his sixties was a very experienced Aviator; he had flown sorties with the Allies against the Germans during WWII.

After one of the training sessions, I approached John, asking him if he could assist me with an application as co-pilot, together we assembled my resume, in as much I was no dummy, I was well aware how an application should be constructed and written, however John made some valuable suggestions about the style of the document, he was well versed about some of the content of the motivational elements that had to be embraced in the letter of application. During the entire time that I was training with John, he never revealed that he was flying for TAA.

Friday 26 March 1971, the interview process at Trans Australian Airlines (TAA) was scheduled for 08:30, the lady at the reception accompanied me to the board room where the interview team was waiting; Captain Cole Evans, the Chief Pilot of the company, also the leader of the panel, Tim Avery the HR manager, Fleet manager David Smith, John Goss Director of Flight Operations, Nevel Wilson the Training Manager responsible for internal training, formed part of the interview team.

At some point after the introduction CPT Cole smiled, asked me if I knew a fellow by the name of John Smith, I explained that I was currently working with John, practicing IFR procedures in the Link-trainer at the old Essendon Airport, I was left to assume that John Smith was working for TAA but nobody among the interview team committed themselves to an answer, nor was this the time to get bogged down with details that weren't relevant at the time. The day was clearly structured; the usual how do you do's, getting to know the people around the table, whom they are and what they are responsible for within the company, though it was somewhat daunting trying to guess the amount of professional knowledge and skill that was gathered around this table, the setting was designed in a very professional manner, structured and yet I felt very comfortable, the personal address was informal, on a first name basis as it was not unusual in Australia, but most of all, the fellows gathered here wanted to get to know this greenhorn who wanted to work as a pilot in their airline, understanding how he ticks, trying to find out if he fits into the TAA environment, wanting to know in great detail what he knows about flying.

The "crossfire" lasted around two hours, a session that is fastidious in itself, any of the members of the interview board, at random placed questions relating to the theoretical aspects of aviation, rules, laws, processes and procedures, questions pertaining to cockpit procedures during the specific phases of the flight, during the second part of the day I was checked out for my practical knowledge and skills, beginning with the aspects of the pre-flight planning, meteo, navigation, fuel, weight and balance calculations, alternate airport management in the event of an emergency, than I was checked out in the simulator, the setting up of the aircraft for an IFR flight from Melbourne's Tullamarine International to Sydney, a bird strike simulation in the number two engine and an en-route emergency situation, all designed to establish my personal ability to function within a team, to find out if my approach to different situations was structured, and to observe my behavior when I was getting poor or indeed incorrect instruction.

Throughout the day's activities, during the different checks and tests, I didn't hesitate to demonstrate my abilities, my skills and knowledge; I clearly radiated self-confidence, I wasn't presumptuous as if I knew everything but I was high spirited, even cocky, sure of myself.

It was a Monday, 5 April, five days before my father's birthday I started my training at Australian Airlines as a co-pilot.

## The First Flight on the DC-9-31, 1971

My flying career began on a narrow body Douglas DC-9-31, designed as a short to medium haul aircraft, it has a seating capacity for 127 passengers, depending on its configuration, 2 Pratt and Whitney turbo fan jets each with 16000 lbf output, with a cruising speed 485 kts-889 km/h, cruising altitude 35,000 ft-10,668 m, an operating range of 1421 NM-2632 Km, the empty weight 64675 lbs-29,336 kg, max take-off weight 121,000 lbs-54,885 kg, max landing weight 110,000 lbs-49,895 kg, for someone that hasn't flown a jet before—a reasonably complex aircraft with good flying characteristics.

I clearly recall my first commercial flight as the Co-pilot of a jet aircraft, how I stood before the mirror that morning, making sure that my hairstyling was just the way the hairdresser had arranged it the day before, one last look, ensuring that my shave was flawlessly clean, that my neck tie was perfectly bound and centered, making sure that the two bar Epaulettes were sitting correctly on my shoulders, ensuring that the Trans Australian Airlines wing chest plaque was fastened on my jacket just the way it should be, the LONGINES Pilots chronograph was secured correctly to my left arm, my Ray-Ban aviators slipped into the chest pocket in such a manner that it was clearly visible with the signature facing up, the pilots bag packed with all the relevant nav charts, manuals and computing tools, ready to be picked up on the way out, most of all—I was ready for it, I was feeling like I belonged to the coolest bunch of people on earth, wishing that my father could see me now.

At the airport, in the cockpit crew room I met up with Cpt David Smith, a cool fellow about twice my age, very calm and composed, I expected the atmosphere to be tense, but the contrary was the case, before our pre-flight briefing he invited me to relax for a moment with a cup of coffee and a couple of cigarettes. For this particular flight we were allocated the DC-9-30 VH-TJP, inaugurated as "Charles Kingsford-Smith," at that time a high-tech short haul Jet with an all-economy configuration of 105 passengers.

Cpt David took care of the aircraft walk around, then he held a briefing with the cabin crew, whereas I had begun with the setting up of the Aircraft; the APU (Ancillary Power Unit) was already running when I got on board, the ground engineer had started it around fifteen minutes prior, I set the lights, pre-setting the communications radios, the tower and the departure frequencies, obtaining current information from the NOTAM, setting the frequencies for the initial Nav stations, I set the local runway altimeter setting, QNH as required below the transition level, input the auto pilot data, set up the initial configuration in preparation for take-off, ready for the cross-check with the Captain.

Both, the load sheet and the fuel doc, had not arrived at that point Cpt David was leading through the pre-start-up checklist, here and there questioning, discussing the purpose of particular settings, me reading back the call, in detail he discussed the emergency procedure on take-off, ensuring that I was clear about the sequencing of events. Finally, the fuel doc had arrived, we were able to cross-reference and confirm the kerosene requirement and the actual quantity on board for this short-haul from Melbourne to Canberra.

The aircraft is equipped with three fuel tanks, a total capacity of 24.649 lbs. (11180.5 kg or 11.18t) with the main wing tanks each having a capacity of 9.286 lbs. and the center wing tank a capacity of 6.077 lbs., each of the fuel tanks equipped with two AC booster pumps installed and each of them capable to supply both engines at take-off power. Fuel cross-feed from either main tank or either engine is available on this aircraft, but it doesn't have a fuel transfer option. The DC start pump installed in the right main tank is used for the APU or the engine start in the event that AC power is not available. Considering the fuel capacity of 24.649 lbs., taking into account take-off weight, fuel burn during the different phases of the flight, cruise altitude, temperature and humidity, wind and anticipated LW, this aircraft has a range of 1500NM / 2.800km.

Considering the distance to YSBB, the wind direction from 333°, (wSpd dev. 39), Temp 2° (dev+2°), TAS 270 during the cruise phase, the speed settings for the climb and descent, GS 263, on Track 57° (WCA-8°) MH 37°, Dist. 253.8, ETE 57, we had ordered 10.000lb of fuel, allowing for the alternate plus twenty minutes of holding pattern if required, on our cross check the fuel document received corresponded to the quantities indicated on the gauges, now, with the load sheet on hand as well we were able to calculate V1, V2 and consequently the VR speed in the preparation of take-off. I had already consulted ATIS on 114.1 and noted all meteorological information, visibility, temperature / dewpoint, QNH, active runway, take-off and landing, Notams and closing remarks.

As per our schedule, prior to the take-off time at 06:30, the outside temperature was 17°Celsius, the humidity 56%, the runway visibility 1.6km, a north easterly wind at 15kts, around 28kmh, we could anticipate to be advised to the north-south runway 34 for our departure. The system showed that all the aircraft doors were locked, Cpt David had made the usual announcement to our passengers, the cabin crew was informed to prepare the aircraft for an immediate departure, the rotating beacon switched on to indicate to all service staff on the ground that we were ready to leave the gate, the ground crew confirmed that all service vehicles were clear of the aircraft, the bridge was about to be retracted, upon our request, the tower had given us clearance for push-back and start-up, just the way it should be, within our allocated slot time for an on-time departure, Captain was communicating directly with the tug driver for the release of the ground steering lock and the handbrake.

After the pushback, the tug had disconnected from the nosewheel, the driver indicated to the Captain that he was now clear of the aircraft, he was in his stand-by position in view of the Captain, waiting for the engines to be started.

In the preparation for the start of number one; on the central overhead panel are the controls for the APU located, showing that the system is operative, both switches were on EXT L&R off, indicating that it is supplying the electricity to the aircraft, to its right are the pneumatic controls supplying the air to the air conditioners as well as the air for the start of the engines. Further to the right are the controls for the air conditioning system which is shut off to start the engine because the APU cannot supply sufficient air to run both, the AC and the air supply required to start the engine at the same time, all of the air that the APU is producing is used to start the turbine, a standard procedure for basically every aircraft.

The right air conditioning unit is feeding the cabin, whereas the left system is partially feeding the cockpit as well as the cabin. To start number one; at the lower left side of the overhead is the ENG panel with its PUMP off / on, FUEL HEAT off / on L&R, the Pneumatic Pressure gauge, L&R Start off / on and the IGN OVRD, Pneumatics control, turn off the AC, open the start switch observe the rotation of the engine on center panel, at 18% of N2 rotation move the fuel lever up, watch the fuel flow around 800lb (no more than 1100lb), then scan to the engine temperature, not to overheat it, check the EGT exhaust temperature, no more than around 550, scan back down to the RPM, at 35% release the starter switch on the overhead ENG panel, the RPM is expected to climb to around 50% idle, and then you follow the same procedure to start number 2 engine.

On 121.7 MHz Melbourne Ground provided us with the clearance to taxi to runway 34, we were number six in line, before moving off, Captain wanted to do a crosscheck on the cabin pressure, the system had to be adjusted manually for the climb pressurization. As we had been instructed to taxi to holding point K, via taxiway A we went through some last cross-checks, as we got to be number two in line, we completed our before take-off checklist, we had now become number one.

Departure control on 129.4 MHz: "TN718 you are cleared to line-up."

Cpt: "Departure Control, TN718, lining-up," checking, making sure that there was no aircraft on final before turning our machine onto the tarmac, holding clear of the threshold, anticipating our clearance.

Very shortly after, "TN718, you are cleared for take-off, wind from 023 at 15kts"; "maintain heading, report at 1500ft."

Cpt: "Roger, TN718 is cleared for take-off, maintain heading, report one five zero zero."

I released the brake, moved the throttles forward.

Cpt: "Standard take-off thrust setting, EPR crosscheck ok."

Cpt: "80 knots" (V1, the speed at which we commit to take-off, or not in the event of a discrepancy).

Cpt: "Rotate," with a smooth movement I pulled up the nose of the aircraft to 18°, a couple of second later the lift-off followed, Cpt: "Gar up," monitoring engine performance instruments—I called "positive rate" and moved the gear up, I set the initial climb speed at V2 + 20 knots, and activated the autopilot. Cpt: "Autopilot engaged," as we passed through 1000 I reduced the pitch and pulled back the acceleration slightly, and called for "flaps up."

Cpt: "Retract flaps"—I called for "slats retract"—Cpt: "retract slats"—I called for "set climb power"—Cpt" "set climb power set" and called the clean maneuver speed—I confirmed "maintain clean maneuver speed" and called for the after take-off checklist—Cpt: "After take-off checklist complete."

A few minutes later, Cpt: "Melbourne Departure from TN718, established on one five zero zero"—"TN718, make a right turn, heading 046°, contact Melbourne en-route control on 127.2 MHz, goodbye." Cpt: "Melbourne Control from TN718, en-route from Melbourne to Canberra, just past 1500, abeam Elden Weir VOR, heading 046°"—"TN718 from Melbourne Control, good morning, you are cleared to 21 thousand, report TOD"—Cpt: "Roger, cleared to 21 thousand, will report TOD." As we reached cruise altitude, levelled off and adjusted the speed, through the intercom Cpt informed the cabin crew accordingly, on the PA he made an announcement to the passengers regarding the cruise conditions, and the expected weather upon arrival in Canberra.

It is the nature of a short haul flight that the moment you have completed the cruise configuration its nearly time to prepare for descent, but we had a brief moment to grab a coffee and discuss some particulars about the flight thus far. To keep us busy along our route we had a number of way point checks, Mansfield NDB on 284 Khz, Corryong NDB on 386 Khz, and shortly thereafter, a couple of NM before 67NM out from the Church Creek NDB 386Khz we had to report our approach to TOD and get our descent clearance no later than 67 NM out from the NDB that facilitates the holding pattern which we might be directed to in the event of some kind of traffic or other difficulties ahead of us.

We had gone through the preliminary checklist, consulted ATIS about the general approach conditions as well as the NOTAM; Runway in use 35, wind 350/12, RVR 1.600, clouds broken at 600ft, QNH 1019.1, the details of the VOR approach was discussed, the chart tucked safely on the yolk clip, the anticipated point of descent was 82 NM out from the Canberra VOR-DME 116.7 Khz which is positioned at the end of runway 35, the anticipated rate of descent had been calculated at idle power 280KIAS, anticipating the need for anti-icing in this configuration, to maintain a 3° descent profile our calculated descent was around **1890ft/min** down to the transition level, then to reduce the power to 170KIAS, or as instructed by approach, with the aim to reach Delta15 at 6000ft, to intercept the glidepath slope, the NAV radios were set for the ILS, slat and flap settings discussed, go-around procedure revised.

Cpt: "Melbourne Control from TN718, altitude 21 thousand, heading 046°, established top of descent"—"TN718 from Melbourne Control, roger, you are cleared to descent, maintain heading, report at 10 thousand"—Cpt: "Roger, we are cleared to descent, maintain 046°, report 10 thousand," Cpt called for the reduction of speed, reconfiguring the aircraft in the preparation of our descent, idle power with a 3° pitch, speed 280 kts, maintaining a 1890 ft/min rate of descent, me as the PF, Cpt as the PNF monitoring the instruments and the progress of our approach, making the calls as we passed through the different phases.

At that point, in the preparation of our descent Cpt adjusted the cabin pressure manually, setting the outflow valve indicator fully aft, indicating that the butterfly outflow valve is fully open to depressurize the aircraft as we descent. We were approaching the transition level, Cpt called, "Set area QNH"—I set the change in accordance with the data that I got earlier from the local ATIS "QNH 1019.1, set"—Cpt: "Melbourne Control from TN718, established 10 thousand"—"TN718 from Melbourne Control, roger, contact Canberra approach on 125.9, goodbye"—Cpt: "Canberra approach from TN718"—"good morning TN718, go-ahead."

Cpt: "IFR from Melbourne to Canberra, heading 046°, passing through 10 thousand"—"TN718 from Canberra approach, you are cleared to six thousand, QNH 1019.1, runway in use 035, maintain 170 kts, report Delta 15"—Cpt: "Roger, QNH 1019.1, runway in use 035, maintain 170 kts report Delta 15."

Cpt: "Canberra approach from TN718, established on six thousand"—"TN718 from Canberra approach, left turn to glide slope on 348°, continue approach, wind 350/10, report outer-marker"—Cpt: "roger, left turn to 348°, continue approach, wind 350/10, will report when established on the outer-marker."

Cpt called for the preliminary check—"seatbelt sign on"—"checked"—"cabin pressure"—"checked"—"hydraulic system" "checked"—"altimeter"—"checked"—"shoulder harness"—"on"—"cabin and flight attendant information"—"complete." Missed approach procedure discussed; MDA 3.5, full throttle, turn right—track 005° and climb to 5.000 or as directed by the ATC. In the event of Communication failure, squawk 7600 and adhere to the last instruction.

Cpt: "Ignition"—"both"—"gear down"—"gear down, three green"—"spoilers, light out"—"armed"—"flaps / slats"—"blue light"—"annunciator panel"—"checked"—"select flaps to 15°"—"flaps 15."

Cpt: "Canberra approach from TN718, established on the outer marker"—"TN718 from Canberra approach, roger, you are cleared to land runway 035, wind 352/12"—"roger, cleared to land runway 035, wind 352/12."

In accordance with the landing gross weight configuration chart our approach speed was to be 135 kts, Cpt made the call, "Flaps/slats setting 25°"—"flaps/slats 25°."

The orange light, together with the middle high-pitched sound indicated that we were now passing the middle marker, Cpt: "established on the middle marker"—"middle marker, glide slope clean"; Cpt: "speed 129 kts, flaps 40"—"speed 129 kts, flaps 40"—Cpt: "approaching MDA at 3250 ft, with 3.5 NM to go, runway in sight, landing"—"confirm, landing"—Cpt: "reduce to 125 kts, extend flaps to 50"—"125, extend to 50."

Cpt calling, "1 thousand"—"5 hundred"—"4 hundred"—"3 hundred"—"2 hundred"—"1 hundred"—"50"—"20"—"retard"—reading back "retard"—Cpt calling, "revers thrust"—reading back "revers thrust."

"TN718 from Canberra approach, on the ground at 07:52 next turn right, contact ground on 121.7, goodbye"—read back "121.7, goodbye."

Cpt called, "remove revers thrust, apply brakes"—call back "revers thrust removed, brakes applied"—Cpt: "anti-skid, off"—read back "anti-skid, off"—Cpt: "ice protection, off"—read back "ice protection, off"—Cpt: "ignition, off"—read back "ignition, off"—Cpt: "flaps, 15"—read back "flaps, 15"—Cpt: "radar and transponder, STBY"—read back "radar and transponder, STBY"—Cpt: "after landing checklist"—read back "completed."

"Canberra ground from TN718, good morning"—"Canberra ground, good morning, you are cleared to the apron, follow the follow me at Alpha"—read back "roger, will follow the follow me."

Once we had come to a holt at the parking bay, Cpt announced "ladies and gentleman, we have arrived at the gate, please remain seated until the seatbelt sign is turned off" "the current temperature is 11° Celsius" "on behalf of the crew, we thank you for flying TAA, we wish you a great day."

Then we began to prepare the aircraft for the 50-minute turn-around to Melbourne, Cpt called, "parking brake, set"—"parking brake, set"—Cpt: "electric system, set"—"electric system, set"—Cpt: "ice protection, set"—"ice protection, set"—Cpt: "fuel control leavers, off"—"fuel control leavers, off"—Cpt: "fuel pumps, off"—"fuel pumps, off"—Cpt: "air conditioning, set"—"air conditioning, set"—Cpt: "anti-collision lights, off"—"anti-collision lights, off"—Cpt: "flaps/slats, up/light out"—"flaps/slats, up/light out"—Cpt: "hydraulics pumps, off-hi-off"—"hydraulics pumps, off-hi-off"—Cpt: "emergency lights, off"—"emergency lights, off"—Cpt: "windshield heat, off"—"windshield heat, off"—Cpt: "electric system, set"—Cpt: "electric system, set"—"electric system, set"—Cpt: "battery switch, on"—"battery switch, on"—"parking checklist, complete."

The checklist is an account of meticulously documented events that take place during a flight cycle, beginning with the technical external "walk around" performed by one of the pilots, ensuring that there are no obvious damages that might influence the safety of the flight, to the setting up of the initial aircraft configuration, the safety and power on, originating / receiving, before start-up, after start-up, before take-off, after take-off, cruise, preliminary landing, landing, after landing, parking and securing the aircraft.

The pilot flying (PF) requests the Normal Checklist, and the pilot non flying (PNF) reads it. The actions asked for in the checklist are known as a "challenge and response" type actions. The PF "responds" to the "challenge" only after checking the current status of the aircraft. In the event that the configuration does not correspond to the required checklist response, the PF must take corrective action before giving a "response" to the "challenge," and if a corrective action is not possible, the PF must modify the response to represent the actual situation, and if necessary, the other crew member must crosscheck the suitability of this response.

The challenger (PNF) must wait for a response before continuing with the checklist. For "AS RQRD" items on the checklist, the response must be corresponding to the real condition or configuration of a system. After the reading of the checklist is completed, the PNF must declare "Checklist Completed."

The purpose of the standardized terminology and procedures is to reduce the pressure of in-flight planning, and it promotes clear communication and understanding among cockpit crew as they work through the different processes and procedures. The standard procedure checklist reduces the risk of unsafe practices, carelessness as well as the development of personalized procedures on the flight deck, the four-eye principle is ensuring that all important safety points have been accomplished correctly.

The McDonnell Douglas DC-9-30 were designed as a short-haul aircraft in the early sixties and achieved airworthiness certification on the 23$^{rd}$

November 1965, powered by two Pratt and Whitney JT8D turbofans mounted under the T-tail, rated at 14.500 lbf (64 kN) of thrust, providing a range of 1500 NM, fitted with a two-crew flight deck and a built-in airstairs. The series 30 was a stretched version of the series 10, seating 115 passengers in an all economy configuration, its take-off weight was limited to 110.000 lbs., the leading-edge slats improved take-off and landing performance considerably, compared to contemporary aircraft that are fitted with fly by wire technology, the DC-9-30 fitted with analogue electromechanical instrumentation with graphics display, Air Data Inertial Reference Unit (ADIRU) to align the aircraft position after power up of the unit, GPS, CDU screen and pads, glass cockpit and other fly by wire technology had not been designed at that time.

This generation of aircraft required a lot of intricate knowledge and experience to operate the different systems, mechanical functionality and settings, a lot of complex fiddling about and fine-tuning was required from time to time, any pilot that had the honor to fly the DC-9 at some point during his or her career will be able to tell you that she was a challenge to handle, that she demanded to be pampered, but she sure was fun to fly.

Though fly by wire was developed by General Dynamics, produced by Lockheed Martin, and first used for the F-16, trials took place and the first operational system was introduced in 1978, eventually the glass cockpit was replacing the conventional analogue electromechanical instrumentation with graphics displays, and the full glass system appeared 1988. Fly by wire was first used by the 777 Boeing to replace the conventional manual flight controls with its first flight in June of 1994.

During the early part of my career with Trans Australian Airlines from 1971 to 1986 when James Strong, our new CEO transformed TAA and rebuild the airline as Australian Airlines, I was regularly flying the DC-9-30 whom had been inaugurated as "Charles Kingsford-Smith." The DC9 received its airworthiness certification in November 1965, as TAA we were operating 12 of them, the VH-TJP, was ferried between 6 to 8 February 1970 from LBG-HNL-PPG-BNE-MEL, and inaugurated as "Charles Kingsford-Smith" and was in our service until 1986 when the aircraft was finally leased to Sunworld International Airlines USA, in 1988 the lease agreement was extended to Midway Airlines USA, during 1992 the aircraft was released to Ross Aviation USA, the following year she was leased to NASA USA in August 1993, registered as N650UG, and finally in July of 1989 this aircraft was leased to

*TAESA LINEAS AEREAS*, a Mexican company with its hub in MEX / MMMX. This company was founded in 1988 and ceased operation 21 February 2000; the aircraft crashed on 9 November 1999 shortly after take-off at UPN Uruapan General lgnacio Lopez Rayon.

TEASA XA-TKN725 (former DC-9-30 "Charles Kingsford-Smith" from TAA) a scheduled flight originating in Tijuana International Airport, terminating at the Mexico International Airport—with intermediate stopovers in Uruapan and Guadalajara, crashing shortly after its departure on 9 November 1999, killing its 18 passengers and crew. Apparently, the crash caused the company to ground all its aircraft, and operation was suspended one year later in 2000. The accident investigation team determined that the crash was the result of pilots having used the wrong checklist prior to their departure, and confusion and disorientation during the climb-out phase of the flight.

With the published production information data; the Manufacturer serial Number 47418, the line number 570, together with the production site at Long Beach (LGB), I was able to track the aircrafts career to its very end—the Aircraft Type McDonnell Douglas DC-9-30, Age 29.9, Airframe Status, Written Off.

**One** Boeing 727 and five Airbus **A300B4-203** also formed part of the TAA fleet; the first one A300B4-203, VH-TAA with its home base in Melbourne, Tullamarine, delivered in June 1981, and in March 1984 the aircraft was leased to the German company Condor. This wide body aircraft was designed, as a twin, capable to land with one single turbines in the event of an engine failure. This production version featured a center fuel tank for increased fuel capacity (47.500kg) and new wing-root Krüger flaps, a conventional but high-tech cockpit with lots of electronics, configured to 247 economy class passengers, with a MTOW of 165.000kg (363.763lb), a range of 2.900 to 4.050 NM, powered by two GE CF6-50C2 turbofans developing 230kN (52.000lbf), a cruise speed Mach 0.78 (450 kts / 833km/h) at FL 350.

In 1986 **Australian Airlines CEO** James Strong began with the acquisition of 32 B-737 (16 X **B737-300** / 16 **B737-400**), the first ones with analogue instrumentation, an FMS flight management system, which included electronic flight controls and navigation; some machines were retrofitted after July 1986 with Electronic Flight Instrument System MFD (glass cockpit) and later, after 1988 additional digital display options were added. The first of the B-737 that was delivered October 1986 was registered as VH-TAV in a 3-class configuration of 12/36/60, as a response to the growing demand for up-market business travel.

At the conclusion of my first day as a commercial airline pilot with TAA, together with Cpt David Smith I spend the entire day flying the DC-9-30 "Charles Kingsford-Smith," charged with emotion as I prepared for the initial setting up to the aircraft configuration in readiness for the flight, experiencing the excitement of the ignitions of the jet engines, the trill of the take-off, navigating the aircraft on its first leg from Melbourne, configuring the aircraft for its descent, feeling the suspense of the final approach, sensing how the tension vanished after the almost perfect touch-down at Canberra, experiencing the sensation of the shut-down of the systems and the debriefing with Cpt David Smith before preparing for the next sector, CBR to SYD, and from there the days operation continued with flights sectors from SYD to BNE, BNE to CNS, CNS to BNE, BNE back to our hub Melbourne.

I was longing to talk to my father, I wanted to tell him about the most wonderful day in my life thus far, beginning with my personal preparation in the morning, how it felt, knowing that today was going to be my first commercial flight as the Co-pilot of a jet aircraft, how I stood before the mirror, making sure that my hairstyling was just the way the hairdresser had arranged it the day before, ensuring that my shave was flawlessly clean, making sure that the amount of after shave felt refreshing but not dominating, assuring that my neck tie was perfectly bound and centered, making sure that the two bar Epaulettes were sitting correctly on my shoulders, taking care that the TAA wing chest plaque was fastened on my jacket just the way it should be, the LONGINES Pilots chronograph was secured correctly to my left arm, how my Ray-Ban Aviators slipped into the chest pocket in such a manner that the signature was facing up and clearly visible, the pilots bag packed the day before with all the relevant nav charts, manuals and computing tools, ready to be picked up on the way out, but most of all, how I was ready for it.

I was feeling like I belonged to the coolest bunch of people on earth, wishing that my father could see me now, how I was appropriately groomed for the day, how bloody smart I appeared in my uniform, proud of the two bars on my jacket, very much aware of how the pilot hat with the aviator's wings fitted perfectly on my head.

I wanted to tell my father about the exuberating experience, tell him every little detail about today's flight operation – I felt the need to tell him how much

I loved him, and how I recognized everything that he had done for me, I wanted him to know that I appreciated the relentless support that he gave me to realize my dreams, I wanted him to confirm that he was proud of my achievement's. I would also have appreciated if Aunt would have been able to discretely accompany me for the duration of this day, secretly wishing that she too would have been proud of me, despite the fact that during my teenage, from time to time she used to tell me that I was stupid.

I was wondering if Aunt would be capable of a positive acknowledgement of my achievement, or if she would contemptuously confirm that my achievement was merely all right, how desperately I wanted to believe that she would be able to demonstrate enthusiasm and excitement. On the other hand, my expectations about Aunt's thoughts and comments were very humble indeed, though still vividly remembering how Aunt treated me from the moment she shifted in with us to the point in time that I left the family home was still haunting me, I still felt hurt, the manner in which she used to torture me mentally, how, with her vicious tongue she used to belittle me, how she used to smirk at me with an apparent pleasure when she was interrogating me about some stupid thing that she insisted that I had done or broken even though I had nothing to do with the issue that she was talking about; I still carried a lot of anger and hate toward her in me.

Still, I recall clearly how as a teeny when I was suffering from Aunt's maliciousness way of handling me, the viciousness with which she used to talk to me most of the time, the ruthlessness of exploitation of my emotional innocents, and how she deprived me of at least part of an uncomplicated, happy youth, and yet I never told her that she had to take care of my fundamental needs, nor did I invite her to come and live with my father and myself, she simply turned up and began to broaden her personal sphere in my life without asking me how I felt, it wasn't her intrusion that bothered me as a kid, it was the manner in which she did it, unintelligent with ignorance and often with intense force and psychological violence, nor was Aunt capable of sharing her love with a child.

Though I believe that children are not bad by nature, their behavior might become peculiar, bizarre, perhaps downright bad if you tell the child often enough how stupid he is, if you try hard enough to show unjust behavior toward the child on a regular basis, you can be sure that the child will show rebellious behavior toward you, without a doubt, in time the child will learn to use every possible opportunity to muck about, he will test your nerves to the limit and take the piss out of you were ever he can, and I was no exception to the rule; in time I had figured out how Aunt is ticking, I made use of every opportunity to undermine her authority, deliberately mess around, knowing that she would be angered by my buggering about.

However, I also recall distinctly that on different occasions throughout my teenage there were moments where I felt immense irritation and resentment toward Aunt, and at the same time I perceived inner rage, I sensed feelings of anger toward my father for having married this horrid lady which I was asked to call mum. I also remember vividly the resentment that I felt toward Aunt, how much I had learned to hate her, and how I began to seriously forge tangible plans about how I was going to take personal revanche for having had to endure a lot of misery during my teenage, knowing that my conscious decision to create a return match would also adversely affect my father; already as a teeny I had decided that the moment that I would leave the family home I would deliberately isolate myself, shut myself off from Aunt and Dad with the intention to upset, in an endeavor that Aunt might reflect on the behavior that she chose to display toward me and eventually realize the reason for my silence.

Despite the enormous desire and the need to call my father after my first day as a commercial airline pilot with TAA, flying the DC-9-30 "Charles Kingsford-Smith," I was grappling with my consciousness, knowing that the making of this call would be the proper thing to do, but the feelings in my heart were dominant; not calling was part of my infantile teenage plot which I was pursuing, and so I didn't call, perhaps punishing Aunt, and hurting my father as well as myself at the same time. Retrospectively, my decision to take revanche in the way that I did at that time may have possibly turned out to be part of our fate later in our lives, setting the emotional landscape that was going to change actions and dealings between our relationship irrevocably.

# Summer of 1973

The summer of 1973, chief pilot, captain Cole Evans, my boss with whom I had had become good friends was telling me about the grazing property adjacent to his farm, apparently the quality of the soil was excellent, most of the two hundred acres were covered with Lucerne, a grass strain that needs a healthy soil, it sends its roots several feet into the ground, getting its water and nutrients from deeper areas compared to most other grass, which is ideal for the dry conditions that prevail during the Australian summer, the fences in very good order, a creek was running through the property assuring fresh water almost all year round, and it featured an old stone house, a barn and several in-ground water tanks. The farm was in Elphinstone, situated around one hundred Kilometers North West of Melbourne's Tullamarine Airport.

It was mid-summer, Cole invited me to stay with him and the family at his farm, both of us had a couple of days off at the same time, he was keen to show me his neighbors' property, I got the feeling that he would have appreciated me as the new fellow next door. Together with his family, Cole had bought their farm about fifteen years prior; with the assistance of another farmer colleague next door, he was breeding Aberdeen Angus cattle, his heard consisted of over one hundred heads, not counting the bull and the calves, and he was keeping a couple of hundred Marino sheep which he used for the production of high-class wool.

The couple of days that I spend country side with Cole and Elise were fabulous, on the job he was very professional, correct, but he kept people around him at a safe distance, he was the kind of boss that maintained his life outside of work hidden, the reality that he invited me into his private life revealed that he trusted me, getting to know something about Cole's personal life and his family was a privilege, and the beginning of a friendship that I treasure to this day.

For much of the first day that I spent at Cole's place, we were on the road, in his old HOLDEN Utility (Holden, made by General Motors Australia) exploring the village and its Surroundings, Elphinstone is situated on the crossing of the former Calder Highway between Malmsbury and Castlemaine, in the vicinity of the villages Taradale and Chewton, the village featured a primary school, a post office, a garage, a railway station, a milk bar, a local corner store were you could register your purchases in a book and settle your debt on pay day, and pub, a real pub.

At that time, all over Australia it was customary that only men were allowed in the public bar, women, families or men accompanied by women were served in a separate room next door; in the lounge, in smaller pubs there was a hole in the wall at navel's level, about 50X50 cm, just large enough to pass through an order of beverages or indeed something from the kitchen, for most people not high enough to see the fellow in the bar next door, to see his face you had to bend down, and as soon as you received your order the little door was shut, larger pubs had a lady looking after the lounge.

The pub wasn't simply the place to refresh yourself with a cold beer, at the same time it was a meeting place to discuss all kinds of issues, exchange ideas as well as a base to converse about and conduct any kind of business.

The Elphinstone pub, a lovely old Victorian style building, with its large veranda along the entire front, its corrugated iron roof concealed a particular interesting history, some of its background a little weird as the publican behind the bar was telling me; the building was constructed on a bluestone foundation in the 1860s, from that time until now (1973) the pub was managed by fifteen different licensees, in 1922 a public telephone and exchange were also accommodated in the building, the smaller parcels of land on the South East corner of the pub was used as the customers horse paddock, and as more and more guests were able to afford a motor car the horse paddock was converted to the parking lot, all of it interesting information about the history of this place, but the juicy bit he left till last, he continued "before the time of refrigeration, during the period where the cellar was used to store goods that kept better in a controlled, cool environment the beer barrels were stored down there, and if someone had passed away in the broader neighborhood, the bodies of deceased locals were brought here to be stored before the burial."

I raised my glass of fosters draft and told him, "an interesting business concept assuring customer loyalty, in this way you make sure that the mourning celebrations of the wake will be held in your pub, but I trust that my beer wasn't stored alongside a corps." He understood my bent sense of humor.

After our visit to the pub, we dilly-dallied through the surrounds of Elphinstone's terrain with its undulating hills and gently winding roads, with the exception of the main road most of them were dirt roads, with its typical flora and fauna, gum trees, blackberry hedges, the occasional koala, the gray kangaroo could be seen late evenings in particular, field rabbits, even hares were sited from time to time, and the brown snake, a fellow I preferred not to meet.

The village was home to barely two hundred people, other than the publican, the postie, the telephone exchange operator, the auto mechanic, a couple of school teachers, the lady that operated the milk bar, and some rail workers, everybody was involved in farming, in particular cattle and sheep were raised here, cropping was common and a four of five orchards were operating, producing apples and pears for which the area had earned a good name for itself.

The areas where horses and sheep were kept could easily be identified, even if there was not a horse to be seen on the property, their fencing contained no barb, whereas paddocks used for cattle generally were built with wooden poles with iron stabilizers in-between and both plain and barb wire were used in its construction.

From the two hundred acres of land that Cole was proposing to me, most of the paddocks were partitioned by dry stone walls as they are typically built throughout Great Brittan to separate fields and lanes of rural England, however, this particular wall was constructed by someone whom originated from Cornwall. Apparently, dry stone walling is dating back as far as the Iron Age, not only did they serve as field dividers, they also provided wind shelter for the animals within its boundaries.

From the dirt road leading to Cole's place, a smaller road was leading up to an old two story bluestone house, maybe one hundred years old, set back from the track by twenty yards, slightly elevated from the rest of the ground, from what I gathered the house was constructed on a bluestone foundation, featuring a large cellar underneath, the terrace with its brick floor was built around the entire house, the wood frame carrying the corrugated iron roof provided lots of shade and space for the old-fashioned rattan lounge chairs which were in good order, they merely needed to be cleaned, and every couple of yards there were very old brass lams hanging from the veranda beams.

The house was in desperate need of renovation, at a closer inspection it became apparent that the stonework was in excellent condition, the slate roof needed the attention of a professional, the wooden window and door frames were rotting away quietly, the front door with its two led-light glass panels mounted in the upper part merely required to be cleaned, the wood sanded and an application of fresh stain, and from what I was able to ascertain through the windows that hadn't been cleaned for years, the interior promised a lot of potential.

Old houses possess an enchanting touch of romanticism, there is something mysterious about them, this place invited me to take a look into its past, perhaps for a short moment to be part of its mysterious history, it didn't take very long until I was convinced that this was the place where I wanted to spend a little, maybe more than just a little time; I was fascinated by the bush, I was absorbed with the local people, most of them farmers, though some of their ideas and opinions arcade, but honest and down to earth, I was enchanted with the way of life that this area had to offer, I was also aware that life could be very humble for those that earned little money, I had fallen in love with the rugged environment that confronted those that dared to live here with the laws of nature and its consequences.

Understanding that for me it was easy to love this place, as a pilot I was able to enjoy all of the good things that this wonderful country had to offer, I was able to do and afford things that many country folk could only dream of; I am aware that I had a different view of things, I experienced a different reality.

It's been a couple of years since I had arrived down under, not a day passed without a thought about my father, wishing that he could experience the things that I did, I missed him, on occasion I would have been glad to have consulted him, and yet I had not called, nor written since the time I arrived in Australia.

I can't recall my thought processes, nor do I understand my egocentric behavior at that time, I can understand that I might have still been offended by the way Aunt had treated me as a kid, but time had passed, I had become a grown up person, despite the hard time that I had as a kid I had become a person that didn't have to claim respect, I received it because of whom and what I had become, I had no reason to be sulking, the contrary was the case, I should have been proud about my achievements and thankful to those that facilitated it, primarily my father as well as Aunt. I don't understand my behavior, I can't provide a reason, and I ask myself if I was attempting to punish them? Frankly speaking, I don't know.

Elphinstone, the house and its surrounding countryside I have come to consider as the right place to raise a family, not that I was in a hurry to get married and the thought of having children had not evolved at that stage, but it was a thought that I wasn't opposed to, I was rather thinking of my dear friend Ursula.

Cole had made an appointment with the estate agent for the following morning, he also organized an appointment with his bank the same afternoon, he knew the manager personally, as a young pilot, having Cole as your reference, getting the place financed was no problem; a couple of weeks later the property had been transferred into my name.

The finance was composed so that the basic renovation could take place over the next twelve months or so, the shaping of the garden and the acquisition of the life stock was going to be funded from my monthly salary.

I would have appreciated if my father could have been with me to supported with his vast knowledge as a tradie when I was meeting with the builder to discuss the renovation work for the house; sure, I was no dummy either, I had developed a solid vision about this house, I knew what I wanted this place to be at the end of its renovation, and I had a good understanding about the technical aspects, I knew what was structurally possible and what not, but my understanding of the particulars of the building trade was limited to my common sense.

We decided that Bill, the fellow that was recommended to me as builder would begin with the roof; the ridge plate, some of the common rafters and purlins had to be replaced, a few pieces of slate needed to be renewed, at the same time the entire roof was insulated, a new fascia (face board) was installed, the old one was totally destroyed from the water, and new spouting and down pipes were put into place.

Once the roof was weather proof again Bill and his team began with the sand blasting, some of the interior stone walls had to be freed from all kind of filth and bad repair work from past times, all doors and their frames as well as other timbers that had been smothered with countless coats of oil paint, which was now flaking off in parts, all of it was stripped back to the natural look of

232

the wood, the old front door with its colorful let lights was renovated to its original old charm, and all window and frames had to be renewed, using a modern double glazed window with its old fashioned cross bars.

The old pine ceiling boards were also covered with several layers of oil paint, dark in color, they too were sanded back to the natural wood, providing the rooms with a bright appearance.

In part this place featured a natural limestone floor pavers, in particular in the area of the entrance hall and the kitchen at the back of the house, the bathroom downstairs had a well maintained checkered tile floor, along the base line of the room there was a line of dark red square tiles two deep, the center was filled with larger square tiles laid diagonally to the perimeter, dark red alternating with creamy colored tiles, giving the impression of a large checkerboard, the limestone pavers were sanded, polished and sealed, they looked like they had just been laid, the tiles in the bathroom were merely cleaned and polished but all the wall tiles had to be replaced.

The remaining floor downstairs as well as the entire first floor was made from old, Baltic Pine – it had a very rugged look but it was very fitting with the bluestone and red brick interior, the floor was sanded and sealed to give it a fresh look.

The sparky moved in next, the wiring was a remnant from the last century, no longer considered safe, the local building authority had ordered it to be removed, the new cables were laid according to an elaborate plan, considering a more as adequate power and light supply throughout the entire house, many of the existing light fittings we were able to utilize, some of them had to be re-fitted, I had also bought some antique ones that fitted the style of the house, but my sparky had also some very innovative ideas, in a very clever manner he used modern spots to play with the illumination, highlighting particular areas of the house, or indeed the different building materials used.

At about the same time the plumber had removed the old iron water lines, a gas hot water service was installed at the back of the kitchen, providing not only cold but also hot water to the kitchen, the bathrooms down and upstairs, in parts, where appropriate, we left the copper water pipes exposed, and in most areas solid brass fittings were installed, water lines were laid to the outside of the house in the preparation of the garden that was planned to embrace the house, water supply line for the pool that I was going to build at a later stage, the down water from the roof area was diverted to a water catch from which the water tanks could be filled, and finally the plumber had to replace the septic tank system, apparently the old one had been leaking.

The kitchen, I believe it to have been an addition to the house in the early twenties, bluestone walls, sandstone floor, a couple of windows and a door to the veranda, fitted with a large stone sink, an old wood fired stove built into a brick alcove from which the brick chimney protruded through the corrugated iron roof, and a huge solid wooden table in the middle. The old wood stove, in excellent working order, with its surrounding brick work and chimney, the sand stone floor and the stone sink were retained in the new design, a new stainless steel gas stove, a rather large copper above it formed part of the kitchen, the old corrugated iron roof was replaced with a concrete slab which served as a terrace for my bedroom upstairs, parts of the wall, in particular in the wet areas we installed new, old fashioned tiles, as well as the cupboards were replaced, making this area aesthetically beautiful, functional, and easy to clean at the same time.

All the veranda posts and its roof structure as well as the corrugated roofing iron had to be replaced, the only part that remained was the red brick pavers and the sandstone retaining wall that embraced the entire veranda, a couple of water taps on each side of the house were installed, some external power points, the external wiring and light fittings were renewed.

In the cellar we merely cleaned out the rubbish that had gathered dust and cobwebs over the past decades, added some gravel on the floor, installed some fly wire on the ventilation openings and added wooden storage racks.

## Chewton Bushlands 1973

During the 1960s, the hippie movement began to hit Australia as it did other places around the globe, influenced through what was happening in American politics as well as their social and cultural issues, driven by an increasing disagreement particularly among young people for Australia's involvement in the Vietnam war. It was also evident that the effects of this war were becoming damaging to the U.S. economy, setting off a cycle of inflation in the country, and at the same time, it appeared that there was a tendency of negative reporting from the printed, the broadcast media, and stories from returning military staff that spread throughout the community, undermining the populations support of the war.

It was a period when youth started to reflect on social values and began to experiment and as new countercultures began to pop up; those involved were not scared about what people thought of them and this became the new social norm for many youngsters at that time. Inspired by the new style of music from bands like Richie Havens, Joan Chandos Baez, Janis Joplin, Grateful Dead, Creedence Clearwater revival, Crosby, Stills, Nash and young, Santana, The Who, Jefferson Airplane, Jimi Hendrix, the hippie ideals of love and human fellowship seemed to have gained real-world expression, at a time when disaffected youths from all over the country gathered, ostensibly to celebrate peace and free love.

Wanting to break out of the "norm," many youngsters dropped out of school, to do their own thing, with a focus on the cultural values, "make love, not war," endeavoring to achieve a higher level of consciousness through the consumption of narcotics, discovering themselves through the use of psychedelic drugs like marijuana and LSD.

At the time, there was an influx of young people, intending to pursue an alternative lifestyle in the Chewton bushlands which formed a triangle between Chewton, Faraday and Elphinstone as well as the area along Fryers Road, heading in a Southerly direction from Chewton. The people that came to the area were as diverse as is the area itself, some had abandoned school, left their studies and yet others had swapped their trades and professions for a hippie lifestyle in a harsh environment, living on a minimum of financial outlay provided by the "Dole" considered a government "handout consisting of pittance," in fact an unemployment and sickness benefit introduced in 1945 by the Menzies government, from which you could barely live.

Some of those youngsters had abandoned high school renouncing their further education, perhaps just for a little while, whilst others never went back to school, there were university students that had interrupted their studies to join the hippie movement, and there were ordinary working-class people, tradie's and academics that were convinced of this alternative lifestyle.

Some of the "hippies" were living in commune type arrangements in precarious accommodation; tents or makeshift huts put together from whatever the natural surrounding had to offer at the time, sharing love, alcohol, drugs for a little while until they realized that there had to be mor to life than sex and getting smashed out of their brain, whereas those that were serious about an alternative lifestyle began to prepare for a future with an option, building a home with a garden on crownland, settling in areas that were difficult to get to, difficult to find, somewhat obscured, out of sight of the ordinary people so that they could maintain privacy and grow their dope without being detected.

At the beginning, most of them lived in large army style tents until they were ready to start with the building of their mudbrick houses, digging out the circumference of the dwelling perhaps one meter deep, some even deeper depending on the terrain, particularly those that build on the slopes that were generally well drained, the dugout area serving as cellar which was providing an area for storage as well as keeping the place cool during the hot Victorian summer. The soil that had been dug out was blended with loam and water, some straw was added to keep this mixture nicely together, than rammed into wooden forms about 30 cm long, 25 cm wide and 12 cm high, left to dry, depending on the weather conditions for around one week.

Some of them built their mudbrick houses in the same way as you build a brick home, one brick on top of the other, overlapping the keys, others build a timber frame construction from second-hand timbers, anything that they could find in the demolition yard, even old railway sleepers were used in some, than the roof; usually a timber construction covered with second hand corrugated iron was completed so that the filling in with mudbrick and the finishing work of the interior which was equally as simple as was the exterior, most of them didn't install a floor, nor wall tiles, the shower was a simple construction outside of the house as was the dunny, and most of the houses had at least two corrugated iron water tanks, one of them to catch the rainwater off the roof, and the other was used as a kind of hot-house which provided plenty of warmth and humidity to the marijuana plants and concealed them at the same time.

To keep out the moisture from the walls, having an insulating effect at the same time, fresh cow dung was smeared all over the wall. Most of those houses didn't have electricity, those lucky enough to have built close to one of the main tracks were perhaps able to tap onto one of the power poles, until they were caught, most of them lived without electricity, the light was provided by candles and household kerosene, whereas the water had to be collected during the winter, depending on the summer season, additional water had to be carted in, and to suit the style of the house as well as the budget, an earth closet was constructed on the exterior.

A few of those people I got to know personally, particularly the ones that had settled permanently in the Chewton Bushlands. On those occasions where we went for a meal in one of the local pubs, we got to know some of those characters; one evening, in the Chewton pub we shared a table with David and Buffy. David, a fellow that was previously working as a merchant in one of Melbourne's large department stores, and Buffy was a nursing sister; both of them had decided to opt for an alternative lifestyle, both of them left their "nine to five" jobs in Melbourne, lived in a tent whilst they were building their own mud house not far-off Minors Hut Road in the midst of the bush.

Eventually, Buffy worked in a pub a couple of days per week and in her spare time she was making candles which they were selling on different markets within the district, and David was initially occupied with the building of their house and later engaged in assisting others with building projects and eventually pursued one of his hobbies, leather work, neither of them was opposed to the occasional party with all the trimmings that the hippie lifestyle had to offer.

Huxley was a high school teacher whom had also opted for a change of lifestyle, I appreciated his intellect, an interesting fellow to have a serious discussion with, he had a small antique shop in the neighboring village Chewton which I discovered early in the peace as I moved to the bush, getting old light fittings for the house in Elphinstone from him. Huxley was one of the few that remained loyal to the lifestyle that he had chosen during the hippie period.

Then there were Ramon and his lady Maggie. The only thing we ever got to know about his past was the fact that he was originally from Austria, and that his father was a teaching fellow, lecturing Psychology at the University in Wien. In the district, Ramon was known as that crazy guy that would take you apart if you got on the wrong side of him; apparently, a group of young yobbos attacked him in the streets of Castlemaine and beat him until he was bleeding from his nose, the moment Ramon realized that blood was all over his face, he got to be irate, in his furious attack he grabbed one of the fellows and bit off one of his ears.

Indeed, I got to know Ramon as an eccentric fellow, his lifestyle appeared to be somewhat muddled up; he would go on a psychopathic binge that would last for days, dowsed with alcohol and drugs, but if you got a hold of him after you left several messages around the different pubs in the district, he proved to be one of the best stone masons that you have ever come across, he built most of my stone retaining walls as well as other stone and brick projects in

Elphinstone. In contrast, Moggie was the kind of person that everybody enjoyed meeting, lovely to be with, enjoying a glass or two consuming the occasional joint to stimulate the mood, as the daughter of an undertaker, she was expected to take over daddy's business in time to come.

In Fryers road, not too far from the Wattle Galley gold mine, with her daughter, Mary lived in an rudimentary, old timber miner's cottage featuring a hipped roof and an old-fashioned picket fence, the kind of places that you used to find all over during that period, the front door leads directly into the kitchen, the only sign of contemporary fitting was the wash trough with a cold water tap and the old fire place that had been refurbished fifty years ago with a wooden stove, next to it was the parlor with its traditional U-shaped timber ceiling and the interior timber wall cladding had been sanded, featuring the natural look of the wood, next to the window there was an open fireplace; together with the wood-fired stove in the kitchen the only source of heating.

Then there were two small bedrooms, a traditional dunny in the backyard and a reasonably new timber shed which was Mary's workshop. Prior to getting involved in the creating of pottery, Mary was a high school teacher, a profession that she still perused one or two days per week on a part time basis, which allowed her to dedicate herself to her great passion—making pottery by hand. Though she got around town in her hippie style rags, she appeared to be living a life of solitude.

Mad-Cat, when he was reasonably sober, which wasn't very often was working as a carpenter around the district to supplement his habits, he was extremely eccentric, even dangerous when he was intoxicated, often he would threaten someone to kill him, behavior that many affected the fellows that returned from Vietnam as War Veterans. Many of those that returned from the Vietnam War deployment back in 1975 were hailed as heroes by some, and yet others responded with hatred and revulsion, this, together with the trauma that they experience left many of them with mental disorders—Mad-Cat was one of those.

Steward and Sherly, both of them in their mid-twenties, on their one-acre property which was situated on one of the main bush tracks in the middle of the Chewton bushland established a market garden, focusing on growing products without the use of herbicides and pesticides without making a lot of noise about it, they were selling biologically grown produce on virgin ground.

Jim, the middle-aged bachelor, inconspicuous, very calm, enjoying his privacy as he did the occasional party, he had a part-time job as a dishwasher in one of the local pubs, and he was doing odd jobs all around the place.

Dingo-Harry was another character in the area, he had established himself in the Chewton bushlands a couple of years before the area had become desirable for those that wanted to live an alternative lifestyle. About a mile along Eureka Street, somewhere between Chewton and Fryers town he lived basically the life of a hermit on a piece of land that he borrowed from the Crown, he had staked out a couple of acres underneath the Poverty Gulley water channel from which he siphoned the fresh water that he needed. The place was well fenced, dug into the ground deep enough, and yet sufficiently high so that his six dingo's that he kept couldn't escape from his property.

The dingo is a wild hound that is used to live in a pack, he is known to be cheeky and dangerous, not suitable to be kept as a pet, in fact a license to have dingo's needs to be obtained from the authorities; nobody in the area knew how Harry had acquired the animals, and how the local authorities never interfered. However, local gossip had it that anybody that came to close to Harry's property was threatened with a shotgun.

Though there were some of them that did little to nothing for their livelihood / survival other that grabbing the government hand-out, most of them were busy supplementing their subsistence by doing odd jobs around town, handy man's work, gardening, dish-washing in the pubs or some other casual, odd job opportunity that they could find, and the majority of them pursued hobbies from which they could earn a few dollars by selling their products at the weekly markets in neighboring villages and townships.

During the '50s, the time when the cold war between the Soviet Union and the United States was taking place the Vietnam conflict was the product of the Viet Cong rebels in the South that fought against the South Vietnam Government and its ally, the United States. Whilst the Soviets were supporting the communist ruled North, the Americans were allied to the Southern part of the country, concerned that that part of the region might become infested with communism, which eventually set off the beginning of the actual war on 28 February 1961; after over more than two decades of violence and conflict that devastated Vietnams population, killing an estimated two million Vietnamese, wounding over three million and rendering twelve million refugees the war ended on the 7th May 1975, killing some 57 thousand Americans, not counting the Ally's. For the duration of the Vietnam war around 60 thousand Australian Airforce, Naval and Army personnel participated of which 520 of them lost their lives, three thousand were wounded, and many of them that returned developed permanent psychological handicaps.

Protesting the war was a mutual goal that held the hippie movement together, but toward the end of the '70s when the war ended, members gradually began to dissipate. After momentarily having dabbled with the hippie ideology, those who survived the movement matured and moved on to pursue "normal" vocations, in the "real" world.

Some maintain that social history is cyclic, because this is an elegant explanation to map highs and lows of societies tides it can be argued that the cultural fluctuation between utopianism and apocalypticism, an oscillation between the spirit of the sixties which promised a better future, and the threads of uncertainty, fear, doom and gloom. Utopianism of the 1960s might only have been a short segment of social improvement, whereas a few years later the hippie movement had been superseded by violence and murders at the climax of the civil rights movement; Martin Luther King was assassinated, and with Bobby Kennedy that was murdered, the revolution would prove anything but a guarantee of equality which does not necessitate that there cannot be social progress.

## Winter of 1974

At the beginning of winter 1974, I finally was able to move into my country home, a wonderful moment and yet odd, almost bizarre to live here all alone, somehow it was a scary thought. Toward the end of the summer of 1971 I had moved out from Peter's house in Brighton, I had joint a bunch of pilots and flight attendants that were renting a large house in the midst of South Yarra, one of Melbourne's suburbs, an up and coming "inn place" to be at the time, as a group we were renting this old mansion; to get to the Yarra River we merely had to cross Alexandra Avenue, a narrow strip of parkland ant the Main Yarra Trail, a lovely place to enjoy a beer with your mates after work.

Life in this commune was interesting, amusing at times, though we were all different as people, and we had different interests, all of us shared a mutual commonality, flying, a professional activity that kept a commitment to each other that was almost unconditional, our association to each other was respectful regardless of gender or rank. As it is the case in any group of people, there are those that for some reason or another you feel closer to, those that you feel more comfortable with, a number of sincere, straightforward, uncomplicated friendships had developed from this bunch, and it were those that regularly stayed with me during their days off, enjoying Elphinstone and its surrounding.

One evening down the local pub I met Ryan, he appeared to be somewhat eccentric, he had withdrawn from the public life as a journalist; moved to the bush in Elphinstone, on a few acres of land he was endeavoring to live a self-sustaining, solitary life, almost like a recluse, he was particularly interesting to talk to, focused on the laws of nature, he loved simplicity, loathe pretentiousness, hated people that were boasting without substance.

Ryan seemed interested in what I was doing, he agreed to come and see my property perhaps he was able to assist me with the design and construction of my old-fashioned English cottage garden.

The slope on which the house was build provided the natural shape to construct terraces, thus creating a garden on different levels, the outside of the terrain enveloped with a naturally shaped sandstone wall, constructed without cement, bonded together with earth. To provide strength and stability to the wall a trench about a foot deep was dug which formed the base of the foundation, the larger stones were placed on the bottom, on a slant, leaning in the direction of the soil, making sure that the stones were overlapping each other just like a brick wall, filling the gaps with moist earth, ramming it down to add firmness, in this fashion building up the wall to about two feet above the ground.

Sandstone walls were constructed all around the house, terraced at the back and the sides, a three foot wide red brick footpath was laid throughout the garden, overcoming the slopes with naturally shaped, large slate plates, the different colors and textures and shapes from the brick, the slate and the sandstone provided a lovely front for the plants in the garden, some of the walls were built in a straight line, other parts were rounded and others yet followed the natural shape of the landscape.

Once the paving and the retaining walls were completed, the soil was prepared; at first, with a small machine the earth was tilted, compost and mulch turned in at the same time before the planting could be started, deciduous as well as native plants, shrubs, flowers were planted, avoiding obvious rows of plants, different shapes and colors—taller plants at the back and toward the center of the bed, shorter ones from the middle onward to the edges, not ridged, packed full, the spaces all jumbled, and in-between we placed different kind of herbs and some vegetables as well.

Soon after I bought the property, I realized that I had to get a vehicle that was suitable for this kind of terrain, most of the farmers around me were driving utilities, either Ford or Holden, fitted with a tow bar so that they could hook up a trailer. Perhaps my reason for wanting to buy a Land Rover was misguided, maybe it was satisfying a little boys dream, long wheel based, two door and a tailgate with the upper part opening upward, three hard seats at the front, four-wheel drive; freewheeling hubs at the front, painted in the color yellow, no leather, no interior lining, no luxury at all, merely a very solid, functional vehicle made to work, it made sense; I had to have one of those, brand new of course. Looking back at this period now, I am convinced that the vehicle was very useful for a hobby farmer and more importantly, it felt good to be seen with the Land Rover.

A suitable two axes trailer with aluminum body with a hydraulic tip device driven electrically was part of this outfit.

During the time that the house was being renovated I was flying on the domestic sectors, and if I was on the late shift I got home before 23:00, a couple of my work buddies whom also were going on days off were already waiting, the boys were going to work with me, whereas the girl's interest was more focused on the interior of the house and the garden. My dear friends provided the labor; I assumed the responsibility for the transport, a roof over the head, the ingredient for whatever we were going to prepare together, the icy cold beer, wine from the cellar, cigarettes and whatever else that we needed. Usually, shortly after midnight we arrived at the house in Elphinstone, we didn't have to be concerned about disturbing any neighbors, nobody was going to hear or bother us either, depending on the mood, some wine was brought up from the cellar, the chilled beer was taken from the fridge, somebody would make sure that the sleeping areas were ready and the rest of us took care of the tucker, usually something from the grill, served with different salads, making sure that the traditional Australian coleslaw was not missing from the selection. It was unusual to have hit the sack before 03:00, there was always a lot to be gossiped about, but often we had very stimulating discussions about everything and anything, having a good time was more important than catching up on sleep and it didn't matter if we started our projects a couple of hours later either.

Breakfast was prepared by whomever was first up, and it wasn't me either, toast made from the typical Aussie pre-cut square loaf that kept fresh for at least four days, butter, jam, baked beans out of the can, grilled bacon and eggs fried in plenty of salted butter, sometimes when a meat-head was in our company the bacon was supported with lamb chops or steak, or indeed both, tea and coffee was part of the standard.

During the early parts of the renovation, after breakfast the fellows and I, used to drive into the bush, gathering different sized stone for the retaining walls in the garden, one of us driving the Land Rover, others were collecting suitable rocks, possibly with one reasonably flat face and throwing them in the trailer, driving them back to the house to dump them as close as possible to the spot where they were used for the construction of the wall.

With a few exceptions, most of the ladies preferred to get involved in projects indoors, sanding paint from the old timber ceilings, frames and doors, dado wall paneling, old cupboards and other wooden objects, the staining of wood, the hanging of wallpaper in the bed rooms, and one of them had an excellent touch with tiling, under the guidance of the builder she covered the kitchen and all the wet areas with new, old-fashioned tiles, and once the garden stonewalls were completed, the ladies also got involved in the planting.

Very near the house, a long time ago there was a small wooden cottage; the only thing that reminded of this building was the old fire place with its chimney half fallen down, overgrown with a large blackberry bush from which we were gathering plenty of fruit to make jam, the red brick from the chimney were still laying around the ground, waiting to be picked up to rebuild the old structure. Once the blackberry bush was cut back, we could see that the base of this fireplace was still intact, from the number of bricks that laid on the ground we were able to work out the original height of the chimney which was an important factor, ensuring that the draft produced was going to be correctly configured; a colleague and I designed the structure to be rebuild in such a manner that the chimney had made a full twist to the top of its outlet.

For the base structure the local blacksmith created a steel frame and rack which we were using as a grill, and at the back of the fire box he installed a steel cabinet with racks and hooks which was used as a smoking chamber. This particular area was now converted to a proper BBQ place, with a slate floor surrounded by a sandstone retaining wall which formed part of the garden, and an old wooden table, a couple of bunks and a large pergola were providing comfort, once the grape-vine was bearing its foliage.

During the entire winter right up to the end of November, spring time we spend a couple of days in Elphinstone every week, much of the interior renovation work was done, all retaining walls for the garden completed, the construction of the BBQ area integrated in the garden and sufficient sandstone was lying near the area where the pool was going to be installed. Working outside during the winter with average day temperatures of 10 degrees Celsius was indeed cold, considering the mean temperature during the summer was around 30 degrees Celsius, but pleasant to get the retaining walls build and some of the planting done.

Now that the summer was near, we began our work early morning, finishing around midday to avoid the heat of the day.

The excavator was organized to be on site for the following week, a couple of us had three days off, we wanted to be at Elphinstone when the excavation for the pool was going to be done, the builder, together with the plumber were set to begin with the setting up and pouring of the foundation, the framing and pouring of the walls with the integrated plumbing was going to be started immediately after the hole was dug, the pool was going to be 25 meters long, 10 meters wide and 2.5meters depth at the deep end, fitted with a salt converter. We were kind of hoping that a couple of days after the hole had been excavated that we were able to enjoy the refreshing water of the pool, clearly we had been dreaming, the building team did a great job, a couple of weeks later when we arrived at the property, the tiled shell had been filled with water, the pump and salt converter were running, natural slate plates had been placed around the pool about two meters deep, all that remained for us to complete was the brick paving from the house to the pool and the retaining walls for the garden around the wet area.

I think that my dad would have been proud of all that I achieved down under thus far, during my working time in the cockpit I was a responsible, well respected fellow and privately I had adopted an alternative lifestyle that some might have described the life of a flower child, indeed I lived my life at its fullest, cigarettes and alcohol, too much at times, but none of my friends, nor I ever consumed any drugs of any sort, I was certain that my father would have approved what I was doing, perhaps even admired my eccentric, sometimes crazy lifestyle in this rugged country, I often thought about him, wondering how he would have solved a particular problem, I missed him, and yet deliberately I had not contacted him since I had arrived in Australia. Aunt on the other hand would not have approved of my private life; admittedly I had no way of really knowing this, I was merely assuming that she would identify lots of issues that she would have condemned. Though I was aware that I had no contact with dad and Aunt, I don't believe that I consciously or deliberately decided not to communicate with them, I simply refrained from calling or writing, and yet fully aware of that they would have been concerned for me.

My father took care of me, made sure that, as he used to say "you need to do well at school so that you may become someone," and I knew that he loved me, and I was now behaving like a spoiled child?

Christmas day of 1974 I was flying, I was celebrating the festive season on Boxing Day, a few of us drove up to Elphinstone, accompanied by a large turkey, a couple of legs of lamb, fresh veggies, a couple of life lobsters and a plum pudding with its vanilla sauce which one of the flight attendants mum had prepared for us. Sue was in charge of cooking, as a true Aussie girl she knew how to cook the life lobster, served with mayo and cocktail sauce, and she used to assist her mum at Christmas, she had prepared the stuffed turkey many times before. My colleague and I had to prepare the veggies for the roast, the medium-sized potatoes peeled and cut into quarters, the garlic and the onions merely peeled and left whole, whole tomatoes with the stalk and the core removed, and most importantly; the pumpkin had to be peeled, halved, the seeds and the stringy / sloppy fiber removed and the pumpkin flesh cut into similar sliced pieces as the potatoes.

All of these veggies were going to be placed in the baking tray, together with the whole turkey, lightly salted and seasoned with freshly ground peppercorns and a couple of twigs of fresh Rosemary and savory from the garden, ensuring that sufficient fat or oil was in the pan, so that the veggies were able to slightly caramelize on the outside.

The fresh green beans were cooked separate in lightly salted water, with the heads, tails and the strings removed.

I didn't get to see how Sue was preparing the stuffing for the turkey but she explained that the main ingredient was frozen chestnuts with lots of diced onion and garlic, lightly glazed in butter, an array of secret herbs from the garden, salt and pepper, a little cream to bind and a splash of Cognac from the kitchen shelves, not the good Courvoisier from the bar.

All of a sudden, from the other side of the kitchen we could hear a loud shriek from Sue, she appeared to be horrified, pointing at the turkey that had been waiting on the bench to be stuffed, as we got close to it trying to understand what Sue's irritation was all about, from her facial expression we gathered that she was shocked, with her trembling index finger she was pointing at the Turkey's opening at the back where a crawling mess was clearly visible.

I had heard about it but it was the first time that I saw a piece of meat being blown. These flies live typically in the bush, they are easily identifiable through their rather large size, the loud buzzing of their wings and their unprecedented persistence to get to food, they are particularly attracted by the smell of rotting meat for which they are very useful in the bush, clearing the countryside of dead animals, once they have found their pray the flies lay their eggs and within twenty four hours the larvae or maggots as they are commonly called appear, at the beginning they are similar to tiny, pale worms, scoff themselves on the meat during approximately five days, by then they have grown to around 5 mm and are ready to shed their skin, but they are not fussy, they are not indisposed to a turkey waiting in the kitchen to be stuffed—our turkey must have already been infested when we bought it, instead of getting stuffed it got thrown away—at a fair distance from the house in the compost bin.

For city folk like me at the time, flies in the bush were annoying, particularly when you were working outdoors, they are attracted by decaying organic matter, rotting meat, filth, scum, moisture and human feces, not necessarily in this order either. Desperately trying to rid myself of these irritating creatures I, like others used to smother my body liberally with a repellent, not knowing that the spray contained some toxic matter; at that time nobody was concerned about **Roundup** and similar chemical substances either, among farmers it was a welcome household word.

There was one person among my acquaintance that was aware of the potency of chemicals used in the farming community, aware of the force at which many of them were assaulting our environment, but most were not interested. In the design of my garden, Ryan had reserved very deliberate areas to plant the purple flour, lavender bushes and basil, knowing that by its mere nature these plants would be useful to keep away flies. He also noted for me that vinegar placed in the kitchen keeps ants and other insects away, and coffee grounds, camphor, garlic, Indian Lilac oil, lemon, eucalyptus and holy basil all are supposed to be natural remedies for mosquitoes, and by now I also understood why everybody in the bush had fly screens installed at the windows and doors.

The leg of lamb took the place of the turkey in the baking dish, the chestnut stuffing had to bake separately, wrapped in aluminum foil and the veggies didn't seem to care either, it didn't appear that they were upset having to bake next to the lamb, and frankly speaking I wasn't unhappy with this configuration, I wasn't too fond of turkey, I much preferred to get my teeth into the lamb, and finally, the boiled lobster served with its homemade mayonnaise as a hors d'oeuvre and the plum pudding with vanilla sauce all contributed to a late, but yummy Christmas dinner.

In one of the rooms downstairs the renovation was not completed, the stone walls had been cleaned with a wire brush, the loose material removed from the in-between of the stone, the tuck pointing completed, the window and its frame had been replaced, the wooden door together with the frame were sanded back to its natural timber, the stone floor had yet to be cleaned and one of the walls had to be re-done, it's stone structure, though solid but aesthetically not very nice to look at, with one of my brave colleagues Jim I was going to re-plaster the wall, I was convinced that it couldn't be that difficult, I had watched the builder doing it a couple of times before; three to one, a large cup of lime and sufficient water to make the mortar mixture slightly sloppy.

And so, we tackled this challenge early morning, straight after breakfast, three shovels of brickie's sand, one shovel of cement and a large cup of lime to each of the four shovels until the wheelbarrow was three quarter full, I dug a hole in the center as if you were making a dough by hand, poured the water in and began to mix the ingredient together to a slightly sloppy mixture. Just like I had observed my builder plastering one of the walls next door, with a broad paint brush, cold water in a bucket, I dipped the brush into the wet, slapping it as evenly as possible over the area of wall that was going to be covered with mortar, holding my large flat face finishing trowel upside down in my right hand, my colleague piling some mortar onto it, me with a rather elegant swing quickly guiding the trowel toward the wall about to be covered with mortar, the finishing trowel slightly slanted away from the wall so that the mortar could slide down onto the wall as I moved my arm in an upward direction, firmly pasting the mortar onto the wall so that it would adhere well.

I was confident that my method, my action must have been correct, just like I had observed with Bill the builder, and I was confident that my motion looked professional, indeed elegant, but the mortar tended to stick for a short time only, I was able to watch it move in a downward direction, eventually falling onto the floor. Again and again I tried to get this stuff to stick to the wall, getting pissed off at the same time, my buddy Jim didn't dare to laugh either, I am sure he was about to burst out in laughter at this spectacle but he didn't dare; eventually, after lots of guessing and trial and error we managed to cover the entire wall with mortar in an orderly fashion, a professional would have done the job in a good hour, we spend the whole morning on this job, it must have been comical if anybody had watched us, but I learned a great deal, not only about plastering, just as much about myself.

Near the end of the summer of seventy-four I had organized a fellow by the name of Johnny, he had a good name as a fencer in the district, a true local, with his wife and two small children he lived in an old caravan, for some reason or another he refused to live in his parent's farm cottage, he drove an old 1951 Ford F1, the gray paint had long faded, and the countless dents and scratches on the bodywork were an indication of the trucks age. Johnny wasn't available all year round, from late spring into early summer he was travelling with a small team from farm to farm, shearing sheep, he had a reputation of handling around 200 heads a day, whereas most shearers managed about 100 heads per day.

At different times of the year, he was also working as a stockman, commonly known as a Drover or Jackaroo, in the States he would have been known as a cowboy, moving livestock, cattle, sheep or horses on the hoof from one grazing area to another, earning his living. Johnny, a true bush craftsman checked all of my wire fences, straining the ones that had become slack over time, here and there replacing wooden posts that had become fragile, thread and fixing new plain wire in some areas, and he constructed a new wooden gate at the bottom of the house, hinged and hung on a huge timber pole anchored about three feet in the ground on either side.

Some of the wall timbers on the hay barn at the back of the house had to be replaced, on the corrugated iron roof a couple of sheets were renewed, the guttering mended ant its down pipe connected to the underground water tank

248

system. Both, lights as well as a couple of power points had been installed recently, and Johnny build a barn door, large enough for the tractor and trailer with a load of bailed hey could enter, I was told to make sure that the hey barn was closed, apparently the kangaroos were well known to use open hay storage like a supermarket to provide themselves with fodder, particular the Lucerne was valued by them during the hot, dry summer period.

The machinery barn was also brought up to standard, the necessary repair work completed, the power lines replaced and new doors fitted to the main access area and the workshop. At that time nobody locked their sheds, nor the houses, pilfering was not heard of, nor would anybody have dared to take something that didn't belong to them.

An old Massey Ferguson TE20, fitted with a four cylinder Diesel, painted gray, the only shelter was provided if the driver was wearing a hat, the cockpit was open, the only instrument on the panel was an oil temperature gage, mounted at the back of it was a device to hook up equipment and a power take off shaft and a gadget to which a tow bar could be mounted, this old lady was in perfect working condition, she started at the first attempt every time, but she was desperately waiting for a little TLC, to remove some of the rust and to give her a paint job, which I eventually did in my free time.

A hay wagon, also out of the fifties, its chassis was constructed from an old truck, front and rear wheels and tires also from a heavy-duty vehicle, the towing fixture was welded together with heavy T iron and the loading bridge had been made from heavy hardwood bolted together, this together with the tractor and a hand full of tools were the only part of the inventory of the machinery shed.

## Kolkhoz System, a Consideration as an Alternative

Equipping the farm with machinery needed very careful thought, as part of Cole's business proposal we discussed the notion of sharing the capital investments on the basis of need, based on the number of acres of land that each of us was operating; the purchase of tractors, grass cutting and similar farming equipment, holding and loading facilities for livestock, would be shared on a percentage basis, a bit like the Kolkhoz system that was implemented in 1917, after the October revolution in the former USSR agribusiness.

Kolkhoz is the abbreviated name of *kollektivnoye khozyaynstov,* or in English; collective farm, a cooperative agricultural enterprise operated on a state-owned land by peasants from a number of households.

Initially, the Kolkhoz were operated by individual farmers on a voluntary basis, this however was changed when Joseph Stalin implemented his five-year plan in 1929, farming within the Kolkhoz system had become compulsory for individual independent farmers, juridical they were placed under collective personal responsibility, Kolkhoz were formally the collective owners of equipment used for the production but not the land itself—this was owned by the state—the government took the liberty to influence the decision-making process, determining production targets, quality agreements, and the sales prices for each product, and as part of the system individual farmers within the Kolkhoz were allowed to use a couple of heads of livestock as well as a small garden for their own use.

Entire areas stretching over 6,000 hectares of land, covering several villages, an area of around 60 km square with its livestock and fields for cropping were part of a Kolkhoz; its mere size should have assured many cost savings, synergies and financial success.

Already as a teeny at high school I was fascinated by the notion of the Kolkhoz, the words **cooperative**—to cooperate with each other, **helpful**—prepared to help others, **collaborate**—to work with others, **companionable**—respecting others, **useful**—to be valuable to others, to the team, all of them are wonderful, indeed powerful words, if their true meaning is implemented as action, we have the basis of a cooperation that can be successful, the foundation of any good business.

And yet, as a kid I had become aware very quickly that most people in my neighborhood were terrified of Communism, at the time I was told that there were people around us that actively kept an eye on folk that behaved different from others, with the belief that they might be commies. The ordinary folk in the street were scared by Communism, but nobody was able, nor willing to explain what Communism is about, and why one had to be so fearful about them.

What was so threatening about cooperating with each other, to be prepared to help others, to be prepared to work with others, to respect others, and to be valuable to others, to the team? I had no idea, and still, during the same period all sorts of different **Cooperatives** were evident in our own country, in fact they had become an integrate part of the farming community, as I recall when I spend my summer break on the farm, we used to drive down to the dairy cooperative with milk every morning, at the same time we brought back cheese and butter, each delivery was measured and registered and the consumption of the dairy products that we took with us noted, so that the account could be settled at the end of the month.

The business model was very fundamental, the **Cooperative** gathered the milk from the farmers within the district, produced butter, cheese, yoghurt and other dairy products from the milk and took the responsibility for its marketing. With this system the farmer merely had to produce the milk, he didn't require additional equipment, nor the specific skills, and he was assured a fair market price.

One of Switzerland's largest food retail stores started its operation over 150 years ago, introducing a mobile platform, selling food items from small trucks, trailers and later out of converted buses, and eventually opening its first self-service shops. The notion of the cooperative was simple, an association of persons who join together to reach a common economic, social or cultural goal and to satisfy their own aspiration through the creation of a collectively owned, democratically run business.

Knowing from historic reports that the notion of the Kolkhoz in the USSR was successful in its first years of operating, but it is of no secret to those that have been engaged with the subject matter that after a while it cease to function; perhaps I am presumptuous but I suspect that reason for its failure was the fact that people were forced to work in this collective, and at the same time they had no say about anything; they had been demotivated, incentives had been removed and their spirit shattered, they had learned not to care, had this system been effective, it wouldn't have been obliterated during the 1960s.

However, preconditions to get involved in a kind of a Kolkhoz were fundamentally different, I wasn't politically motivated, my participation was voluntary, I, together with my business partner could determine the characteristics as well as the specific aspects of our cooperation, through mutual agreement we were able to alter the modus operandi, and we agreed that in the event that either of us felt that this system was not workable, we were able to discontinue without a financial loss, without compromising our relationship.

For two fellows like Cole and I, people that were able to agree to disagree in a discussion, the sharing of farm machinery made good sense, both of us were willing to give it a go, if the project was successful, we could endeavor to work with the same kind of agreement with a cooperative workshop, both of us were looking forward to our Kolkhoz project.

For this kind of project, it is essential that all involved respect each other, they must necessarily believe that it can work, they must be able to think liberally and broad.

Consider for a moment that you are a partner in a cooperation, the heavy-duty electric drill has just packed in, and now it needs to be replaced immediately, the drill is only a couple of years old and you have used it a couple of times for light jobs over a year ago, the cooperative agreement states that you have to participate with 50% of the replacement cost—not fair? Perhaps not—but that's how it works.

If you are not willing to accept this state of affairs, if you believe that this scenario should be settled in a different manner—leave your fingers from cooperation, and do your own thing.

Because Cole had considerably more acres compared to me, for the large farming equipment we set up a cooperative agreement that was based on the number of acres on a percentage basis, allowing room for changes as they became necessary or desirable.

Our Kolkhoz was successful for many years, the agreement was disbanded when I finally left Australia, its success can be attributed to generosity, tolerance, respect for each other, and the sincere friendship that we had developed between us.

The principle of our cooperation was very simple; the fundamental rules were determined by both, Cole and I in writing with the option to make changes through mutual consent, and we agreed to maintain a protocol—an auditable document. A business bank account requiring the signature from both of us was also established, Cole's wife was nominated as the bookkeeper, one of the public accountants and taxation specialist in the next near larger place, around 48 km from Elphinstone, in the city of Bendigo was our accountant and auditor, periodically we took our bookkeeping document to his office from which he would prepare the taxation return for the period beginning 01 July ending 30 June of the following year, as it is required in Australia.

As a registered Cooperative we raised Merino Sheep, principally for the production of wool, and Aberdeen Angus Cattle intended for the meat market, cultivated Lucerne on our paddocks as grazing fodder for the livestock, some of which was cut, dried, bailed and stored in the barn for times of drought so that we had the ability to feed our stock during the poor times without having to purchase fodder at high prices.

The Merinos had a good blood line, they were pure, well-bred sheep, free running with an open barn available to them during the very hot, the wet and the cold weather as a sanctuary, and there were a number of old, very large native trees that provided additional refuge for the livestock, the sheltering of the sheep was one of the elements that supported a superior quality of wool, we aimed at a fleece fiber smaller than 16 diameter micron, a wool that produced a soft handling fabric used by designers and tailors that produced high quality textiles for luxury goods which earned a higher margin. Unlike most other wool producers that sold their product at the classical auctions, our fleeces were bought through the farm-gate sales system, Cole had built up a very particular private clientele over the years.

Though, at the time Cole had been involved in farming for over fifteen years, and then there was me as a greenhorn, the farming intelligence, the know-how and much of the hard work wasn't provided by Cole and myself, the entire husbandry operation, the crutching, the dipping of the sheep, the different treatment processes to minimize the impact of fly strike, lice and worms, the rotation of the livestock, land management and the maintenance work was provided by John, a very unassuming fellow, supported by his wife Patricia, our neighbors, managing over 1.000 acres of farm land were our managers, the foundation of our business. Sure, Cole and I were also on the property on the days when we were not flying, assisting John.

The Cooperative wasn't merely an engine to make lots of money, and to create as many taxation advantages as possible, primarily it provided us with an unprecedented lifestyle, embracing nature, we recovered strength, were able to relax despite the work involved, and most of all, we had fun.

## A Moment of Devastation

Early March of 1974 My colleague Hans Peter, with whom I shared the classroom during my time at the SLS contacted me a couple of years after I had left Switzerland and informed me that after a short period of suffering from cancer, his sister—my dear friend Ursula had passed away—together with a vinyl record from the Piccadilly six she had given me a copy of Taillard's book about evolution as a farewell present, after a period she stopped writing to me—I kept asking myself again and again why she had ceased to reply to my provocative letters that I had written to her about Taillard's theory of evolution.

Throughout the first eighteen months of my time in Australia we had written to each other every week, talking about personal experiences, stimulating, indeed provoking each other with exhilarating thoughts, to the point where we began to scheme that she would join me down under, we shared mutual thoughts about a future together. The news that she had passed away was very tragic, indeed devastating to the point where it had characterized my future behavior for some time.

## Whyalla

Saturday afternoon, together with friends we were sitting around the BBQ fire in our backyard, spinning yarns, one of my mates' brother whom was working as a welder at the shipyards of Whyalla was telling us tales about his work which at the surface appeared to be very funny but in reality, these stories were detrimental to this business. John was new to the shipbuilding industry, he had been working for this company for nearly two years by now, though he enjoyed his work, he had difficulties accepting the very stringent rules that the trade union was imposing on its members.

The Whyalla shipbuilding yards were established by BHP in 1939, beginning to build ships for the Australian Navy, with the first order being the corvette HMAS Whyalla which was launched on the 12th May 1941. At a later stage, BHP also began with the building of ships for its own use, the Iron Monarch with a dead weight of 8.158 tons was the first tanker to be launched in October of 1942. The production continued throughout the forties but at a slower rate because of a shortage of skilled labor, a problem that was solved through immigration, bringing in the necessary skilled people from overseas, but at the same time strikes caused by the trade unionism, organized stop work claiming better working conditions and better pay contributed to the demise of the yard.

For a while, the company was able to continue with its production, with the adoption of the all-walled method during the late fifties the company was gradually able to increase the size of the ships that they build. As a result of this the slipway was extended to accommodate the ever-larger ships, and the crane capacity was eventually increased which enabled them to implement the prefabrication technique. During the early sixties the Whyalla Shipbuilding and Engineering Works engaged in a Technical Co-operation Agreement with Ishikawajima-Harima Heavy Industries Company of Tokyo which provided the company access to its partners technical resources.

However, industrial problems coupled with increasing labor cost began to slowdown the yards production, as these issues affected other areas of Australia at the same time. April 1970 a disastrous fire gutted the then half build 66.800-ton tanker *Amanda Miller*, a further setback to the company. Finally, the *Iron Curtis*, the sixty fourth and at the same time the very last large ship build in the Whyalla yard was launched in January of 1978, and then the yard was shut down.

John explained what happened to him that time, when after he had waited for over two hours for an electrician, he decided to move the electrical cables himself so that he could get on with his welding instead of wasting time, and as he was about to connect the cables to the power station closer to where he was going to continue his job, one of the union representatives had caught him, and immediately called for a stop work meeting over the entire yard. As John was telling us, as a worker in the shipbuilding yard you weren't allowed to exercise any task outside of your area of competency as stated in your job description, a welder wasn't allowed to move an electrical cable, or change an electrical fuse, this was not part of his job, and the unions would take serious action if one of the rank and file were caught doing something outside his area of responsibility, making sure that their jobs were protected.

Apparently, on another occasion one of the painters was found drunk on the job by one of the supervisory staff, whom ordered this fellow to accompany him to the administration office immediately. On the way, the intoxicated painter was kidnapped by members of the union and moved from the yard before the supervisor was able to present him to the management. When the "kidnappers" were questioned by management about the abduction of the drunken painter, they explained to the manager that this fellow wasn't drunk at all, he was suffering from the effects of medication, hence they decided to take him to his home. The drunken painter had been ordered to front up at 09:00 the next day in the meeting room of the admin building.

When this fellow turned up the next day for his meeting with the human resource manager, he was either still, perhaps again drunk, unable to get up the stairs to the HR manager's office, he had to be supported by the union representatives, virtually being carried up onto the first floor. When the HR manager told the painter, "It appears that you are still drunk," one of the union representatives replied to the manager, "Are you a doctor? How do you know that this man is drunk?" and he continued, "In fact, this man is so dedicated to this company, he came to work despite the fact that he is very ill; the man is suffering from the effects of strong medication."

Needless to say, the man was able to keep his job, as a result of the union's audacity and boldness, they had the upper hand during that period, able to do, or indeed not do, just about anything that they cared.

May 1927 the ATCU, Australian Council of Trade Unions, the dominant association and governing body of the trade union movement in Australia was established, governing some 46 unions.

The rise and decline of Australian Unionism began during the 1820s (Bradley Bowden 2011), between 1921 and the 1950s unionism in Australia claimed a central place in society, even during the years of the great depression union density never fell beyond 42.5 percent, 1948 reaching the peak with 64.9 percent of the workforce, remaining around the 60 percent up until the early 50s. However, there is no doubt that many blue-collar workers had joint only because of the union's preference clause, being forced to join if you wanted a job. Unionism was socially anchored in the working people's lives.

Bowden goes on to say that the acceptance of collectivist union values was a reflection of the little change in Australia's class structure during the first half of the twentieth century. During that period, few blue-collar workers were able to aspire to a successful business or professional career, at best they could become one of the union officials, or indeed a Labor parliamentarian. The stability of this unionized working-class society, and the collectivists values embedded within, were underpinned by two government mandated policies, the tariff protection which insulated manufacturing from the depressions worst effects.

Equally important was arbitration, playing a significant role in maintaining union strength as the award system gave unions the ability to regulate working conditions even during unfavorable economic times. At the same time, the union preference system ensured that mass defection from its organization were not possible. However, the preference system was abolished in 1932 by the incoming government. Structural changes in the economy between 1954 and 1971 were responsible for the membership decline in the unions, in particular in the areas of shipping, stevedoring, mining, agriculture and pastoralism, rail transport and in the building industry, the mechanization of many of those areas, the switch from steam to diesel in the railways, the change to bulk-loading reduced employment, whilst the strength in the manufacturing industry remained stable, and some of the growth was due to the increase in part-time jobs which were largely because females that entered the retailing and hospitality jobs.

The sustained fall in union membership was turned around in 1970, which can be explained as substantial gains among the white-collar workers had come on board, as well as members of the teaching and nursing profession that were traditionally well unionized. Arbitration and the enforcement of union preference clause was also instrumental in this movement. Major employers in retailing, banking and the insurance business also agreed to enforce the compulsory unionism. The most spectacular advances occurred in the public sector where unionism was well established.

In 1970, the McMahon Liberal government introduced automatic deductions for union fees. The Whitlam Labor government was overly pro-union, threatening to withhold an extra week's annual leave from non-unionists in 1973, greater white-collar militancy and marked gains in working conditions also increased the recruitment.

Imports rather than home-made goods increasingly began to fill the retail shelves. Another mining boom based on the open-cut mines in Western Australia and Queensland caused the value of the dollar to hike, causing imports to be cheaper. A 25 percent tariff cut introduced by the Whitlam government in 1973 made imports even more attractive. Then between 1974–75 and again in 1981-83 the economy slipped into a recession, decreasing the union membership by early 1982.

Australian workers had one thing in common, they believe that they could gain more through collective action than they could by acting alone. In the final analysis, unionism survived and grew because the members of this working class believed it delivered them a benefit. From the early 1950s, however structural change in the economy brought about the gradual disintegration of the working-class constituency that had long championed unionisms. By the

1970s barely half of the workforce belonged, after a series of recessions curtailed a brief rebound in unions fortunes, industrial labor found itself best by new problems. From the 1980s the deregulation of the industrial regulation, a growth of precarious employment and employer anti-union strategy, as well as further structural changes in the economy, all combined the support of less than 20 percent of wage and salary earners.

Militancy, industrial, sometimes personal threats were part of the union's bargaining power, created for the purpose of securing and improving pay and better working conditions. However, this was often exaggerated, unnecessary and often self-destructive. On the other hand, one needs to recognize that prior to the union movement, Victorians worked up to 14 hours per day, six days a week, there was no sick leave, no holiday leave, and employers could sack staff at any time without giving a reason. The union movement also supported occupational health and safety, they were fighting against precarious work, and assisted with the restructuring of work processes.

## Elisabeth 1977

John, one of my colleagues whom was also flying for TAA, both of us had just gotten our endorsement on the B727-726/Adv at that time had invited me to his birthday, at the age of twenty-six he was still living with his mum and dad in a rather grand Victorian style two story manor in Toorak, one of Melbourne's best suburbs. His mum was a doctor at the Royal Melbourne Hospital and dad was the owner of one of Melbourne's most renowned chambers of law at that time. The party was taking place in the outdoor area of their villa, a rather large, breath-taking, lavishly but tastefully decorated garden, round tables covered in white cloth, the crockery, cutlery and the glassware to suit, the beverages served by a professional team of waiters and waitresses, the food, fresh, nothing but the best and plenty of it in the form of a buffet that was taken care of by a couple of chefs dressed appropriately in their whites with rather tall chefs hats, all of it very elaborate.

John was getting around the crowd, mingling with those that had been invited, making sure that he spends a little time with each, and at some point, he grabbed my hand and dragged me along, to introduce me to some of the party members and his parents in particular, both of them very pleasant, down to earth people. As we moved around, being introduced to different folk I realized that the majority of these people belong to the beautiful ones of

Melbourne, some of them were high-ranking members of the industry and commerce, academics and intellectuals from the university, members of the local and the federal government as well as other influentials, clearly his parents were very well connected in society.

Meeting so many influential people in one place is certainly unusual, Dr. Osborne, the researcher that played a major role in the shaping of the local as well as the nation's social, and cultural profile, the fellow that worked with the cardiologist Dr. Christiaan Barnard in Cape Town when he, on the third of December 1967 performed the first ever human to human heart transplant, Patrick Jeannette Tweeddale from the Liberals, elected on the 20 March 1976 a member of the Victoria Legislative Assembly, Child Gloria Joan Liles whom was elected into the Commonwealth House of Representatives in 1974, Federal Attorney-general Senator Peter drew Durack, Sir Peter Abeles, a business giant involved in TNT and Ansett Transport Industries which included the domestic Airline Ansett, as well as many other important people.

Having met so many influentials was indeed very impressive, but I never felt the urge to tell others about this particular experience. During a quiet moment, over an icy cold beer in the one and a fag in the other I was talking about a recent incident during our approach to runway 16 where the fellow with his B747 from Cathay Pacific, immediately before us, descended his aircraft below a segment minimum safety altitude, a little fellow about six years of age had come to sit with us, calling my mate uncle John.

John introduced his nephew, the little boys name was Edward, his fascination was airplanes, for quite some time he kept quizzing us about flying, what it was like to be sitting upfront in the cockpit, when suddenly this lovely lady joint us in this conversation, Elisabeth was her name, she claimed to be the mother of this very pleasant little boy, and consequently she was the older sister of my buddy.

I don't know if this was coincidental or if my friend John had deliberately promoted these situations, after his birthday, on a number of occasions at different parties and gatherings I came across his sister Elisabeth, in a positive manner there was something eerie about her being, very attractive, she moved like I can imagine an angel would do it, she was very graceful, self-assured but not arrogant, assertive and inquisitive at the same time, intelligent and her interest embraced a wide range of subjects, simply a person that you wish that you could get to know better.

On the other hand, I had to consider that you don't go chasing married ladies, I was well aware that Elisabeth had two children but at some stage I found out she was separated from her husband, apparently, he had walked out on her and the children, now living with a younger lady whom had not yet been tarnished by the physical traces that the birth of a couple of kids leave behind, as he apparently declared to her. Knowing this changed my opinion all together, it had become legitimate to cease my restraint behavior toward her, it was now time to show Elisabeth that her friendship was important to me.

We had now met on different occasions over a period of six months or so, mostly her kids Edward and Jacqueline were there as well, and I was growing rather fond of those joint gatherings, looking forward to the next weekend day that I wasn't on duty, an opportunity to meet again, when spontaneously I invited Elisabeth and her kids to join me on the farm in Elphinstone for the next available weekend.

A couple of weeks before Christmas, after my last flight on the Friday afternoon I got into my car and headed in the direction of the bush, making a detour to Castlemaine the place where I mostly did my shopping at one of the local supermarkets, the Greek greengrocer, the bakery and on the way back I stopped in the neighboring Chewton, opposite the old post office there was a milk-bar, next door to it Mr. Archer had his butcher shop, a meat-shop that should have been either renovated or shut down a long time ago, exposed brickwork and a timber construction that had lost its paint in the working areas, the workbench a greasy old wood block totally indented from the butcher's chopper, sawdust on the old dirt floor and some of the meat hanging on raw iron hooks attached on a rod suspended from the ceiling, unrefrigerated.

As a customer you didn't get into the shop, you were standing under the open veranda which was covered with its corrugated iron roof, about half of the shop area was fitted with louver glass panes and fly wire which were opened during the winter time, Mr. Archer would than open this tiny flap door through which in the end the meat would be handed to you. Mr. Archer, a fellow well over sixty at that time understood his trade, despite the diabolical conditions of his shop, his meat was of excellent quality, he would age his products during different time frames, just like the butchers of Europe had done it for ages before him, it was best to place your order in advance so that you could be sure to get what you wanted, which I did on that Friday, I wanted to make sure that my hospitality skills were not neglected.

The little house in Elphinstone was going to rock for the weekend, some of my mates from Australian had already arrived when I got home, a couple of the girls vacuuming the pool, getting it ready for a party, and my colleague John was getting the house ready, he was aware that his sister and the kids would arrive on the late evening train; I got the feeling that he was as excited about this as much as I was. Because the train didn't make a scheduled stop at the Elphinstone station, I picked them up in Castlemaine, a township around fifteen kilometers from Elphinstone, I recognized the kids first, they were out of the carriage well before Elisabeth, embracing me as if we hadn't seen each other for a long time; then I noticed that Elisabeth was struggling with the luggage but I could not assist her because I had two excited kids clinging onto me; eventually, she joined us in this hearty welcome.

That was one of these wonderful moments in life that I enjoyed immensely, at the same time I thought of my father, curious about what he might have thought of my situation right this moment, would he approve, would he be sharing the same sentiments as me, or indeed would he have shared words of wisdom with me? I was curious to know but it didn't matter what dad or anybody else thought, the situation felt right to me. I also thought about the time when my colleague Hans Peter whom had gone back to Switzerland contacted me about his sister, to inform me that my dear friend Ursula had passed away, but I knew that one day I had to conclude the period of mourning which didn't mean that I had to forget, but I had to allow myself to let go and to get on with life.

Several joint weekends were to follow before both of us decided that we were right for each other, that together we would like to share our lives. Both Jacqueline and Edward were enrolled in a coeducational private school in Melbourne, not far from Albert Park where Elisabeth lived in an old, beautifully renovated Victorian Style home—just one street away from the beech promenade of Port Philip Bay. The kids' school wasn't far from their home, Elisabeth was in downtown Melbourne within fifteen minutes or so, she held a partnership in her father's law firm, and I operated out of Tullamarine, Melbourne's International airport; for the drive to the airport I had to calculate about thirty minutes for an early morning start. Essentially it was sensible that we lived in Melbourne Monday to Friday, and the weekends we would spend on the farm in Elphinstone.

The prospect of becoming a step-parent had now become a matter that deserved very careful thoughts, considering Elisabeth as being the right partner did not suffice, I wasn't getting involved with just one person, Jacqueline and Edward were going to be an integrate part of this as well, I was aware that I couldn't have Elisabeth as my partner without the kids, I had to be convinced that I was able to love the kids as if they were my own. I was scared, thinking about my own childhood, the way in which I experienced my step-parent, how aunt Lulu appeared to be a good person at the very beginning.

About at the same phase, as I had gotten to know Jacqueline and Edward until now, I felt that they liked me and enjoyed my company, I also know that they were aware about my feelings toward their mum and I liked them, enjoyed being with them, I never had the feeling that they were in our way, the contrary was true, and yet the memories about Aunt kept haunting me, contemplating how she, as an apparent good person gradually evolved to be very dominant, unloving, how she had become a severe stepmother that exposed me to mental torture almost on a daily basis.

Because I had savored Aunt's torture during my childhood, I had good reason to be very honest, even though with myself, taking myself to trial, asking if I was sincerely prepared to be a part in the raising of children, ascertaining if I was capable to assert the responsibility of an educator, asking myself what kind of a father I would be. Time after time tormenting memories which I experienced during my childhood pursued, even clouded my thoughts, I recall clearly, at that time how Aunt tried very hard to influence my personality, how she unremittingly attempted to shape my being, and how I, with a great deal of tenacity, arrogance and self-confidence refused to be molded by Aunt. Can a step parent love his or her partner's children as if they were their own?

I think that one has to differentiate between men and women; I believe that a woman that has not carried the child in her womb, a woman that has not experienced natures gift of the muddle of joy and pain at the same time that the process of giving birth provides you with cannot truly have the same feelings for a child as does the woman that has, which doesn't mean that she is incapable of loving another woman's child, but the feelings cannot be the same. As for blokes, I believe that the moment we have "made" a child we know that we did, not because we are aware of the act of making but because of the incomparable, spiritual feeling that captures our heart which is imparted to your own child, a very special kind of love that you can only feel for your own, which doesn't exclude you from loving another man's child, but it's not the same, understanding that there can always be the exception to the rule, I have accepted this point of view as a notion that I can comfortably live with.

The prescription that made our family a well-functioning ensemble was fundamentally founded upon the elements of trust, respect, tolerance, honesty, clear communication and the love for each other; from the outset we maintained an honest and open communication, listening to each other, letting each other know how we felt, mutual respect, respecting the fact that little people have the right to an opinion, we allowed each other to have time out, and we respected each other's need for privacy, we understood that respect is something to be earned, it cannot be demanded, we were honest with each other, but never brutal, we involved the kids in our daily lives, sharing the chores to be done around the house as we shared the fun things, we focused on the things that matter, we discarded the nonsense and the things of no importance, the kids involved me in some of their activities, the kids consulted me about things that appeared to be difficult for them, and they shared the good moments with me, as I shared as much as possible with them, supporting them, supporting them in the decision making process, to shape some of their ideas, views and opinions on their sometime delicate but precious journey to become adults. Sure, each one of us had to learn how to handle the other, not everything was perfect either.

In contrast, the family in which I grew up was dis-functional, the relationship that I enjoyed with Aunt was fundamentally founded upon the elements of mistrust, disrespect, no tolerance, dishonesty, clear one-way communication and the hatred for each other; in time I learned that an honest and open communication led to interpersonal difficulties, listening to each other was limited to me listening to Aunt, letting each other know how we felt wasn't an option, it didn't interest Aunt at all; mutual respect meant that Aunt demanded my respect, she didn't believe that that little people deserve to be respected as well, nor did she accept that they have the right to an opinion.

Aunt allowed myself to have lots of time out, and she respected my need for privacy, during the week I had lots of time to myself, even on those occasions that I would have appreciated if someone would have been around, Aunt simply wasn't there, she was out enjoying herself with my father; I had learned not to be honest with Aunt, honesty was often punished with some kind of disciplinary action by withdrawing one of the very few privileges that I ever had; Aunt involved me in her daily life, my daily chores included my assistance in the kitchen, predominantly pealing, scrubbing, washing, drying and putting away, I was involved with the shopping, I was instructed to sweep, mop, vacuum floors and other surfaces, clean the carpets and comb their fringes so that each of them looked like a little soldier all pointing in exactly the same direction, I had to dust everything and anything around the house, clean the windows—the old-fashioned way with water, vinegar and old newspapers; I had to work in the garden—pulling weeds, watering, sweeping the pavers.

I was expected to do anything else that popped into Aunt's vivid mind— from time to time, Aunt had involved me in fun things but those occasions I can probably count on one hand; Aunt focused on the things that mattered to her; the things that seemed to be important, the does, the don'ts, where were you, what took so long, why isn't this done properly, do this, do that, hurry up, you are lying again, I know the truth, I know everything, rarely did we share good moments, I don't recall to have been understood nor listened to by Aunt, I don't remember anything of immense value that she has shared with me, but I learned how to run a household, I learned how to handle foodstuff, and how to prepare a range of meals.

I believe that as a step-parent you cannot love someone else's child in the same way that you can your own, but I don't think that this is all that significant, merely assume your responsibility as a parent and handle the child with respect, do whatever it takes to guide the child through its childhood, be sure to be there *when the child needs you, with lots of love and understanding show him the way to become an adult, support the child in his endeavor to reach its maximum potential, and all the rest will follow naturally.*

## My Best Friend Clive

During the Summer of 1974, with a couple of mates from work I was messing around in the Chewton bushlands, the car we had parked at the post office, heading down the Pyrenees Highway in the direction of Castlemaine, right into Farran Street and right again into Colles Rd up to Moonlight Flat where we stopped for a cold beer at a friend's place whom was spending a few weeks at home, as a mariner he enjoyed the privilege of two months at sea, and two months off, a fellow that was rich with yarns that he brought back from his journey's, perhaps a little far-fetched from time to time but nonetheless thrilling.

From there we headed in an Easterly direction, mostly following tracks that joint up with Fairbairn Street which eventually leads back to the Pyrenees Highway in Chewton, West of the General Store. On the way, somewhere in the vicinity of the desolate bush track called Fairbairn Street, a road that you can't pass after heavy rain, perhaps fifty meters further into the bush we discovered a small opening, closed in with a fence constructed from natural bush pols near to one meter fifty high, pounded into the ground about one meter apart, the in-between filled out with suitable twigs kind of woven into each other like braided hair, and on the side a simple gate, not hinged, it was the kind that you had to lock into a particular position to block the entrance to what was once a vegetable garden, badly neglected, obviously abandoned some years ago.

Near the side of the fence was an old agricultural water pipe ¾ Inch gage (19mm diameter), a relic from the old imperial system that the country began to change in stages, beginning in 1966 through to 1974, for the first couple of meters it was exposed but then disappeared underground, I guess it was running up to that beautifully concealed, rather large dam that we came across a few hundred meters further up the road, providing fresh water for whom ever was living here. Tucked on to a large gum was a shack about four by three meters, in part constructed from milled timber as well as natural bush materials, its foundation walls were built from handmade mud bricks held together with sloppy dirt, the old door was open, a tatty but still intact, old sash window fitted on the west side of the building, provided some day light and a clear view to the main track.

The roof was made of corrugated iron overhanging the walls by about a meter which was designed to protect the mudbrick and timber walls from the wet and the heat of the Victorian summer, a six thousand liter water tank had been placed directly on the North side, connected to the roof guttering, the old cast iron wood stove was placed against the mudbrick wall, its flue was leaving the hut directly through the wall then made a ninety degree angle, pointing up to the sky, an old bank, a wooden table and a chair and a few cooking utensils was all that was left behind. Covered with an old army cover, tucked against the hut were several old doors, windows and other building materials, waiting for someone to make good use of them.

The place had a pleasant spookiness about it, somewhat unearthly, even eerie; soon after we had arrived, I got the feeling that this place was sacred, that we shouldn't be there at all, some innate voice told me to get the hell out of there. A few hundred meters down the track we walked onto a stone wall that provided wind shelter as well as security to a two-acre property that appeared to be taken up with a huge garden, a couple of stone sheds scattered around the property and two houses built very close together both of them made of local sand stone.

As we were about to pass the front gate of the property, a heavy haired, full bearded fellow with a deep voice, a British accent asking us where we had come from, and in no time we got involved in a conversation, feeling very comfortable, I think even intellectually attracted toward each other in a complementary manner, realizing that our interests were much the same, and yet so different as individual people, Clive the long-haired fellow behind the fence, a "left-wing greenie" that has chosen to live a reclusive life up in the bush, whereas my political alliance lays more toward the center, with a preference to make money.

Not very long after our first encounter, we invited Clive and his lady over for dinner; Born on January 14, 1939 in Uxbridge, Middlesex, England, together with his mother he immigrated to Tasmania where he completed his education, and became a moderator on the local 7LA radio station. I don't recall where, nor from which school of acting he graduated but in his early twenties he had moved to Melbourne and became a member of the Melbourne Theatre Company before joining ABC television in Elsternwick, Melbourne, Victoria—playing one of the characters in the soap opera serial (28 August 1967-23 December 1977), set in a small fictional Victorian rural township, producing an incredible 1.562 episodes over the ten years of broadcasting.

After his uncompleted acting career, Clive decided to peruse a different life, a simple existence, living with a minimum of material possessions, materialistic poverty, he moved into the bushlands in the Northern part of the Chewton, Victoria, building himself a simple hut, established a vegetable garden, together with some basic tools, appropriate clothing, writing material and a few books he lived like a self-sustaining recluse for a couple of years, before he met up with the lady a bit further down the bush track, the lady that lived in a sand stone cottage on a couple of acres protected by a superbly constructed stone wall.

Clive never revealed the subject matter that he was examining and writing about, it appeared that he preferred to just get on with it, rather than talking about it and I was prepared not to bother him about intricate questions, but I was very much aware about his intellectual capacity, to me, Clive is a veritable fellow researcher, a person that has the audacity and the mental endurance to peruse his interests and get to the bottom of things, finding out the truth, Clive was also very humble and self-assured, he exerted self-criticism, almost as if he was degrading his own work from time to time, a no nonsense kind of a fellow whom had difficulties accepting stupidity in peoples actions, to the best of my knowledge, unlike the BBC production of Monty Python's comedy, Clive was fascinated by the meaning of life, interested in human behavior.

Clive is no Jesuit, but like Pierre Teilhard de Chardin, he is a paleontologist and a mystic, Clive didn't make five geological research expeditions to China, he conducted his research, in particular remains of organisms of plants and fungi in the old goldmining township of Chewton, Vic. Australia, like Teilhard, Clive dismissed the doctrine of original sin, he believes to be able to bringing together science and religion; it wasn't the Roman Catholic religious order of the Jesuits that presented difficulties to Clive, his problem was the constant disruption of having to earn a living.

Like Teilhard, Clive is honoring both, faith and reason, to participate with God and the process of bringing the universe to its fulfilment in Christ, like Teilhard, Clive through his mere presence has the ability to fill people with a cosmic, earthy vision for life. I wouldn't dare to collate Clive with Pierre Teilhard de Chardin as a person, nor do I intend to compare Teilhard's astonishing achievements with those of Clive.

I am merely fascinated by the physical features and traits that are so similar, the shape of the head, the eyebrows more or less very slightly arched from the nose out to the side of the head, the eyes that seem somewhat covered on each outer side of the skull area as a result of the skin above the eye having become a little saggy, probably the result of the aging process, the nose, relatively long and skinny, the mouth, the ears rather large, tucked firmly against the head, the crow's feet—very similar, the serious look as well as the dry but hearty smile of the two men are uncanny similar; the primary difference of appearance being the fact that Teilhard has a clean, short haircut whereas Clive has a full-length beard and wild long hair, sometimes tied back into a ponytail.

267

Looking at the front cover of Teilhard's (Comment je crois) "the way I believe," if I may make a comparison of facial characteristics with my dear friend Clive; both have much the same look, the classic French Basque Béret is worn by both and in this case their code of dress very frugal indeed.

My best friend Clive and his lovely lady Margret were over for dinner, our kids spent the weekend with their grandparents in Melbourne, Elisabeth and I shared the preparation in the kitchen, pancake filled with a ragout of fresh seafood which I brought home from the Victoria market that afternoon, covered with a Hollandaise sauce according to the recipe of Paul Bocuse, overbaked with a little French Comté.

For the main we served duckling oven roasted on a low temperature over a couple of hours served with an orange sauce created from the roast pan sediment's, freshly squeezed orange juice, a little lemon juice, some zest, a generous splash of Cointreau and equally as much Grand Marnier, reduced to a thick syrup like jus, accompanied by red cabbage and gratin potato, the dessert was composed of fresh berries diced with a raspberry liquor and a superb butter cake, a specialty that Elisabeth's mother made with lots of dried fruits and nuts. Our cellar was well stocked with white, red and other, fortified fluids from my preferred supplier Murphy's in Melbourne's Prahran, for the entrée I chose a Coralinga Sauvignon Blanc, beautifully chilled, relatively young as this particular wine reaches its optimum consumption time after five years, for the duck, to breathe I opened a couple of bottles of Hill of Grace 1961 from Henschke, a red that reaches its peak at age twenty, both wines produced in the Eden Valley, Barossa Valley, and Adelaide hills, and to round off the evening a Tawny Grant Burge Port 1969 accompanied us during several hours into the early morning.

Earlier that week, Clive and I had discussed that after dinner he would introduce us to a séance, a "spiritual table round meeting of a group" that he had not engaged in since the last session that they had with some locals that almost ended up in a tragedy. According to the (National Spiritualist Association of Churches) spiritualism is "the Science, Philosophy and Religion of continues life, based upon the demonstrated fact of communication, by means of mediumship, with those who live in the Spirit World."

Some of the rules in holding a séance require the participants to hold hands to build up the energy in the room, the séance is opened with a prayer, there is to be no light in the room, the light of a candle is sufficient, the participants should include a good mix of females and males, newcomers to the séance must be kept to a minimum to maintain a good balance of energy, sceptics like me and Elisabeth are to be discouraged from attending a session as they tend to decrease the possibility of success, and it is said that the participants should never disturb the medium when he or she is in a trance.

Clive didn't prescribe to ridged rules and regulations, to him a séance, is a meeting of a group of people, a "spiritual table round meeting of a group" with the claim of getting in touch with the dead and the supernatural like ghosts and demons, under the guidance of a Medium in order to receive messages or news from the other side, from the beyond, this also requires the belief that the spirits of the dead exist and have both the ability and inclination to communicate with the living, afterlife, or the spirit world is seen not as a static place, but as one in which spirits continue to evolve, though I never asked him if he truly believed in the notion of contact with the beyond.

Whatever, both, Elisabeth and I don't believe in the notion of continues life, hence apparently getting in touch with anybody out there is for us not plausible, but we were curious to experience this supernatural ritual; perhaps we would be able to discover something that we don't understand, and in the event of an apparent success there had to be some other explanation.

The spiritual table round meetings that Clive was involved in consisted of several, consecutive séance sessions with a couple of well-known locals, one of them a high school teacher from Castlemaine and the other an Artist from Chewton engaged in creating pottery, drawings and paintings, both of them intelligent, open-minded people. Apparently, the initial séance sessions appeared to be entertaining, based on an apparent true story that was part of the pub gossip among some of the oldies in the area, fellow miners that were still around, only too pleased to spin a yarn over a cool Victoria Bitter or two, fellows that actually were involved in some of those mysterious operations; word had it one of the minors stumbled across a small fortune as he was secretly prospecting in one of the NIMROD horizontals, caught by a couple of mining mates whom killed him and buried his body in a disused shaft in the area nearby.

The timeframe of this puzzling crime was confirmed in "The Argus (Melbourne Vic. :1848-1957)" on Friday 24 May 1946, page 18, "an article stated that Chewton Goldmines NL has acquired an option over the NIMROD mine Chewton, north of the Bendigo railway line. The prospecting program at

No. 8 level on the Chewton mine will be suspended, and the mining staff transferred to develop the NIMROD leases. A plan suitable for sinking the shaft to a depth of 200 ft has been purchased, and work will commence on the area immediately. It is expected that operations will occupy a period of six months. The mine was reported on favorably by Mr. M. R. McKeown, mining engineer—it was supposed to have happened in June of 1946, and approximate coordinates had been handed down the gossip line.

As I understood from Clive, the purpose of the séance sessions was to find the location of the shaft where the body of this minor was supposed to have been buried, in their spare time they were actually out there in the bush with picks, shovels and minors' torches. After a number of sessions "the spirit" revealed sufficient information for the team to eventually find the filled in point of entry; over a period of some weeks they progressed to a point where several directional options presented themselves which led to the next séance session from which the team expected to obtain a closer description from the "spirit," but this session was different from all the previous ones, apparently they were urged to drop this subject matter by the "spirit"—as the session was intensified to the point where, without anybody touching them, crockery and glassware were hurled around the room, smashing against the stone walls, falling to the ground in pieces. Clive was telling me that this particular séance session had gotten out of hand, apparently it was convincingly scary, the team was terrified, and ceased the project immediately.

That particular evening, after the seafood pancake à la mode de Paul Bocuse, after we had enjoyed the roast duckling we prepared our very own **Ouija board,** an invention by the US attorney Bond the patentee of 28 May 1890. Unlike the ones that you can buy, the one that we used was merely an old round table, the letters of the alphabet, the numbers from one to zero a yes and now all-handwritten on some light cardboard, each about four centimeters square, neatly laid out on the table, the four of us sitting around it, Clive had placed a water glass placed upside down in the inner circle.

Me wanting to check the integrity of this event; I got up and walked over to the side board, wrote the name of the dog that I had during my childhood, turned the paper upside down and placed it under an ornament that was standing on the dresser and joined the gathering at the table. With a couple of candles placed near the table and a kerosene lamp in the corner, the mood was set for a serious session. "Is there anybody there?" Clive asked, the four of us had our pointing finger placed just above the water glass, kind of hovering without touching it; apparently to transmit our energy to the glass.

I noted that our dog had left my side, she disappeared under the piano in the corner, I had the feeling that she was terrified, trembling, behavior I had never noticed before from my Dobermann, and yet she was noted for her stealth and protective alertness. After a few calls the glass began to move, not always smooth, sometimes slow, hesitant at times and other times it was difficult to maintain our fingers just above it, there were occasions where the glass had moved away independently from the "guidance" from my finger and halted at the letter **K**, next it moved to **E**, eventually on to **L**, it hesitated for a while, suddenly it moved to around the board a couple of times then came back to the letter **L**, this time it moved to **Y** and didn't move after that.

Margarete, on a piece of paper, had noted that the glass had had spelled KELLY. I went over to the dresser to retrieve the note that I had written a moment ago, brought it over to the table and presented it to the séance team, the name of my childhood dog was written on the note—indeed it was KELLY. Elisabeth and I were astonished of the outcome of this particular segment of the session, I was certain that nobody in this round could have possibly known the name of my childhood dog with the exception of myself, it was also impossible for anybody in the room having observed what I had written on a bit of paper several meters away from the table, but it didn't convince either of us that the name KELLY was transmitted through the movement of the glass by a "spirit," the likelihood of this result being coincidental is near zero, there had to be another explanation.

We attempted several trials that required a specific response, some of the outcomes were near right, others rather blurred to the point where similarities or a plausible pattern of behavior could not be determined.

Since the late seventies, the time when this mysterious experience with the "spirit" took place I was annoyed not to have a plausible answer for this mystical event, irritated because I didn't understand this phenomena about the name of my childhood dog, not that I was preoccupied with this subject to the point where I would have pondered over it every day, but the thought of it haunted me until just recently; by mere chance I came across an article written by Tom Stafford 30 July 2013: "The mystery isn't a connection to the spirit world, but why we can make movements ant yet not realize that we're making them," an article that clarifies the phenomena called **ideomotor effect**, an explanation that may well anger those that are staunch believers in the ability of psychics that obtain information derived directly from an external physical source, believers in spirits."

Stafford states that the glass that appears to be mystically moving of its own accord on the Ouija board is really being moved by the participants that have their finger on it, the only mystery is not one of a connection to a spirit world, but of why we can make movements and yet not realize that we are making them. He called this phenomenon the ideomotor effect which you can try out yourself, if you attach a small weight from a string (ideally a bit more than a foot long), then you hold the end of the string with your arm stretched out in front of you so that the weight hangs down freely, holding your arm completely still. Now, the weight will begin to swing in a clock or anti-clock direction, forming small circles.

Don't start this motion yourself, but ask yourself a question, any question at all and tell yourself that the weight will swing clockwise to answer Yes, and anticlockwise for No. Maintain this thought in your mind, try not to make any motions, and you will soon be able to observe how the weight begins to swing, and you can ask yourself if this is magic, it's the ordinary everyday magic of consciousness, there is no supernatural force at work, just tiny movements you are making without realizing, the string permits the movement to be exaggerated, the inertia of the weight allows it to be conserved and built on until they form a regular swinging motion.

So, what happened with the glass that seemed to have moved of its own accord to answer the questions by moving to the letters on our home-made Ouija board, it was my finger -apparently floating just above the glass, but without me being aware my finger actually touched the glass, and small movements caused the glass to be guided toward the letters that build up the name of my childhood dog. The discovery of **the ideomotor effects** demonstrates that there was no mystery underpinning the eerie happening of the seances, merely the effect of delusion. As I have precious little time for nonsense, this is a reminder that we can all too easily fool ourselves, the séance is not some bizarre supernatural event, nor is it a psychic phenomenon that deals with extrasensory perception as in telepathy, precognition, clairvoyance, psychokinesis, telekinesis psychometry and other related to near-death experiences, synchronicity, apparitional experiences, etc., despite a persistent fascination with the paranormal, researchers following rigorous and reproducible scientific methods have yet to prove that psychic phenomena are real.

## The Struggle for Equal Opportunity 1977

In Australia, Victoria was the third state, after New South Wales and South Australia to implement anti-discrimination laws, with its first Equal Opportunity act back in 1977, Australia's structure and organization to protect the rights of humans has evolved to meet contemporary times. The first Equal Opportunity Act was aiming to eliminate discrimination based on sex and marital status, established the Equal Opportunity Board which was headed by the Equal Opportunity Commissioner.

The legislation which protected people with a disability followed suit in 1983, and one year later further protective elements against discrimination had been added, religion, political beliefs, ethnic origin, race, de-facto spouse and sexual harassment, and the Equal Opportunity Act 1995, further expanded its protective attributes to age, industrial activity, parental status, physical features, pregnancy, religious belief or activity, and personal association with someone that is perceived to have one or more of these attributes, with the acts being reformed continuously, whereas the principle of equal rights of man and woman in Switzerland was established on 14 June 1981 written into the Swiss federal constitution, and yet, in Switzerland, nearly forty years later we are still debating the same subject.

Not only has Australia began with its implement of anti-discrimination laws earlier than Switzerland, it has embraced the notion of equal opportunity much earlier whereas in Switzerland we adore to talk about the subject matter, but in practice often the result leaves much to be desired, a possible reason for this difference may be multicultural society that Australia already was at that time whereas Switzerland's cultural behavior was still a little unobtrusive, reserved.

One of the first and most compelling equal opportunity cases handled by its commissioner in Victoria was the case of Deborah Wardley whom had applied with Ansett Airlines in 1976. It was in 1971 that Deborah Wardley, at the age of 18 gained her PP license, a couple of years later she had accomplished the Commercial PL in 1973 and with 2600 hours of stick time she became flight instructor and charter Pilot in 1976. Then she applied to Ansett Airlines in 1976, finally in 1978 she was invited for an interview but was rejected. Deborah Wardley wasn't satisfied with this answer and took the case to the Victorian Equal Opportunity Board, challenging Ansett on the basis of sexual discrimination.

Reg Ansett, the founder and owner of the airline denied the allegation of discrimination but admitted that it was his strong personal view that woman are not suited to be airplane pilots, which led to public demonstration marches during August 1979. As a result of Ansett's perceived views about woman, many successful ladies at the time transferred their business travel to QF in the first six months, Ansett lost more than 50 percent of its business travel at that time—many of them never returned. In a letter to the woman's electoral lobby the general manager of Ansett wrote: "Ansett has adopted a policy of only employing men as pilots. This does not mean that women cannot be good pilots, but we are concerned with the provision of the safest and most efficient air service possible. In this regard we feel that an all-male cockpit crew is safer than one in which the sexes are mixed."

Reg Ansett's views about women was widely viewed as sexist, apparently he once described female cabin crew over the age of thirty as "old boilers," he also claimed that woman were unsuitable to be commercial pilots because of the menstrual cycles, he claimed that the pilot's union would object to woman in the cockpit, even though there was no strength test for pilots, Reg Ansett claimed that pilots needed strength, and that pregnancy and childbirth would disrupt a woman's career to the point where it would jeopardize safety and incur extra costs for the company, rendering women unsuitable—this was Ansett's main legal argument.

The Victorian Equal Opportunity Board ruled that Ansett's refusal to employ Wardley was illegal; it awarded damages of AD 14.500 and ordered Ansett to include her in the next pilot training program. Ansett delayed its next intake and appealed to the Supreme Court Victoria but the appeal was dismissed. Consequently, Ansett appealed the Victorian Supreme Court's decision to the next level, the High Court of Australia in October 1979, but employed Wardley from the 5th of November 1979 pending the outcome of the case. During classroom training, Ansett attempted to sack her by claiming she had been at fault in a near-miss incident during a training flight at Moorabbin Airport despite an inquiry exonerating her and identifying the other pilot as at fault.

However, Ansett backed down after unions stepped in, defending Wardley. When classroom training was completed in December 1979, she was not assigned to a training aircraft despite the male trainees progressing to line flight training. Ansett Airlines had been taken over by Peter Abeles and Rupert Murdoch in late 1979. Wardley had previously taught Murdoch's brother-in-law, John Calvert-Jones, to fly. Eventually she telephoned her former private pilot student Calvert-Jones in early January 1980 informing him of the situation. Two days later Rupert Murdoch, the new part owner of Ansett issued a memo directing that Deborah Wardley was to be treated the same as the male pilot candidates, she commenced flight training immediately and made her first commercial flight co-piloting a Fokker F27 from Alice Springs to Darwin on the 22 January 1980. The High Court dismissed Ansett's appeal in March 1980.

This case is still used as a precedent. However, simply removing the most formal of exclusionary practices did not dissolve barriers in Australia, and so continuing prejudices and putting obstacles in the way of women—female commercial pilots are still rare in Australia.

## Further Education, February 1980

English wasn't my favored subject, though I was in full command of the colloquial language, if you lived in the bush like I did you had to have some knowledge of the Ozzie slang, jargon is inherent in my profession, but I reserved it for that purpose, and the writing of technical reports using cockpit lingo and abbreviations wasn't a problem either; however, the writing of a letter triggered catastrophic anxiety in me, the subconscious part of my brain would take charge of my writing hand, guiding it deliberately to put some illegible scribble to paper, so profound that often I was unable to identify what I had actually written myself, and there was good reason for this behavior, my spelling skills were in a diabolical shape, extremely difficult to correct, particularly if you realized a mistake toward the end of the page, regardless whether it was written by hand or machine typed, either you applied liquid paper which invariable looked very smudgy, or you started all over again—either choice was tedious.

It wasn't until 1983 when I bought my first Japanese NEC APC III; the rather large "screen box," the keyboard and a dot matrix printer, the desktop CPU with its Intel 8086 processer, a 16 bit memory bus with its 8 MHz was nearly twice as fast as its opponent IBM-PC, with its 2 X 5.1/4 large floppies and to go with it a couple of games for the kids, one of the first spread sheets called multiplan and a word processor that allowed us to format the pages and make changes possible at any time, a true blessing for all of those that suffered from a misspelling disorder.

It was my first check and training flight with Captain Cole Evens since I made Captain on the Friday 28 September, a couple of days before my thirtieth birthday, without letting me know what this was all about, he made an appointment with me in his office for the next day, my check ride was impeccable; hence I knew that our meeting had nothing to do with today's flight performance. However, since I began my career with TAA, from time to time I had the feeling that Cole was tougher with me compared to my colleagues of equal rank and experience but I didn't see this necessarily as a disadvantage, the contrary was true, I had the impression that I was able to squeeze more experience-based knowledge out of Cole than did others.

Cole reminded me a bit of my father, being a no-nonsense kind of a boss, he came to the point very quickly, pointing out some of the processes that I might consider strengthening, and emphasizing those procedures or part thereof that he was particularly impressed with, but he didn't dwell on either of the subjects, Cole paused briefly, he was staring at his desk; it seemed like eternity before he looked up, stared straight into my eyes and said: "I want you in my team, I want you to get involved in the training department," "I want you to become one of my check and training pilots."

Cole went on to propose to enroll me at the Chisholm Institute of Technology at Hawthorn in the Diploma of Technical Teaching, a course that was aimed at tradie's that were aspiring to become teachers in their technical field.

Mid-February 1980 I received confirmation that Australian had enrolled me at Chisholm, and that the course began Monday the 3$^{rd}$ March. The aim of the course was to meet the developmental needs of trainee teachers in respect to their capacities to; demonstrate the essential knowledge, skills and attitudes to enable them to design and implement effective learning experiences for their students; to fulfil a professional role as a member of an educational organization; maintain a program of self-development which will extend competence in educational, specialist and personal areas relevant to their roles as teachers.

The structure of the course was such that students spend one day per week at the college in a learning environment and the remaining work hours in the respective place of work and transpose the knowledge gained under the supervision of a qualified instructor. The core subject of study in both, year one and year tow consisted of; Principles of teaching, Educational Psychology, Communication / English, Mathematics and computer studies, the personal as well as the professional backgrounds of my class mates was as colorful as is Australia's society; all men, most of us in the late twenties to early thirties, the personalities as diverse as it can get, each of us fundamentally different but there was one common denominator, all of us appeared to be very dedicated professionals in our own right; fellows from the electrical trades, metal fabrication, masonry, fitting and machining, electronics trades, and myself from the aviation industry were sharing the class room.

Attending a classroom, being confronted with task-oriented learning, delivering performance at the higher end of the yardstick was something that I was used to, frequent refresher as well as advanced training courses on the ground as well as in-flight were part of my profession, I was looking forward to get involved in the subjects, I was highly motivated and self-disciplined to learn independently, though keen to learn more about the intricacies of the subject Communication and English, I was horrified of the thought of having to write an essay or a report, if possible without spelling mistakes, in a handwriting that can be decoded by the teaching staff.

Our English lecturer was a lady by the name of Anne Baine, not only did she value, but she insisted that we used the British spelling rules and not the American, in fact she got mad with us if we dared to use the US spelling method, Anne was of the opinion that the American way of spelling had no rules, that only those that couldn't spell would make use of US grammar. My problem wasn't the choice between British or American; despite considerable efforts back at school, my English grammar was modest, which was the reason why I tended to write the letters very close together, particularly in those cases where I wasn't sure about the spelling so that nobody had a chance to identify if the spelling of a word was correct or not, as a result some of the words couldn't be identified at all.

It didn't take many classroom sessions at all before Anne realized that one of her pupils had difficulties with spelling, she asked me to "loosen up" my writing so that she would be able to assess my work, not very long after that I was obliged to confess to Anne that I was embarrassed about my spelling, that it was for this reason that I had developed my very own style—"compact spelling" as I called it at the time, a method to hide spelling mistakes. For a long time, I was hiding from this problem because it was easier to conceal the reality rather than confronting the truth. Through this experience I realized that; because I was prepared to be honest and share my shortfalls, I was able to liberate myself from a problem that caused extreme anxiety and discomfort from time to time, and with the assistance of my lecturer I was able to move forward.

Part of the core program at Chisholm was Communication, a subject I got to appreciate as the content began to intensify, I began to realize how much I had learned about communication as a kid without having realized it; by now I was able to ponder over the mental torture that Aunt used to subject me to without getting emotional. Already as a youngster I was aware that people could read very different things into the choice of words and the body language, as a result, neither of them will have the same understanding as the person that is communicating—"open-ended" face to face messages in particular are difficult to decipher because of characteristics like the eye contact or the lack of, the general body language, the manner in which we are dressed, the perfume that we ware, our facial expression together with the modulation of our voice that we utilize are making it difficult to interpret the message the way it is intended, whereas "close ended" messages tend to be better understood by most.

There was usually no confusion about Aunt's verbal communication; regardless whether it was a non-emotional statement about some trivial matter or a clear instruction, an opinion that she expressed, regardless whether I thought it to be fitting or not, regardless if her opinion or statement was true or false, and there were the special moments, the highlights of her verbal communication skills, the times when Aunt was particularly inspired by her vivid phantasy, inventing stories about what I was supposed to have wrecked or caused, standing over me with all of her impressive physical dimension, putting on her scary face, staring at me with her sinister eyes as if she was about to swallow me in one hit, yelling and screaming at the same time.

However, as the course progressed, I realized the significance of the non-spoken communication, I began to understand the signals that we send out in anticipation that the receiving person understands the message as it is intended, though this does not assure that the person has really understood what I was trying to convey. Interpreting Aunt's non-verbal messages wasn't difficult, surely they weren't well meant, nor were they intended to be caressing or affectionate, whereas I don't know how Aunt interpreted my non-verbal answer in response to her scolding, I could merely guess that she was looking for a reaction because more often than not she would demand "don't look at me in this way" or she would invite me to answer her question which indicated that she had been observing my behavior, how I was feeling uncomfortable, sometimes squirming, looking at me with her filthy smirk, as if she could see how my entire inside was trembling, as if she was amused if I appeared to be scared.

But I don't know if she was able to imagine how over the years I had learned to be terrible with her, without being conscious about it I had acquired very sophisticated non-verbal communication skills, standing in front of Aunt, letting her pour her verbal diarrhea all over me, my posture conveyed that I was scared, I was able to put a terrified look onto my face as if I was sorry about something, and at the same time I was talking to myself; reminding myself to be courageous and patient, telling myself that the time would come were this kind of suffering would come to an end, that one day Aunt would be sorry for what she did to me, I would look at her and quietly mumble in my thoughts "I hate you," "you will never know the truth," "you can kiss my ass you stupid cow"—this kind of caressing thought helped me to get through difficult times.

During the communications course, we also examined the role of the media and the manner in which Journalism influences our lives, how the media is shaping public perceptions and opinions about significant political and social issues. It is widely accepted that what we know about, think and believe about what happens in the world, with the exception of personal first-hand experience is influenced, perhaps orchestrated through the manner in which these events are reported in newspapers, on the radio, TV and more recently through the social media.

We also examined how the topic of school discipline was covered in some of the Australian major newspapers, reports on discipline and related topics such as behavioral management, disruptive and antisocial behavior in schools were examined for a particular period. The analysis focused on the types of topics covered, evidence of bias and the "message" conveyed in the reports about this important and highly controversial subject, the paper concluded with a commentary the relationship in schools and how educational decisions and policy might be influenced by such reports.

The role of the media in forming public perceptions and opinions about significant political and social issues has long been subject of much speculation and debate, it is broadly accepted that what we know about, think about and believe about what happens in the world, with the exception of personal experience, is shaped and orchestrated by how these events are reported in the media, the reality that nowadays each one of us has the potential to act as a reporter or influencer is terrifying.

*Sociology,* the scientific study of social patterns of social relationships, social interaction, and culture of everyday life was one of the key subjects taught; there were two major issues throughout my time at Chisholm that we analyzed in some detail, the first subjects that were of particular interest to me was the laissez faire education method that had started in Summerset England in the sixties.

It was sometime during 1969 when I came across a book titled "Summerhill," written by the Scottish educator (A.S. Neill, November 1960 by the Hart Publishing Company). Regularly, this book used to hang about on the kitchen table of the apartment that I shared with my flat mate Ursula during my pilots training in Zürich, the literature was all about the co-educational Summerhill founded in 1921 by A.S. Neill, a school that was described as the original alternative "Free" School in Suffolk, England.

Having enjoyed a classical post-war WWII education with a pure autocratic leadership, both in the home as well as out in the education system, Neill's "laissez-faire" education, the opposite to the education that I had undergone, in Neill's concept the parents behave rather in a passive role in the education whereas children are essentially left to make decisions themselves, a notion that wasn't merely an exciting novelty, it appeared to be an alternative to what I had experienced.

Highly controversial then, as it is now in the 21st century, Neill's educational philosophy can be summarized in the following manner; he believes in the basic goodness of the child, Neill set the happiness of the child as the goal of his education, he thought that educators must take into account what the child wants, not just what others want from him, Neill is adamant that discipline should be kept to a minimum, Neill is of the opinion that the child should be allowed freedom, not license, respecting the rights of others, he persists that teachers are honest and sincere toward their pupils, Neill proposes that the child is cutting its ties to his parents, making the schools his home, he says that we should avoid giving the child guilt feelings, and he refrained from teaching children religion.

"Summerhill is a democratic, self-governing school in which the adults and the children have equal status. The daily life of the school is governed by the school meetings, usually held twice a week in which everybody has an equal vote. The school's philosophy is to allow freedom for the individual, each child being able to take their own path in life, and following their own interests to develop into the person that they personally feel that they are meant to be. This leads to an inner self-confidence and real acceptance of themselves as individuals. All of this is done with the school's structure of self-government through school meetings which are at the core of the school and emphasize the distinction between freedom and license.

Living life in a community is of great importance to the pupils. Through this they learn to compromise, communicate, negotiate and assume responsibility. It also teaches them empathy and a consideration for the feelings of others. The adults and children have equal status in the school but, of course, they have different roles. Everybody in the school is aware of the responsibilities that the adults have and which the children are not subject to. The atmosphere of the school is informal and first names are always used, the school is international, reflecting the extent of A.S. Neill's continuing influence in the world.

The Summerhill School provides an environment where children can grow up happily, free from many of the anxieties and neuroses of the outside world. They can take part in a caring and active community and assume real responsibilities as they learn more and more about the running of the school is that these lessons are not the central concern. Neill's notion of freedom in education, an idea that was considered to be controversial in its time, influenced many progressive educators that came after him, like John Holt (an American author and educator, 14 April 1923-14 September 1985) who headed the "unschooling" movement was popular among those that wanted to promote the process of educating children at home rather than at a public or private institution; at the Donahue Show, 1981, Holt was asked to describe how to fix schools in one sentence, he responded, "the schools would be a lot better if they were a lot smaller, if the teachers were their own bosses in the class room, which for the most part they are not, if there was a wide variety of schools, and if the parents could choose the schools they wanted."

Back in 1969, when for the first time I got mentally entangled in Neill's educational philosophy I sympathized with many of his ideas; finally, there was somebody that believes in the basic goodness of the child, someone that set the happiness of the child as an educational goal, Neill's thought that educators must take into account what the child wants, not just what others want from him, how refreshing, the idea that discipline should be kept to a minimum I can appreciate, Neill's opinion that the child should be allowed freedom, not license, a healthy portion of freedom can be beneficial, though too much might be unhealthy in my view, his demand that teachers are to be honest and sincere toward their pupils I perceive as an obligation, Neill's proposal that the child is cutting its ties to his parents, making the school his home I believe to be preposterous and unhealthy; I don't grasp his reasoning to refrain from teaching children religion.

To realize the outcome of Neill's "laissez-faire" approach to education, fostering freedom and the abolition of authority, his anti-academic method, the willingness to sacrifice brain for heart, his attitude to hold books and formal learning in contempt I perceived as daring, perhaps reckless; but I knew that it would take at least twenty years or so before I would be able to enjoy a report about the outcome of this form of education, learning how these children developed into adults and what they achieved in their lives.

The second major Sociology issue was a study of interaction between the Ethnic groups that make up Australian society, with particular focus on religious believes. Most contemporary Australians, 67.4% of them can trace their ancestry back to the British Isles with the Irish representing 8.7%, Aboriginal and Torres Strait Islander account for 3.0%, Italians 3.8%, Germans 3.7%, Chinese 3.6%, Islam 2.6%, Indians 1.7%, Greek 1.6%, Dutch 1.2%, Judaism 0.4% and Others 2.7%, of the total population, a melting pot of cultures.

According to the **ABS Census of population and housing 2016,** the religious makeup of the Australian citizen represents 52.1% Catholics, Anglicans, and other Christians-Dreamtime-Islam-Buddhism-Hinduism-Judaism and other believes amount to 8.2% and the 30.1% of the non-religions include secular and other spiritual beliefs.

*Catholics*, account for 22.6%

*Anglicans*, make up 13.3%, part of the Church of England, considered firmly Protestant, despite similarities with the Catholic Church.

*United Church,* founded on Christianity with some believes that are fundamentally different from the Catholics and the protestants, *Presbyterian and Reformed*, emphasizes the sovereignty of God, a form of Protestant Christianity which has its origin in Great Britain, particularly in Scotland, *Eastern Orthodox*, a religion that is aligned with Catholicism, *Baptists,* a Christian religion group belonging to the Protestant movement of Christianity, *Lutheran*, one of the largest branches of Protestantism that is aligned with the teachings of Martin Luther, together these Christian believes make up 15.2%, the balance of the 35.9%.

*Dreamtime,* 3.0%, it is with respect and awe that I begin with the people that are native to this country, the Aboriginal and Torres Strait Islander from whom is said that they inhabited the historic region of Arnhem Land in the North Eastern part of the Northern Territory, a place that was first discovered by the Dutch East India Company by captain William Joosten van Colster in 1623, before the first fleet of British ships arrived in Sydney NSW in 1788 whom established the penal colony. At the time of colonization, the majority of Aborigines were living in the areas along the Murray River which rises in the Australian alps, then meanders across Australia's inland plains where it forms the natural border between NSW, Victoria, flowing northwest into South Australia, at Morgan the river turns South and eventually runs into the ocean at lake Alexandria.

With the colonization of Australia, Aboriginal and Torres Strait Islanders were exposed to a collapse of the population, principally from a disease brought in by Europeans; *smallpox* an infectious disease that reached epidemic magnitude three years after the arrival of the British settlers. However, conflicts that led to frontier wars between the indigenous people and the British settlers some months after the landing of the first fleet in January 1788 resulted in the massive killing of Aboriginal and Torres Strait Islanders, a subject to an ongoing public discussion where the characterization of this violence as genocide is debated.

Aboriginal *Dreamtime*, the foundation of Australia's native people which dates back some 65.000 years is probably the oldest religion known to man, the story about how the universe came to be, explaining how the Creator intended humans to function in this world. (Aboriginal Service Branch. (2009) *Working with Aboriginal People and Communities:* A Practice Resource. Ashfield, NSW Department of Community Services)

*Islam*, 2.58%; Is an Abrahamic monotheistic religion teaching that there is only one God (Allah), and that Muhammed is a messenger of God. With 1.8 billion followers It is the world's second largest religion in the world after Christianity, around 24% of the world's population known as Muslims; apparently, it is also one of the most misunderstood religions. My description of Islam is an interpretation of the meaning, and not the exact word for word definition, in an endeavor to understand this religion; Islam, an Arabic term which means to submit one's life to the will of God, Muslims believe that Islam is the true religion of God revealed to humanity, that it is a universal religion that can be practiced by anyone at any time, in any place, the principal concept being that this way of life is total submission to God.

Islam is a holistic way of life, covering all aspects, it teaches how to behave personally, socially, materialistically, morally, ethically, legally, culturally, politically, economically and globally. It is said that a Muslim is anyone who submits their will to the one and only true God who is worthy of worship, "Allah" (God). Some sources advocate using "Allah" as the word for "God" in Islamic contest tell us that the word "Allah" is simply a noun used to describe a divine being just as the word "God" is a noun used to describe a divine being in English (which does not answer the question whether Allah and God are one and the same divinity).

Muslims believe that Allah is the name God Almighty has given himself, he has no partners in divinity, he is the originator and sustainer of the universe, and that he is the creator of human beings for one purpose only—to worship him alone. Fundamentally, the believe taught in Islam is that human beings are unique from God's creation, that we have the ability to think freely and that we can behave in any way we wish. It is also believed that Allah has delegated prophets to each nation to guide them to the truth.

*Buddhism*, 2.41%; nearly half a million Buddhist that live in Australia, about two thirds are descendent from families originating in Asian countries whom have immigrated to this country in recent decades, practicing Eastern Buddhism, the remaining quarter of Buddhists are Australian-born Caucasian probably grown up in either a Christian or humanistic family. Buddhist are generally peaceful and non-threatening, their basic teachings of Buddha which are core to Buddhism are the four-noble truth's—*the existence is suffering, suffering has a cause,* namely craving and attachment, *there is a cessation to suffering, and there is a path to cessation of suffering.*

It is also said that Buddhism characteristically describes reality in terms of process and relation rather that entity or substance (cause and effect), that followers of Buddhism don't acknowledge a supreme god or deity—they focus on achieving enlightenment, a state of inner peace and wisdom, when the spiritual echelon is reached, they have experienced "nirvana," its numerous philosophies and interpretations within Buddhism, making it a tolerant, evolving religion which is said not to be an organized faith, it is essentially a way of life or a spiritual tradition.

*Hinduism*, 1.88%; the followers believe that there are a number of different ways to reach God, Hindus believe in the doctrines of *"samsara"* (the continuous cycle of life, death and reincarnation), and *"karma* "(the law of cause and effect), and *"atman,"* (the believe in soul). Hinduism is the world's second oldest religion, dating back some four thousand years, with its around 900 million followers, Hinduism is the world's third largest religion behind Christianity and Islam.

Hinduism embraces a number of different religious ideas; hence it is often referred to as a way of life, most Hindus are henotheistic, worshiping the deity known as "Brahman," Hindus believe that peoples actions and thoughts directly determine their actual as well as their future life, Hindus aspire to reach "dharma," a way of living which emphasizes good conduct and morality, Hindus consider cows to be sacred and worship all living creatures, many Hindus are vegetarians, most of them don't eat beef, nor pork, Hinduism is closely related to other Indian religions which include Jainism, Sikhism and Buddhism.

*Judaism*, 0.39%; Judaism, a monotheistic religion developed among the ancient Hebrews. Judaism is characterized by a belief in one transcendent God who revealed himself to Abraham, Moses and the Hebrew prophets and by a religious life in accordance with Scriptures and rabbinic traditions. Judaism is the complex phenomenon of a total way of life for Jewish people, comprising theology, law, and innumerable cultural tradition.

Jewish people believe that there is only one universal God, that he is the creator of the world, consequently there is one universal morality, that God is incorporeal, that all matter comes to an end, that all matter has a beginning, that God is not in nature, that nature is not divine, that God knows each of us and that he is moral, just and compassionate, that God is the God revealed in the Torah, that his primary demand is that people be good; the Jewish people believe in afterlife but he wants us to be preoccupied with this life, that there will be reward in the afterlife ("heaven") available to all good people, not just good Jews, that human beings are not born basically good, hence evil comes primarily from within, that all people are created in the image of God, hence racism is theoretically not possible, the Jewish people believe that God created the world for man, that the Torah is from God, they believe in trinity, God, the Torah and Israel, the Jewish faith rests on two pillars—creation and exodus (the departure of the Israelites from Egypt under the leadership of Moses), and that Judaism is a religion of distinction—God and man, good and evil, man and woman, holy and profane, life and death, and the believe that Judaism can ennoble anyone, hence, any non-Jew is welcome to embrace Judaism and become a member of the Jewish people, but no one needs to become a Jew to be saved.

*Other spiritual beliefs*, not specified in the Census 0.46%

*No religion,* according to the ABS Census of population and housing 2016, 29.63%

*Inadequately described*, 9.57%,

Out of the surveyed people, those that did not indicate their ethnic, nor their religious background are not included in this statistic.

I consider Australia as a melting pot of cultures, a place where people from different cultural backgrounds and diverse religious makeup live together without major problems, the multicultural makeup has enriched the Australian society over a number of decades, and enabled the country to move forward, few social problems have occurred in the country with the exception of non-English speaking immigrants who have a difficult time finding high-level, skilled jobs.

Social and class association was once prevalent among Christians but this is no longer the case, though it is common to find ethnic and national churches that act as a cultural hub, a center for different cultures, for example, the *Eastern Orthodox* churches have become a cultural meeting place for Russian, Serbian and Greek communities, and the *Oriental Orthodox* churches accommodate Armenian, Ethiopian and Egyptian Coptic communities, and

*Wesleyan Methodists* churches that are affiliated with Samoan, Tonga and Pacific Island nations.

The majority of Australia's Jewish community live in Melbourne and Sydney, their settlement and community activities, kosher food stores, Jewish schools and other facilities tend to be established around the synagogues whom serves as the hub to the community, providing a great sense of support and awareness of togetherness, an ethnic group that tends to isolate themselves from the rest of the community. (Barker, R (2019) State and religion: the Australian story. New York; Routledge)

Muslim communities in Australia differ from what I have experienced in other countries. Australia's contemporary Muslim population reflects its divers linguistic and ethnic migration background. Some of the country's mosques were originally founded along ethno-linguistic lines, Turkish, Egyptian and Lebanese communities. Though, a shift among second generation Muslims has been evident, often mosques in Australia are very multicultural, acting as social and cultural hubs for different migrant communities, providing a sense of universal connection to the Muslim world. (Deen, H., 2009) Muslims in Australia 1901-75. (In J. Jupp (ed.), *The Encyclopedia of Religion in Australia.* Melbourne: Cambridge University Press.)

In Australia, many Buddhists that have their roots in Asian countries, but there are also *Anglo-Australian* Buddhists as well as those that migrated from English speaking western countries, a great deal of diversity of practices can be identified in the Buddhist community. Some are part of teachings and sects that were established centuries ago, and others belong to newly emerged schools, each having different meditation centers.

Hindus migrated to Australia during the nineteenth century, mainly as hawkers, farm hands and cameleers alongside the Muslin communities. Many of them had to return to their countries as a result of the introduction of the "white Australia policy" in 1901. However, as gurus, yogis and swamis began to introduce various expressions of Hinduism in Australia, a wave of political refugees, political migrants of Indian descent begun to arrive around 1986. Various small community groups celebrate cultural events either in homes or temples.

The "white Australia policy" was an approach to immigration by Australian government enforced from 1901 up until mid-20th century. Changes to the Migration Act sought to effectively prohibit immigration from non-

European countries, particularly neighboring Asia. Subsequent Australian governments gradually abolished the policy, with its official removal in 1973.

The Australian society is made up of different cultural or ethnic groups, Christianity with 51.2% being the dominant fraction; although they live alongside each other, but each cultural group does not necessarily have engaging interaction with each other, the multicultural neighborhood people may frequent ethnic grocery stores and restaurants without interacting with their neighbors from other countries. In some cases, the differences between the cultures may be understood and acknowledged by some, and this can bring about individual change but not collective transformation. Considering broadly the fundamental elements and principles underlying each of those religions, it is evident that Christianity emphasizes the sovereignty of God, that the Aborigine's "Dreamtime" explains how the Creator intended humans to function in this world, Muslims are teaching that there is only one God (Allah), and that Muhammed is a messenger of God, Jewish people believe that there is only one universal God, that Buddhists believe in the divinity of Buddha, and that Hindus are henotheistic, worshiping the deity known as "Brahman."

Considering the fundamental elements and principles, teaches supernatural gifts of the holy spirit such as divine healing, prophecy and speaking tongues, a version of Christianity the Eternal Creator in an endeavor to live a blessed life on earth and inherit eternal life; "Dreamtime," the beginning of knowledge from which derived the laws of existence fort the Aboriginal People, representing the time of the ancestral spirit and how they evolved over time and created life, an explanation of how the Creator intended humans to function in this world; Islam, the principle concept being that this **way of life** is total submission to God, a holistic way of life, covering all aspects, it teaches how to behave personally, socially, materialistically, morally, ethically, legally, culturally, politically, economically and globally.

It is said that a Muslim is anyone who submits their will to the one and only true God who is worthy of worship, "Allah" (God), the four-noble truths of Buddhism, the existence is suffering, suffering has a cause, namely craving and attachment, there is a cessation to suffering, and there is a path to cessation of suffering, a way of life; Hinduism embraces a number of different religious ideas; hence it is often referred to as a way of life, most Hindus are henotheistic, worshiping the deity known as "Brahman"; Judaism is the complex phenomenon of a total way of life for Jewish people, comprising theology, law, and innumerable cultural tradition.

Though there are elementary differences between these religions, each founded upon distinct convictions, some varying slightly in their fundamental believe whilst others are more complex in their composition, all of them serve the same purpose; to provide clear guidelines and rules by which we live our daily lives, how we are expected to behave toward the **deity** that we believe in, and how to function within our community.

However, Catholics follow the teachings of Jesus Christ and the authority of the Pope, with more conclusive conviction as do other Christians, the Protestant in contrast is **free to accept** or reject individual teachings and interpretations of the bible, whereas the Aboriginal and Torres Straight Islanders follow the teachings of the Dreamtime in an **uncomplicated** manner, the Torah isn't merely the bible of the Jewish people, it is a way of life with **very stringent rules** to be followed on a daily basis, Buddhism is a different kind of spirality where nothing is permanent, and the path of enlightenment occurs through the practice and development of morality, meditation and wisdom, a way of life, Hinduism embrace many religions ideas as part of a way of life, in contrast, Protestants are free to accept or reject individual teachings and interpretations of the bible.

The 1960s was a period of decisive change in the religious history of Christianity in the western world, including western Europe, the United States, Canada, Australia and New Zealand. Between 1958 and 1974 in the religious history of the West, these years may come to be seen as marking a rupture as profound as that brought about by the Reformation. Nearly every western country saw a decline in church members, attendance and a drop in the number of clergy and other religious professions. In many cases the drop was severe, for instance; 825 secular priests had been ordained in France in 1956, by 1975 the number had fallen to 181 per annum, the proportion of Dutch Catholics attending mass diminished by half in just ten years between 1965 and 1975. During this period large numbers of people lost the habit of regular religious worship, and the social significance of priests and nuns decreased because their numbers had diminished considerably.

At the same time there was a weakening of the processes by which Christian identity and knowledge of Christianity had been passed on to the younger generation. In some countries there was a substantial fall in the proportion of infants baptized, children attending Sunday school or catechism classes, and adolescents confirmed. In England for instance the latter statistic fell by half between 1956 and 1975, religious education in schools continued, but it seems likely that this was less effective as a means of Christian socialization that religious teaching in the home and institutions such as Sunday school, directly connected with the church, as well as a drop of the number of clergy and other religious professions. (Hugh McLeod, the Religious Crisis of the 1960s, Amazon.de)

After the inherent "religious cleansing" that occurred around the Western civilization during the 1960s, the Australian Catholic church, between 1971 and 2016 lost 4.4% of its congregation, and the Anglicans, in the same period lost 17.7%. During the same period in Switzerland the Catholic church has lost around 10% of its congregation, whereas the loss for the Protestants has been a near 50% of its congregation, apparently in favor of people without religious affiliation.

A recent study conducted as par to the National Research Program, "Religions, the State and Society in Switzerland" that one in 11 people attend religious ceremonies each week. 38% attend **Catholic** churches, an average of 38.1%, in some cities well over 40%, in the city of Basel an astonishing 73.7% attend **Evangelical** (Non-Protestant) Churches (compared to 1.2% in 1970), 14% attend **Protestant** churches and 11% attend Muslim gatherings. (Samuel Haber, Rédaction Francophone, development of the religious communities).

In Switzerland we enjoy freedom of religion, hence, since the 1970s there has been a rapid growth of **Evangelical** churches, the so-called Free Churches attract twice as many worshippers as do protestant churches, they are profiting from favorable social and economic conditions in our country, not only but particularly from those of the lower socioeconomic segment of our society. The development of this movement also owes a lot to migration and the growth of ethnicity in our country, ethnic churches are an attraction for African and south American migrants in particular, they represent a place that offers essential personal support, and the services are conducted in their language, accompanied by the music of their home countries, providing them with a sense of being understood, being listened to in a place far away from home.

Some of these free, reformed churches operate with doctrines that don't deviate greatly from that of the Protestant church. However, **Pentecostalism** the **Restorationist** movement within Christianity teaches supernatural gifts of

290

the holy spirit such as divine healing, prophecy and speaking tongues, a version of Christianity that gained recognition in the United States during the seventies as the preacher and "Rock-n-Roll musician Jimmy Swaggart, through radio and television popularized his teachings as well as the Worship Center in Louisiana's capital city Baton Rouge. Then there are some of those that claim to teach Evangelism, though their way of practicing faith is more than questionable.

It is estimated that in Switzerland more than one thousand Esoteric, Christian and New Religious groups are operating alongside the traditional mainstream churches, and it is estimated that around 200 of those sects and cults operate in an abstruse manner, their methods of recruitment and modus operandi is obscure, many of them profit financially from people's fear, personal misfortunes, often exploiting the week and the underprivileged, youngsters with growing pains as well as those that apparently suffer from mid-life crisis, the misguided, and those that are seeking entertaining "religious" spectacle, a sensationalistic "spiritual" experience. Regrettably, sometimes peoples need for help is so great that they suspend their critical judgement as well as their brain and open themselves to commercialized "religious" messages.

The religious landscape in Switzerland is experiencing an ongoing process of change, it is clear that traditional churches are losing popularity, whereas the new spiritual movements are up and coming which may in part be the result of globalization, economic circumstances, and the feeling of enjoying more anonymity and liberty, free to choose the religion that we prefer, a religion you feel more comfortable with.

However, the current situation begs the question about the future of Christianity in Switzerland, but in particular the Protestants whom after the inherent "religious cleansing" during the sixties until now have lost near 50% of their congregation, many of them to those without an apparent religious affiliation, it seems to be unclear as to the action being taken by the Protestant Church, if any at all, it appears as if those responsible are merely watching in astonishment how one by one the congregation disappear from the churches, but continue to practice what apparently has worked well for centuries, failing to grasp that times have changed, failing to understand that talking at people from the superior height of the pulpit does not suffice to render the church as an attractive place of worship, and yet I dread to imagine what the world will be like with Christianity being a minority Religion.

With fondness I look back to the eighties in Australia, I recall those Sunday mornings that I was able to spend at home, for an hour or so watching Jimmy Swaggart on TV; it wasn't his teachings of supernatural gifts of the holy spirit, nor his notion of the divine healing, nor his prophecy and speaking tongues that grabbed my attention, I was fascinated to watch how this man was able to attain the trust and utter focus of his congregation, knowing that I didn't agree with the content, but the method of delivery was exemplary.

I don't think that any one person has the ultimate solution for the Protestant church. However, if the Church aims to survive this century as a key Christian authority it has to give serious thought to how it is going to present itself to its current, but more importantly its potential future congregation. Considering one of the fundamental differences between the Catholics and the Protestants; it is evident that Catholics follow the teachings of Jesus Christ and the authority of the **Pope**, with more conclusive conviction as do other Christians, the Protestant in contrast is **free to accept** or reject individual teachings and interpretations of the bible, the "free to accept or to reject" is an invitation to liberty and a laissez faire attitude, in itself a loose concept for a religious believe that ought to provide us with clear behavioral directions and guidelines for our lives.

Perhaps extraordinary times necessitate innovative thoughts and ideas; solutions that have not been considered thus far; in lieu of waiting every Sunday for folk to turn up at church, make me feel as if you were in touch with reality, show me that you understand the particulars of my daily struggle to survive, show me that you care, don't preach to me legends and tales from the Genesis, Exodus, Leviticus, and Deuteronomy because I don't understand the relevance between happenings then and now, don't tell me about Joshua the leader of the Israelites, I fail to grasp what he has to do with my life in today's world, instead, show me how I can improve my life, involve me in your activities, play the kind of music that I understand, perhaps you need to consider alternative resources in order to reach me, perhaps you could consider that it might work better the other way around, if you come to me, wherever I am, at a time that is convenient to me.

*Educational Psychology,* the scientific study of the human mind and its functions, the learning environment, the study of memory, the conceptual process, and the individual differences and strategies pertaining to the human learning process was also an integrate part of this course of study, the learning environment, the study of memory, the individual differences and strategies pertaining to the learning process, facilitating the instructional process and development of teaching strategies which enhance the retention of the subject matter.

Having been fascinated by some of the greats, Sigmund Freud, Carl Gustav Jung, Abraham Maslow, Erich Fromm as well as some of the more contemporary psychologists like Elizabeth Kübler Ross since my time at high school, the study of psychology was an invaluable, complementary subject to the course; the study of human learning, the learning processes, both, the cognitive and behavioral perspective, individual differences of the students, motivation, instructional design, classroom management, assessment required for the various airline specific educational settings in the classroom, in the simulator and in the aircraft.

*Method*—the key subject of the course which taught us *how to* teach and instruct. Different methods and approaches to teaching and instructing were discussed, however in our profession there is no room for an experimental approach, nor is there a need for a lot of classroom discussion, in our business we talk about technical issues pertaining to the aircraft and its application, particular processes and procedures for all phases of the operation, there is no room for philosophical debate.

It was clear that an instructor must have a considerable breadth and depth of the subject matter in order to teach others, and this requirement I was able to fulfil entirely, after all, my boss had told me that I was a bloody good pilot, an excellent team-player in terms of cockpit management, suggesting that my success as an instructor would be at the same level, and as a result of his opinion my appearance was accordingly which some people interpreted as arrogant, but in fact I was merely very proud of my achievements.

For the preparation of a lesson, three key elements are considered the *Performance;* what is the student expected to do, to simulate a take-off at the MEL Tullamarine Airport, on runway 34. The *Conditions;* by which the student is expected to execute the required performance, prepare the DC-9-31aircraft motion simulator with 127 passengers on board, at max take-off weight 121,000 lbs., in accordance with the checklist, follow the instruction given by the Tower's ground and departure control and execute the take-off.

And the *Standard*; to which the student must achieve the required performance, the aircraft is correctly configured for max take-off weight, all systems are checked, indicators analyzed, settings correct in accordance with the check-list, take-off emergency procedure discussed and agreed, all procedures carried out correctly, internal and external communication clear and precise, and the take-off carried out as instructed, which might be a simplified depiction of the PCS's.

## Airbus Industries Toulouse, Summer of 1981

June 1981, as part of a team I was commissioned to assume an addition to the fleet, the A300B4 which we were to fly from Toulouse in France, home to Australia. The team was to leave one week before the pick-up date, Airbus was going to put us through a familiarization program with the aim of an aircraft type endorsement at the end of the course.

I had not been back to Switzerland since my arrival in Australia, so I asked for a week of recreation leave before joining my colleagues at Airbus in Toulouse so that I would finally have the opportunity to visit dad and Aunt.

My other two team colleagues that were travelling the week after me had a confirmed first-class ticket from MEL to FRA, and from there open arrangement to TLS, with my ID90 I was booked on a QF flight to Frankfurt. Because the flight was overbooked, every seat was taken up by full fair paying passengers, I took the option of the jump seat for the round eleven-hour sector between HKG and FRA, not in command, merely as an observer and passenger, a mighty achievement for anybody, though during the cruise phase you can get up and stretch your legs in the galley for a moment, but getting some sleep in a jump seat is very difficult.

Having arrived at Frankfurt around 09:00 in the morning, I was too tired to make the onward journey to my home town; I decided to check in at the Steigenberger Airport Hotel Frankfurt, to get some sleep and to enjoy some of the night life a little later, before heading for Basel the next day.

It wasn't just the sleep and the Frankfurt's night life that I wanted to enjoy, I was a little concerned about the reception that I would get from dad and Aunt, since the time that I left Switzerland in 1972 I never phoned home, only on two occasions I bothered to write, the first time to let them know that I arrived safely in Melbourne, and the other time a couple of years later when I was moving into the countryside, so that dad and Aunt knew where I was living.

I clearly recall, my silence was not coincidental or indeed sloppiness on my part, it was deliberate, I wanted to make a statement, it was important for me that both, dad and Aunt would take the opportunity to reflect, to wonder about the reason for my silence, perhaps they would realize that for the most part of my youth I had been treated in an unfair manner, particularly from Aunt.

In the meantime I also had some time to think about the feelings that I had about the growing up time that I spend under the sometimes brutal guidance, the guidance that I perceived as savage, even bestial, but I had not considered the positive aspects of this period, the wonderful bachelor time that I spend with dad, the fact that dad was a good father, he provided me with stability and character, he taught me how to become a striving, valuable member of our society, he made sure that I had everything that I needed and more, he financed my entire education right up to my CPL license, and Aunt taught me how to take care of a household, how to prepare a meal, as well as lots of forms or behavior that one should avoid, but now the time had come to forget all this negative stuff—to strive for peace and a good relationship for the future.

From the hotel I called dad's office, I was told that he was not available, he was out with a client but the lady asked me to hold the line for a moment, she was going to get Aunt to take the call, eventually I had Aunt on the phone, it was now that I realized that I was unable to retrieve my German language skills from my memory, the language that I spoke fluently until some nine years ago, it was a moment of embarrassment, I spluttered a few words but I was unable to put together a sentence that Aunt could understand, so I began to speak to her in English, a language that she was not in command off. Eventually Aunt handed me back to the receptionist, her translating so that I was able to make arrangements with Aunt for my arrival the next day.

If I was going to stay with dad and Aunt for the duration of the entire week, I would have taken the train from Frankfurt to Basel, but I wanted to take the opportunity to take a quick tour through Switzerland and spend a couple of days with mum, her husband Paul and my brother William, to give me flexibility with my travel, I hired a car for the week.

The 330 kilometers From Frankfurt to Basel should have taken me around three and a half hours to drive, not being used to drive on the wrong side of the road anymore, together with a refreshment break at Offenburg the trip took nearly five hours and another thirty minutes until I finally had navigated my way around town until I reached dad's office.

## Meeting My Father Again

Dad was walking toward the front door of the building when I drove through the front gate into the properties car park; as it should be for a young, successful fellow like me, slightly arrogant, I was driving a dark blue 1981 BMW E12 TURBO 528i with off white leather upholstery, and all of this with German number plates which aroused the curiosity of my father, at first he stopped at the stairs that lead up to the door, with his forehead slightly frowned; eventually he approached my car as I was pulling into a vacant slot. At first, he didn't recognize me, but as I stepped out of the car, he realized whom I was, sincerely hearty, he was firmly squeezing my hand, hugging each other at the same time, returning home was truly fabulous, now I was curious about Aunt's reception.

We spend the entire Tuesday together, talking about my mission to Toulouse, life in Australia during the past few years, we reminiscent about the past, we discussed certain aspects of the future, and indeed, at some point we did talk about the why question, the reason for my long, unjust silence, which I tried to illustrate as the huffy child that was sulking over some aspects of his childhood that didn't suit him at the time, that this child felt the need to sulk for a while until he realized how childish and ungrateful his behavior was, but now it was time to put all of this behind him and to get on with life. I believe that this explanation was understood and accepted by dad whereas Aunt was non-committal about my confession.

## Tour de Suisse

Wednesday morning I took off on my rapid tour de Swiss, heading toward Lausanne and then onto Montreux where I was meeting with one of my friends that I had not seen in a long time, she was working as an assistant to the director of the Montreux Palace, the hotel that I was staying the night, we had a dinner date to which I was very much looking forward to, I was a secret admirer of hers back then during our teeny age, now I was curious to find out how she had developed as a person and what she had achieved since we last met.

The next day I was only a very short drive away from my next destination, six kilometers in fact from Montreux; the cemetery at Villeneuve, I wanted to visit grandma to place some flowers on her grave, to dedicate a prayer to her, to shed some tears that might trickle down to the place where she had been put to rest, and to pay my last respect which I was denied at the time she was buried, an act that I had planned for some years as an important part of my grieving process, as Elizabeth Kübler Ross would have explained, this was the fifth stage of the process of grieving—acceptance.

After my visit to the grave, before heading up the Rhône valley toward Brig I took a little detour to the house where grandma was living, to the place that had given me some of the most beautiful memories of my childhood—this was also part of my saying good bye to grandma.

In Brig (canton Vadt) I loaded my car onto a specially designed low bridge freight wagon where the cars could drive directly on to; the track was leading through a tunnel, a forty minute ride, on to Frutigen (canton Bern), driver and passengers of the cars remained in their own vehicles, kind of spooky; you are sitting in your car, the train begins to pull away slowly, then begins to accelerate, you can hear the squeaking caused by the wheels rubbing on the rail, then the train reaches the tunnel and suddenly, it is dark, you are moving but you are not in control, you are merely an observer, you perceive the rapid left and right tilting which is caused by the unevenness of the trusses.

You could feel the banking of the train as it entered and drove through a bend, the smaller and larger gaps between the spots between the rails can be felt and at the same time you hear and feel the hammering sound presumably caused by the unevenness of the rail, from time to time there was a light rushing by from the maintenance molds in the tunnel, and when I opened my window slightly to let the smoke of my cigarette escape, despite the smell of the burning tobacco I could smell the stale air of the tunnel coming through the opening, this journey was pleasant as an experience but I was glad when the train arrived in Kandersteg where I disembarked with my car.

I had an appointment with a couple of mates from my college time in Neufchatel, we were going to have lunch at the See park Restaurant in Thun, there were six of us, our table was reserved out in the garden, overlooking the lake, comparing notes about what each one of us had achieved thus far was simply fabulous, reminiscing about the time at the college, but also observing how each one of us had developed as a result of our different professional and private experiences—I wanted to make sure that I was going to maintain contact in times to come.

Mum's place near Bern I reached late in the afternoon; I was also pleased to see that my brother had turned up for the occasion as well, both William and mums husband Paul were more interested in my professional aspects, wanting to know lots of technical staff about the operation of an aircraft and the social experiences as a long-haul crew member, there was little opportunity for me to find out anything about them, the only thing that became apparent that Paul and William were working for the same company, in the same position, doing the same thing as they did ten years ago.

Mum, as usual, a very warm and humble person, she didn't miss an opportunity to let the neighbors know that her son had become and airline pilot neither, a profession that was considered an enormous achievement that only a few of the chosen ones could realize at that time, but she was more interested about me the person, and how my private life in Australia was developing in particular.

I had the feeling that lack of contact over the past years had driven us even further apart and I felt responsible for this, accepting that during my childhood I had no opportunity to influence the frequency of my visits to mum, but from my late teenage when I was living with her for a year, I was in charge of my own decisions as I am responsible for my decision not to visit her earlier.

I was able to see her love in her actions and affection in her eyes when she looked at me, knowing that her blood was also circulating in my veins, I had the feeling that the other part of my make-up for which dad was responsible, together with the education and the guidance that I received from him was the dominating factor in my behavior.

I began to realize that I had become a different person, I was no longer capable to appreciate mums love, I didn't sense the closeness and affection that I once had for her, I had to digest this perception and endeavor to change it.

On the Friday morning I got back to Basel, I had planned to spend the weekend with dad and Aunt.

Dad had decided that we would leave for the village around midday so that we could enjoy an extended weekend; Aunt's sister Tabea whom I very much appreciated when I was a teenager was joining us for the weekend, I thought that she could ride in my car which would have been an opportunity to find out a bit more about what had happened during my years of absence, but dad was adamant that I was to leave my rented BMW in his garage.

I didn't understand why I couldn't drive the car to the village, but dad explained their weekend hideaway was an old farm house that he had restored, situated in a tiny village with around three hundred residents, all of them strict Catholics, many of them with strict, very old-fashioned views and opinions about life, a lot of them had not forgotten the WWII and all the sufferance that this had brought about, the German folk was still not accepted, thus my luxury car with its German number plates would have only appeared as provocation in the village. The socio-economic makeup of the village residents was farming people, some professionals that were either retired or they were working in the neighboring township of Porrentruy, and a considerable amount of folk that were living on the fringe of society, people living on the pension which wasn't sufficient to live a dignified life.

As I gathered in the short time that I spend in the village, anybody whom was operating a little corner store, or indeed someone like dad whom was the major shareholder of a large print-house in the big city was considered a wealthy person. Both, dad and Aunt were respected people in the village, but Aunt in particular was very popular, she was well known for her generosity; she would take care of some shopping for her eighty-nine year old neighbor whom was struggling to survive on her small pension without asking for any money, in the rear of the car she had a large case of fresh fruits, chocolates and other goodies for the family of nine that lived at the back of our farm, she had some fresh meat for one of the neighbors skinny farm dogs that was chained to the house for most of the time, and she had a package of fresh fish scraps from the market which she had gathered for the stray cats that would visit our house on weekends. Aunt had this wonderful gift to share some of her wealth with those that had less, with those in need of a little help, an attribute that I was not aware of when I was living at home as a teenager.

It was for the first time that I got to see Dad's and Aunt's weekend retreat, a beautifully Jura style farm house located about one hundred meters before the bitumen road came to an end, on the right-hand side; the roof covered the two-story residential part which was located on the left, the center part where the house entrance and the garage were situated, as well as the part on the right-hand side where dad's workshop was housed. The residential part was constructed from natural stone, covered with a rough cast render painted in off white right up to the roof line, the ground level of the center part was also natural stone, rough cast render and painted off white, its upper story featured a traditional balcony constructed of dark stained timber tucked in under the roof line, the palings of its fence were decorated with the shape of a small hearts cut out of each, hanging from the top of the railing were narrow troughs filled with blood red Geranium (Geraniales), together with the rounded, slightly hairy leaves they depicted a homely contrast against the dark stained heavy timber.

The bottom part of the left side of the building was also natural stone, rough cast render and painted off white, the garage door constructed of heavy, dark stained timber, on its left, on the second level was a sturdy wooden loft, just like a balcony, covered with upright wooden slats with spaces between the them a bit like a fence, this was the place where the fire wood was stored, covered by the roof and yet half open so that the air could dry the split wood in readiness for the next winter season.

The front of the house was surrounded with an old-fashioned stone fence with a large timber gate in the middle of the bit that was facing the bitumen road, behind the stone fence grew a boxwood hedge, deep green in color, about two meters in height, providing a little shade as well as privacy for the front garden, orange colored shutters that could be extended way over the pergola, the place where the garden furniture was placed during the summer was creating a warm ambiance and shade at the same time, a couple of Damascene trees, a tree that carries small plums that is particular to the regent Ajoie (a particular area within the canton of Jura / Switzerland), according to one of the local sources, crusaders brought the kernels with them from Damascus, the capital city of Syrian, however there are also other opinions about their origin. The Damascene is a small fruit, its skin is red, although not uniformly the same all round, the predominant color is pink on the sunny side and rather yellow to orange on the shady side, the fruit exudes an extremely strong and a very pleasant odor.

Like then, the ripe Damassine plums are picked up from the ground and processed as fruit tarts (Wähen), and jam, however the most important use of the fruit is the production of alcohol, a very fine spirit (eaux-de-vie).

Dad had also planted two Boskop trees, a very old apple species that is used for cooking in particular, a rather large apple, very sour in taste, the skin rather rough and dull, not so pleasant looking, but lovely to eat as a cooked product, in fact it was dad's favorite apple. In-between the free-flowing path through the garden and up to the front door of the house there was a beautifully groomed lawn with small garden beds along the stone wall, filled with all sorts of flowers, herbs and other greens, rendering the front garden just perfect.

Walking through the front door, there was a large, square hall way, featuring natural stone walls, the original wooden beams were exposed, the door frames constructed of heavy, stained timbers, from the center the wooden stairs lead up to the first floor, to the left there was the living room, the external walls left with the original exposed stone work, the internal partitioning covered with beautifully French polished wooden panels, the ceiling with the original exposed beams and boards behind them, the floor was a new concrete construction covered with natural stone plates, the light fittings and the furniture were reflective of an old farm house.

Connected to the living/dining area was the kitchen. Understanding Aunt's passion for cooking I should not have been surprised, but I was overwhelmed when she showed me the piece de resistance, a natural stone floor, original exposed timber ceiling, against the back wall a large, all stainless steel cooking battery; the left part could be wood fired with a cast iron top, then there was a small water operated Bain Marie (hot water bath to keep things hot), a four gas burner stove and oven underneath, then four electric hot plates with an oven underneath, and next to it a large electric grill with stowage space for pots and pans, the back and both sides of the battery fully dressed in stainless steel, mounted on the wall was a commercial salamander, and covering the entire cooking range was a copper hood with the exhaust extending to the roof, the rest of the kitchen was covered with old-fashioned white kitchen tiles, on the wall opposite the window was a large commercial stainless steel refrigerator and deep freezer.

On the other side, a wall-to-wall stainless steel work bench with under as well as above storage areas, and immediately near the cooking battery was a floor console furbished with drawers and a stainless steel work top, on its side stood a wooden butcher's chopping block, a wet area for the preparation work as well as the washing up, and all areas were appropriately lit, the equipment cupboard was fitted out with everything from the electric mixer, an ice cream machine, the dough breaker as well as any other imaginable gadget, the entire outfit just like a small commercial kitchen. The only thing that remained to say was "WOW."

The stone steps in the kitchen were leading down into the larder part of the cellar, the entire area was fitted out with shelving, most of it suitable for dry goods, others designed for the storage of vegetables and fruits, there was yet another fridge and freezer, the entire area stocked to the brim, one could have operated a small corner store from there. One of the neighboring parts of the cellar was used as general stowage space, and the other was fitted with special shelving that accommodated several hundred bottles of red and white wine from French origin in particular as well as a rather large selection of spirits, just as you would expect to see in a pub.

Adjacent to the kitchen was the guest bathroom and the door that lead to the garage, large enough for two cars and workbench with all the tools that you might need to maintain your vehicle at the back of it, and the workshop set up like a joinery / furniture workshop, but based on the other machines and equipment I gathered that in this place you could fabricate anything that was required for the house and its surrounds, plumbing, carpentry, furniture manufacturing, metal work, electrical, tiling and other odd jobs around the house.

Going upstairs there was a large hallway, leading to the master bed room, a couple of guest rooms, each with its own bathroom, a work room for Aunt and a small office, like in the lower part of the house, the outer walls were kept in natural stone and the inner partitions were masked with polished timber panels, the floors were natural stone plate covered concrete, the ceilings featured the original wooden beams, at the end of the hallway were the French doors that lead to the balcony, the light fittings were suitable for an old farm house and the furniture throughout the house was matching the surrounding style.

The entire roof structure had been left as original, where required beams and supports were renewed or supported, and the old slate had been replaced, this area was once the hay loft, large enough to build three apartments under it.

Both, house and garden were carefully restored, a reflection of Aunt's and dad's taste as well as an expression of their artistic abilities.

Aunt had just started to smoke, whenever she was taking a break from whatever she was doing this particular weekend she would look out for me, invariably I was tied to the shadow of my dad, in the workshop or somewhere in the garden exchanging thoughts and ideas, Aunt would be looking for a puffing partner. Meeting her now as a grown-up man, a man without any inhibitions about the past was almost pleasant, she had become an acceptable conversational opposite, over a cup of coffee and a couple of fags Aunt and I were able to conduct reasonable discussions.

The feelings of discomfort and hate that I once had as a teenager I had put aside, now I was prepared and ready to face Aunt on my own terms, even though with the appropriate respect, I was talking to her without any insecurity, without being shy, not hesitating, speaking honestly without any consideration for possible consequences, I had freed myself of Aunt's psychological violence that I had to endure as a child.

At the time I didn't have any presentiments that she might dig up some of this stuff that I was talking about at a later stage, much later, in fact some thirty years later she surprised me with some of the things that I told her then.

In particular I was glad to spend a little time with Solange, Aunt's elder sister whom supported, even sheltered me from some of Aunt's anger attacks when she and her younger daughter were living with us the year before I joint the boarding school in Neuchâtel, she was like my second mum to me, something that Aunt could never have claimed to be, I very much enjoyed her company, catching up with her and gathering a bit of gossip.

To get reconnected with dad was uncomplicated, in no time we had found each other, we were able to have intensive discussions about anything at all, we were able to challenge, even provoke each other, together we could conduct a war of words, we were able to discuss controversial issues, be of a different opinion without losing the respect for each other, just the way a relationship between father and son should be.

As far as I was able to tell during this short weekend together, the relationship between Aunt and dad I had estimated as healthy, both of them appeared to be happy, which was important for me to know. With all that I was allowed to experience with my folks that weekend I got a positive feeling about the future, believing that as a family we would be able to work out our differences and move forward to be able to mutually enjoy each other's company in the future, the brief acquaintance that I was faced with in this short time left me with an irrefutable impression that spontaneously prompted me to invite dad and Aunt and her sister Solange to Australia for the coming year.

## Toulouse, Our Mission

On the Monday morning I returned to Frankfurt, my flight was booked from the companies travel department, FRA-CDG-TLS, in Toulouse I joined my colleagues to start the familiarization training on the A300B4 on Tuesday morning, the technical aspects from the point of view of the maintenance was going to be taken care of by our fellows from the engineering department whom had arrived a few weeks ahead of us, it was their responsibility to master all aspects of the scheduled as well as unscheduled maintenance work back home.

The A300B4 was considerably different from other aircraft that we were operating at that time, there were differences in construction and the assembly of the fuselage; in contrast the airframe as on the A300B4 had become more sturdy, because of an improved aerodynamic design of the wings the aircraft enjoyed an improved airflow and at the same time it had become lighter, with the same powerplant performance we were able to increase the payload, the aircraft steering was of mechanical nature, cables and steering rods attached to a hydraulics setup which was connected to the control surfaces, each of these was activated by three independent systems, flaps and slats were also hydraulically operated, the aircraft trim was activated electrically, the rudder could be trimmed manually, the navigation system had become extremely complex, and the auto pilot functions were unique at the time, this aircraft was fitted with an approved automatic landing system.

As a member of the cockpit crew, we also had to be aware of the technical aspects, how they function and how interact with each other but from a different point of view compared to our engineers. As we progressed with our training it became apparent that this aircraft was going to be different from others that any of us had flown thus far, because of its enhanced wing design and the improved flap and slat configuration we were able to operate this aircraft much closer to its limits during the take-off and landing phase.

During our training, one evening after our dinner together with our instructors we were heading to one of the local pubs, over a chilled beer our buddy Max was telling us the story about how he got from Paris to Toulouse some days ago. I personally never made this experience, but apparently the flight on which Max was booked from CDG-TLS was operated with an airbus. After a little waiting time, which is not unusual at the mega airport the check-in was strait forward despite the fact that Max is not acquainted with the local language, the fellow on the desk spoke good English and was rather pleasant, his luggage had disappeared in the bows of the airports handling system, with his travel documents in hand he now was ready to move through customs, and on to find the boarding gate.

As he was sitting there in the assembly area, waiting for the boarding call he once more checked his documents; then suddenly realized that his boarding pass showed all relevant flight information but there was no seat number allocated. In the meantime, the counter staff had announced that the boarding could begin, without any additional information, even on a domestic flight one might expect that the Business Class passengers, the mums with small children and the elderly have priority, none of that.

Eventually, Max got to speak to one of the boarding staff about the fact that there was no seat number indicated on his boarding pass, with a smile he was told that this flight was operating as a shuttle, there were no particular seat allocation, passengers merely boarded the aircraft and grabbed the first available seat, and so it was, by the time Max was ready he was the last one on board and had to take the one that was left over, the door had already been closed and the push back in progress. Max had made his way toward the rear of the aircraft, checking on both sides of each row if there was a vacant seat and by the time he reached the last row he realized that there was no seat for him, he informed one of the flight attendants in the rear galley, she walked to the front of the aircraft and back again and confirmed that indeed there was no seat left, the cabin crew jump seats were no option either, for safety reasons they had to be occupied by the flight attendants during take-off and landing.

In the meantime, the purser had been alerted of this situation, she summarized; we have one passenger to many on board, our departure has been delayed, the push back is in progress, the only option that I see is the toilet during take-off and landing. The flight time from Paris to Toulouse is one hour ten, for nearly the entire time of the flight Max had no choice but to remain in the closet; at first this story seems amusing, but it could have had very serious consequences for the airline company, had something gone wrong.

The following week we were ready to fly back our brand-new aircraft, TLS-KLL for refueling KLL-HKG fuel stop, HKG-SYD where our engineers took the aircraft in their care.

# Dad and Aunt's First Visit
# to Australia, 1982

The preparation for Aunt and Dad's visit began a couple of months before they arrived, we made sure that the garden and the surrounding outdoor areas were well groomed, though the house was always in good shape we had organized a spring cleaning frenzy, making sure that Aunt could not find any hidden grime anywhere, we made sure that every nook and cranny had been well scrubbed, the kitchen, its cupboards including its content checked, we made sure that the toilets and the bathrooms were shiny as if they were brand new, the living area was turned upside down, ensuring that there was no dust nor any other dirt to be found, and special attention was given to the guest room that we had reserved for Aunt and Dad; Elisabeth had even bought new bed linen for this occasion.

We were truly looking forward to their visit, we wanted to make sure that they would experience a wonderful time with us. I recall clearly, at that time I thought that I had forgotten all this negative stuff that I experienced during my youth, that I had put behind me the hate that I perceived toward Aunt long ago, but I had to realize that small traces of discomfort were still apparent when I thought of Aunt, and I suspected that this visit would be associated with a silent audit, which would be well documented in Aunt's memory, biased and prejudice on my part prevailed indeed, and I knew that I had to work on this problem.

The kids were excited, looking forward to this visit, as Jacqueline stated one evening over dinner, "I am glad to finally meet grandma and grandpa from Switzerland" a statement that no doubt came from her heart, a message that touched me deeply, whereas Edward was more reserved, perhaps a little concerned that now, at least for a few weeks he wouldn't get the usual full attention.

Although Elisabeth and I were not married, I regarded her parents Marlise and Bill as my in-laws, both of them solid, uncomplicated, down to earth people, no doubt they would have appreciated if Elisabeth and I had consolidated our living together in the name of the all-mighty, but they acknowledged our relationship and treated me as their son. I was glad to hear that they accepted our invitation to join us for the weekend in Elphinstone when Aunt and dad were arriving.

It was Saturday morning, I was at Melbourne's Tullamarine International Airport, waiting for the arrival of Singapore Airlines, on my side was Marlise my mother in-law, she had offered to accompany me because we anticipated Aunt's sister as well which would have been a little more luggage than I could have managed to carry in my car, Bill had already left for Elphinstone; Elisabeth had asked him to do some last-minute shopping in Melbourne, a few things that she had forgotten.

Once they collected their baggage and had cleared customs, we could finally greet them, Aunt was astonished that Elisabeth's mom was at the airport to welcome them, she was over the moon when I suggested that she and her sister could travel in Marlise's car, Dad and I in mine. Aunt's eyes lit up, she showed that she was pleased with this arrangement, I knew that she would feel important if she could be driven by Mrs. Doctor, and I wasn't unhappy to have dad to myself either.

At the time when I designed our kitchen there were ten to twelve people in the house on most of my days off, all of them adoring food and some of them had transformed cooking to their passion, so I decided to create my kitchen accordingly, but some of my mates commented later that I had exaggerated with my cooking equipment, that I was suffering from delusions of grandeur; I had installed a stainless steel commercial gas stove equipped with six burners, a grill plate with a splash board on the back and both sides, on the right side there was a deep fryer, on the left side of this battery I had a hot water Bain Marie to keep food hot, underneath the cooking area I had two ovens; one of them large and the other smaller, opposite the stove a couple of work benches were fitted, constructed with stainless steel surfaces and stainless drawers underneath and stainless cupboards above, and on the other side, against the wall were a reasonably large stainless upright deep freezer and a refrigerator, as you might expect to see it in a small restaurant.

For this particular weekend Sue and Peter, both of them very good cooks had volunteered to run the kitchen; to take the responsibility for the cooking and the serving; under the pretense that we could spend more time with our parents, but I had the distinct impression that meeting our parents was as important as the culinary treats that they would provide us with—regardless, a very considerate thought indeed. Saturday, just in time as Marlise and I returned from the airport with our visitors, the kitchen team had presented us with their buffet creation, a number of compound salads which included the "Aussie Coleslaw," freshly cooked crayfish, a couple of different meat pâtes and terrines from the French fellow at the Victoria Market, fresh Snapper from the grill, well hung Porterhouse steak from Mr. Archer's butchery in the neighboring village Chewton, grilled to order, fresh bread, baked in-house that very morning, a variety of Australian hard and Tasman soft cheeses, and a home-made Pavlova for dessert.

The wines were selected by Bill, he was a member of the wine and food society whom met regularly at the Two Faces Restaurant, at that time one of Melbourne's best eating places, as one of their Wine Masters he was extremely knowledgeable about Australian as well as French produced liquid gold; I knew that he was going to be a match for my father who was also a connoisseur of wine and spirits.

The late evening meal on that day was equally as scrumptious as lunch; a couple of large legs of pork which Marlise had bought at her local butcher's, oven roasted together with bits of pumpkin with their skin on potatoes cut into quarters, whole medium sized onions, whole tomatoes, garlic and fresh herbs from the garden, all presented on large silver platters which Peter had borrowed from one of his friends, carved at the table by Sue and Bill, served with a butter mounted gravy, cheese and fresh fruits for dessert. After dinner Elisabeth introduced the couple responsible for the culinary delights that had been served, making sure that the two of them were celebrated as her brother and a dear friend, and not as kitchen staff.

Sunday began with a breakfast buffet, home-made bread rolls, fresh croissants from the bakery in Castlemaine, fresh fruits, jam, honey from the hives of a local farmer, the flavor clearly characterized by the local flora, salted butter, baked beans on toast, grilled bacon and eggs which were to be ordered in the kitchen, prepared to your liking, as an omelet, scrambled, hard or soft boiled or indeed fried, coffee and tea.

For lunch—late lunch—I had invited everybody to the neighboring township of Castlemaine, at the local Chinese the cuisine, though somewhat modified to the Aussie taste, the chef had found a rather pleasant blend of local adaption of Chinese food and authenticity, tucker that was appreciated by all.

Throughout the weekend the mood was heartily, I had the feeling that Dad and Aunt felt comfortable, Marlise, a lady whose behavior was generally very calm and guarded appeared to have a ball, as usual, my father-in-law Bill enchanted the ladies with his natural charm; he and Dad got on with each other like a house on fire, Elisabeth wasn't merely the usual perfect lady of the house, Dad and Aunt thought that she was simply gorgeous, and the kids savored the attention that they received from everybody. If sore facial muscles are an indication about the amount of enjoyment one had, then my weekend was great.

Everybody laughed a lot, not necessarily about the content of the conversation, often we had to giggle about the linguistic challenges from both sides, the Aussies trying to patch together something in German, and some of our Swiss visitors' pronunciation of the English language at times was hilarious. The house was rocking, the atmosphere was very jolly, it appeared that everybody got on well with each other, the kids enjoyed being pampered by their two Grandpas, Aunt's sister didn't speak a word of English; Elisabeth and Sue were the only one that took care of her to make her feel a little welcome in our house, and it appeared that Aunt was in her element—being surrounded by doctors, lawyers and airline staff, this was a proper treat to her soul.

Despite this wonderful atmosphere I couldn't repress the fact that for the first time since my teenage that I was to live under the same roof with Aunt, knowing that it was for a foreseeable time; I tried very deliberately to repress the memories that were still present from that time, wondering what it would be like and at the same time praying that we would have a good time together, that this time would pass without any severe incident, for a moment I could feel the repressed mood that I experienced then during my youth, I was surprised, a little shaken to realize that after all these years Aunt could still set off an negative impression within me, but I realized that this was only possible because I was terrified not being able to please her; as a consequence she might have influenced my father to the point that we would not see each other on a regular basis.

To regain a healthy state of being, I had to remind myself that in the meantime I had reached thirty-three years of age, that I was a successful Airline Captain, that I was well established in my professional as well as my private life, that I was well integrated into the Australian society, that I was in a solid relationship, where one respects the other, and that I was a father figure of our two children whom adored me.

During Dad and Aunt's visit Elisabeth wasn't always at Elphinstone, having anticipated their stay with us she had made sure her appointments were centered around my parents, but there were preorganized commitments that she had to take care off, during the week the kids were at school, and I had also made arrangements with the company to have some days off, wanting to make sure that there was somebody at home during most of the time of the visit. At the beginning of the following week, Dad and Aunt together with her sister Tabea had booked a week on Kangaroo Island, situated 13 kilometers from the Southern tip of Cape Jervis.

Together with the kids, Elisabeth and I made this trip the year before, we drove down to Anglesea on the Bass Strait, to the tip of Cape Otway, along the Great Ocean Road, overnighted in Robe South Australia and went on to the port of Adelaide the next day, covering around 730 kilometers the first day and 350 on the second, admiring various bits of nature on the way including the Seven Apostles. We were embarking the ship late afternoon, our car stowed in its bow, we spent the night on the upper deck in airline style seats, Elisabeth sleeping, the kids mucking around for much of the time, and me running to the toilet regularly—attending to my stomach cramps caused by the motion of the ship—arriving at the port of Kingscote just in time to watch the sun rise.

I don't know if this particular service still exists today, but I do know that in recent years a modern 50metres catamaran is providing a service between Cape Jervis and Penneshaw, taking you to the island and back within forty-five minutes. Alternatively, there is a flight that operates between Adelaide and Kingscote or Penneshaw, taking around thirty minutes. Dad had booked a flight from Melbourne to Adelaide, on to Kingscote because Aunt's sister wasn't sure that she would feel comfortable on the boat.

On the Sunday before their departure, Dad was well instructed by Jacqueline and Edward about all the places that they had to visit; Flinders-Chase National Park, Seal Bay, cautioning that they should maintain a reasonable distance between the seals, Edward reminding his Grandfather that he was chased by a seal bull, that he was very lucky to escape just in time, Admirals Arch, absolutely spectacular, the picknick in the wire cages designed for people to be able to take shelter from the inquisitive Kangaroos, the fancy shaped rocks, the Koalas, the huge Goannas, the different birds, and the drive on the tail gate of the Land Rover, feeding the Kangaroos whilst we were driving slowly with condensed milk out of the tube, all of them very important things to experience, so the kids explained to Grandpa.

Our visitors were back the following Tuesday, 26 January, just in time for the National Day Celebration, I met them very briefly at Melbourne's airport as they were disembarking only minutes before I had to board my aircraft which I was going to fly to Adelaide, on to Perth and back, but Elisabeth was waiting for them, she had the day off work. From what I was able to gather in this very short time, Kangaroo was well worth visiting, my folks enjoyed it very much.

A couple of days later I had an appointment with Ray Riley the manager of the Wattle Gully Gold Mine in the neighboring village Chewton, Ray was going to give us a private tour of the mine facilities, assuming that the ladies would also be interested to see how gold was gained but I wasn't sure if they would also join us in the underground operation, in particular I wanted to surprise Dad with this outing. The drive from Elphinstone to Chewton is a mere nine kilometers, rugged bush on both sides of the road leading through the Chewton bends, once you reach the Red Hill Pub, you take the next left, Wattle Gully Road, continue under the railway bridge, a couple of kilometers further on you turn right and follow the road for a couple of hundred meters until you reach the mine.

Wattle Gully was central of the Gold Rush Days back in 1851 into the 1860s, throughout the seventies and eighties the production of gold was not continues, it was coupled with the price of gold, I recall, there were periods when the price of or was low, the production was halted until the price had recovered, the impact on the minors wasn't that detrimental, most of them were locals that were farming at the same time. None of us were too keen to spend a lot of time exploring the broader part of the surroundings of the mine, the temperature had reached around thirty-eight Celsius.

A couple of years ago when we were still renovating the old house I was stomping around this area, I recall some of the devastation that the cyanide had caused with the environment surrounding the mine was indeed not a pretty sight, water dams that had been used as holding basins, almost dried up, the natural vegetation in the vicinity ill looking, dead in part, and the little water that remained was stagnant and had an unpleasant odor.

On the surface, Ray showed us the crushing facility with its conveyer system, the elevator tower and the machine room adjacent to it where the motors and the winding gears were housed; the cable drums around two meters high, several hundred meters of steel cable wound up on it, mounted on the side of the winches there were two large clock faces that indicated the position, the depth of the lifts, the two electric motors powering the winches, the large workbenches and spare parts laying all over the place, the control mechanisms for the lifts and the ventilation system—all of it remnants from the 1930s.

As I thought, the ladies were not keen to explore the underground section of the mine, Aunt and her sister were invited to join Ray's wife at the mine's residence adjacent to the lift tower, enjoying a cup of tea with freshly baked scones, whipped cream and jam.

Together with Ray, Dad and I boarded the steel cage at shaft No.3, beginning our descent down to level 350 which represents 350 feet in depth, the platform of this lift is designed to accommodate four miners, all of them standing face to face, then the safety gate was closed, Ray communicated to the crew member in the machine room that we were ready and the cage began to move—at the speed of a slow lift—we descended into the shaft, the daylight began to vanish, the only light that we realized came from the head torch fitted to our safety helmets and the dim light reflection that escaped from the different levels as we drove past them, we were told to keep our hands close to our body.

Had I poked my finger out of the cage just a little I would have touched the rock wall that ran past my face, I was able to hear the sound of the draft created by the descending platform and the particular smell of the underground became more and more evident. As the lift came to a holt, for a short moment you could feel a very slight up and down bounce that was caused by the slackness of the steel cable, after which Ray opened the front security guard in front of us, we turned into the shaft on our left, barely two meters high and wide enough to accommodate the rail system with a small margin on either side, the temperature was around 38 degrees Celsius, the humidity 97 %, the entire shaft system not airconditioned, merely ventilated.

Walking on the sleepers of the narrow gage rail system was the safest way of moving along the shaft which was sparsely lit by bull-eye lights covered with a wire basket, mounted on the heavy timber post and rafters that were installed as safety guards every five meters or so, being supplied through heavy insulated electric cables suspended from the wall. In part we had to be extremely careful as we got to passages with unsecured downward shafts on our left, some of them filled with ground water, others were lit—used as ventilation shafts—after around six hundred feet into the shaft we had reached an area that had been dug out, about ten foot high with a radius of about thirty foot, heavy duty drills operated with compressed air, minors picks, shovels and other tools and materials were stored in this area in readiness for the next attack on the vein that the miners were following.

Ray pointed out the vein that they were following, explaining in some detail how the miners will go about this, and to my amazement I had to realize that what we were looking at had no resemblance to gold. Standing there admiring what didn't look like gold reminded me at a situation the previous year, not far from the Wattle Gully Mine, around two kilometers along the Pyrenees highway we turned into Eureka street in Chewton, over the railway bridge, heading in a Southerly direction along this bush track looking for suitable sandstone rocks for my garden wall when we stumbled onto a small opening on a rock formation, densely covered by bushes; Peter and I walked along this shaft for a couple of hundred feet, carefully checking the surrounds with our torches as we eventually reached this cavity, perhaps ten or so feet high, we weren't sure if this was a cave or indeed a cavern, the whole area was glittering, Peter and I just about went berserk, believing that we had hit the jackpot—we found gold.

Despite our very profitable discovery we eventually got on to gather a trailer load of stone before heading back to Elphinstone. On the way home Peter and I were contemplating an elaborate plan, how we would inconspicuously get to and from the mine, how we would extract this precious metal from the rock without being noticed, and we had agreed that we would sell this stuff to someone in Melbourne to avoid that the locals would become aware of our fortune. Although we weren't sure that this shiny metal was indeed gold, still hoping that it would be, a couple of days later Elisabeth took our mysterious treasure to a fellow that was knowledgeable with precious metals, carefully placed into a small black cotton bag with a string on its neck as a closing mechanism I had placed this lump of mineral, a rock the size of my fist containing clusters of brass like, yellow to silver-colored, sparkling, shiny, metal, through closer examination it became evident that nature had formed this metal in spectacular polygon shapes like pyramid, prism, rectangle, hexagon, decagon, and similar as if time had provided them with natural sharp edges that had been flattened and polished.

The examiner's diagnosis of our treasure was pyrites a mineral that got its name from the Greek language "fire," because it produces sparks when knocked together—pyrites is also commonly known as "Fools Gold," apparently, some value the mineral against negative energy, for their personal well-being—indeed we were fools to believe that we had found our jackpot.

Breathing had become a little difficult at 350 feet underground, the high temperature and humidity had made itself noticed, though fascinating to get a glimpse of a miner's work environment, I wasn't unhappy to head back toward the lift to get up to the fresh air.

A couple of days later, together with Dad and Aunt we visited Sovereign Hill, an open-air museum in Golden Point, a suburb of Ballarat, Victoria, around 84 kilometers from Elphinstone. In this instance, a gold mine together with its small township, an entire infrastructure has been faithfully reconstructed in the manner that it might have been at that time, creating a breath-taking atmosphere for its visitors, showing how this town was designed and functioning during the gold rush period in the 1850s.

The museum boasts to be providing fun for kids, but big kids whom are inquisitive about the Australian history and the way people lived during that period will have a ball as well, on this 25-hectare area you will see the conical wood construction, the tower for the shaft lift, below the tower is the little cottage from which you can step into the little train that takes you around some of the shaft systems, on an old four horse drawn carriage you can take a ride around this historic town.

At the funeral parlor, you can admire the horse drawn wooden hearse featuring glass panels on both sides and in the same shop different style coffins were displayed, the one that is constructed from raw planks assembled like a cheap packing case for some machine part, the other with the traditional coffin shape, the timber joint stained and finished with a reasonable good polish, walking along the dirt roads past the different buildings, some constructed as traditional weatherboard with the large verandas spanning right up to the cobblestoned water trench, others still full double brick business houses with very sophisticated Palladian central superstructure decorated with ornamental cast stone figures, dentils, brackets, columns and lovely balustrades.

Then there is the foundry were you can watch the blacksmith how he forges a horseshoe, witness how the lathes spins metal into gold pans and household wares and for a small fee you can try your talent as his apprentice for the day, a little further down the road you can get involved in the making of candles, or you can be one of the spectators at the old Victoria Theatre, if you are feeling a little peckish you can get a pie or pasties at one of the local bakeries watching the activities in the bake-house at the same time, or you go to one of the pubs were you are served a traditional Aussie roast with vegies and thick gravy.

If you are a little weary, you can catch the horse-drawn coach to your next destination, you can stop at the local goldsmith, watch how she pours a gold ingot, stop by the Chinese village, tent housing made from wooden poles covered with cloth, all of them furbished as it was the case back then, relax at the water pumping system from the mining shafts, visit the big shed and watch the rock crusher driven by the wood fired steam engine, spend a little time with the skilled craftsman in the wheelwright and coachbuilding workshop, put yourself back into the 1800s and watch how the fellow in the saddlery makes all kind of harnesses and other leather articles using traditional methods.

Drag your kids to the confectionary shop and witness how the boiled lollies are made, visit the ladies lounge in one of the old hotels, browse through the grocery store—admiring the simplicity of the range of products and its packaging—a true inspiration for those whom despise the amount of superfluous wrappings, enjoy the different spectacles that are performed just about at every street corner—all of the actors dressed in period clothing, or simply get involved in the panning of gold along the creek that runs through the property. Though commercialized, Sovereign Hill should be on everybody's travel list, providing that you are interested in the history of Victoria.

Having lived down under for many years, being just like one of them, having had the opportunity to extensively travel to places that the average tourist doesn't get to see; I conclude that Sovereign Hill reflects the architecture, the mood and to some point the way of life that still exists today in many places outside of the principle agglomeration in Victoria in particular, the old weatherboard, double brick houses and cottages have perhaps been renovated, the internal cooking area improved, a gas heater installed in the old fire place, the outhouse, rather the "dunny" with its tin can as the Aussies have named it turned into the garden shed and a modern toilet installed in the house, the leaky tin roof replaced with new corrugated iron sheets, some of the dirt surfaces of the roads have been covered with bitumen, the kerosene lamps have long gone, the candles have remained merely to provide a romantic atmosphere and the streets are lined with wooden masts that serve for the suspension of the electric cables that are hanging all over the place like overcooked spaghetti, the bridle hooks and rings are still mounted on the wooden veranda railing in front of the shops but they no longer serve their purpose.

The horses that remain are kept in the paddocks and used merely for pleasure, the horse drawn carriages are not to be seen in the streets anymore, the modern utility has long replaced it, the modest range of groceries and other fundamental consumables has changed, replaced with commercially processed staff embellished with food coloring, artificially flavored, enhanced with preservative, presented in lots of unnecessary packaging, apparently environmentally friendly, the greasy shop is still selling fish and chips, burgers with grilled bacon and fried egg and other junk food delicacies but the shop has become more sophisticated and its blackboard menu boasts health consciousness, woman are no longer wearing the long dresses with broad shoulders, narrow wastes, flared out on the hips, hoop skirt, petit cote, detachable cuffs, removable collars, and the men do not wear the fancy vests, the long coats, the baggy trousers tucked into the high boots, nor the top hats and the broad neck ties.

Fashion consciousness through on-line shipping has become an integrate part of the bush folks life, sitting in front of a cool beer with friends in the pub is not in vogue anymore, the mobile smart phone has aroused excitement among the younger generation out here as well, to the point that a one-to-one conversation has become the exception to the rule. Outside the main agglomeration, from Melbourne across to Nelson on the West coast, back up to Lindsay Point at the Northern part near the Murray River, across to Mildura down to Swan Hill, Echuca, Albury, down to Gabo Island near the border of the East Coast you will find places just like Sovereign Hill, places that still radiate a similar atmosphere, places that set off excitement and emotions.

Throughout Dad and Aunt's visit I didn't perceive any obvious differences or potentially severe disagreements among Aunt, any member of my Aussie patch-work family or myself, perhaps the odd occasion where I thought that Aunt might be observing a situation or trying to follow a conversation that she might misunderstand because her English was very limited, but I was aware that often she would clinch a word or part of a sentence that she thought that she had understood and made up the rest of the story as she thought it was appropriate, in this was very often constructing a story that was contrary to the actual facts, but I didn't believe that any of that could develop into a drama.

Sometime in my early twenties, for some reason or another I began to develop an interest in psychology and among others my curiosity to disassemble and to decipher the soul, Sigmund Freud had grabbed my curiosity, his psychological theory, the theory of the analysis of dreams as wish fulfilment that provided Freud with models of the clinical analysis had aroused my inquisitiveness, understanding that some of his analytical processes and underlaying mechanism were highly contested and debated with regards to its efficiency by his professional colleagues.

I am being presumptuous, but when I discretely observed Aunt as she was watching someone in a particular situation or when she was trying to follow and understand the content, perhaps the gist of a conversation in English, I was able to recognize how she had interpreted a scenario or a discussion, once she commented upon the subject matter immediately thereupon or indeed sometimes long after the event, sometimes I had the feeling that Aunt had been pursuing the process of Freuds clinical analysis to reach a conclusion. Aunt with her apparent ability to interpret an action, on this particular occasion, she insisted that; because, after a two-hour breakfast session where she expected that everybody took part, my partner dared to get up and began with the tiding of the kitchen in her own household, Elisabeth was being disrespectful toward her, that it felt as if she was no longer welcome.

I am well aware that every society assignation has its do's and don'ts surrounding its expected social behavior, most of it is common sense, underlaying a rational, meaningful notion of behavior, demonstrating respect and appreciation toward others, and it may also be true that within the different socioeconomic background particular sets of behavior are not only expected, they may well be a condition, a requirement in order to belong.

However, I could never realize Aunt's social behavioral values, nor do I understand how she got to accept them; as far as I can gather her upbringing at home was rough and ready, social behavioral expectation during her stint at the convent was merely very strict, and during her apprenticeship she would have experienced nothing other than behavior that can normally be expected in our society. So, where did these bizarre ideas and expectations come from? Where did she acquire them and when did she decide that they had to be implemented? I suspect that Aunt had developed her own set of behavioral values over a period of time, and those around her were expected to guess what was expected in which situation, and what was, and what was not tolerated, and yet much of the time Aunt's own behavior was bordering on vulgarity and disrespectfulness.

At the time when Elisabeth got up from the table after the two hour breakfast session, Aunt did not mention the fact that she had perceived my partners behavior as disrespectful; it was merely a couple of years later when Elisabeth and I spend a few days with Aunt and Dad back in Switzerland, one afternoon when for some reason or another Elisabeth wasn't around for a moment, Aunt and I were sitting at the kitchen table when she suddenly said, "You know, remember that time when we were visiting you in Australia, that particular morning when Elisabeth suddenly got up from the breakfast table to clean the kitchen? Do you realize that I was very close to get up and pack our bags?"

Aunt sat there all puffed up, her cheeks slightly red, both of her hands on the table, clenched into fists with the knuckles beginning to turn white, her eyes wide open, staring into mine and then continued, "You simply don't do this sort of thing when you are having visitors, and you know this," pausing and then got on to with her arrogant, educative manner, "In any case, I think that you ought to consider doing something about this lady, teach her about manners."

Me, being absolutely speechless, my head was spinning, I was very angry at myself for not reacting immediately, to get up and pack our bags, but Aunt kept on going, "I have discussed this also with Dad and he agrees with me, I don't think that Elisabeth is the right lady for you." I was glad that we were leaving a couple of days later anyway, I never talked to Elisabeth about this particular incident with Aunt, she would have declared instant war with Aunt.

It was this particular incident with Aunt that made me realize that our relationship was as if she had a spell over me, I felt as if I was condemned to do as she told me to, just like when I was a kid, I felt that she was manipulating me, as much as I tried to oppress this kind of thought, I realized that Aunt was still the bitch that I despised very much, there were short moments where I thought to have relived my childhood horror.

Food was a significant aspect during this visit, Dad was very appreciative of most meals that we provided at home, he was happy with some good cheese, fresh bread and a glass of Aussie red, whereas Aunt was a finicky eater, she would have preferred to be pampered in one of Melbourne's fine restaurants every day. Dining out in that particular period was relatively uncomplicated; the choices were fine dining, relatively expensive, and we had to travel an hour and a half to get there from Elphinstone and the same to get back home, and the other choices were relatively affordable Greek, Italian and Chinese food, most of them reachable within half an hour from home.

On average we surprised Dad and Aunt with a fine dining experience once per week and a couple of times we treated ourselves with some hearty junk food; fish and chips from the greasy shop, wrapped in greaseproof and newspaper, pizza from the Italian fellow, Chinese or some take away from somewhere, and on Fridays we visited the Victoria Market in Melbourne, getting our weekly supply of fresh vegetables and fruits, different kinds of meat and poultry, fresh seafood from our fishmonger, pâtes, terrines and cheese from the Frenchman and any other kind of groceries that we needed, paying close attention to Aunt's every culinary desire and wish, making sure that she had sufficient time to snoop around, knowing that she adored food markets.

Though she didn't comment at the time, I suspected that Aunt wasn't too keen about our cuisine, much of the time she asked for leave salad, vegetables, avocadoes and mangos from Queensland under the pretense that this was just right for her diabetes.

After breakfast on the Sunday morning my in-laws Marlise and Bill were heading back to Melbourne with Dad and Aunt, they had invited them, spending the day at their beach house at Port Sea, at the Eastern tip of Port Philip Bay, and on Monday morning bill would take them to the airport, they had reserved a trip to the Great Barrier Reef. Dad and Aunt had booked an early flight from Melbourne to Brisbane where they boarded the Queenslander at the Roma Street Station, around noon.

As I understand, today the Queenslander has been taken out of service some years back, but during the eighties it was a train configuration that had been partially renovated, used as a theme train from time to time, featuring "Murder on the Orient Express" where actors had been invited to set the scene

319

for an entertaining six-hour trip up the East Coast and back again, and at some point during the night the train would stop to allow the ambulance, with all of its attributes—the red light and siren to pick up the "body." However, Dad and Aunt were booked through to Cairns, from Brisbane along the Sunshine Coast to Maryborough; 30km from Hervey Bay and Fraser Island, a further 110km up to Bundaberg, famous for its Original Ginger Beer and the production of the "Bundy"—Bundaberg Rum which is made from the locally grown cane sugar across the road, on to Gladstone about 540km North of Brisbane, a town just across from Facing Island.

The much larger Curtis Island, Gladstone has the fifth biggest deep see port in Australia, particularly geared for the export of coal and aluminum which has characterized the town, than a further 108km to the beef capital of Australia, Rockhampton which is situated on the Fitzroy River, apparently the Aboriginal Cultural Centre at Rocky is one of the best on the East Coast of Australia together with the Heritage Village featuring the period between 1850 to 1950, 186km further to St. Lawrence, a two horse town with a population of around 390, other than a general store, a pub, post office, police station, a school, church, a bowling and a golf club, a caravan park, a swimming pool, arts and craft shop, and the railway station there isn't anything to see but it's worth making a stop to get to know the other side of Australian life.

Then on to Mackay, the capital of the cane, two thirds of Australia's sugar is produced in this regent, the Bluewater Lagoon, the Botanical Garden and the Great Barrier Reef are well worth visiting, 126km further up you reach Proserpine one of Australia's youngest towns in the midst of the Whitsunday Region, founded in 1890 as the administrative center of the region, from there within a mere 25km you are at Airlie Beach in the midst of the Great Barrier Reef, also known as God's Country, from where Australia's most famous Long Island, Hamilton Island, Whitsunday Island, Lindeman Island, Mansell Island, Swan Island and others can be reached within a short time, a further 265km up the coast to Townsville—famous for its glorious beaches, and finally 347km further on to Cairns.

Aunt and Dad returned to Elphinstone after their ten days trip up and back the East Coast, raving about the charm of the countryside, talking about the adventures that they had experienced, the beauty of the Reef, the lousy meals that they were served in some of the pubs, the great food enjoyed in the hotels and the resort, and the lovely people that they had met along the way.

During the week I had a couple of days off, Elisabeth was working and the kids were at school in Melbourne, Jeffrey and Shirly I had not seen for some months, but the last time we spoke I promised to introduce them to Dad and Aunt sometime during their stay with us. Both of them of British descent, Shirly an English teacher at Castlemaine High, talking with a medium sized plum in her mouth, Jeffrey was an arts teacher at one of Melbourne's High Schools, both of them intellectuals, lovely to be with, and over a glass of red pleasant to argue about some meaningful stuff. Shirly would have preferred to remain in Melbourne where they had lived and enjoyed fame in the "Arty" scene of the big city, Jeffrey had become a successful local artist, they were able to live very comfortably from the sale of his paintings and collages, but Jeffrey was more a down-to-earth fellow, he was yearning for the simple life that allowed him to draw energy from mother earth, and so they bought an old miners cottage on a few acres in the historic township of Maldon in the midst of the Victorian Goldfields.

Maldon is situated around 130 km Northwest of Melbourne a thirty-minute drive from Elphinstone, its population about 1400, it has been designated as "Australia's first notable town," notable for its 19th century appearance that it was able to maintain since the gold-rush days. At that time, I didn't realize that Jeffrey was one of the contemporary ancestors, partly responsible for what Maldon was to become a couple of decades later, he was not a trendy, he was a down to earth fellow that realized the towns environment as an underlaying stimuli for his life, and in deed for his art.

Since the 1850s the heart of Maldon is basically unchanged, it has become of historic and architectural importance as a result of the variety of building styles, the old gold mining fields, and since recent years the town is now sustained by its appeal as a retreat and retirement venue for artists and writers, it has also become somewhat trendy, today several annual fairs are held—the Winter Fair, the Easter Fair, the Art Shows, and the Folk Festival.

As we reached the end of the Maldon Road/C282 I turn the corner to the right onto High Street and then into the Main Street, the stretch of road that appears not to have changed for the past one hundred years; as I have experienced Maldon, the only change that has taken place is that the folk from then have long gone, the place is now occupied by another generation. To capture the local ambiance and its architectural beauty I pulled up on the side of the road, I wanted to stroll through the street with Aunt and Dad.

With its typical Victorian style architecture, in part old weather board structures with a wide veranda in front, a timber structure supported by wooden posts, corrugated iron roof, some of the roofing iron showed considerable signs of rust, iron railings, the red brick chimney visible from the street, most of them painted in pastel colors, some a little dilapidated, others well taken care off, the façade of the red brick buildings, some with bay windows, stained glass in windows and doors, some roofs made of slate, sash windows—they open by sliding the lower part up, often the sanitary facilities were limited to flowing water in the kitchen, the toilet outside, some featuring the raw red brick façade with the window frames highlighted in a white / creamy color, left-overs from the gold rush time.

In the business sector of the main street façades were often very elaborate, some of them had rounded superstructures build in the shape of a half circle on top of the front, others with the shape of a pitched roof, merchandise displayed outside of the shops, benches for the public to use, the street drainage channel laid open adjacent to the footpath, its bed covered with cobble stone, elaborate cast iron sections decorating the balconies and the roof structure, often the same material is used as a barrier under the balcony railing, wooden power posts from which the powerlines are hanging like spaghetti—in part it looks like they needed a bit of sorting out as if they were not sure where they had to go next in a Criss cross fashion, beautifully crafted business signs, many constructed of wood, others with flat metal sheets, the writing written by hand in different fonts and sizes, using different colors just as if they were having a competition.

The Palladian central semicircle superstructure on the top of some of the façades had no structural function at all, it was merely a visual deception making this particular place look grand, important; often, behind these elaborately constructed façades, falsified designs, decorated with ornamental cast stone masks, rosettes created from plaster, dentils and brackets, columns and balustrades, round as well as square shaped, frontispiece, often treated as a separate element of the design and highlighted ornamentation, there was a ramshackle, tatty wooden construction fitted with Sash windows, fancy window hoods, carved cornices, projecting member at the top of the exterior wall, a decorative terminal form at the top of a feature, decorated columns, the bulkhead, the area between the sidewalk and the display windows crafted from wood, the transom, the upper window of the store front clear, embellished with cast iron rosettes.

From our home we headed in a North-westerly direction to Chewton, Castlemaine, Muckleford driving through the rugged countryside on to Maldon; on the way over I had plenty of time to tell Aunt and Dad a little about Shirley and Jeffrey, how we met them, what they were doing professionally and the kind of lifestyle they were perusing so that they would not get a cultural shock once we got there. Their cottage is situated off the bitumen road, the level of comfort that you experience on the last couple of kilometers depends on the past weather conditions; if a lot of rain has fallen in recent days you will find a lot of pot holes in the track which the shire grader operator will fix as soon as he gets around to do it, sometimes this can take weeks, in which case you might have to head down the pub, buy him a beer and remind him politely.

In Australia, statements like "I'll be there straightaway" doesn't necessarily mean now, it's a mere acknowledgement that the person is aware; he or she will be coming soon, perhaps later today, perhaps in days to come. Though Shirley and Jeffrey's place was as clean as you can keep a household in the bush, on a dirt track in the midst of summer, the place was very comfortable and the ambiance homely, but it was no glamour mansion either, enjoying life had precedence. Dad was uncomplicated, the character of people was of prime importance to him whereas Aunt was a little more complicated as this; if a place wasn't presented in accordance with her ideas, she wasn't able to enjoy the moment, she would then be focused on the little things that didn't suit her.

Shirley had prepared a traditional leg of lamb, roasted with its potatoes and pumpkin, served with gravy and sautéed greens from the garden, a salad of fresh berries with ice cream, and plenty of red to go with it, Dad had a ball with the hosts, he was keen to learn about their alternative life style, and Aunt tried very hard to decipher the British accent.

Aunt was ecstatic over the horses; their daughter was involved in dressage and show jumping, Pricilla had just completed a one-year internship with Bill Roycroft, one of Australia's most famous equestrian rider whom was part of the Australian Olympics team that participated in Rome in 1960, winning Bronze in the team events at Mexico City in 1968 and 1976 took part in the Montreal Games, and at the age of 61 he had become the oldest Australian competitor at the 1976 Games. The Roycroft stable was in the township of

Camperdown in the Southwestern part of Victoria. Self-assured, with her assertive manner, Shirley showed Aunt around the luxurious boxes at the back of the cottage, explaining that these horses came out of Australia's finest stables, indeed from a member of the world breeding federation, out of a registered breeding program, that they are very valuable, and this coming from Sherley, a lady with an imposing presence, with her magnificent British accent sounded very exciting.

To gratify the breeding standard of the horses, a beautifully crafted float with every conceivable comfort for the animals was parked in the shed, of course painted to match the brand-new Land Rover, the property was fitted with safety fencing and barriers with the horse's comfort in mind, Pricilla's personal competition accessories, only the best was good enough, including the Louise Epstein Jacket, the R.M. Williams riding boots, the helmet and other important equipment and gadgets which she proudly exhibited.

The prestigious lifestyle, her daughter mingling with the best of Australia's horsy elite, the husband a successful artist, living in one of the trendy places desirable by the Artie's and the would like to bee's was very dear to Sherley, it was this kind of perceived glamour that Aunt adored, I know that the old cottage wasn't her thing, the leg of lamb she would have prepared better, her sauce would not have been thickened with commercial gravy powder, the jus would have been reduced and the viscosity achieved by whisking fresh lumps of butter to it, and the table would have been decorated to perfection, but Jeffrey's fame, the daughters success and the charming British accent in which Shirley spoke made this visit to one of our successes during their visit in Australia.

On another occasion we headed up the Northern Highway up to Axedale, Goornong, Elmore, Rochester on to Echuca, with its 130km one way from Elphinstone, this outing can also be very suitable for a memorable daytrip. Echuca is situated on the river Murray which was one of the most important freight ports right up to the end of the Victorian Goldrush, positioned around 220 km northwest of Melbourne the Murray forms the natural border between the northern part of Victoria and the southern part of NSW, crossing over to South Australia, at Murtho, beginning to run in a south westerly direction down to Wellington (South Australia) flowing into Lake Alexandrina, and near Mundoo Island it runs into the great Australian Bay about 30km from Victor Harbor, from the source of the river which is situated in the Southern part of the Victorian Alps, to its final destination at the Great Bight, the Murray, Australia's longest river has covered 2520km of very diverse and contrasting landscape.

Echuca is just like many other Australian country towns, contemporary facilities and buildings have since been established since the last time that I visited the township, but the core of the town with its Victorian style heritage buildings has been beautifully maintained and restored, with the old Wharf being the highlight of this place.

Originally, the natives of this area were the Yorta Yorta people whom were dispossessed by the European settlers during the early colonial period. Henry Hopwood, an ex-convict was the founder of this town as we know it today, the then small settlement by the name of Hopwood's Ferry in time became the township of Echuca around 1850, and by the 1870s it had become Australia's largest inland water port, supplying the communities on the Murray-Darling water system between New South Wales and Victoria, all being part of the Murray-Darling Catchment.

The rivers Culgoa and Barwon, tributaries become the Darling River in the northern part of NSW between Brewarrina and Bourke from where it continues on to Louth, Tilpa, Wilcannia, Menindee, Pooncarie, Para, down to Wentworth were the river flows into the Murray. The paddle steamers that navigated upriver back then were loaded with fencing wire, galvanized iron, glass, windows, general building supplies as well as household goods, provisioning store keepers and glaziers along the way, and on their way back they were loaded with bales of wool in particular, mostly destined for Britain. However, the navigability of the Darling was limited, very much dependent on the seasonality's, the flow of water was extraordinarily irregular, unpassable during drought periods, in fact the river dried up on some forty-five occasions between 1885 and 1960, to the devastation of the outlying communities who also depend on the river for drinking water as well as for agricultural use, whereas the paddle steamers heading to Goolwa which is situated on the Channel near the Murray Mouth in South Australia, approximately 100km south of Adelaide, were carrying wool that was transferred onto sea freighters.

Because of the traitorous point of entry of the Murray Mouth, the point where the Murray joins the Sanders Reef in the Great Australian Bay the continuation of the waterway to Port Elliot and Victor Harbor was impossible, the inland goods were transported on a horse drawn "railway link" to Port Elliot and Victor Harbor.

In the meantime, the Echuca Wharf has been classified as part of the National Heritage of Australia, with its 75.5 meters in length and 24 meters deep, constructed with locally felled and milled river redgum it is an impressive sight as you walk onto its timber deck, much of it still in its original state, its waterfront side slightly bend like a banana, following the shape of the river, railing all around its edges, toward the waterfront there are a couple of old heavy iron cranes mounted on the surface, a large cargo shed sits on the easterly side of the deck, built with a heavy timber frame construction cladded timber on its base and corrugated iron above it—functioning today as a museum, leading to the cargo shed—the old railway line with its steam train can still be admired today, on the side of the shed is a wooden stare that is leading into the inner life of the wharf.

On the waterfront, you can see the heavy river red gum uprights about 10 meters from the ground to the top of the wharf, fitted in accordance with the grade of the land slope, getting shorter as they approach the end of the slope, all of them braced with heavy struts, providing stability to the structure, as you reach the bottom of the stairs a gangplank is providing access to the paddle steamer. The descent to the boarding level has an eerie feeling about it, from time to time you can note the creaking and groaning of the slightly moving timber, and if you listen very attentively you can almost hear the hustle and bustle from yester year, at the time when the in-bound barges were unloaded and the outbound ones provided with goods. During the summer period when the Murray isn't carrying a lot of water the boarding level is lower compared with the winter time, and in times of a drought it can happen that the boats can't navigate up and down the river.

Both my in-laws, Marlise and Bill, had joint us on this outing, spending a couple of nights on the river boat, it was clear that the eight of us had to travel up to Echuca in two cars; for some reason or another Aunt suggested that the girls should share one, and the boys the other car, a proposal that I thought was rather unusual, somehow this didn't appertain Aunt's usual behavior as I knew it, though I was aware that Marlise's car was perceived as being on the higher end of up-market vehicles, indeed very comfortable, and she appreciated to be seen with Mrs. Doctor, whereas my Land Rover didn't impart the same prestigious value, nor did it provide the same emotion of luxury, probably a significant issue in Aunt's decision making.

However, from the point of view of conversation this wasn't a bad decision, Jacqueline was learning German as a foreign language at school which provided her with the opportunity to translate the dialog between her mum, Aunt Lulu and her sister Tabea. Had we travelled as mixed couples, the conversation might not have been the same; there are things that are of interest to all, the things that can be observed as you pass through the countryside, the questions and answers about the things of interest along the way, or indeed the kind of things that concern our lives in general, with some exceptions to the rule, generally the ladies are less inclined to be interested in the type of high technology Keihin FCR Racing Carburetor that you fitted to your car, the fact that the flat slide throttle on roller bearings with its progressive linkage ensures smooth operation and control, whereas generally speaking, the fellows are less disposed to discuss the instantaneous result of the best beauty care product for the skin—I am convinced that the ladies had a ball, as did I with my father, Bill and Eduard travelling together in my car.

Once we arrived at the base of the Wharf, ready to board the "EMMYLOU," a reproduction of an original, authentic paddle steamer that began its operation as a passenger boat on the Murray River during the midst of the seventeenth century, the building of this little seven-ton beauty began a couple of years prior, in 1980 and had just been launched merely a couple of weeks before our visit. The "EMMYLOU," for reasons beyond my comprehension was named after the famous American Country singer and song writer Emmylou Harris whom has a résumé of very high distinction, I would have thought that an aboriginal name would have been more fitting, worthy of its history.

I know that the ladies adored the two day tour on the "EMMYLOU" but the boys enjoyed it from a different view point; sure, floating past the world heritage wetlands, marveling at the old river red gums on both sides of the river with their crackling sounds being produced through the breeze, listening to the rustling of the gum leaves, observing the odd koala lazing around high up in the tree forks nibbling on the olive green eucalypt delicacy, listening to the pounding sound of the wooden paddles hitting the water on both sides of the boat, with the very particular scent of the Victorian bush pronounced by the dry heat, feeling the slight breath of refreshing air wafting past our faces, enjoying the nostalgic impressions and emotions of a time long gone, for a moment we had been immersed into a very different world.

However, besides the sentimental experience of this trip, the boys were also fascinated by the technical aspects of the "EMMYLOU," in particular Bill whom was a Board Member of the Victorian Steamrail Inc., a non-profit organization dedicated to the restoration and operation of vintage steam, diesel and electric locomotives and carriages, here was this highly successful lawyer that relived his childhood dream of becoming a steam engine driver, his enthusiasm together captured the boys attention, as we had gathered alongside the railing that closed off the open engine room on the main-deck where the engineer was busy checking the grease pots providing the lubricant for the two pistons.

Up until that point in time, I didn't know that Bill was a steam enthusiast, he never talked about this little secret but now that I could see how his eyes had lit up, with great passion and enthusiasm he began to explain to us that this two cylinder double action horizontal steam engine was made by MARSCHALL SONS and CO Limited CAINSBOROUGH LONDON 1906, burning one ton of wood during a day's operation, requiring 250 liters of water per hour to convert it to steam, being pumped directly from the river, filtered before directed to the boiler, with its large fire box and boiler and the two pistons fitted on top to the boiler immaculately painted in British Racing Green, that the highly polished gages and other fittings were made from brass, Bill remarked how clean and neatly groomed the entire engine room was despite the fact that the fire wood was stored in the same area, how this engine develops 12kph with the engine setting at 120rpm, causing the paddlewheels to turn at 30rpm.

I kept an eye on Edward, noting how attentively he was listening to the way his grandfather explained the technical peculiarities of this boat, it was an aspect of Edward that I had never observed, apart from his fascination for flying, usually his interests were rather of academic nature. Bill, as if he had been engaged as our very private tour guide continued to explain; that the "EMMYLOU" had been designed by a leading Sydney marine architect, drawing his inspiration from the old paddle steamers that used to play the Murray, with the propulsion system build in a solid steel hull, the entire superstructure constructed of machined river red gum timber, the main deck features crew facilities toward the bow, the closed in kitchen forward center, the dining room toward the rear with an open lounge facility positioned at the stern, two Queen Class cabins, two Double cabins and two twin cabins are located on the upper deck with a veranda all around, superbly furbished with contemporary comfort without compromising the nostalgic atmosphere of the last century, and the wheelhouse is positioned above the upper deck.

Bill was telling us how, back then the paddle steamers were built as tugs with flat-bottomed timber broad beam hulls for greater stability, usually they had two or more decks, driven by steam engine paddles, some at the rear but more often at the side, and they were designed to tow wooden barges loaded with up to two thousand bales of wool stacked in the hull and piled in several tears above the deck, a large iron helm was connected to the rudder by ropes and chains, the towlines between steamer and barge was 100ft long on the Murray, and 50ft on the darling because of its tighter curves. Bill went on to explain further that by regulation, the steamers had to stop before dark, but by moonlight many of them continued to operate throughout the night.

Apparently, there were also the hawking boats, fitted as travelling ships which called at isolated homesteads and timber cutting camps, until 1920; another was the "Etona," she was equipped as a travelling mission boat to provide religious instruction to the isolated settlers along the Murray until 1912, it featured a small chapel accommodating around 20 people. According to Bill, the P.S. Adelaide, today the oldest wooden hulled paddle steamer still operating anywhere in the world was built in Echuca in 1866 for J.C. Grassey and Partners, now moored at the Echuca Wharf and used for special occasions, history also is telling us that boat building is still an important industry in Echuca today.

Since our outing on the "EMMYLOU," she has been refurbished, offering one-to-six-day river boat trips from the port of Echuca, up and down the river, featuring luxury accommodation and comfort, with its riverside dining, camp side BBQ along the way, the on-board restaurant and bar offering great dining using local produce, serving morning and afternoon tea, lunch and dinner, offering Australian wines and beer in an environment that represents the emotions of the past century.

On this particular trip, from time to time I began to note that Aunt got on like wild fire with my mother in-law which touched me deeply, but I also observed moments when Aunt was discretely watching Elisabeth. Back home Aunt was correct, a little reserved, enjoyed the house, the garden and the pool in particular; she also wanted one of those, loved the animals, the Aberdeen Angus cattle, the Marino sheep, the horses, the cats and dogs; from time to time I noted that Aunt did observe the kids' behavior, how they interacted with their mother and myself as well as with Dad, but in particular I noticed how she was watching Elisabeth, I would have loved to know what she thought of her, wondering if she would gather information so that she could form an opinion which no doubt at some point she would share with me, whether I wanted it or not.

I recall how uncomfortable I felt that Aunt was secretly observing Elisabeth, hoping that she would not notice Aunt's behavior, and at the same time curious to know the remarks that Aunt would make. I was well aware that Elisabeth's house-keeping attributes did not match those of Aunt, both ladies were fundamentally different, their backgrounds could not have been more distinct, one of them enjoyed an elementary school formation and qualified as a sales person, the other had the fortune to have been cultivated in a good home and was able to enjoy a university education and had become a lawyer.

For the duration of the visit Aunt was noncommittal, she didn't comment about my partner Elisabeth at all, we tried to make this stay with us as comfortable as possible for Aunt, but we didn't do anything that we would not have done normally, however during my next visit Aunt began to indicate that she was appalled by the lady of the house.

## Unacceptable Grades

It was one of those moments, Dad and Aunt left to go somewhere with my in-laws Marlise and Bill, Elisabeth and the kids had gone shopping, and I was alone at home with Aunt's sister Tabea, sitting at the poolside with an icy cold soda, suddenly she began a conversation that I didn't understand at first, hinting at something in a polite manner without actually saying what she meant, her non-committal verbal diarrhea blended with innuendos that had no clear context got on my nerves, eventually I asked her politely to be clear and straight forward, to explain what in particular was bothering her. Almost bashful at first; she thought that for Aunt's next visit I must make sure that the house would be better prepared. I asked her if Aunt had been commenting about something in particular.

"No, I'm merely telling you," Tabea responded, beginning to talk about the things that she had apparently observed; I found some crumbs in the corner of the cupboard where you keep the plates.

"That is to say that you are snooping around our cupboards when nobody is around," I responded.

"Not really," Tabea replied, her head was tilted slightly away, it appeared that she was unable to keep the eye contact with me. She went on to say, "I picked up some doghair from underneath the stairwell"—and this despite the fact that I don't like dogs, they don't belong in the house anyway, dogs should be kept outside and besides this you must know that Aunt doesn't appreciate this. And she went on to explain, "Please don't be angry with me, I am merely telling you this for your own good. I also noted that the veranda could do with a bit of scrubbing, there is a lot of dust out there."

"I don't intend to justify myself in any way," I said to Aunt Tabea, "We live in the midst of the Australian bush, it gets to be windy out here, dust is a way of life but we sweep the veranda daily."

"The exhaust system above the stove should be washed down—I have detected a slight film of grease," Aunt Tabea commented. "For some days now, there is some hair in the shower recess that I am sharing with Aunt and your father, you know that isn't very hygienic," Aunt Tabea continued, "and the toilet bowl in our bathroom isn't clean either."

As if Aunt Tabea was in a stage of intoxication, she appeared to have this urge to tell me about all the things that she perceived as negative during the stay at our house, between her describing the stuff that she identified as being disturbing assuring me that she was telling me this because it was for my own benefit. "I don't know if you have noticed," Aunt Tabea continued, "Aunt doesn't appreciate if your wife is cooking, she prefers if you prepare for us, instead letting Elisabeth do the cooking you should consider dining out as an option if you don't have time to take care of the kitchen."

I was overwhelmed by the account of Aunt Tabea's observations, surprised at the same time about the stupidity of her behavior, but I was equally astonished about her honesty; at first, I wasn't sure if I should simply ignore her remarks or if I should insult her severely, knowing that if I opted for my second thought she would be entirely offended. For a brief moment I consulted my feelings, reminding myself that I was a teeny when I first met Aunt Tabea,

I never spent any time with her, the only time when she got to see me was at grandpa Robert's place sharing the traditional Sunday roast once in a while.

I don't recall ever having a conversation with Aunt Tabea before she visited us in Australia, I asked myself if she hadn't noticed that the teenage pickles had left my face long ago, did I forget to tell her I am in my thirties now, didn't anybody tell her that I was an airline pilot and that I had assumed the responsibility for my family, that together with my partner Elisabeth I was taking care of the well-being of a couple of kids, nurturing them progressively into adulthood? For a short time, I was also wondering if Aunt Lulu shared the same thoughts as did her sister, a thought that brought back some memories of my childhood, briefly pondering over the mental abuse that Aunt Lulu had exercised on me on a regular basis which raised feelings of insecurity for a brief moment.

After what seemed to have been for a long time of reflection, I settled for the second option, deliberately I had chosen to be arrogant in my approach to Aunt Tabea, looking at her profoundly, beginning by saying, "I didn't invite you to come to Australia—you invited yourself, I was merely informed that you were coming—we had no problem with you tagging along with Dad and Aunt, in fact we were looking forward to see you, I thought that we made you feel welcome in our home, where possible—Elisabeth, her parents and I have taken time out from our jobs to make sure that Aunt, Dad, and you can enjoy a wonderful time with us, thus far we have made sure that you are comfortable, making sure that there is always decent tucker on the table, a decent drop of Aussie gold is always available from our wine cellar, when we go out for dinner you don't have to pull your wallet out of your pocket either—then you snoop around the place to see if you can find something that isn't up to Aunt's standard—you are welcome at our place but I never promised anybody a five-star hotel with its fully serviced rooms, you are complaining about the shower that is provided for you is not clean—I would have thought that you could wipe down your dirt yourselves, and if some of your ploppies get stuck in your private bowl, I would have thought that you make use of the brush that is kept on the right side of the pot for exactly that purpose; the dogs are part of our family—we have decided that they have access to our home, something that we are not going to change now because you believe that they are a nuisance, and no—I haven't noticed that Aunt doesn't appreciate Elisabeth's cooking, and please if there is anything else that bothers you about our house—keep it to yourself."

During my verbal throwing up, having deliberately chosen a harsh approach, using straightforward language, having chosen my words very carefully, deliberately making sure that Aunt Tabea would be left with a clear message, I noted that her eyes had become watery, gradually Aunt's face began to change color, her rather pale skin appeared to be transformed, the tiny blood vessels began to flood her cheeks, filling them with an intense deep red blush, she began to turn her head away from me as if she was trying to conceal herself, her head was slightly dropped by now, her mouth slightly opened; eventually tears began to roll down her cheeks and her sobbing had become more intense.

At that point, I handed Aunt a couple of disposable hankies which she took almost begrudgingly, I nearly felt sorry for her, I was certain that I had surprised her with my response, I was sure that she didn't expect this from me. Watching Aunt Tabea's behavior was pathetic, the person that tried to criticize and scold me a moment ago was now a miserable sobbing mess, and at that moment, for some reason I remembered that years ago my father had nicknamed Aunt Tabea "the Carp"—apparently because under the water the Carp is holding open its mouth for most of the time, this provided Aunt with a kind of an unintelligent look. At the same time, I questioned my integrity in this particular case, asking myself if I would have reacted in the same manner if Aunt Lulu or indeed my father would have held this conversation with me; would I have been as candid with them, would I have been as straight forward and deliberate in my approach?

Without having to reflect for too long, frankly speaking, I don't think so, my thought processes would have been the same, I would have felt just as angry, but I would have chosen a different approach. My reaction in this case begs the question, why did I dare to scold Aunt Tabea in a manner that I would not have behaved toward my father or Aunt Lulu? I think that the answer is straightforward—my father was a figure of authority by default, I felt connected and held a lot of respect toward him, Aunt Lulu was also a figure of authority, by force, I merely respected her because she was the wife of my father, I had no respect for her as a person, I didn't feel connected to her, at no time ever was she a substitute for my mother, nor did I love her.

I believe that the harsh reaction that I exerted toward Aunt Tabea was conceivable because she never represented a figure of authority for me despite the fact that we knew each other since my teen age, Aunt was merely a person that I got to know as the sister of Aunt Lulu, and I wasn't prepared, nor obliged to accept her behavior.

## Miss Fox

One of our neighbors, an eighty some year-old lady, whom lived in a ramshackle, very neglected old minor's cottage bordering on one of our Westerly fence lines, apparently, she had a water tap out in one of her paddocks but this particular pipe was not connecting to her home; Elisabeth discretely used to keep an eye on the old lady, making sure that she would maintain her dignity and that she didn't feel as if we were trying to interfere in her life. In the village the street wisdom had it that Goldie, as we used to call her when she was not around coming from a well to do family, her father was the owner of a flower mill in one of the riverside rural village located on the Goulburn River, a major inland perennial River of the Goulburn Broken catchment which is part of the Murray-Darling basin, around 150km North of Melbourne.

Goldie was the black sheep of the family, the odd one out, she had no interest in her parent's business, her passion was the land and the animals, she was described as the strange old lady that lived with her animals in isolation, a solitary life, didn't get involved with anything or anybody, she was reserved, didn't trust anybody either, nor did she confide in anyone, she was somewhat odd, shy and eccentric.

Elisabeth invited her on a regular basis, I don't know how she convinced this old lady to take a bath or a shower at our place before taking a seat at the dinner table, knowing that she would not groom herself out there in the paddock in the company of her cows and sheep, knowing that if she didn't scrub herself before coming over it would have been an unpleasant experience for our olfactory senses, very ugly indeed. Sometimes, when Goldie was over for dinner and I had the chance to be home at that time, enjoying chatting with her, and I hit the right buttons, assisted with a little South Australian Red she would become talkative, she was extremely knowledgeable about nature, wild and domesticated animals, the weather, as if she had spent some time living among the indigenous people of this land.

Goldie knew a lot about the Aborigines and the Dreamtime, she had learned to read natures behavior, she was able to make predictions about the weather based on the way the sun had set, from the way the gum leaves were dangling from the trees she could forecast the amount of rain that could be expected in the hours to come, from the behavior of the crickets Goldie was able to construct some other prognosis; Goldie had a lot of reverence for the land, she was able to read nature, she knew how to conserve the environment, how to develop sustainable agriculture, ensuring how to secure the continuity of the food supply, Goldie had a true adoration for Aboriginal skills, she understood the philosophy about environmental and the ecological skills, i.e., the burning of the land, Goldie explained the meaning of "sensing" the world / our environment beyond our body through cognitive agility, being able to put yourself into the viewpoint and perspective of creatures, rocks water, clouds, or indeed other Materia.

It was going toward the end of Aunt and Dad's visit, in preparation of this particular evening where they were to meet our dear old friend from next door, Elisabeth had supervised Goldie's mandatory hygiene service in one of our bathrooms, then providing her with a lovely outfit, covering her sunspots with a touch of discrete make-up, finishing off with a splash of her eaux de perfume, transforming her into a presentable person in the hope that she would be socially acceptable for Aunt to share the dinner table with her. I thought that Elisabeth had done a tremendous job; Goldie all dressed up to the nines, looking just lovely, chatting about the subject that she knew best, the land, the environment and her animals.

From my observation, Aunt wasn't overly thrilled having to share the evening with a person that wasn't worthy of her standard of living. It wasn't until years later that Elisabeth told me how much effort that she had put into the making of Goldie's acceptability on this particular evening, that from the moment she met Aunt, Elisabeth realized that Aunt had a strong need to exhibit her assumed nobility and social status to others.

Goldie Fox, a lady that was never married throughout her life, the alternative lifestyle on the land, taking care of her twenty cattle, about fifty sheep and zig fowls without the support of anybody else had taken its toll on her body, no longer did she stand straight, her posture was slightly stooped forward, she had become fragile, and yet she wasn't prepared to give up farming, retirement without her animals was an option that she would not have chosen, this would probably have been the end of her.

I have many good memories about Mrs. Fox, I will always treasure the stories that she had to recount, the wisdom and the purpose of spending time on this earth that she personified; our gatherings weren't intellectual discussions in a corner of a paddock or indeed over dinner at our place, Goldie wasn't the kind of person that would debate a particular point of view, nor would she criticize anybody's opinion, she merely had a great deal of experience with life and lots of fascinating yarns to tell. I also have memories of Goldie that weren't particularly delightful. I had just returned from Tokyo on a night flight, I was tired, preparing a light breakfast before hitting the sack for a few hours, when suddenly a nasty smell which seemed to be carried by a stream of smoke came wafting through our house—this was no BBQ either.

The stench was drifting in our direction from the west, in my four-wheeler I was heading in the direction of what I believed to be the source, eventually reached the dirt track that was leading up to Goldie's place, a couple of hundred yards up the track I was able to locate the reason for the smoke. As I pulled up, there was Goldie, in her hand she had an old half gallon metal kerosene container from which she had poured its content all over the cow, apparently lying dead in a water channel on the side of the dirt track since the night before.

Upset and clearly mourning over the loss of her elderly pet cow, Goldie had kept her scope of reality, out in the bush or in the outback nobody would have bothered about a dead cow, the animal would have been left for nature to take care of its body, but here in our rural farming community it was customary to engage an excavator to bury the dead animal, not out of sorrow or because we would have wanted to respect the death of the animal, it was merely a question of public hygiene, despite her grief Goldie had chosen an unemotional, pragmatic solution which didn't affect her pocket, it merely disturbed her immediate neighborhood.

On another occasion, Goldie had asked me if I could take a look at her water supply which was positioned in her back paddock around fifty meters away from her cottage. To reach the location of the water tap, the quickest way would have been to take the path from her backyard but for some reason Goldie preferred for us to take the long way; shortly after we had reached the trough it had become evident that the absence of the flowing water must have its source elsewhere, the brass tap and it's fitting was operative. Goldie and I followed the old iron pipe and it became obvious that we were heading toward her cottage, I was able to feel that Goldie would probably have preferred that this wasn't the case, and as we had reached the fence line to her backyard, I began to understand why she was trying to avoid this scenario.

The rear gate leading into Goldie's backyard had long ago lost its hinges, hanging crooked on a rotting wooden corner post that should long have been replaced, the top part of the rusted iron gate was hanging on a piece of fencing wire tightly fixed to the post, the bottom part stuck loosely in the ground and the gate was secured to the opposite post with the aid of a kind of rusted ring made of a piece of fencing wire. Because Goldie was predominantly rearing sheep, her fencing was constructed from mesh wire, some of it broken in parts, held together with hay bind.

Those of you that have travelled through rural Australia will know what I am talking about, it is not unusual to come across badly maintained fences, patched and held together with different colors of hay bind, I have seen repair work on fences that resembled a cobb web, very funny indeed but it is an effective, an inexpensive short-term solution for many farmers that are a little short on cash; frankly speaking I have also resorted to this method from time to time.

Although from where we stood, I could see parts of the cottage roof but the rest was obstructed by scrub that had grown out of control and some half dead fruit trees that should have been pruned a long time ago to maintain their fertility, as finally Goldie had managed to open the lopsided gate I felt as if I had been led on to a horror movie set, the back shed in which the out-house was incorporated was leaning heavily to the right, the weatherboard was patched here and there with odd bits of timber, the part where the nightman used to remove the can at the back of the outdoor toilet was overgrown with blackberries; clearly the dunny had been inoperative for a long time, in other parts of the wall corrugated as well as flat galvanized sheeting were covering the damaged areas, on the roofing iron rather large patches of rust was clearly visible, several rusty old 44Gallon drums, some still intact, others had the top removed, filled with water, slimy green organic growth on the interior, others were used as garbage disposal containers, old newspapers and heavily discolored plastic spread all over, firmly imbedded the ground, defective rusted tools, empty cans of cat food that had been badly marked by the weather over years.

Wherever I looked I could spot a cat that looked at me in utter distrust as if they had never met anybody but Goldie during their life time, empty plastic containers tarnished by the sun, remains of perished animals, cats, fowl even a rather large dog, the entire place looked as it was the local councils tip, a dumping ground for unwanted things, on the other side of the shed I could see a couple of water tanks constructed in a traditional manner from corrugated iron one of them still in working order the other rusted through, the scrub that had taken over what once was the vegetable garden. For a moment I was preoccupied with this dreadful sight, Goldie was standing near me, pretending that she had not seen the same thing as I did—this filthy mess had perhaps ceased to be a problem for her long ago, I was not certain that Goldie was ashamed.

Around the neighborhood, for some reason Goldie didn't have a good reputation, it was said that she was selfish, antisocial, prepared to take but not to give in return, folk from the surroundings had stopped to help her out. It is true that Goldie kept to herself, it is also true that she was eccentric, as far as I was able to ascertain she was paying her bills, perhaps not always on time, and I asked myself what on earth the local people expected from this elderly lady, she was in need of assistance from time to time, but other than her personal time she had nothing to give, she simply didn't have anything other than her rundown farm.

Cole's family and the four of us were the only folk that assisted the dear old lady in her struggle for survival, where possible we maintained her fences from time to time, Cole ploughed a few acres of her land and cultivated Lucerne hay, a sturdy grass variety that drives its roots several meters into the ground to draw water from the deeper areas, thus providing a high quality fodder all year round including during most drought periods, between us we made sure that Goldie's animals had sufficient to feed, shade and plenty of water, we organized the crutching, shearing and the dipping of her sheep, giving her a hand with the selling of her farm products.

On this particular Saturday morning, Elisabeth and the kids had come up from Melbourne, on the way, before they reached our farm house in Elphinstone they stopped at Goldie's weatherboard cottage, the weekend before she had asked Elisabeth if she could get her some special goodies from the big smoke, Elisabeth respecting the fact that Goldie didn't appreciate if people came to the front door, she called out to her from the front fence. The fellow that lived opposite Goldie's place eventually came out from his house, telling Elisabeth that he had not seen the old lady for a couple of days, but he didn't bother to see if she was ok either.

338

Elisabeth kept on calling out to Goldie, eventually getting to the front door, it wasn't locked, though she was able to push the handle down, the door could not be opened, it appeared to be blocked from the inside, but eventually she heard what sounded like a soft whimpering which appeared to be coming from the window on the right-hand corner of the cottage. Elisabeth, having to be careful not to fall over the bits or rubbish and junk that was scattered on the front veranda as she made her way down to the window on the far corner, from the outside she was able to push up the sash. The place was in total darkness, Elisabeth could not identify an outline of any furniture, it appeared that the entire room was filled with unidentifiable stuff, plastic shopping bags with something or another, hessian bags; as she described to me later; it looked like Goldie was laying somewhere in the midst of all this rubbish, responding to questions in a very week, uncoordinated manner, but it became evident that something had happened that rendered Goldie's speech near incomprehensible, slurring like she never did before.

Elisabeth asked Lawrence; the fellow on the other side of the road to call "000" the number for the emergency services; ambulance fire and police. Around twenty minutes later the ambulance from the Castlemaine Hospital pulled up; the chief of the medic's team commented that even for experienced professionals, this particular rescue deployment had been very special, one that he would never be able to forget—he suspected that Goldie had suffered a mild heart attack, he was of the opinion that she would pull through.

I didn't get home until Sunday morning, still tired from the night flight but I soon forgot my fatigue when Elisabeth began to tell me the story about Goldie's misfortune, I got changed into some old working rags and we headed off to take a look at her small weatherboard cottage just down the road from us. Elisabeth had explained to me that the front door was not accessible, the rescue team got Goldie out through the front window on the far right, but I had decided to try the rear door first. I had done a couple of odd jobs for Goldie some months earlier, it was a while back since the last time that I was anywhere near her cottage, but it was evident that more rubbish had been accumulated around the place since then.

The back door was not locked but once the handle had been pushed down in its opening position it took a little pressure to carefully force it open until the gap between door and frame was sufficient to squeeze my way in, from the sound that was caused by the opening of the door I gathered that empty cans had been obstructing the door and this was confirmed as I entered the kitchen, near evenly distributed all over the entire kitchen floor, almost up to the level of the small table that stood a couple of meters ahead of me on the left side the entire area was covered with empty cat food cans, most of them mold covered on the inside, caused by the scraps of food that had remained in the cans, the smell was unpleasant but the sight was simply unbelievable—how can anybody possibly allow one's kitchen to become filled with empty pet food cans?

Did Goldie value her cats more than the place that is designed to prepare one's food? I guess that Goldie hadn't prepared a hot meal for some time, next to the old fire place which was opposite the kitchen table was an old wood fired stove, most of it also covered with cans. Next to the table stood a lovely old kitchen larder, likewise, covered to the working top with cans, the bottom doors could not be opened anymore and the top part contained moldy food matter which could not be definitively identified, it had long perished beyond recognition, and the same was true for the couple of cooking pots that were laying around, both the front and the rear doors to the kitchen featured each two stain glass panels on the top part, they had been concealed with old-fashioned, embroider curtain material, covered with filth.

The ceiling was constructed in the fashion of an A frame lined with lining boards heavily muted with smoke from the open fire place which served as a heater during the winter period, almost entirely covered with cob webs, the old oil paint was peeling from the walls in part, on the right side there was a doorway which had been covered up with a sheet of unpainted plywood nailed to the door frame, which added a sense of mystery to this little cottage, as if Goldie was hiding some kind of secret behind this door. From the kitchen I began to wade my way into the next room on my left, it was dark, the window had been covered with ply wood from the outside, the beam from my small torch was the only direct light source supported by a glim of brightness that entered the room from the kitchen door.

As I was scanning the room systematically with my torch I couldn't cease to be astonished, on my left there was a lovely old four door Victorian Mahogany sideboard, a small sofa with a dark leather cover on its side and near the window a table with four Victorian oak balloons back dining chairs, some old photos were hanging on the wall, neatly arranged and cleaned it could have been a comfortable lovely small parlor. As I took my second step into the room the wooden floor boards and the underneath of the carpet that I stood on had given way, together with the floor cover I fell about a meter through the broken floor onto the ground on which the house stumps had been embedded.

As I recovered from the shock and struggled back up into the room I was able to identify that much of the floor boards had rotted, in fact the entire floor area was soaking wet, it didn't appear to be water either, the smell of urine was very strong, the parlor was likely to have been used as a toilet, as I continued to scan the room with my torch I noted the rather large nails had been driven into the wall on the East side on either side of the window, on them, Goldie had suspended plastic shopping bags, as I carefully touched one of them it felt very soft, on closer but careful investigation I realized that they were filled with human feces and partly the urine was still enclosed in those bags that were still intact, with others the liquid had escaped the leaky bags and had run down the wall.

The walls were covered with stained tongue and groove bead board up to about three feet high, capped off by strips of horizontal molding to finish off the seams of the bead, and above that there was a very old pastel colored wall paper decorated with lovely, red flowers, but it too had seen better days, it was torn in different parts. Just like the kitchen, the parlor was also covered with dust and the cobwebs had taken over large areas of the room. From there, I was moving forward very gingerly, being aware that the floor may not support my weight which was probable near twice that of Goldie's, getting into the last room of this cottage; the bedroom wasn't going to be simple either, beginning at the doorway stuff that appeared to be a blend of clothing, old hessian bags, bedding material, rags and bags of things, in all about half a meter high and somewhere in among this stuff must have been Goldie's bed, or at least the place where she was sleeping. This room was no different, the place was dark and smelly like the others; everything covered with dust and the spiders had woven a gigantic network of traps which provided them with nutritious goodies.

At that time the council didn't provide its citizens with a garbage disposal service, it was assumed that everybody had a vehicle to take their rubbish to the local dump, a large hole in the ground, located close to the edge of the bush, the term "re-cycling and the separation of different materials and substances" didn't belong to our vocabulary then, everything, food scraps, carton and paper products, plastic, glass, metal, old gone hard paint, residue of cleaning agents, simply anything that was unwanted landed in the ditch and on a regular basis a council worker came by to light this cocktail with the assistance of some kerosene and a match, providing the neighborhood with an awful stench, depending on the direction of the wind at the time.

In the rural areas the local council didn't provide its citizens with a sewerage system either, in a period long gone, in rural Australia as well as in the suburbs of cities each house had an outdoor dunny, they were usually one meter wide and a little more than one meter deep, consisting of a more or less solid timber frame, lined with weatherboard or corrugated iron and an appropriate roof to protect this important facility, depending on the owner, the outdoor dunny was a pleasant to look at construct, but it could also be a ramshackle hut constructed from scrappy materials. The earth closet, a hole in the ground about two meters deep, as soon as the ploppies had been finished the user would sprinkle some sawdust together with a pinch of bicarbonate soda down the shaft which would ease the smell and at the same time it assisted the crap to decompose nicely was the preferred system by some, others had a large can placed underneath the seat, its content was collected and emptied once a week by the "Nightman," a fellow that came around with his small truck to empty all the cans filled with the "night-soil," in rural Australia as well as in the suburbs this was common practice right into the fifties.

In more recent times laws had been passed that obliged folk from the suburbs to get connected to the mains and those living in the rural areas had to construct a septic tank system for their waste water. However, Goldie didn't have a car and none of us that lived in the vicinity of her cottage had thought to help her out by collecting her rubbish on a regular basis, it didn't occur to us, nor did Goldie have a septic tank system, the "Nightman" had stopped to call many years ago—I fully understand how the old dear got into trouble with her "night-soil" and her garbage in general, she didn't have the means to keep up with the changes that modern society had brought about, nor was anybody taking care of her, guiding her, to stand by and to assist her with the transition into modern times.

Knowing that Goldie would be in the care of the Castlemaine Hospital for at least a couple of weeks, we decided that she couldn't possibly move back into her home in the state it was in. Elisabeth called one of her lawyer colleagues whom had a chamber in neighboring Castlemaine, she also knew that he was a Rotarian, a service organization whose stated purpose is to bring together business and professional leaders in order to provide humanitarian services. Within an hour, this fellow by the name of Rodney was knocking on our door, together we drove down to Goldie's place, for him to get a first-hand impression of the gravity of this situation, and to figure out how we could make this place fit for a human being to live in.

Sunday afternoon, within a matter of a few hours Rodney had mobilized a team of volunteer's, in all about twenty men and woman, all members of the Rotary Club of Castlemaine, State of Victoria; one of them was charged with the responsibility of the team leader, a lady by the name of Joanne had pulled up with a ten-ton tip truck, also part of the clean-up and renovating team, by mid evening the entire cottage including the front and back yard had been completely cleaned out, all garbage and other stuff that was useless to Goldie removed, carted to the local dump, the place was now ready to be fixed up, prepared for the professionals to move in in the morning.

The volunteer's team provided their professional experience and their time where as others donated cash or building materials required to fix the place. On the Monday morning, four utilities fitted with large trailers, a ten ton tip truck driven by Joanne pulled up at Goldie's; a carpenter team began by replacing the floor stumps that had been removed the day before, digging the new, sump oil treated hardwood stumps firmly into the ground, placing the new hardwood timber joists, insulation bats and foil was installed on the joists, the pine floor boards installed and the skirting board fixed, the other carpenter team began with the replacement of external weather boards where necessary, replacing uprights here and there, getting the kitchen ready for its new sink and work surfaces, fixing the odd timber construction of the veranda, and building the framework ant its lining for the new bathroom which was to consist of a shower, a hand basin and an indoor toilet in the area that was concealed behind a plywood board in the kitchen.

At the same time the electrician removed the old wiring system, installed new wires for the lights, their switches, power points, all connected to a power company approved mains board, the plumber pulled out the old iron water pipe that led from the main supply pipe in front of the cottage into the house, installed an all-copper system to the kitchen, the bathroom as well as a cold water tap each for front and back yard. The plumber also checked over the roof, replacing corrugated iron sheets where required, renewed the entire spouting system with a direct connection to the water tank at the back of the house.

The following day, both interior as well as the external weather boards had been prepared for a fresh coat of paint, the windows were replaced, the doors mended, the tongue and groove panels and the skirting surfaces lightly sanded and re-stained, the wall paper above removed, replaced with a similar design, the ceiling surfaces washed down, also repainted with a near white color to add brightness to the rooms, on the third day the kitchen facilities and the new bathroom were completed, a gardening team had organized the garden, cut and pruned trees and shrubs and placed large pots with flowers along the front and the rear veranda, new, second hand furniture was moved in, curtains suitable for an old, renovated Victorian Miners Cottage were installed, some new cooking utensils, a set of crockery, cutlery and glass ware placed in her restored larder as well as other gadgets positioned around the place, making sure that the owner would be truly touched by the effort that the team put into her little place.

The following weekend Elisabeth and a couple of other ladies from the village spent another couple of hours in the cottage, putting clean bed sheets on the bed, generally tidying up after the renovations and completing the last finishing touches.

## Ash Wednesday, 16 February 1983

I was on early duty, departing Melbourne at 06:05, on a direct flight to the East Coast of Queensland, arriving in Cairns at 09:25, with a thirty-five-minute turnaround we were cleared to take off shortly after 10:10 heading toward New South Wales, arriving in Sydney at 13:05, during our short break at the crew room we learned that a large bush fire was raging in the Mount Macedon area, a township that I passed everyday going to and coming back from the airport when we weren't staying in Melbourne, I didn't have a lot of time to listen to this news, I had to consult the meteo office and complete our flight plan in preparation of our departure at 14:00, heading back to my home base Melbourne.

From about 80km out of Melbourne we were able to see the huge smoke cloud moving in our direction, though for a short moment I was able to feel a wave of emotion coming over me, but this wasn't the time, nor the place to be thinking about a bush fire not so far from home, I had to focus on the flying of the aircraft.

During our approach phase we received the instruction from the tower to descent to 4,000 ft, and to approach the holding pattern ZUVOM from the south; for this purpose the controller send us in a South Westerly direction, out over Port Philip Bay, cleared to 2,000 ft, then to turn onto QDM 359°, as we flew over the FIX, applying a procedure turn to enter the holding pattern with a right turn, levelling out at heading 274° about 6 NM from JENOV, the outer marker.

Earlier, before the approach phase began, we consulted the Aircraft Manual, reconfirming that our calculated landing configuration was within the operating limitations, I was a little concerned about the ambient temperature at the airport, it was reported at 43° with a cautioning for a possible increase; I had to keep this scenario in mind and be prepared to react during the final approach phase.

The aircraft was configured for the approach, our airspeed indicated 163 kts, the landing gear had been extended, we were reading three green lights, flaps were set at 30, the nose slightly raised, we had received our clearance to descent to the OM (outer marker) which we were expected to intercept at 1,500 ft on heading 274°, the VOR centerline indicator was placed in the center circle and the glide slope dial began to stabilize in the center circle as well. In those days the IFR (**I**nstrument **F**light **R**ules) were flown with the ADF (**A**utomatic **D**irection **F**inder) and VOR (**V**HF **O**mnidirectional **R**ange) coupled with a DME (**D**istance **M**easuring **E**quipment), GPS and integrated flight systems had just been developed and introduced in the early 80s, but our aircraft was of an older generation and had not been retrofitted.

The lighting up of the blue light confirmed that we were established on the outer marker, speed around 160 kts, reducing, rate of descent about 700 fpm, speed brake in the ARM position, the orange light confirmed that we had reached the middle marker, flaps increased to 40, only very conservative, provident power adjustments, throttle to idle at about 50 ft, at 30 ft we initiated the flare, the main gear touched the tarmac almost simultaneously, we lowered the fuselage to the point where the nose wheel touched the surface of the runway, applied the brakes very gently, initiated the reverse thrust, released and eventually rolled off the runway, along the taxi way to the terminal.

If there is such a thing as a textbook landing, this one would have been worthy of describing, but I don't think that our passengers noticed this performance, I suspect that all of them were preoccupied with the bushfires, particularly those seated on the right side of the aircraft, they would have had a good view of the devastation of Mount Macedon.

Over the intercom we had just bid our passengers goodbye, pulled the parking break, cut the engines, competed the shutdown procedure, and had gone through our debriefing when the gate agent knocked at the cockpit door, he wanted to provide us with an update on the bushfire, he knew that both of us had to drive through this area to get home, Paul Williams, my Co-Pilot on this flight lived in Woodend, a township about 13 km out from Mount Macedon, and I had to head up the Calder highway as well to get back home to Elphinstone.

Wednesday 16th February 1983 has been described as Ash Wednesday by history since. I was up at 03:30, getting myself ready to leave for work, the 105 km drive from Elphinstone took me through Taradale, Malmsbury, Kyneton, Woodend, Macedon (the township in the Wombat State Forest, commonly known as the Black Forest) Gisborne, Sunbury, on to Melbourne's International Airport, Tullamarine, just under the hour. Windows down, listening to good music in the background, a cigarette in my right hand, mostly lit on the same spot during every drive, at least four or five between home to the staff parking lot at the airport, pursuing my thoughts, the long drive to work was for me a great way of preparing myself for the day, and the world seemed to be in great shape as I drove through the Black Forest early that morning.

By 05:00 I was in the office, grabbed a cup of coffee, checked my in-tray and the notice board for news and general information, Paul Williams my Co-Pilot for the day prepared the flight plan, together we consulted the fellows at the Meteo, by 05:30 I had completed the exterior check whilst Paul was configuring the aircraft for the take-off on the first leg MEL-SYD, ETD 06:05.

Neither of us could have known that Victoria was going to be hit by one of its most horrific bush fires in some hours to come—a series of fires that hit the State, it got to be known as the Ashe Wednesday bush fires.

Leading up to this day, we had extremely little rainfall over the winter and spring period, and the summer rains were 75 percent below from the previous year, almost drought conditions, the humidity had fallen from the standard 45 to below 15 percent and the temperature had risen to 43° accompanied by occasional winds higher than 100km per hour that day.

A front of cold air was located in the Great Australian Bight off the coast of South Australia, causing the hot air in the center of Australia to be drawn southward, creating a hot, dry Northerly wind over Victoria. Many smaller bushfires were reported by mid-morning and toward early afternoon most of them were well established.

By mid-morning the official fire danger reporting system had forecast the fire danger to be higher than 100 probability factor for different areas of the states Victoria and South Australia.

Around mid-morning, in Trentham East, a small township West of Macedon, apparently twigs of eucalyptus trees were rubbing on power lines causing sparks. The Eucalyptus tree, commonly known as the "blue gum" is native to Australia, as the tree ages their bark peels of in long streamers and eventually fall to the ground, together with falling eucalyptus leaves are building a dense carpet of highly flammable materials providing additional fuel that draws ground fires up into the leaves, creating an opportunity for massive, fast spreading crown fires.

At the same time the eucalyptus oil contained in the gum leaves give the trees their characteristic spicy fragrance—it is a flammable oil, this combined with leave litter and the dried bark strips gathered on the ground, combined with dry, windy weather can turn the ground fire into a terrifying explosive firestorm in a very short time.

Concurrently, some professionals from the CFA (Country Fire Authority) Victoria were speculating on how the fire in Trentham East could have started by tree branches rubbing on the overhead powerlines, and they concluded that; Eucalyptus oil which is extremely flammable vaporized in the heat, their oil left a smoggy haze—not unlike vapor hanging over the eucalyptus groves, this combined with the electric sparks caused by the twigs rubbing on the electric wire, causing the start of the bushfire in Trentham East.

As a rule, on most days after work, like other colleagues I used to call in at the office lounge, a place that the airline provided for crew to relax in comfort during their breaks, but on this particular day I was in a hurry to hit the road, I could feel the mood of the airport workers that I met, heavy, even depressive and some of them appeared scared, many lived in and around the areas where the bushfire were raging, I knew that Elphinstone and its surrounding townships had not been affected by the fire, but I was afraid for the people, the livestock, the countless species of wild animals that called the Wombat State Forest their home.

Typically for this area, public buildings and most of the homes from the previous century were constructed from large, local stone blocks and bricks, from the same period some weatherboard homes and cottages, mostly delightfully renovated formed part of the architectural charm of Central Victoria, and the contemporary brick veneer houses which is principally a weatherboard with a cladding of brick on the outside; I feared that many of these timber homes would not have been able to escape the rage of this fire.

The distance between Melbourne's International Airport and Gisborne, the township before Macedon is around 46 km, a thirty-minute drive, though focused on my driving and the traffic; this was usually a time to reflect, to follow and to consolidated stimulating thoughts and ideas, to begin to relax, but not on this occasion, I was nervously excited, lighting one cigarette after another, listening to the newsflashes that both, the local radio stations and the ABC were broadcasting as news about the bush fires became available, trying to imagine the extent of the devastation up ahead, scared of what I thought that I would be about to discover, I finally reached the township of Gisborne.

Gisborne had already suffered from bush fires that destroyed over six thousand ha of farming land, some 1.800 ha of Stat Forest and fifty houses on the first of January of that year, and again the township had been hit hard, the 28 km railway track between Gisborne and the neighboring Kyneton in the North West was destroyed, the wooden sleepers burnt and the steel tracks bent and buckled, effectively disrupting the train connection between Melbourne and the township of Mildura situated in the North West of the State, in the vicinity of the border to New South Wales.

Immediately after Gisborne the police had set up a road block, stopping every vehicle travelling North, wanting to know the purpose and the destination of each with the intention to keep out sightseers, voyeurs and opportunists that might have been ready to pilfer, or to capturing pictures as souvenirs without any consideration to the people directly involved in this misery, only residents of Macedon and it's district, emergency services and supplies were permitted to head in that direction, fellows like me that had to head up the Calder Highway were cautioned to remain on the main road.

From the roadblock to the beginning of the Black Forest was a mere nine kilometers, a six-minute drive, the car windows were down, already from the distance I was able to suspect some of the devastation that had taken place in this area, on the radio the air temperature was indicated at around 43° Celsius but I was convinced that locally it was considerably higher, increasing as I got near to the forest, high clouds of black smoke with deep red, in parts dark yellow shooting flames coming out of them could still be seen to the East of Macedon as the fire had moved away from the township, and as I eventually got to the forest a spectacle of unprecedented horror began to unfold itself; for a few more minutes I kept driving, uncontrollably tears were running down my face, and eventually I pulled up on the side of the road and got out of the car.

Surrounded by hundreds of acres of forest burned to the ground, as far as I could see the entire foliage of the gum trees gone, the undergrowth and the earth burned right up to the bitumen of the road, the edges had become very soft leaving a kind of sticky layer of tar on the tires, the tree trunks from the larger trees badly burnt and heavily scarred on the outside, some of the trunks twisted as if Superman had disformed them deliberately, most of the smaller gums reduced to a large stick without branches in the ground, still smoldering, the heat was almost intolerable, the air was filled with smoke, creating an eerie atmosphere, rubble and debris, metal parts that had been softened and bend from the heat of the fire, destroyed corrugated roofing iron and entire water tanks, burnt out cars and trucks.

Having seen this unbelievable devastation, I also became acutely aware of my other senses; although the fire had been put out by the local voluntary fire people, in part the undergrowth was still smoldering, in isolated areas causing tree trunks to take up flames from the ground and beginning to burn again; the rustling of some of the debris that was moved about by the hot breeze still blowing from the West, the crackling of the smoldering sources on the ground as well as on the timber above the ground provided a further dimension to this extraordinary experience, in the distance, from time to time I was able to hear the voice of a human, calling out the name of a missing pet, hoping to find it, and the sound of sirens from the emergency vehicles was still evident.

Actually, under normal circumstances the smell of the burning fire induces pleasant ideas, the thought of a fire burning in the fire place in the living room, providing a cozy atmosphere, or the smell of the charcoal glowing in the BBQ, together with the fragrance of meats and vegetables being grilled, but the smell of this fire was different, it brought about emotions of horror, not far from the road where I was standing I could see what appeared to be a cow and a couple of sheep, laying on the ground, singed to a horrific death – the smell that came from that direction was miserable, even pitiful, with each breath that I took I was able to smell and at the same time sense the sweet-bitter sensation in my nose and almost simultaneously, the bitter smell of fire was aggravated through the dry soot, and the vapors caused by the wet soot which had been caused through the water that was dispersed by the fire fighters had a sickening smell about it.

On both sides of the Calder Highway where I was standing, about 50 to 100 meters in to the bush I was able to see dozens of homes, all of them burned to the ground, the only object remaining in an upright position were the chimneys, surrounded by debris, some of it twisted and buckled beyond recognition, roofing iron, water tanks, vehicles and life stock that couldn't be saved, and then there was the horrific thought of the people that had lost their lives. I didn't have to feel the ground, the glimmering heat rising from it together the blurred view into the distance were an indication of the heat that still prevailed in this area.

I didn't stop in this area because I was inquisitive, curios to get a glimpse of another people's misery, I was deeply frayed by what had happened in my neighborhood and genuinely concerned for everybody involved, the folk that lived here as well as for those that came to assist, the life stock, the flora and the fauna that perished. I don't remember how much time I spend just standing there on the side of the road, I was totally captured by the emotions that were guided by what I was seeing, hearing, smelling and feeling.

Back home in Elphinstone, on the evening news the extend of Victoria's Ash Wednesday devastation became even more apparent; the local TV station reported that around mid-morning in Trentham East, a village about 10 km West of Macedon, in the district of Shire of Hepburn and Moorabool, the alarm bells went off as arching power lines started a bush fire, out of control, drifting fast toward Wombat State Forest, life recordings of Macedon's fire at the height of its rage showed how house after house was gutted as the flames gathered strength.

According to one of the fire fighters, he observed 10-inch trees that were literally twisted off, apparently the Cross on top of Mount Macedon which has been watching over the area for over one hundred years remained unharmed for some reason, as if the man upstairs wanted to spare Jesus that was nailed to it the physical anguish, as if he was forced to watch this horrific spectacle, for some reason, whilst everything around it got burned.

Macedon is an area that became famous in 1900 when the story about the picnic at Valentine's Day began to unfold, during 1975 a movie was shot about this bizarre Australian legend, using the basis of regisseur's Peter Weir's book.

Macedon is only a couple of miles away from Hanging Rock were the famous film "picnic at Hanging Rock" was produced, the township had been wiped out, all that remained was a couple of homes and the Macedon Town Hotel, which became a place of refuge to over 300 people on that day. Gary Nish, whose relatives owned the Macedon hotel at the time was out fighting the fire when he got the call that his family might have perished in the fire, he was on his way back to provision his fire truck with fresh water and was able to confirm that the local pub and its owners were busy assisting hundreds of local residents.

Indescribably touching scenes were featured on the news; standing among debris, surrounded by burned down gumtrees, a fire man was standing, his overall torn in parts, his boots smudged with dirt, his safety helmet littered with filth, his face covered soot like a chimney sweeper, in his arms he was holding a koala whom was hugging this fellow tightly—like a two-year-old desperately hanging on to his father—the tears that ran down the fireman's cheeks where evident, and from his eyes you could read that this fellow had gotten a glimpse of hell, a face filled with a lot of emotion.

One of the firemen that were interviewed was explaining that in parts, the fire was between one and a half to two tree height, the sound was incredible, as loud as an approaching train, but one of the most tragic stories of the day was the news of 13 members of the volunteer fire brigade lost their lives during a deployment mission, their fire truck got surrounded by heavy fire to the point that they were unable to save themselves, some hours later it was left to their dazed colleagues to remove the burned bodies from the area.

The most devastating factor in these bush fires occurred shortly before nightfall, heavy wind began to blow over South Australia and Victoria at speeds in excess of 110 km/h, through this abrupt change of direction of the wind the fires were dramatically intensified, fires that had moved in a Northerly direction during the day, now suddenly were moving toward the East; virtually the entire upper Beaconsfield was burned down, 25 lives were lost; 13 of the firefighters that got killed whilst trying to put out the fire with their water trucks, Belgrave heights, one of Melbourne's Eastern suburbs near Dandenong, Cockatoo—a village about 6km East of Belgrave six lives were lost, other areas along the Great Ocean Road, Aireys Inlet, Anglesea and Lorne, were totally devastated.

Tornado like fire twirls and fire balls from twigs of Eucalyptus, creating flames of 3meter high, unstoppable fire storms were born, the gases from the Eucalyptus spreading the fire fast. The changes of temperature, together with the altering air pressure was so high that sometimes houses exploded before the fire actually arrived. Members of the Victorian CFA were of the opinion that the melting metal was caused by a heat energy of 60,000 Kilowatt per m2, which can be compared with values measured after the bombing of Hiroshima and Nagasaki.

Victoria's Ash Wednesday bush fires on Wednesday 16th February 1983 claimed 47 lives; destroyed 2895 homes and countless livestock, breeding cows, sheep, horses, poultry, family pets, flora and fauna of immense, irreplaceable magnitude, in the areas of Cudgee, Ballangeich, Otway Ranges, Warburton, East Trentham and Mount Macedon, Belgrave Heights, Upper Beaconsfield, Cockatoo and Branxholme.

On the same day, South Australia's bush fires were also raging, 28 people died including three CFA members, more than 1500 people were injured, 383 homes and 200 other buildings had burned down and were destroyed 160 thousand hectares of land were extinguished.

Official investigation revealed that in some areas sparks from powerlines were the source of some of the bush fires, others were started as a result of tornado like fire twirls and fire balls from twigs of Eucalyptus that moved about, driven by strong winds, and it was also speculated that some of the fires had been lit deliberately.

The lost lives—both human and animal—cannot be brought back, the emotional torment that relatives and friends from those that perished in these tragic events cannot be swept away or comforted with words, the suffering of their pain and grief will continue for some time to come. This is however different for the environment, Eucalyptus trees have the advantage over other plants; their seed capsules open up when burned, and the seedlings thrive in freshly burned ash-rich soil.

At the time when the native people, the real owners of this vast Continent, the Aborigines as part of their deliberate land management still today "burn-off" land in the Western part of Australia, the Martu's, like other tribes that still peruse traditional life style, deliberately light fires, as soon as the fires are burning, they get out there hunting.

An old tradition of the aborigine's, the hunting fires in the outback, there are no environmental, mining, pastural, or other interests that would inhibit them from burning the land, through the fire the hidden homes of goanna's, rabbits, snakes and other smaller animals that live in the desert are revealed, with this method the Aborigines can get food in an extremely efficient manner, about 1.500 Calories per hour can be gathered, compared with around 130 Calories per hour without the hunting fire method.

The hunting fires are not merely an efficient way of gathering food, the fires have a dramatic impact on the desert ecology, encouraging a cycle of vegetation growth which in turn acts as feed for everything from Kangaroos, bush turkeys and all the other smaller species that are native to the bush, the one hundred or so hunters from the Martu tribe that are out there starting hunting fires to gather food are maintaining landscape just through their daily practice that increases the biodiversity of that massive regent simply by going out and spending a few hours a day acquiring food.

It has also been realized that the manner in which the Martu's are burning the land builds a buffer from the huge wild fires that are caused by lightning, protecting the Aboriginal's habitat from burning uncontrolled. The intentionally lit hunting fires are critical for the health of the desert environment; we should pay more attention to the ecological knowledge and practices of the Aboriginal people, none of their methods are incorporated into formal ways of our land management strategies.

## Environmental Sustainability

For the first twenty years of my life, my colloquial language was German, some of my education I completed in the western part of Switzerland, an area called Romandie where the spoken language is French, English was the second foreign language I dealt with throughout my secondary and tertiary education, and from that time onward I spoke nothing but English, with some rare exceptions, when Aunt and Dad had come to visit in Australia, or the other way round—when I visited them in Switzerland.

As an Australian, the word "Sustainability" has long been part of my vocabulary, but I don't recall that this word was used in the colloquial German language during my college time, to the best of my knowledge it's only a couple of years ago since the word "Sustainable" has become an everyday slogan in Switzerland and in Europe in general, in particular in connection with the environment, whereas in Australia the environment movement began outside institutions, in the minds and actions of ordinary and great people who perceived environmental issues and problems that were largely ignored by mainstream politics. Since the late 1800s until now, advocacy and action have been primarily driven by people with the passion and commitment to conserve and act as custodians for nature, ordinary people achieving significant and **lasting / sustainable** outcomes.

During the 1960s and 70s, campaigns led to protection of some of Australia's unique and special natural places. In the 1970s and 80s, the proposed damming of the Tasmania's Franklin River mobilized tens of thousands of Australians achieving not only the protection of the Franklin, but of most South-West Tasmania. Since the late 1980s, climate change has emerged as a key issue, major issues of the time which is being fought by hundreds of individuals as well as grass-roots organization and larger conservation groups. The global nature of contemporary environmental problems such as sustainability and climate change has seen an international focus by Australian based organizations. The current movement has become a complex driver of change, supported by the professional strength of committed research staff and the ongoing commitment of volunteers.

Some sources claim that the concept of sustainability as we know it today appeared in 1987 for the first time in the famous Brundtland Report, the **Brundtland Commission,** dissolved in December of that year after the release of "Our Common Future" also known as the **Brundtland Report**. The document popularized and defined the term "Sustainable Development"—the report describes how the concept of sustainable development could be achieved, *sustainable development that meets the needs of the present without compromising the ability of future generations to meet their own needs.*

Back during the mid-eighties I was flying to and from Hong Kong on a regular basis, generally overnighting at the Grand Hyatt, it was usual for some members of the crew to take a stroll in the neighborhood, have dinner at some place, sometimes we permitted ourselves exquisite, first class Chinese, more often than not we headed for the place around the corner that was famous for its authentic local tucker, and from time to time junk food was on the wish list, and to conclude the evening we would usually take a nightcap at our hotel bar, often meeting colleagues that flew for other airlines.

Richard, a B747 captain that was flying for one of Americas largest Airlines, positioned at the New York-JFK hub at the time was telling me this hideous story, how his airline was proud to be working with branded products, in particular; each economy meal tray featured a pre-set, branded plastic water couplet produced by a well-known French Mineral Water producer throughout the network, on all in and outbound sectors, the same water brand was on offer in the JC and FC—served from the one liter bottle.

This natural mineral water, a rainwater product that has made its journey through to local rock system filtered through an underground source, a product protected from the human influences, reaped from the earth's natural reservoir's deep in the ground. The producer has stated that from this unique source to the end consumer the companies untiringly efforts to assure the waters extraordinary quality, and that all legal regulations pertaining to mineral water in each country where it is being sold are fully met. The producer goes on to claim that their longstanding commitment to the environment, to be in harmony with nature and to consider sustainable process during all facets of the production cycle.

Once the mineral water was bottled, packaged in cartons and arranged on pallets ready for the dispatch, it was trucked from the source in France to the sea port Le Havre, around 800 km, from the French seaport to New Orleans it had travelled a further 8600 km, from there it was again loaded on a truck to be carried to the Airlines Warehouse in Minneapolis USA, a further 1600 km, a total of 11 thousand km from the source to the distribution center from where the pallets of water were flown to other hubs and their outstations, for example from Minneapolis MSP to Tokyo NRT, an additional 9576 km that is in excess of 20 thousand km that this water cuplet has been transported before it could be enjoyed by passengers that valued this famous French Mineral Water, it is likely that most of them didn't give any thought to the $CO_2$ footprint that this marketing gag had caused our environment.

The groundwater level of this particular Mineral Water Source is being diminished fast, through the water that is reaped continuously by the producer, each year the ground water level is reduced by thirty centimeters. The local authorities have indicated that the reason for this vast loss is nature, the rainwater that seeps through the different layers of rock to slow, ant that the heavy extraction, in particular by the Mineral Water company that owns the rights to the source since the mid-60s are the cause of the reduction of the water volume.

I cannot fathom that it has taken nearly 60 years before environment and consumer protectionist have begun to try to stop this company from reaping the peoples water so that it can be cart it all over the world and to generate respectful profits from natures product, and if this is not hideous enough, it is known that the locals don't have sufficient water for their private use, nor is there sufficient for the surrounding agriculture, fresh water is being trucked in from other areas to assure the minimum requirement of water, apparently the local authorities have even considered to build a pipeline in order to provide the locals with fresh water from other areas. The Mineral Water company indicated that they would support the construction of the pipeline to promote a sustaining solution to the water resources.

Understanding that because the Mineral Water company is the largest tax payer and probably the biggest employer of the area with a population of around 5,000, the local authorities as well as its resident may have felt obliged, indeed they may have been intimidated to the point where they accepted that one of our most pressures resources on this earth be permanently raped over a period of nearly sixty years, giving preference to their personal, financial gain. The local authorities, the employees responsible for the wellbeing of its citizens, the legal guardians of our heritage and the environment also favored the income through the taxation system, and chose to ignore the reality, in the first place justifying the diminishing ground water level by arguing that nature was to slow with its natural replenishment, knowing that the Mineral Water company through its shameless exploitation of the source is the only cause of this problem, and then the misguided decision to build a pipeline, importing the water from another area to remedy the local situation.

Nearly forty years ago, on that particular evening when I was sitting at the Grand Hyatt's bar with my colleague Richard, talking about this Mineral Water Brand that was shipped and flown half way around the world before it was consumed, neither of us were aware of the disastrous effects that this would have on the regional environment and the local population nearly four decades later, neither of us would have thought that mankind can be so irresponsible, stupid as a matter of fact to ignore this problem for all this time.

Nearly forty years have passed since that time when Richard revealed the story about the Mineral Water to me, and still today I realize lots of other practices and habits that have consequences of similar magnitude on our environment; for some time now we are tempted with good quality Avocados all year round, because of its beneficial properties, including a richness in antioxidant vitamin E, monounsaturated fats, carotene and useful minerals such as iron and potassium, this fruit has become an important part of our trend food. As I understand that some 60% of our Avocados that we consume in Switzerland are grown in Chile, at the Petorca Province in the Valparaiso region who has a Mediterranean type climate, with its highest precipitation from May to August, the remainder of the year the rainfall is relatively low, rendering this area unsuitable for a sustainable production of avocado.

However, since the end of the 1990s, investors have taken a liking to the Petorca Province because of the cheapness of its land, this combined with the generous revenue that avocados provide has encouraged the development of large Avocado plantations in the region, reducing dramatically the availability of water to its local inhabitants, limiting the cultivation of beans, corn, potatoes or livestock that they used to produce on their lots, setting off a series of unprecedented consequences for Petorca and its inhabitants, effectively eroding their fundamental subsistence for their lives by removing much of their water.

This particular problem is not limited to the Petorca Province in Chile, in many parts of the world Avocado trees cannot be grown without supplementing natural rainfall with irrigation, correct water management is arguably the most important tool in achieving high yields of quality fruit. In the dry regions of Chile where Avocado farming is especially water intensive, some **320 liters** of applied water are required to grow one Avocado.

This, compared with the water footprint of tomatoes produced in Spain, is around 236 liters of water per kilogram which equates to around **50 liters** for each tomato, as a simplified contrast. In addition to the water that is required to produce an Avocado, indeed any kind of produce or product at all, the cost of shipping including the carbon dioxide footprint must be considered as well; if there were a direct flight between Zürich, Switzerland and Laguna Verde in Chile, the distance would be around 13 thousand km, and yet, the Avocados from Chile continue to be a trendy part of our lifestyle, we continue to import, indeed to demand that they are available for us all year round, without giving any thought to the environmental cost, nor do we care about those ordinary folk in Chile that are severely deprived of an adequate supply of water as a result of our appetite and pleasure for this delightful fruit.

Now that we have arrived in the age of digitalization and instant news, most of us have access to this kind of information; most of us should be aware about the effects that our consumer behavior has, and yet we continue to ship personalized parcels of goodies around the continent, demanding that strawberries are available at Christmas despite the fact that in our part of the world they are out of season, we insist that the flight from ZRH to LHR for the weekend is really important, that stroll through large food halls at Harrods, drawling over the finest foodstuffs and comestibles, the elaborate backdrops created with lots of imagination at the toy department are truly worthy of seeing, and the visit to the fish and chips shop round the corner are not to be missed either.

Our son's shopping habit, a reflection of contemporary behavior, he preferred to snoop around online catalogues, placing an order for what he believes to like, with the option to send it back if it doesn't meet his expectations, which is often the case.

The undue shopping tourism that prevails in our country, particularly families with a low earning capacity are prepared to drive the seventy-six roundtrip kilometers once or twice per month, apparently to reduce their household budget, with some of the products a money saving of 60% can be achieved. Though not part of the low-income earners, as part of her lifestyle, Aunt would undertake one or two trips each week to the neighboring France to get most of her food and other household needs.

The (FiBL, department for socio-economics, Switzerland) has published an article, stating that two million tons of foodstuff are either used as animal fodder, turned to biogas or is indeed disposed of through our garbage disposal system each year, having an effect on the production costs and the sale price. The study carried out by this department has shown that between the field and the shop shelf, around half of the carrot harvest in our country is lost, for this reason the farmer has to deliberately overproduce. Around 14 to 45 percent of this waste is caused on the farm, through the sorting of the carrots, as they do not fit the quality standards set by the detail trade, a reflection of consumer behavior.

Out there in the supermarket I have observed that I am no different to most other folk, meticulously examining the fruits and vegies, picking out the best looking, the ones with the perfect shape, making sure that there are no signs of spots, blemishes of any kind, no signs of decay, that they have reached the perfect degree of ripeness, that the touch is appropriate, just the way I am expecting it to be, and that the smell of the product is rich and intense; after all, the price of the commodity is the same, near perfect or not. Our growing expectations together with a continues desire to raise the quality standards of our lives, indeed that of the products and services that we consume are potential contributing factors to our self-destruction.

So far, nature has not managed to provide us with the perfect fruits and vegetables, that is why since decades, under the pretense of progress, we are endeavoring to alter the way nature produces sustenance for the food chain of mankind, genetically modifying plants, animals or microorganisms, altering its DNA in a manner that does not occur naturally by mating and, or natural recombination, consequently risking the cause of some common toxic implications such as hepatic, pancreatic, renal or productive effects which may alter the hematological, biochemical and immunologic parameters, and then we go to argue that genetically modified food is mor nutritious, tastier, that the plants have become disease and drought resistant, that fewer environmental resources (water and fertilizer) are required, that we use less pesticides and herbicides as a result, that we have increased the supply of food and reduced costs at the same time, that the shelve life of many products has been increased, and that plants and animals grow faster, to introduce new trait to plants and animals which does not occur naturally, to change its characteristics, to render the plant more resistant to pests and environmental stresses.

According to the Swiss Federal Office of Environment, between 2008 and 2016 the sales of herbicides and insecticides for the Swiss agriculture industry amounted to about 2.200 tons per annum, however the sale of insecticides is outpacing that of the herbicides. The controversial herbicide product Glyphosate still being one of the products that is most applied to combat problematic weed orchards, viniculture, agriculture in general as well as in public park facilities.

We are altering the natural traits of animals, plants and microorganisms, changing the way nature has intended them to be, arguing that we have made progress, made the product better, even improved their taste, and at the same time for many of us the taste buds have become accustomed to convenience foods.

Most of us have become accustomed to the idea that our everyday food should be prepared with ease, without too much effort and time, the food manufacturing industry has provided us with an enormous range of convenience foods from which we can select the degree of convenience to suit our preparation skills, the time that we have available to prepare a meal, as well as the type of meal that we want to eat. Both, canned and deep-frozen convenience foods permit us to present a relatively well balanced meal on the table within around twenty minutes or so, cold as well as hot ready to eat food can be served within minutes, preparing a meal with the aid of some semi-finished products allow us to exercise our cooking skills as well as our creativity and imagination, without having to spend a lot of time in the kitchen, cleaning and peeling fruits and vegetables, being able to directly influence the flavor.

To further complement the availability of convenience foods and fast food, from the sit-down restaurant to take-out, take-away or indeed food that is delivered directly to our homes. However, it would be smart to inform yourself about the additives that are used in the food manufacturing industry, through closer examination of convenience products, antioxidants, leavening agents, emulsifiers, food-dye / food color, firming agents, humectants, fillers, gelling agents, flavor enhancers, preservatives, flour treatment agents, minerals, acidifiers, foaming agents, foam retarding agents, melting salts, stabilizers, sweetening agents, propellant gases, excipients, release agents, coating agents, thickening agents, and vitamins can be found.

By law, food additives must be declared on the packaging with an E-number, alternatively a precise description of the added content is necessary, but I suspect that few of us read this information, and fewer still understand their purpose and potential impact on our health. Whilst some health authorities claim the most of the additives are inoffensive and harmless, and yet others caution that some of the substances added to convenience foods may be dubious, indeed questionable, suggesting that some additives may be harmful to our health, that they are suspected to cause intestinal inflammation, headaches, diarrhea and nausea in those of us that are generally sensitive with the consumption of some food products, as well as this some sources argue that they may promote allergies—even cancer.

Preserving food is not a particular characteristic of contemporary time, already in the 7th century in ancient Greece, during the time of the Roman Empire as well as in Chine around the 3rd century sour white cabbage was consumed, using salt as the preserving agent, legend has it that vinegar was "discovered" by the Babylon's 5000 BC, used for the preservation of pickles, and around 430 BC applied to manage wounds by the Medic Hippocrates, the smoking of food as a preservation method can be tracked back to the primitive caveman, the dehydration and sun drying of food is also a prehistoric method of preserving, preserving food with sugar as well as the method of immersion in alcohol are also ancient methods; most of these natural preservation techniques are safe, but some of them may well be less innocent, potentially releasing pathogens like listeria, but all of those are probably far more harmless compared to modern methods.

It is difficult to think of an industry that does not use plastic in its manufacture or use plastic as a packaging material. Though, plastic has lots of useful characteristics; the crumple zone build into cars are potentially saving life, the durability of some food items can be prolonged by covering them with a plastic film, plastic containers used for the packaging of food as well as take away items that have simplified our shopping, the convenience that plastic bottles has given us, in particular the PET products, the vast range of plastic packaging for our cleaning agents in the industry as well as in our homes, the plastic toys that can be manufactured at prices that have become affordable for most of us.

Diapers, for most families, a product that is near inconceivable to raise the baby without them, all the household and commercial products constructed fully or in part from plastic, the countless parts of the cabin furnishing and equipment in the airline industry which have contributed to the fuel efficiency of the aircraft, the old concrete pipes used in the sewerage system that are systematically replaced with plastic ones, the long lasting materials used in the building industry, the electronics industry that is utilizing affordable, long lasting plastic in the production of computers, television sets and cell phones, much of the sports safety gear that is produced from plastic; many of these products have had a positive effect on us, has made our lives safer, more comfortable and more pleasant. However, there is also a downside to synthetics which is not negligible, we must consider the disadvantages, their effect on society and our environment very carefully.

If the average life expectancy of eight years or 150 thousand km of cars would be considerably increased, the use of plastic in its manufacture might make sense, much of the plastic used to cover food in supermarkets could be eliminated, for take away food items, alternative packaging products could be considered, plastic bottles could be replaced with glass, their return assured through a deposit, wood and metal could be used for the manufacturing of toys, cloth nappies could be re-introduced, replacing the disposable ones, we could design and build household and commercial products with a higher life expectancy, and it should be made mandatory for all plastic to be recycled.

The plastic footprint that is inherent to our throwaway culture is caused in part by the booming production of plastic, in part because of the demand of single-use items such as disposable plates, cups and cutlery, water, soda bottles, disposable nappies, plastic bottles, circuit boards, drinking straws, cleaning agent containers, food packaging, toothbrushes, toys, medication, bags, bottles, containers, packaging film, the mobility industry, and the manufacturing industry. 300 million tons of plastic is produced each year from which around 50% is for single-use-purpose, from that eight million tons of it is dumped into our oceans each year (Plastic Oceans International 2019), distressing our environment.

Some sources state that only 9% of all plastic ever produced has been recycled, about 12% has been incinerated, having released harmful chemicals into the air and the remaining 79% was accumulated as landfill, in dumps or simply disposed of in the natural environment, plastic that will take anywhere between ten to one thousand years, (plastic bottles around 450 years) to decompose, because bacteria do not appreciate plastic, it is likely that a piece of plastic, over time, can turn into lots of little pieces which don't go away, nor do they transform themselves into useful matter, the tiny particles of plastic will continue to be harmful to our environment.

The current debate about the climate change does not reveal anything that we didn't know about long ago, during the last 650,000 years there have been several cycles of glacial advances, both, growth and retreat with the abrupt end of the last ice age around seven thousand years ago, the beginning of the modern climate era and that of the outset of the human civilization. Most of these climate changes were brought about by very small alterations in the earth's orbit which have changed the amount of solar energy that our planet receives.

However, there seems to be no doubt that increased levels of greenhouse gases are causing the earth to warm, and this is the responsibility of mankind as a result of our activities since the 20$^{th}$ century, caused by the rising temperature, around 0.9 degrees Celsius since the late 19$^{th}$ century, largely driven by an increase of carbon dioxide as a mand made emission to the atmosphere. Warming in the oceans, the top 700 meters warming by around 0.4-degree Fahrenheit. The shrinking of ice in the Antarctic the Arctic for which the greenhouse gas is predominantly responsible.

The melting of the glaciers, the decreased snow cover in the northern hemisphere over the last four or so decades, the rising sea level, around 20 centimeters in the last century, and the extreme meteorological events that have occurred. However, a deeper understanding of these processes and their incorporation in climate models have progressed rapidly since the 1990.

The term climate change has become part of our daily lives in one way or another, some are of the opinion that the public outcry has developed into a hype for the green and mostly but not only the younger generation, whom are taking part in organized demonstrations, protesting and others have participated in strikes and yet other are presenting solid scientific facts, all of them trying to reach the different fractions of the political system locally as well as on a federal level, attracting the attention of the media; television, radio, the printed media, and the social media platforms which has made it possible for each one of us to be a trendsetter and a news maker.

And yet with all this attention and focus the climatic disaster the destruction of our environment goes on; most of us continue to be tempted by the cheap flights that the airline industry is offering, we continue to be tantalized by the new gadgets that seem to appear on the market from a bottomless barrel of supply, the fashion industry which doesn't promote the notion of long term sustainability keeps arousing the desire to need the latest scream, and most of us seem to want it too, the automotive industry that keep on creating the four wheelers ever so loaded with heaps of new electronics, fitted with economical high powered engines, four wheel drive SUVs with all the comfort that you can desire, we are not prepared to abstain from the online platforms on which we can look at just about any product or service that we can think of.

From the comfort of our homes, we can order these goodies without having being able to assess their quality traits, to see, to feel, to smell, to touch, the "made abroad" often in places where "labor law" is a foreign word are then delivered directly to our door step, and if it doesn't suit our idea we can send it back where it came from, an inexhaustible range of convenience products continues to be on offer in our supermarkets, assuring that with a minimal effort we can whip up a fast meal at home, our insatiable desire for ready to eat fast food and beverages goes on as it were never ending, and to satisfy our perpetual need for plastic products and packaging, the world continues to produce in excess of around 320 million tons each year, only about 25% or less of that is being recycled according to some sources—a sobering thought.

Some of the discoveries and inventions accomplished during the last couple of centuries have influenced our lives dramatically, having allowed us to make the transition from a peasant subsistence to the existence that we enjoy today. In the 18th century Benjamin Franklin, after extensive research discovered electricity, electrical engineering was developed by some of the greats like Alexander Bell, Thomas Edison, Galileo Ferraris, Werner von Simens, Nikola Tesla and George Westinghouse, Luigi Galvani, Alessandro Volta creating electricity, and around 1819 the electric motor was invented by Hans Christian, Andre Ampere and Michael Faraday, 1879 Thomas Edison, the inventor of the direct current electricity invented an incandescent (white glowing) light bulb, some years later the first electric bulbs were used to light the streets of Cleveland, Ohio, a tool that has become indispensable in our lives.

In 1764, James Hargraves invented the Spinning Jenny which became instrumental in the development of the industrialization of weaving, and the rag industry.

The Old Farmer's Almanac; its premiere issue was published in 1792, a reference book that was updated annually featuring weather forecast, astronomical data, planting charts, predictions on trends and articles about folklore, astronomy, predictions about fashion and food trends and prognosis about technological development, the invention of the Moldboard Plow, in many ways its publication was instrumental to the development of modern farming.

364

Thomas Newcomen invented the first steam engine in 1712, it was further developed by James Watt whom in 1776 introduced his new engine commercially—the beginning of modern mobility.

The 19<sup>th</sup> century continued to provide us with lots of significant discoveries and inventions; Alessandro Volta invented the battery in 1800, the British merchant Peter Durand first patented the idea of preserving food in cans, in 1812 the steam locomotive was invented by Richard Trevithick, and twenty five years later George and Robert Stephenson designed the most advanced locomotive of its day which became the future steam locomotives for the next 150 years, Joseph Nicéphore created the first permanent photograph in 1826, the Swedish chemist Alfred Nobel gave us Dynamite in 1826 intended for the mining industry, and we managed to apply this product to destroy each other, the first ship build from steel was built by Jonathan Laird during the 1830s, 1834 the electric motor was invented by Michael Faraday.

Telegraph communication was born and demonstrated in 1837 by Sir William Fothergill and in 1844 a wire connection between Baltimore and Washington DC had been established, in 1846 the Sewing Machine was invented by Elias Howe, during the 1850s the rifle was invented, the first manned glider was airborne, build by the British engineer George Cayley in 1853, the Escalator was invented in 1859, in the same year the first internal combustion engine was invented by Etinner Lenoir, further developed by Nikolaus Otto, Parkesine was discovered by Alexander Parkes, one of the earliest forms of plastic, cellulose nitrate being the basic substance in 1862.

In 1867, the typewriter was invented, Alexander Graham Bell gave us the telephone in 1876, in 1878 toilet paper was invented by the British Perforated Paper Company, rendering the trip to the loo more pleasant and hygienic, 1879 Thomas Edison created the first commercially practical incandescent light, Coca Cola was created in 1886 and still today it is one of the most popular soft drinks, in 1876 Alexander Graham Bell had won the first U.S. patent for the telephone; at that time he had no idea that some one hundred and forty years later just about everybody is walking around with one of those in their pocket, 1884 Richard Jordan Gatling's machine gun was used during the American Civil War, Wilhelm Maybach and Gottlieb Daimler build the first gasoline driven car in 1889, and in 1892 the motion picture was invented by Edison and Dickson.

The 20<sup>th</sup> century gave us the first mass produced car which was built by Oldsmobile, and Henry Ford developed the mass production of cars as we know it today, 1903 the Wright brothers made the first flight with their Kitty Hawk—their first powered aircraft—today we are able to fly from Zürich to Singapore with an A380 which in a one class configuration carries around 868 passengers, with a flight time of 12hours and 15minutes, Radar was invented in 1904, 1907 the invention of plastic by Leo Baekeland, during 1901 to 1907 the vacuum cleaner, the air conditioner, the electrocardiogram, the radar, radio broadcasting and the electric washing machine were created, during the 1920s the automobile, airplane, the washing machine, the refrigerator, garbage disposal, the instant camera, the jukebox, television, the pop culture, height clubs and jazz were created, 1921 Robots and Insulin were invented, 1924 the quick freezing of food was developed, a couple of years later, 16 March 1926, the first flight of a liquid propellant rocket took place, Alexander Fleming the Scottish scientist discovered Penicillin in 1928 which has been instrumental with the saving of lives, in 1930 the jet engine was invented.

The past three centuries have provided mankind with lots of remarkable discoveries and inventions, most of them we have evolved to the point where they have become essential parts of our lives, several have taken over the hard-physical labor that man used to perform, others have fundamentally changed the way we do things, and some of them have provided us with personal delight, others we developed so that we are able to conduct warfare to establish military superiority over others, yet others have emerged and are now aimed to exercise intellectual grandeur over individuals or groups, and banking institutions and tools have considerably unfolded to better control the Financial Markets, many of these discoveries and inventions have brought us pleasant, useful changes that greatly improved the quality of our lives, but equally as many have been applied as tools to abuse, misuse, mistreat, to exploit, or to use as a threat of sorts as a sign of superiority.

Our insatiable lust for power, greed for mightiness, the need to reach a social status of significance and the need for personal recognition, our innate drive and curiosity for the unknown, the desire for adventure, our fascination for progress together with the requirement for economic growth have contributed to the desolate shape that mother earth has reached, and yet we continue to state with conviction that we do care about our environment but it seem that our achievement are very modest indeed.

I believe that the notion of economic growth is one of the obstacles that prevent us from moving forward with serious corrective actions that dramatically reduce the harmful greenhouse gases, the apparent need to apply herbicides and pesticides which are devastating to the water systems and the food chain, the constant mining of natural resources, the continues production of more and better gadgets and products and the lack of serious recycling, in the absence of economic growth we talk about economic stagnation, ignoring the fact that growth is always at the cost of something or somebody else.

Simplified, economic growth is the amount of goods and services produced per head of population over a period of time, factors that influence economic development of a country are its capital formation, the amount of capital we have for the purpose of development, an abundance of natural resources, which is essential for growth, surplus agricultural products that can be marketed to other countries, we need favorable conditions of trade, a clever economic system, preferably a command or mixed system, a strong economy needs a skilled labor force to develop the country, a high level of education and excellent technical know-how, political freedom is essential, social organization, the process of structural change with ongoing innovation, improvements of infrastructure and increased labor productivity.

I do understand the fundamental principles of economic growth and I am aware of the possible causes for the economies stagnation, but I am curious to know how long we can continue to remove the natural resources from the ground, for how long can we proceed to harvest vast areas of rainforests and the natural habitat, how long can we continue to keep pouring poisonous chemicals, antibiotics as well as huge amounts of fertilizers into our food chain, how much more plastic products that haven't been recycled can we dump into landfills or indeed into our oceans, how much more $CO_2$ can we release into our atmosphere before the point of no return is reached—the point where mother earth is no longer able to recuperate the impurities and filth from the water system, the point where mother earth is no longer able to convert the polluted air, the point where mother earth no longer has the ability to cleanse and salvage the ground in which we grow our food.

For years now, scientist are presenting us periodically with solid research data, pointing out how much our ecosystem is threatened; the world population has nearly doubled in the past 38 years, the meat production has increased by 15kg per person per annum since 1980, the $CO_2$ output per capita has grown from around 4 to 4.4 tons, the carbon dioxide output has risen from 330 to nearly 410 CO2 parts per million, the methane output has changed from around 1650 to 1850 between 1984 and 2018, the trend of the temperature surface change is on the increase, around 0.8 degree Celsius in the last decade.

During the past twenty years, the sea level has changed by nearly 5 cm, the Greenland ice has been diminished by about 2900 Gigatons within a period of 10 years, and the loss per annum is on the increase, and the extreme weather events around the world has more than doubled in the past thirty eight years, cautioning us, if we keep ignoring the profoundly troubling facts and indicators that are affirmed by science periodically, if we don't begin to change our way of living, if we don't change the way we think, if we refuse to realize that sometimes less of something is more, if we are not prepared to secure a sustainable future on this earth, the time will come when it will be impossible for our delicate ecosystem to recover, perhaps we ought to consider the notion of economic growth and pose the question—do we really need it?

## James Strong Takes Over TAA in 1986

1986, TAA was taken over by CEO James Strong. I am not the kind of person that bitches behind the back of my employer, nor is this an attempt to grumble about the airline, but in the mid-eighties it had become increasingly more embarrassing to work for TAA, many of its staff were dissatisfied, unmotivated and didn't give a hoot about the profitability of the company, many had lost respect for the management and didn't believe that they were able to change things either. Airline employees were heavily unionized in Australia, extremely well organized, the management was often stone walling on issues rather than working out real solutions, in fact both, management and union representatives often took an approach that wasn't solution-orientated—both pig-headed and obstinate.

Coming from Switzerland where folk don't just go on strike, where in general folk negotiate directly with the company's representatives, having grown up in a family where my father was the owner of the firm, I was absolutely astonished about the behavior of both, the unions and the company representatives, I loathed the way they were handling disagreements, I didn't understand the frequency at which they met in front of the Arbitration Commissioners Officers.

Corruption, cheating and stealing during the mid-eighties was ramped in the airline; it had become usual for staff to falsely punch work mates in or out in an endeavor to increase ones earning capacity, duty free articles, liquor minis and meat products in particular disappeared from the flight kitchens, the value at Melbourne only was in excess of two million Dollars per annum, from the warehouse areas expensive spare parts had been removed to be sold on the black market, the fellows from the cargo area were known to frisk passengers luggage and search through general freight to remove valuables wherever they could.

It appeared that the employees of the airline had lost their plot, more and more the TAA service had become a second choice for the flying public.

At that time, TAA (Trans Australian Airline) which was founded in 1946, many of its employees were still living in an arcade world where one had forgotten the reason for being; its customers were merely a necessary evil needed to pay the bills.

I recall sitting in the Business Class of a DC9 as Crew on duty, from Melbourne to Sydney, I was being repositioned to operate a flight SYD-BNE-CNS and back again. As usual, for take-off the flight attendant was sitting on her crew seat which was mounted to the back of the cockpit, facing the passengers, with the curtain of the doorway between the cabin and the galley open and tied back on its side, just the way it should be for the take off and initial climb phase, I could observe the purser how she was busy with her nail care, totally oblivious of the fact that passengers were able to watch.

The Australian humor is not dissimilar to that of the British, some Aussies jokers thought that it was amusing to change the name of TAA which stood for Trans Australian Airlines, they nicknamed it "Try Another Airline," frankly speaking, from a passengers point of view as I witnessed from time to time, the statement wasn't far from the truth; often, from the purchase of the airline ticket, to the check in, the reception on the aircraft, the safety instruction from the cabin crew, the on-board service, the food, the only decent thing about the flight was often the alcohol that was begrudgingly offered as if it had been bought from money of their own pockets, the mood of the cabin crew that bid their passengers good bye was as if a huge suffering had ended for them, the assistance upon arrival for those passengers that needed it was often poor. All in all, if indeed I had not worked for TAA, I would not have hesitated to try another airline, and the price of the ticket in those days was not cheap either.

The street talk was that at TAA the service was atrocious; very often the scheduled departure, respectively the arrival times were not achieved, the on-board product and service were appalling, many of the cabin as well as ground crew treated customers with disrespect, much of the cockpit crew was arrogant, the only thing where you didn't have to worry about as a passenger were the safety aspects pertaining to the aircraft maintenance and the cockpit crew.

In the mid-seventies as a young co-pilot, I met a cabin attendant by the name of Sue. She was a little older than me, she reminded me of one of the Salvation Army ladies that used to perform at the pub where I earned myself some pocket money as a student. Her facial features were hard and yet angelic, her nose was thin, long and pointed.

At the beginning she appeared somewhat scary to me, but as I got to know her better, I realized that I had met a good-hearted person.

Sue was known as a hard liner in the FAAA (Flight Attendants Association of Australia). Her view of the company, her ideas about what could reasonably be expected from her as a cabin crew member and an employee of the Airline was limited to the pre-flight cabin check, the boarding of the passengers, the safety processes and procedures before, during and after the flight, and the de-boarding, beyond this, Sue didn't accept any other duties as a flight attendant that would have made the flight a more enjoyable or indeed more comfortable experience for the passenger, her opinion was no exception to many other cabin crew.

## Cultural Differences in the Aviation Industry.

Like other Australian companies at that time, TAA for whom I was flying before joining Qantas had a very powerful, safety orientated Cockpit Culture; formalities that were expected to be respected and maintained, the fellow in the left hand seat had to be addressed by his title, **Captain**, there is no doubt his status wasn't given to him either, he had earned it, his word was absolute, not to be questioned, almost intimidating for the cadets and younger crew members in particular, a culture that couldn't be accepted in contemporary cockpit management.

At the same time, the captain's sovereign approach to decision making, founded on immense experienced gained during WWII and the Vietnam war, characterized by an Air Force style mentality and leadership in most cases, the discipline prevailing in the cockpit was a solid contributing factor to flight safety in Australia at that time, recognizing and understanding that Australia has a very solid air safety record, it is the country with one of the world's safest airlines, the national airline Qantas has never had a fatal jet airliner accident since the beginning of its operation on 16 November 1920—a remarkable achievement indeed.

To further celebrate the captain's perceived aura, at times when we had to overnight at an out port, the cockpit crew was driven to the hotel in a limousine. Rumor had it that captain was lodged at least one floor above the rest of the crew so that none of them was able to accidentally witness which of the flight attendants slipped into captains' room for the good night story, a matter that was openly discussed by some crew members, at the time, others discretely secluded this indictment.

However, soon after I joined TAA back in 1971, the flight crew management, in an endeavor to further develop its corporate airlines safety culture intended for all activities on and around the aircraft on the ground as well as in the air, with particular focus on the cockpit crew; our senior check and training pilots, together with the training and development specialists began to generate and construct a crew resource management tool that was implemented in the mid-seventies as part of the initial as well as the ongoing cockpit crew training program which was the turnaround for our cockpit culture, shifting the focus away from the autocratic cockpit crew management approach, now emphasizing the human performance awareness;

To be aware, understand and be able to deal with professional, organizational and national culture, and to recognize the potential threats as well as the benefits of a cross cultural crew environment.

- Be aware of the different types of leadership approach, gradients of authority, understand and know how to eliminate barriers that may affect and influence team work.
- To be able to identify different levels of stress, understand how this affects your performance in the cockpit, and know how to overcome stress and fatigue.
- To understand human error, explore different types of unsafe behavior, be able to trace errors and be able to comprehend the cause and effect thereof.

- Be able to handle error management, be able to develop appropriate cockpit management tools to eliminate threats, to monitor, detect, prevent, ant to recover from errors.
- To understand the "Situation Awareness," to be able to realize "red flag" situations and to know how to deal with them appropriately.
- Understand the application of automated cockpit systems and know how to apply these to optimize processes and procedures.
- Be aware of potential communication barriers in the cockpit environment and develop effective, assertive communication skills.
- Understand the different techniques and their prioritization in the decision-making process and know how to apply these in the cockpit environment.
- Understand the different elements of risk management before, during and after the flight and realize its consequences.

The implementation of this training package was the beginning of an ongoing process, though not understood, nor appreciated by everybody concerned at that time, but it brought about fundamental changes in the way we functioned within the team; the hierarchy of the command was maintained without questioning its integrity, the cockpit culture had become less authoritarian, and co-pilots were encouraged to question captains if they observed mistakes without any kind of fear of consequences.

Though it has to be recognized, the Australians had always been innovating leaders of the Aviation Industry, but the fact remains—the "official" CRM (Cockpit Resource Management) training, together with its changes that it has presented over time did originate in June 1997 in a meeting conducted with the support of NASA sponsorship, partially because of United Airlines flight 173, December 1978, a scheduled flight from JFK International Airport to Portland International Airport Oregon with a scheduled stop in Denver, Colorado, operated by a DC-8 with three cockpit crew, five cabin crew and 173 passengers on board. The en route time for the first sector was estimated at 02:26, the fuel requirement was 31.900 lbs., the actual fuel on board was 46.700 lbs., a very generous safety buffer indeed.

On approach to Portland, as the landing gear was lowered the crew identified an abnormal vibration and yaw of the aircraft and the absence of the three green lights which indicate that the gears are locked into position. The crew requested to fly a holding pattern so that they could diagnose the problem, the holding pattern was flown for about one hour whilst the crew was trying to identify the cause of the malfunction, preparing for a potential emergency landing. During this time none of the cockpit crew effectively monitored the fuel consumption which had become compounded by the fact that the gear was down and the flaps were set at 15 degrees during the entire time flown in the holding pattern, significantly increasing the fuel burn rate.

As the aircraft was configured for the final approach of an emergency landing into Portland, number one and number two engines were lost as a result of a flame-out, at that point the approach was declared as Mayday, the aircraft crashed into a wooded section of a populated area of suburban Portland, about 6 NM southeast of the airport. The crash investigation report showed that the flight crew failed to relate the fuel remaining and the rate of fuel flow to the time and distance from the airport because their attention was almost entirely focused on diagnosing the landing gear problem. As a result of this accident, "only" 10 fatalities were caused.

However, the "official" CRM (Cockpit Resource Management) training that has its origin in the States wasn't so different from what the Aussies had developed back in the early seventies.

The present-day captain is still the boss in the cockpit, however, he or she is no longer idolized as some divine being, captain has become the person in charge of an aircraft and anything that is concerning its operation on the ground and in the air, gone are the days of lordly behavior, lower ranked officers are expected to come forward and report anomalies and point out potential danger.

CRM had become a global standard in the 1990s, but not all of the cultural differences were resolved with its introduction as Malcom Gladwell in his books "theory of cockpit culture" debates by referring to the circumstances surrounding the crash of Korean Air, flight KE801 06 August 1997, explaining that modern airplanes with their sophisticated systems are designed to be piloted by a crew that works together as a team of equals, not being afraid to point out mistakes or to disagree with the captain, he goes on to say "in addition to several misfortunate problems, the weather condition, an off line warning system, outdated charts, and a co-pilot that was afraid to question the poor judgment of his captain—a fatal mistake, whose origin is the result of an authoritarian cockpit culture.

Systematic investigation and reporting of aircraft accidents in Australia since 1995 by the BASI (bureau of air safety investigation). During the seventies and eighties investigation agencies were part of the safety problem themselves because the thinking was focused on the rudimentary operator error, concentrating on the concentration of the "sharp end" factors—pilot errors.

Underpinning much of the work on human error are notions regarding the influence of culture on individual and group behavior, it appears that it is not possible to create a "culture free" work environment, sure, there are a variety of cultures in which aviation professionals carry out their daily duties which impact significantly on the operation of airlines.

**According to Gerard Hofstede the Dutch social psychologist,** "National cultures are classified into four dimensions, two of which can be applied to the flight deck: power distance, which defines the nature of relations between subordinates and superiors, or, how often subordinates are afraid to express disagreement, (which is debated in Merritt Ashleigh (May 2000). "Culture in the Cockpit, do Hofstede's dimensions replicate?") and whether the culture is collectivists or individualist in nature. Western cultures are individualistic and pave a low power distance, whereas most Asian and Latin cultures are on the other side of the spectrum." Hayward, Brent (1997) "Culture, CRM and aviation safety" *The Australian Aviation Psychology Association.* Lower power distance and high individualism in Western culture may have contributed to a better safety record.

An amusing solution to create a culture free environment has been proposed by some; "fill the cockpit with Australians"—(Hamilton 1992) unfortunately for the Aussies, in practice this does not work, it is evident that we are all, to some extent culturally bound in terms of our behaviors and attitudes. (Brent Hayward the Australian aviation psychology association) culture; "the collective programming of the mind which distinguishes the members of one group from another"

To better understand the significance of a healthy cockpit culture, an environment by which the hierarchy of the command is maintained without questioning its integrity, a culture in which the co-pilot is encouraged to question the captain if he or she observes mistakes, I have chosen to illustrate a Korean Air flight conducted in August 1997. The transcript of the cockpit voice recorder that was secured from the aircraft wreckage of this flight is not recommended for the faint-hearted, but it is not intended to serve those that might be seeking thrilling sensations either, the transcript represents a series of facts as prepared by the NTSB, it is not intended to draw presumptuous conclusions, nor is it intending to make any kind of accusation toward anybody involved with this flight operation, it is presented with the utmost respect for those directly and indirectly involved with this flight.

The B747-300 from Korean Air HL7468, flight KE 801 departed from Seoul's Gimpo International Airport, 06 August 1997, crashed into Nimitz hill southwest of Guam, approximately three NM short of Runway 06 left at Antonio B. Won Guam's Airport. On board the aircraft; the Commander, a 42-year-old Korean with around nine thousand hours of stick time, he was originally scheduled to fly from Seoul to Dubai, because his breaktimes weren't sufficient to command this flight he was rescheduled to flt. KE801, the first officer a 40-year-old with approximately four thousand hours stick time, the flight engineer, a 57-year-old with 13 thousand hours—all of them locals from Korea, 237 passengers and 17 crew including the cockpit, from which 228 people perished as a result of the crash.

**This transcript was prepared by the NTSB**, "*vehicle recorders division Washington, D.C. 20594 as part of the factual report of investigation of flight KE 801.*

*The reader of this report is cautioned that if the transcript or parts thereof are taken out of context, the information could be misleading. The transcript is merely a tool used in conjunction with other evidence gathered (not exhibited in this report) during the accident investigation. The reader should not construct any conclusions, nor interpretations about the circumstances surrounding this accident merely derived from this source of information.*

*The transcript starts as the crew is preparing for descent from the cruise altitude of forty-one thousand feet into the Guam international airport. The transcript continues as the crew briefs for the approach and discusses the usability of the airport ILS (Instrument Landing System) system. The recording ends shortly after the aircraft impacts terrain and power is removed from the CVR.*"

Incident; 06 August 1997, 01:42 Guam local time. UTC 15:42 (Coordinated Universal Time)

Comment; Cpt—is the Captain, Coplt—the Co-pilot, Engn—the Engineer, and?—is an unidentified voice.

## Intra-Cockpit Communication:

15:11 / 01:11:51, Cpt: I will give you a short briefing, ILS is one one zero three, NIMITZ VOR is one one five three, the course zero six three, since the visibility is six, when we are in the visual approach, as I said before, set VOR for the TOD, I will add three miles from the VOR, and start descent when we're about one hundred fifty miles out. I will add some more speed above the target speed. Well, everything else is all right. In case of go-around, since it is VFR, while staying visual and turning on the right at …request a radar vector. If not, we have to go to FLAKE … turn toward FLAKE … turn toward a course zero six two outbound heading two four two and hold as published. Since the localizer glide slope is out, MDA is five-hundred sixty feet and HAT is five hundred four feet. It was a little lengthy. This concludes my briefing.

## Intra-Cockpit Communication

| | |
|---|---|
| 15:13 / 01:13:33, Cpt: | We better start descent. |
| 5:13 / 01:13:35, Coplt: | Yes. |
| 15:14 / 01:14:35, Engn: | Here it is, landing data card. |
| 15:14 / 01:14:37 Cpt: | O.K. thank you. |
| 15:14 / 01:14:55, Cpt: | Altimeter two niner eight six on hundred thirty-four knots… |
| 15:20 / 01:20:01, Cpt: | If this round trip is more than a nine-hour trip, we might get a little something. With eight hours, we get nothing. Eight hours do not help us at all. |
| 15:20 / 01:20:20, Cpt: | They make us work to maximum, up to maximum … (unintelligible words) |

| | |
|---|---|
| 15:20 / 01:20:28, Cpt: | Probably, this way…hotel expenses will be saved for cabin crew, and maximize the flight hours. Anyway, they make us B747 classic guys work to maximum. |
| 15:21 / 01:21:13, Cpt: | Eh … really … sleepy … (unintelligible words) |
| 15:21 / 01:21:15, Coplt: | Of course. |
| 15:21 / 01:21:59, Coplt: | Captain, Guam condition is no good. |

## Air-Ground Communication

| | |
|---|---|
| *15:22 / 01:22:06, Tower:* | *Korean air eight zero one information uniform is current at Agana now…altimeter tow niner eight six.* |
| *15:22 / 01:22:11, KE801 crew:* | *Korean…eight zero one is checked uniform.* |

## Intra-Cockpit Communication:

| | |
|---|---|
| 15:22 / 01:22:16, Coplt: | Two nine eighty-six. |
| 15:22 / 01:22:26, Cpt: | Uh, it rains a lot. |
| 15:23 / 01:23:35, Cpt: | (unintelligible words) |
| 15:23 / 01:23:45, Cpt: | Request twenty miles deviation later on. |
| 15:23 / 01:23:47, Coplt: | Yes. |
| 15:23 / 01:23:48, Cpt: | … to the left as we are descending. |
| 15:24 / 01:24:00, ? | Chuckling … (several unintelligible words) |
| 15:24 / 01:24:02, Coplt: | Don't you think it rains more? In this area, here? |
| 15:24 / 01:24:07, Cpt: | Left, request deviation. |
| 15:24 / 01:24:08, Coplt: | Yes. |
| 15:24 / 01:24:09, Cpt: | One zero mile. |
| 15:24 / 01:24:14, Coplt: | Yes. |

## Air-Ground Communication

*15:24 / 01:24:30, KE801 Coplt:*　　　　*Guam center...Korean...eight zero one request deviation one zero-mile left track.*

*15:22 / 01:22:06, Tower:*　　　　*Zero one approved.*

*15:24 / 01:24:30, KE801 Coplt:*　　　　*Thank you.*

## Intra-Cockpit Communication

| | |
|---|---|
| 15 :25 / 01 :25:03, Engn: | Descend checklist. |
| 15:25 / 01:25:05, Coplt: | Yes please. |
| 15:25 / 01:25:07, Engn: | Cabin pressurization set ... landing data speed bug one two niner? |
| 15:25 / 01:25:13, | Set. |
| 15:25 / 01:25:15, | One two niner. |
| 15:25 / 01:25:17, | Fuel set for landing ... (several unintelligible words) |
| 15:25 / 01:25:22, Engn: | Seat belt? |
| 15:25 / 01:25:23, Cpt: | On. |
| 15:25 / 01:25:25, Engn: | Altimeters stand by. |
| 15:25 / 01:25:17, ?: | Where is it? ... (several unintelligible words) weather radar |
| 15:25 / 01:25:35, Engn: | Two niner eight six. |
| 15:25 / 01:25:38, ?: | Landing briefing completed ... |
| 15:25 / 01:25:41, ?: | Altimeter two niner eight six. |
| 15:26 / 01:26:09, Engn: | (several unintelligible words) we are supposed to be going out right hand side from here ... |
| 15:26 / 01:26:12, ?: | Yes, request please. |
| 15:26 / 01:26:18, Cpt: | Going right hand side, then getting out of the left-hand side. Next is left hand side. |
| 15:26 / 01:26:21, Engn: | How about GUAM condition? |
| 15:26 / 01:26:23, Engn: | Is it GUAM? |
| 15:26 / 01:26:25, Engn: | (several unintelligible words) it's Guam, Guam. |

15:26 / 01:25:27, Cpt:          (chuckling) good.

15:27 / 01:27:17, Engn: (several unintelligible words) … because.

15:27 / 01:27:58, Engn:          Today the weather radar has helped us a lot.

15:26 / 01:25:59, Cpt:          Yes, they are very useful.

15:28 / 01:28:54, Cpt:          Request heading one sixty.

## Air-Ground Communication

*15:28 / 01:28:56, Coplt:*        *Guam center…Korean…eight zero one request right turn heading one six zero.*

*15:29 / 01:29:08, Tower:*        *Say again?*

*15:29 / 01:29:09, Coplt:*        *Korean eight zero six ah eight zero one maintain heading one six zero.*

*15:29 / 01:29:15, Tower:*        *Eight zero one approved.*

*15:29 / 01:29:16, Coplt:*        *Roger.*

## Intra-Cockpit Communication

15:29 / 01:29:36, Cpt:          Course zero six three.

15:29 / 01:29:38, Coplt:        Set.

15:29 / 01:29:50, Cpt:          If we take this way,

15:29 / 01:29:52, Engn:         Yes.

15:29 / 01:29:56, Cpt:          We should be getting…onto the route. 15:31

/ 01:31:08, Engn:               It is rising instead.

15:31 / 01:31:10, Cpt:          Ye, you are right.

## Air-Ground Communication

*15:31 / 01:31:17, Coplt:*        *Guam center…Korean…eight zero one clear of Charlie Bravo request radar vector for runway six left.*

*15:31 / 01:31:31, Tower:*        *Korean eight zero one fly heading one two zero.*

*15:31 / 01:31:34, Coplt:*        *Heading one two zero … eight zero one.*

# Intra-Cockpit Communication

| | |
|---|---|
| 15:31 / 01:31:39, Engn: | Approach checklist? |
| 15:31 / 01:31:41, Cpt: | Approach checklist. |
| 15:31 / 01:31:42, Engn: | Inboard landing lights? |
| 15:31 / 01:31:43, Cpt: | On |
| 15:31 / 01:31:44, Engn: | Radio and nav instruments? |
| 15:31 / 01:31:45, Cpt: | Set and cross check. |
| 15:31 / 01:31:46, Coplt: | Set and cross check. |
| 15:31 / 01:31:47, Engn: | Radio altimeters? |
| 15:31 / 01:31:48, Cpt: | Set |
| 15:31 / 01:31:49, Coplt: | Set |
| 15:31 / 01:31:50, Engn: | Three hundred ... |
| 15:31 / 01:31:51, Cpt: | Three or four. |
| 15:31 / 01:31:52, ?: | Three zero four. |
| 15:31 / 01:31:55, Engn: | Shoulder harness? |
| 15:31 / 01:31:55, Cpt: | On |
| 15:31 / 01:31:56, Engn: | Approach checklist complete. |
| 15:33 / 01:33:03, Cpt: | Set number one ILS frequency. |
| 15:33 / 01:33:05, ?: | Number one. |
| 15:33 / 01:33:05, ?: | Correct? |
| 15:33 / 01:33:06, ?: | Yes. |
| 15:33 / 01:33:06, ?: | One one zero three. |
| 15:33 / 01:33:07, ?: | One one zero three. |

15:33 / 01:33:09, Coplt: Set.

| | |
|---|---|
| 15:33 / 01:33:11, Cpt: | Roger. |
| 15:33 / 01:33:38, Cpt: | What's the number for Guam seventeen? |

15:33 / 01:33:40, Coplt: Seventeen.

| | |
|---|---|
| 15:33 / 01:33:47, ?: | (several unintelligible words) |
| 15:34 / 01:34:05, Cpt: | Ya, there is a bit CB over there to the left. |
| 15:34 / 01:34:23, Engn: | Is it going to be rough? |
| 15:34 / 01:34:24, Cpt: | It may be better at lower altitude. |
| 15:34 / 01:34:33, Coplt: | Flaps one. |
| 15:35 / 01:35:29, Cpt: | Flaps one. |
| 15:35 / 01:35:30, Coplt: | Flaps one. |
| 15:35 / 01:35:34, Coplt: | One nine nine. |

| 15:35 / 01:35:50, Cpt: | Five. |
|---|---|
| 15:35 / 01:35:51, Coplt: | Flaps five …one seven nine. |
| 15:36 / 01:36:33, ?: | (several unintelligible words) |
| 15:37 / 01:37:07, Cpt: | INS DME … (several unintelligible words) |
| 15:37 / 01:37:09, ?: | Yeh. |
| 15:37 / 01:37:55,: | (Sounds of altitude alerts) |
| 15:38 / 01:38:13,: | (Sound of slight increase in wind/background |
| noise) 15:38 / 01:38:34,: | (Sound of loud clunk) |
| 15:38 / 01:38:37, Cpt: | Flaps ten. |
| 15:38 / 01:38:37, Coplt: | Yes sir, flaps ten. |
| 15:38 / 01:38:40, Coplt: | One five-nine. |

## Air-Ground Communication

| *15:38 / 01:38:49,Tower:* | *Korean air eight zero one turn left heading zero niner zero join localizer.* |
|---|---|
| *15:38 / 01:38:53,Coplt:* | *Heading zero niner zero intercept the localizer.* |

## Intra-Cockpit Communication

| 15:38 / 01:38:57, Cpt: | Turn on the (unintelligible word) |
|---|---|
| 15:39 / 01:39:09, : | (Sound of rattle, similar to that of stabilizer trim) |
| 15:39 / 01:39:12, : | (Sound of slight decrease in wind/background) |
| 15:39 / 01:39:18, : | (Sound of slight increase in wind/background) |
| 15:39 / 01:39:20, : | Ooooh (surprised expression) |
| 15:39 / 01:39:23, : | (Sound of slight decrease in wind/background noise) |
| 15:39 / 01:39:25, ?: | Cool and refreshing. |
| 15:39 / 01:39:28, ?: | (several unintelligible word) |
| 15:39 / 01:39:28, Coplt: | Glide slope … (several unintelligible word) … localizer capture (several unintelligible word) Glide slope … did. |

## Air-Ground Communication

| | |
|---|---|
| *15:39 / 01:39:44,Tower:* | *Korean air eight zero one...cleared to ILS runway six left approach...glide slope unusable.* |
| *15:39 / 01:39:48,Coplt:* | *Korean air eight zero one roger...cleared ILS runway six left.* |

## Intra-Cockpit Communication

| | |
|---|---|
| 15:39 / 01:39:55, Engn: | Is the glide slope working? Glide slope? yeh? |
| 15:39 / 01:39:56, Cpt: | Yes, yes, it's working. |
| 15:39 / 01:39:57, Engn: | Ah, so ... |
| 15:39 / 01:39:58, | Check the glide slope if working? |
| 15:39 / 01:39:59, | Why is it working? |
| 15:40 / 01:40:00, Coplt: | Not usable |
| 15:40 / 01:40:01, Engn: | Six D check, gear down. |
| 15:40 / 01:40:04, Cpt: | Check... |
| 15:40 / 01:40:06, | (Sound of altitude alert) |
| 15:40 / 01:40:16, | (Several unintelligible word) |
| 15:40 / 01:40:21, | (Sound of slight increase in wind/background) |
| 15:40 / 01:40:22, | Glide slope is incorrect. |
| 15:40 / 01:40:22, Coplt: | Approaching fourteen hundred. |
| 15:40 / 01:40:37, Cpt: | Since todays glide slope condition is not good, we need to maintain one Thousand four hundred foot. Please set it. |
| 15:40 / 01:40:40, | Yes. |

## Air-Ground Communication

| | |
|---|---|
| *15:40 / 01:40:42,Tower:* | *Korean air eight zero one contact the Agana tower one one eight point one "ahn nyung hee ga sea you" (goodbye in Korean language)* |

| 15:40 / 01:40:47,Coplt: | *"soo go ha sip si you) (take care in Korean language) ...one eighteen one.* |
|---|---|

## Intra-Cockpit Communication

| 15:40 / 01:40:50, Engn: | The guy working here probably was a GI in |
|---|---|
| Korea before. | |
| 15:40 / 01:40:50, Cpt: | Yes. |

## Air-Ground Communication

| 15:40 / 01:40:42,Coplt: | *Agana tower Korean air eight zero one intercept the localizer six left.* |
|---|---|
| 15:40 / 01:40:42,Tower: | *Korean air eight zero one heavy Agana tower runway six left wind...at zero niner zero seven...cleared to land...verify heavy Boeing seven four seven tonight.* |
| 15:41 / 01:41:14,Coplt: | *Korean air eight zero one roger...cleared to land six left.* |
| 15:41 / 01:41:18,Tower: | *Korean air eight zero one heavy roger.* |

## Intra-Cockpit Communication

| 15:41 / 01:41:22, Cpt: | Flaps thirty. |
|---|---|
| 15:41 / 01:41:23, Coplt: | Flaps thirty. |
| 15:41 / 01:41:27, Coplt: | Flaps thirty confirmed. |
| 15:41 / 01:41:31, Coplt: | Landing check. |
| 15:41 / 01:41:32, Cpt: | (Several unintelligible word) ... look |
| carefully. | |
| 15:41 / 01:41:33, Cpt: | Set five hundred sixty feet. (noise increased) |
| 15:41 / 01:41:35, Coplt: | Set. |
| 15:41 / 01:41:37, Cpt: | Landing check. |
| 15:41 / 01:41:40, Engn: | Tilt check normal. |
| 15:41 / 01:41:41, Cpt: | Yes. |

| | |
|---|---|
| 15:41 / 01:41:42, GPWS: | One thousand (Ground Proximity Warning System) |
| 15:41 / 01:41:43, Cpt: | No flags gear and flaps. |
| 15:41 / 01:41:45, Engn: | No flags gear and flaps. |
| 15:41 / 01:41:45, : | (Sound of altitude alert) |
| 15:41 / 01:41:45, Cpt: | Isn't glide slope working? |
| 15:41 / 01:41:48, Cpt: | Wiper on. |
| 15:41 / 01:41:49, | Engn: Yes, Wiper on. |
| 15:41 / 01:41:53, Coplt: | Landing check. |
| 15:41 / 01:41:55, Engn: | Ignition flight start flight start. |
| 15:41 / 01:41:59, Coplt: | Not in sight? (the runway) |
| 15:42 / 01:42:00, GPWS: | Five hundred (Ground Proximity Warning System) |
| 15:42 / 01:42:02, Engn: | Eh? (astonished tome) |
| 15:42 / 01:42:03, ?: | Stabilize, stabilize. |
| 15:42 / 01:42:04, Cpt: | Oh, yes. |
| 15:42 / 01:42:05, Engn: | Auto brake on? |
| 15:42 / 01:42:07, Cpt: | Minimum. |
| 15:42 / 01:42:07, Engn: | Minimum. |
| 15:42 / 01:42:08, Cpt: | Landing gear down in green. |
| 15:42 / 01:42:09, Engn: | Landing gear down in green. |
| 15:42 / 01:42:09, Engn: | Speed brakes armed. |
| 15:42 / 01:42:10, ?: | Armed. |
| 15:42 / 01:42:11, Engn: | No smoking signs on? |
| 15:42 / 01:42:12, Cpt: | On course. |
| 15:42 / 01:42:12:81, Engn: | Flaps? |
| 15:42 / 01:42:13:64, ?: | Thirty thirty green. |
| 15:42 / 01:42:14:13, GPWS: | Minimums minimums. |
| 15:42 / 01:42:14:70, Engn: | Hydraulics. |
| 15:42 / 01:42:15:45, ?: | Uh, landing lights. |
| 15:42 / 01:42:17:15, GPWS: | Sink rate. |
| 15:42 / 01:42:18:17, Coplt: | Sink rate ok. |
| 15:42 / 01:42:19:04, Engn: | Two hundred. |
| 15:42 / 01:42:19:47, Coplt: | Let's make a missed approach. |
| 15:42 / 01:42:20:56, Engn: | Not in sight. (the runway) |
| 15:42 / 01:42:21:07, Coplt: | Not in sight. (the runway) Missed approach. |

| | |
|---|---|
| 15:42 / 01:42:22:18, Engn: | Go around. |
| 15:42 / 01:42:23:07, Cpt: | Go around. |
| 15:42 / 01:42:23:77, : | (Sound of auto-pilot disconnect warning starts) |
| 15:42 / 01:42:23:84, Coplt: | Flaps. |
| 15:42 / 01:42:24:84, GPWS: | Fifty. (feet above ground) |
| 15:42 / 01:42:25:19, GPWS: | Forty. (feet above ground) |
| 15:42 / 01:42:25:50, GPWS: | Thirty. (feet above ground) |
| 15:42 / 01:42:25:78, GPWS: | Twenty. (feet above ground) |
| 15:42 / 01:42:25:78, : | (Sound of initial impact) |
| 15:42 / 01:42:28:65, : | (Sound of tone) |
| 15:42 / 01:42:28:91, ?: | (Sound of groans) |
| 15:42 / 01:42:30:54, : | (Sound of tone) |
| 15:42 / 01:42:31:78, : | (Sound of tone) |
| 15:42 / 01:42:32:53, : | End of recording. |

## End of Transcript

Lessons learned; complex approaches, especially when executed at night or in bad weather conditions must be carefully and fully briefed, associated procedures and approach constraints must be followed and monitored to avoid accidents (crew resource management) CRM. The investigation concluded that the crew did not conduct a thorough briefing prior to the beginning of the approach, and during the approach the crew lost situational awareness relative to the location of the approach. The captain ordered continually and prematurely increasingly lower altitude selections, resulting in an approach profile that was consistently below the minimum required safe altitude.

Though the crew was aware that the glideslope was inoperative, intermittent indications on the associated instruments caused some confusion among the crew as to whether or not the glideslope might be active to the determinant of proper monitoring of the localizer only approach that was being executed. The intermittent fixation on the glideslope indications contributed to a delayed awareness that the airplane was too low, as a result, the go-around was initiated too late. In the meantime, the performance of the GPWS has been considerably improved in modern aviation, enhanced with graphic displays to avoid confusion.

A decision to go around should have been made without delay under missed approach conditions (failure to visually acquire the runway when the minimum descent altitude is reached is imperative).

According to the findings of the FAA NTSB US American Authority, the first officer and the flight engineer responded to the **GPWS** annunciation of low altitude above ground, the first officer properly called for a missed approach. It was also concluded that once the go-around decision had been made, the captains control inputs were not immediate, and not of sufficient magnitude to properly initiate the go-around, or to arrest the existing sink rate. The captain's failure to reach in a timely manner to the GPWS minimums annunciation and his further failure to immediately initiate the go-around when prompted by the first officer, led to the accident.

The approach was inadequately briefed by the captain. During the approach the first officer erroneously called out that the flight had reached an altitude one thousand feet lower than had actually been achieved, the captain then ordered the next lowest step-down altitude in the approach to be set, and before passing the next radio fix, inappropriately commanded the final minimum altitude to be set, allowing the aircraft prematurely to descent and remain significantly below the specified minimum safe altitudes for several segments of the approach. Coupled with the crew's confusion over the intermittent glideslope signals, the approach monitoring deteriorated and the aircraft was allowed to descent into the ground short of the runway.

Since the night of 6 August 1997, 01:42 Guam local time, where flight KE801 slammed into Nimitz hill southwest of Guam, approximately three NM short of Runway 06 left at Antonio B. Won Airport as a result of unfortunate but complex circumstances; some of my colleagues and I have reason to light a candle every year, in remembrance of the 237 passengers that perished in the early hours of the morning, but also in memory of our buddy, Captain Park Yong-chul, who was in command of the B-747-300 and its crew.

# References

(in no particular order of importance)

Blue Cross, Basel Switzerland The Salvation army

Dr. Ray Pritchard, the doctrine of Trinity, 2010 6 May

Pierre Teilhard de Jardin, Philosopher, born 01 May 1881 in the French town of Clermont-Ferrand, the Phenomenon of Man 1955. The letters of Teilhard de Chardin 1993

Cpt Cole Evens, Australian Airlines

Leonard E Hubbard, The economics of Soviet Agriculture, Macmillan, London (1939) (The Kolkhoz System)

Australian Bureau of statistics 2006

Constitution of the Commonwealth of Australia signed into law in 1900, section 116 – the free exercise of any religion, and no religious observance, or for prohibiting the free exercise of any religion, and no religious test shall be required as a qualification of any office or public trust under the Commonwealth, a sobering reality, which permits the so-called "free churches" to operate freely in Australia

The Scottish educator (A.S. Neill, November 1960 by the Hart Publishing Company) "Summerhill"

(Aboriginal Service Branch. (2009) *Working with Aboriginal People and Communities:* A Practice Resource. Ashfield, NSW Department of Community Services)

The Muslim world. (Deen, H., 2009) Muslims in Australia 1901-75. (In J. Jupp (ed.), *The Encyclopedia of Religion in Australia.* Melbourne: Cambridge University Press.)

(Hugh McLeod, the Religious Crisis of the 1960s, Amazon.de)
(Samuel Haber, Rédaction Francophone, development of the religious communities)

Elizabeth Kübler Ross, Living with death and dying, Macmillan, 1981,

Sigmund Freud, Psychoanalysis

Plastic Oceans International 2019, non profit organisation

James Strong, CEO, 1986 to 1989 Australian Airlines, 1993 to 2001 chief executive and managing director of Qantas

Gerard Hofstede the Dutch social psychologist

Malcom Gladwell in his books "theory of cockpit culture"

Merritt Ashleigh (May 2000). "Culture in the Cockpit, do Hofstede's dimensions replicate?")

**NTSB**, *"vehicle recorders division Washington, D.C. 20594* – Transcript

CPSIA information can be obtained
at www.ICGtesting.com
Printed in the USA
LVHW022359130423
744364LV00001B/3